CW00833779

Ethical Marketing Through Data Governance Standards and Effective Technology

Shefali Saluja
Chitkara Business School, Chitkara University, India

Varun Nayyar
Chitkara University, India

Kuleep Rojhe
Chitkara University, India

Sandhir Sharma
Chitkara Business School, Chitkara University, India

A volume in the Advances in Marketing, Customer
Relationship Management, and E-Services
(AMCRMES) Book Series

Published in the United States of America by
  IGI Global
  Business Science Reference (an imprint of IGI Global)
  701 E. Chocolate Avenue
  Hershey PA, USA 17033
  Tel: 717-533-8845
  Fax: 717-533-8661
  E-mail: cust@igi-global.com
  Web site: http://www.igi-global.com

Library of Congress Cataloging-in-Publication Data

Names: Sauja, Shefali, 1991- editor. | Nayyar, Varun, 1982- editor. |
  Rojhe, Kuldeep, 1977- editor. | Sharma, Sandhir, 1974- editor.
Title: Ethical marketing through data governance standards and effective
  technology / edited by Shefali Sauja, Varun Nayyar, Kuldeep Rojhe,
  Sandhir Sharma.
Description: Hershey, PA : Business Science Reference, [2024] | Includes
  bibliographical references and index. | Summary: "This book strengthens
  the understanding of AI enabled marketing standards and data privacy
  standards for better implementation of AI based marketing analytics"--
  Provided by publisher.
Identifiers: LCCN 2024002245 (print) | LCCN 2024002246 (ebook) | ISBN
  9798369322154 (hardcover) | ISBN 9798369322161 (ebook)
Subjects: LCSH: Marketing--Moral and ethical aspects. |
  Marketing--Technological innovations. | Branding (Marketing)--Moral and
  ethical aspects. | Business ethics. | Artificial intelligence--Moral and
  ethical aspects.
Classification: LCC HF5415 .E798 2024 (print) | LCC HF5415 (ebook) | DDC
  174/.4--dc23/eng/20240227
LC record available at https://lccn.loc.gov/2024002245
LC ebook record available at https://lccn.loc.gov/2024002246

This book is published in the IGI Global book series Advances in Marketing, Customer Relationship Management, and E-Services (AMCRMES) (ISSN: 2327-5502; eISSN: 2327-5529)

British Cataloguing in Publication Data
A Cataloguing in Publication record for this book is available from the British Library.
All work contributed to this book is new, previously-unpublished material. The views expressed in this book are those of the authors, but not necessarily of the publisher.
For electronic access to this publication, please contact: eresources@igi-global.com.

Advances in Marketing, Customer Relationship Management, and E-Services (AMCRMES) Book Series

Eldon Y. Li

National Chengchi University, Taiwan & California Polytechnic State University, USA

ISSN:2327-5502
EISSN:2327-5529

MISSION

Business processes, services, and communications are important factors in the management of good customer relationship, which is the foundation of any well organized business. Technology continues to play a vital role in the organization and automation of business processes for marketing, sales, and customer service. These features aid in the attraction of new clients and maintaining existing relationships.

The Advances in Marketing, Customer Relationship Management, and E-Services (AMCRMES) Book Series

addresses success factors for customer relationship management, marketing, and electronic services and its performance outcomes. This collection of reference source covers aspects of consumer behavior and marketing business strategies aiming towards researchers, scholars, and practitioners in the fields of marketing management.

COVERAGE

- Online Community Management and Behavior
- Cases on Electronic Services
- CRM strategies
- Data mining and marketing
- Mobile CRM
- Database marketing
- Relationship Marketing
- Customer Relationship Management
- Customer Retention
- Electronic Services

IGI Global is currently accepting manuscripts for publication within this series. To submit a proposal for a volume in this series, please contact our Acquisition Editors at Acquisitions@igi-global.com or visit: http://www.igi-global.com/publish/.

Titles in this Series

For a list of additional titles in this series, please visit: www.igi-global.com/book-series

Impact of Teleworking and Remote Work on Business Productivity, Retention, Advancement, and Bottom Line
Harish Chandra Chandan (Independent Researcher, USA)
Business Science Reference • © 2024 • 311pp • H/C (ISBN: 9798369313145) • US $290.00

AI-Driven Marketing Research and Data Analytics
Reason Masengu (Middle East College, Oman) Option Takunda Chiwaridzo (University of Science and Technology Beijing, Beijing, China) Mercy Dube (Midlands State University, Zimbabwe) and Benson Ruzive (Modern College of Business and Science, Oman)
Business Science Reference • © 2024 • 490pp • H/C (ISBN: 9798369321652) • US $290.00

Marketing Innovation Strategies and Consumer Behavior
Belem Barbosa (University of Porto, Portugal)
Business Science Reference • © 2024 • 469pp • H/C (ISBN: 9798369341957) • US $325.00

Corporate Governance and CSR Strategies for Sustainability
Maja Pucelj (Faculty of Organisation Studies, University of Novo Mesto, Slovenia) and Rado Bohinc (Scientific Research Centre Koper, Slovenia)
Information Science Reference • © 2024 • 368pp • H/C (ISBN: 9798369358634) • US $290.00

Balancing Automation and Human Interaction in Modern Marketing
Arjun J. Nair (St. Lawrence College, Canada) Sridhar Manohar (Chitkara Business School, Chitkara University, India) Amit Mittal (Chitkara Business School, Chitkara University, India) and Wasim Ahmed (University of Hull, UK)
Business Science Reference • © 2024 • 326pp • H/C (ISBN: 9798369322765) • US $290.00

Building Strong Brands and Engaging Customers With Sound
Minna-Maarit Jaskari (School of Marketing and Communication, University of Vaasa, Finland)
Business Science Reference • © 2024 • 267pp • H/C (ISBN: 9798369307786) • US $265.00

Globalized Consumer Insights in the Digital Era
Fatih Sahin (Bandirma Onyedi Eylul University, Turkey) and Cevat Soylemez (Kutahya Dumlupinar University, Turkey)
Business Science Reference • © 2024 • 296pp • H/C (ISBN: 9798369338117) • US $325.00

IGI Global
PUBLISHER of TIMELY KNOWLEDGE

701 East Chocolate Avenue, Hershey, PA 17033, USA
Tel: 717-533-8845 x100 • Fax: 717-533-8661
E-Mail: cust@igi-global.com • www.igi-global.com

Table of Contents

Detailed Table of Contents

  Annumeet Nagra, GNA University, India
  Shefali Saluja, Chitkara Business School, Chitkara University, India

The growth of the internet and other IT has altered global ease of necessary material outside of national boundaries. Due to the internet's capacity to disseminate information at a rapid pace, most businesses today are taking advantage of the opportunity to reveal financial as well as nonfinancial material to their stakeholders, such as environmental related content. The sample used in the current study consisted of 100 businesses that are listed on the BSE-500 Index Stock. T-test was utilised as the statistical method in the current study to compare the online and offline modes of disseminating environmental information by Indian businesses and MNCs. MS-Excel Analysis Tool Pack was used as the study's software. Analysis of it has shown that it is a sad situation when some of the top executives of major corporations are found to be withholding any type of information about their environmental performance. In India, online environmental reporting is still in its infancy. Large business houses and markets with high market capitalization do not give much thought to their surroundings.

  Shefali Saluja, Chitkara Business School, Chitkara University, India
  Varun Nayyar, Chitkara University, India
  Shuchi Dawra, Chitkara Business School, Chitkara University, India
  Mansi Jain, Chitkara Business School, Chitkara University, India
  Rishi Prakash Shukla, Chandigarh University, India

The artificial intelligence technological revolution is sweeping across the globe; audit is no exception. The dimension of auditing is about to get revolutionized with not just automation, but intelligence-based automation; the future of traditional auditing, especially manual one, is being redesigned. IAA, or intelligent audit automation, is the next generation of auditing services that encapsulates new auditing business models, new auditing professionals, and new ways of looking at the data creation. With the increase in accounting frauds in the current economic scenario, the discovery of financial accounting fraud detection (FAFD) has become a prominent topic in the field of education, research and industry. The chapter investigates the current economic fraud detection issues and proposes an accounting framework using business intelligence as a viable way to address them. The chapter adopts an exemplary research approach to present how business intelligence can be used in detecting accounting fraud.

Chapter 3
Divya Dang, Chandigarh University, India
Sahil Kohli, Chandigarh University, India

In this chapter, the authors unravel the intricate dance between ethics, data governance, and economics in India's vibrant digital marketing sphere. It's a deep dive into how India, a burgeoning digital powerhouse, grapples with the challenges of protecting consumer data while fostering ethical marketing. The authors shed light on the crucial role data plays in today's marketing strategies in India and ponder the repercussions for consumer privacy. By critically examining India's current data protection laws and stacking them up against global benchmarks, the authors pinpoint areas ripe for innovation. The unique hurdles Indian marketers face in the big data era are laid bare, and the authors explore cutting-edge tech solutions that promise to guide ethical choices and policy shaping. Wrapping up, the chapter casts an eye to the future, envisioning a balanced path for India's economic growth that doesn't lose sight of ethical marketing and robust data governance. It's about charting a course for an economy that's digital-first but ethics-forward.

Chapter 4
Sayani Das, Institute of Mass Communication, Film, and Television Studies, India
Archan Mitra, Presidency University, India

This chapter explores the integration of ethical marketing practices, data governance standards, and technology. Highlighting the importance of transparency, consumer control, accountability, and beneficence, it examines data protection regulations like GDPR and CCPA, and the role of AI and blockchain in promoting ethical practices. Case studies of Patagonia and Unilever demonstrate ethical marketing's potential, while the Cambridge Analytica scandal underscores the consequences of neglect. A comprehensive framework for ethical marketing is proposed, offering guidelines for businesses and policymakers. The chapter concludes with future directions, emphasizing the need for regulatory evolution, technological advancements, consumer empowerment, and cross-disciplinary collaboration to achieve ethical marketing that respects consumer privacy and fosters trust.

Chapter 5
Devesh Bathla, Chitkara Business School, Chitkara University, India
Raina Ahuja, Kurukshetra University, Kurukshetra, India

Customer engagement and customer retention are closely linked, and the metaverse offers a unique opportunity for brands to build lasting relationships with their customers. Metaverse allows brands to create a virtual representation of their stores and to interact with customers in that space. The metaverse offers a platform for community building, where brands can create a sense of belonging and connection among their customers. Brands can create virtual events, social spaces, or games that bring their customers together and foster a sense of community. By building a community around their brand, customers are more likely to feel connected to the brand and to each other, which can increase the likelihood of repeat purchases and brand advocacy. The metaverse concept has been popularised in science fiction and video games but has gained momentum in recent years as a potential next step for the internet.

    Nibedita Gogoi, St. Xavier's College, Kolkata, India
    Rounak Agarwal, St. Xavier's College, Kolkata, India
    Sumanta Dutta, St. Xavier's College, Kolkata, India

This chapter used a bibliometric analysis to assess the leading authors, countries, organisation, and journals in the domain of ethical marketing research while identifying prevailing research trends. Influential authors in ethical marketing research are Gene R. Laczniak and Patrick E. Murphy. United Kingdom leads in terms of ethical marketing research, followed by the findings of this research, which identify influential authors, countries, organizations, journals, and trends in the field of ethical marketing, can inform policy makers, educators, and researchers in India and globally about the importance of ethical marketing to promote transparency and sustainability to build trust and long-term customer loyalty which will help a business to survive in the market and achieve the organisational goals.

    Ankita Sharma, Navrachana University, India
    Varun Nayyar, Chitkara University, India

The chapter focuses on social and ethical concept of marketing, which appeared in connection with the need to bring the business into line with the requirements of both modern market economy and the principles of social responsibility to individual consumers and society. Most modern enterprises recognize the need to implement tools for social and ethical marketing, increasing awareness and consumer protection. The studies suggest that ethical marketing, particularly through the incorporation of corporate social responsibility (CSR) and sustainable development goals (SDGs), can positively impact brand loyalty and promote ethical consumer behavior Social and ethical marketing at its core implements the principles of consumer orientation, innovation, increasing the value of goods, awareness of the social mission, and social responsibility of the enterprise. Increasingly, enterprises are willing to be guided by marketing ethics, such as limiting potential damage, meeting basic needs, economic efficiency, innovation, consumer education and awareness, and consumer protection.

    Prachi Gupta, Chitkara Business School, Chitkara University, India
    Rajni Bala, Chitkara Business School, Chitkara University, India

Electronic word-of-mouth, or e-WOM, has emerged due to the expanding trend of online transactions in every category. This change in consumer purchase behavior has led to the widespread presence of online reviews, which have become a significant reference source before purchases are made. Constant dependence of customers on these reviews has induced marketers to manipulate these to their benefit. They do so by offering discounts or incentivizing customers who readily agree to post false positive reviews of their products. All such fraudulent practices are termed "opinion spam," which undermines customers' trust. The study's objective is to look into the factors and practices that have led to the burgeoning issue of opinion spam and its impact on customer trust. The study also examines the different ethical norms and standards laid down by regulatory bodies and how marketers' actions align with those. The study is based on secondary data, mainly collected and compiled from academic articles, case studies, and industry reports on opinion spam, customer trust, and marketing ethics.

Chapter 9

Priya Jindal, Chitkara Business School, Chitkara University, India
Lochan Chavan, Chitkara Business School, Chitkara University, India

There has been a wide range of technological improvements and breakthroughs, allowing new vehicles to evolve and adapt to changes to obtain a competitive advantage. Consumers' lives have been made easier by autonomous vehicles, such as cybersecurity, the internet of things (IoT), 5G technology, V2X communication, etc. These autonomous vehicles may examine system weaknesses and threats with the use of the market knowledge dimension and the knowledge integration mechanism, and they can then collaborate to reduce all potential risks and vulnerabilities. By concentrating on potential flaws and risks in automotive vehicles, cyber security, and IoT play important roles in advancing the physical world.

Chapter 10

Dharmesh Dhabliya, Vishwakarma Institute of Information Technology, India
M. N. Nachappa, Jain University, India
Ritu Rani, Vivekananda Global University, India
Neha Nitin Karnik, ATLAS SkillTech University, India
Anishkumar Dhablia, Altimetrik India Pvt. Ltd., India
Jambi Ratna Raja Kumar, Genba Sopanrao Moze College of Engineering, India
Ankur Gupta, Vaish College of Engineering, India
Sabyasachi Pramanik, Haldia Institute of Technology, India

In developing India, the traditional coir industry employs 0.55 million people. Production of coconuts and coir is dominated by Kerala. Karnataka and Tamilnadu afterwards provide good coir. India is benefiting from the manufacturing of coir. This is having an impact on the coir sector due to commercial enterprises. This research looked at the effects of two trade reforms on the development, performance, and solution of India's coir sector. Trade influences trade volume and propels growth. Trade growth and volume are impacted by trade liberalization. Two significant trade agreements that had an impact on the coir business were the WTO Agreement on Textiles and Clothing (ATC) and the GATT Multi-Fiber Agreement (MFA). Data for the study came from the Coir Board's annual reports as well as websites belonging to the Reserve Bank of India, Ministry of External Affairs, Ministry of Commerce and Industry, and Coir Board.

Lakshmy Ravindran, Amrita Vishwa Vidyapeetham, Kochi, India

P. Ravindranath, Amrita Vishwa Vidyapeetham, Kochi, India

Studies have shown that excessive use of Instagram can lead to feelings of inadequacy and low self- esteem as individuals compare themselves to the carefully curated and edited lives of others. Additionally, the constant exposure to unrealistic beauty standards and idealised lifestyles on Instagram can contribute to body dissatisfaction and distort one's perception of reality, creating unrealistic beauty standards, unattainable for most people. This can further fuel feelings of inadequacy and self-doubt, impacting mental health and overall well-being. Negative ideas and perceptions of our physical bodies, as well as issues with body image, can cause significant distress and have serious psychological and medical effects. Body dysmorphia and eating disorders were linked to a high level of social media addiction. Educating users about the importance of setting boundaries and practicing self-care while using Instagram can help mitigate its negative effects on mental well-being.

Navreet Kaur, Chitkara Business School, Chitkara University, India

Preeti Kaushal, School of Business Studies, Chitkara University, India

Two factors viz. technology and consumer needs are the main drivers of the marketing evolution referred to as Marketing 5.0. The business philosophy in the present phase of marketing is about a confluence between technology and humanity. The chapter entails a focus on how technology aids human marketers and advertisers to create content and the subsequent emotional experience of consumers. The emphasis primarily is on mind mapping – a dynamic visual representation of a group of ideas clustered around and linked to a single central topic; a tool to unleash creative impulses. The main themes are high-level ideas that radiate from the central image as 'branches' and result in content creation such as slogans and taglines, formulating of marketing strategies, and building of a brand identity. A discussion on transformation in the field of content marketing over the years, the benefits and drawbacks of AI-assisted content creation and the ethical challenges in AI-powered marketing is an integral part of the chapter.

Ashutosh D. Gaur, Mangalmay Institution of Management and Technology, India

This chapter delves into the changing landscape of marketing in the digital age. It examines the evolution of the traditional marketing mix, the proliferation of digital media platforms, the rise of MarTech, and the emergence of P-PACE as an eighth element in the marketing mix. This research highlights the profound impact of technology and the internet on the marketing mix and the emergence of new dimensions such as participation, public opinion, physical proof, process, personalization, and political power. It also explores the acceleration factor, encapsulated in the concept of P-PACE, and how it has become a fundamental element in the marketing mix. The implications and applications of P-PACE and its significance in contemporary marketing are discussed, emphasizing the advantages of harnessing the power of acceleration for businesses.

Chapter 14

This chapter explores the intricate relationship between privacy and ethics in the realm of artificial intelligence (AI). With the proliferation of AI technologies, concerns about data privacy and ethical implications have intensified. The chapter delves into the ethical dilemmas arising from the collection, analysis, and utilization of sensitive data, emphasizing the need for robust frameworks that balance technological advancement with safeguarding individual rights. It examines the challenges of maintaining privacy in AI-driven systems while adhering to ethical principles, offering insights into the current landscape, potential risks, and promising solutions for creating a responsible and transparent AI ecosystem.

Chapter 15

The proliferation of e-commerce platforms has provided customers with a level of convenience never seen before, but it also raises serious questions about how sensitive consumer data is protected. This chapter explores the complex interplay between two emerging technologies, AI and blockchain, with the goal of strengthening consumer data protection on e-commerce platforms. It examines innovative and forward-thinking solutions that handle the complexities of data governance as well as the changing legal aspects of the e-commerce industry by exposing the numerous difficulties and challenges that occur in this confluence. The protection of consumer data is one of the biggest issues facing e-commerce. The combination of blockchain technology and artificial intelligence (AI) acts as a lighthouse, pointing the way for the e-commerce sector toward a more transparent, safe, and morally upright future.

Chapter 16

Human resource management (HRM) is a field that has evolved in combination with advancements in technology and is now operating in a highly competitive market. Augmented reality (AR) and virtual reality (VR) are cutting-edge technologies that have shown promise in several areas. It is a prospective way to assist with HRM operations due to its ability to simulate real-world situations, provide an immersive perspective, and facilitate communication between simulated & realistic environments. This paper attempts to understand better the possible advantages that the use of VR and AR may give to HRM through an analysis of relevant literature.

Chapter 17

Shefali Saluja, Chitkara Business School, Chitkara University, India
Arjun J. Nair, Chitkara Business School, Chitkara University, India

An economy needs a well-functioning banking system—it is crucial for a country's economic growth and progress. With different economic factors influencing the banking sector, both domestically and globally, the role of the banking industry has changed over time. This has allowed the financial sector to explore new opportunities and expand its reach beyond national borders. The banking industry has undergone major transformations in response to shifts in trade and commerce, including the emergence of private sector banks, the integration of technology such as NEFT and smart cards, and changes to capital adequacy standards. These improvements have greatly increased the efficiency and productivity of the banking sector. The Indian banking industry is unique and has undergone three stages of development, from character-based lending to competitiveness-based lending, according to Singh,. Despite the growth and expansion of the banking industry, it faces many operational risks, including various types of fraud and scams.

Chapter 18

Varun Kumar, Mangalmay Institute of Management and Technology, Greater Noida, India
Ashima Dhiman, Gitarattan Institute of Advanced Studies and Training, New Delhi, India

The current study has investigated students' perceptions towards the use of E-commerce platforms. The main focus is on the correlation between the frequency of online shopping by the college going students and their demographical factors like age, gender, and educational attainment. It also covers the various aspects of internet buying and the obstacles that prevent people from making purchases through E-Commerce platforms. In addition to secondary data, a Google form was utilized to collect responses from students at Higher Educational Institutes to an electronic questionnaire. A questionnaire was employed as a research tool to gather information from 208 randomly chosen respondents who were students at Delhi NCR's Higher Education Institutes. According to the results of this study, respondents firmly believe that using e-commerce platforms and online purchasing is practical, time-saving, and useful. But many of them, claimed about online purchasing have been found to be unaffected by factors such as gender, age, educational background, and young generation background.

Chapter 19

Preeti Kaushal, Chitkara University, India
Navreet Kaur, Chitkara University, India

Shoppers take advantage of the retail store to check the product but finally order it online, thus posing a great bane for the offline retailers. Due to the absence of any systematic treatment of 'showrooming.' This chapter discusses the reasons why the customers indulge in showrooming, the reasons to understand why customers visit the offline store and make the purchase online, how the measure is developed to access showrooming and how it will help the retailers to understand and combat this issue, the ethical concerns related to showrooming as the retailer who displays the products in the offline store, provides complete service to its customers, but the customers resort to online buying after availing the services of the offline retailers. This concern has raised not only ethical issues but also issues concerning the survival of these retail stores in future. This chapter will serve as a complete guide to help retailers evade this ethical concern and handle the issue of showrooming with awareness about the reasons of customers indulging in showrooming.

Chapter 20

Parul Kulshrestha, Chitkara University, India
Dhiresh Kulshrestha, Chitkara University, India

In today's dynamic and technology-driven business landscape, the convergence of ethical marketing, technology, and data governance has become paramount. This abstract provides a glimpse into the forthcoming book chapter titled "Strategic Talent Acquisition for Ethical Marketing: Leveraging Technology and Data Governance," which explores the pivotal role of talent acquisition in ensuring ethical marketing success in this digital age. The chapter examines how organizations can navigate the complexities of digital marketing and data privacy while upholding ethical principles. It highlights the strategic importance of talent acquisition in assembling teams capable of not only excelling in marketing but also prioritizing ethical considerations. This strategic approach not only helps maintain brand reputation and customer trust but also fosters long-term business success.

Chapter 21

Gurpreet Singh, Apeejay Institute of Management and Engineering, Technical Campus, Jalandhar, India
Ajwinder Singh, Apeejay Institute of Management and Engineering, Technical Campus, Jalandhar, India

The banking and financial system of any country influences and also acts as the economic indicator of its performance and also helps play a vital role in framing macro-economic policies in order to cope with the current business environment. This chapter highlights the importance of ethical issues in the governance of banking systems, and also discusses the unauthorized use of SWIFT codes which takes the character of swindles in the banking system. Rising NPAs and frauds in the Country like India is weakening the nation's growth both in terms of economic power as well as currency devaluation. The root cause of fraud in a country is not only poor risk management but also the dearth of specialized financial experts with knowledge of nuance of forensic accounting as well as good legal understanding of legal framework. The regulator (RBI), commercial banks, auditors and government of the country need to reconsider their roles and should take more ethical decisions without fear of the political pressures and influences.

Social media has recently become part of people's daily activities; many of them spend hours each day on Messenger, Instagram, Facebook, and other popular social media. Mental health is important at every stage of life. While studies have found a correlation between increased social media usage among young adults and a rise in mental health problems in this demographic, the specific mechanisms linking social media use to these changes remain unclear. This chapter aims to investigate the relationship between social media use and the mental health of young adults. To achieve this objective, the researcher review and consolidate existing literature on the characteristics of social media, the mental health of young adults, and current theories at the social and individual levels that could help explain this relationship.

Preface

Welcome to *Ethical Marketing Through Data Governance Standards and Effective Technology*. In this comprehensive reference book, we delve into the intricacies of modern marketing practices, focusing on the crucial intersection of data governance, technology, and ethical considerations.

In today's digital landscape, marketers face an ever-growing challenge: to harness the power of data while maintaining ethical standards and ensuring consumer trust. Led by Shefali Saluja, Varun Nayyar, Kuleep Rojhe, and Sandhir Sharma, this edited volume offers insights and strategies to navigate this complex terrain.

At the heart of effective marketing lies data governance. Our authors argue that to achieve the coveted status of a single, reliable source of information, organizations must adopt robust data governance strategies. This involves breaking down silos, implementing regulations for data classification, storage, and processing, and embracing emerging technologies such as artificial intelligence (AI).

Indeed, AI has revolutionized marketing, enabling practitioners to glean deeper insights into consumer behavior and craft more personalized, effective campaigns. However, this newfound power comes with responsibilities. As marketers leverage machine learning methods and delve into customer data, they must also consider ethical implications, including issues of privacy, transparency, and fairness.

Moreover, the advent of digital platforms has reshaped advertising standards and practices. From virtual avatars to targeted advertising, companies must navigate a landscape fraught with challenges and opportunities. By studying the intersection of technology, ethics, and consumer psychology, marketers can develop strategies that resonate with their audience while upholding ethical principles.

This book serves as a valuable resource for academics, researchers, management students, and professionals alike. Through its interdisciplinary approach, it aims to enhance understanding and foster dialogue on key issues shaping the future of marketing.

We hope that the insights presented within these pages will inspire readers to approach marketing with a keen awareness of both the possibilities and pitfalls inherent in our digital age. By embracing ethical standards and leveraging technology responsibly, we can chart a path toward a more sustainable and consumer-centric future.

ORGANIZATION OF THE BOOK

In *Ethical Marketing Through Data Governance Standards and Effective Technology*, we present a diverse array of chapters that collectively illuminate the evolving landscape of marketing in today's digital era. Here's a glimpse of the insights each chapter offers:

1. **An Empirical Study of Online and Offline Way of Disclosure of Corporate Environmental Material: A Contrast:** Examining the disclosure practices of environmental information by Indian businesses, this chapter contrasts online and offline modes of dissemination, revealing disparities and areas for improvement in online environmental reporting.

2. **Artificial Intelligence in Forensic Accounting:** This chapter explores the intersection of artificial intelligence and forensic accounting, highlighting the potential of AI technologies in detecting and preventing financial accounting frauds through innovative business intelligence frameworks.

3. **Balancing Ethics and Economics:** Navigating Data Governance in India's Marketing World: Unraveling the complexities of ethical marketing in India's digital landscape, this chapter delves into the intricate dance between ethics, data governance, and economics, offering insights into the challenges and opportunities faced by marketers.

4. **Balancing the Scale - Ethical Marketing in the Age of Big Data: A Comprehensive Analysis of Data Governance Standards and the Role of Effective Technology:** This paper offers a comprehensive analysis of ethical marketing practices, data governance standards, and the role of technology in promoting transparency, accountability, and consumer trust in the era of big data.

5. **Customer Engagement in Metaverse Using Big Data:** Exploring the potential of the metaverse in fostering customer engagement, this chapter examines how brands can leverage big data to create immersive experiences and build lasting relationships with customers in virtual environments.

6. **Ethical Marketing: A Systematic Literature Review:** Conducting a bibliometric analysis, this study identifies influential authors, countries, organizations, and journals in the field of ethical marketing, offering valuable insights for policymakers, educators, and researchers.

7. **Ethical Marketing and Sustainable Development Goals:** This article explores the integration of ethical marketing practices and sustainable development goals, highlighting the positive impact of ethical marketing on brand loyalty and consumer behavior.

8. **Exploring Ethical Dimensions of Marketers' Influence on Electronic Word-of-Mouth and Its Effect on Customer Trust:** Investigating the ethical implications of marketers' influence on electronic word-of-mouth, this study examines the factors contributing to opinion spam and its impact on customer trust.

9. **Exploring Market Knowledge Dimensions and Knowledge Integration Mechanisms in Automotive Cybersecurity and IoT:** This chapter explores the role of market knowledge dimensions and knowledge integration mechanisms in advancing automotive cybersecurity and IoT technologies.

10. **Industry Development at COIR: Trade Reforms and India's Export Outcomes:** Focusing on India's coir industry, this research examines the effects of trade reforms on the sector's development and performance, shedding light on the impact of trade agreements on India's export outcomes.

11. **Instagram and Body Dysmorphia:** Investigating the impact of Instagram on body image and mental health, this chapter explores the link between excessive social media use and body dissatisfaction, highlighting the need for user education and self-care practices.

12. **Marketing 5.0 and the Role of Mind Mapping in Content Advertising: An Analysis:** This paper explores the evolution of marketing in the digital age, emphasizing the role of mind mapping in content creation and discussing the ethical challenges in AI-powered marketing.

13. **Navigating the Digital Frontier an In-Depth Analysis of the Evolving Marketing Mix and the PPACE Acceleration Factor:** Delving into the changing landscape of marketing, this research

examines the emergence of new dimensions in the marketing mix and the significance of P-PACE in contemporary marketing strategies.

14. **Navigating the Intersection of Ethics and Privacy in the AI Era:** This paper explores the ethical implications of AI technologies on privacy, offering insights into the challenges and solutions for creating a responsible and transparent AI ecosystem.

15. **Privacy Matters- Espousing Blockchain and Artificial Intelligence (AI) for Consumer Data Protection on E-Commerce Platforms in Ethical Marketing:** Investigating the intersection of blockchain, AI, and consumer data protection, this paper proposes innovative solutions for strengthening consumer privacy on e-commerce platforms.

16. **Role of Human Resource Management in the Era of Augmented Reality (AR) and Virtual Reality (VR) in Global Market:** This chapter explores the potential advantages of VR and AR technologies in human resource management, offering insights into their applications in a competitive market.

17. **An Analysis on Frauds Affecting Financial Security of Indian Banking Sector: A Systematic Literature Review:** Delving into the crucial role of the banking sector in India's economic growth, this chapter explores the transformations and challenges faced by the industry, particularly in combating various types of fraud and scams.

18. **An Analytical Study on Perception of College Going Students towards the Use of E-Commerce Platforms:** Focusing on the perceptions of college students regarding e-commerce platforms, this study investigates the correlation between online shopping behavior and demographic factors, shedding light on the practicality and challenges of online purchasing.

19. **Showrooming An Ethical Gamble in Marketing:** Discussing the phenomenon of showrooming in retail, this chapter explores the ethical concerns and challenges faced by offline retailers, offering strategies to mitigate the impact of showrooming on businesses.

20. **Strategic Talent Acquisition for Ethical Marketing: Leveraging Technology and Data Governance:** Examining the role of talent acquisition in ethical marketing success, this chapter highlights the strategic importance of assembling teams capable of navigating digital marketing while upholding ethical principles.

21. **Swift Transactions and Unethical Conduct: A Blame Game:** Investigating ethical issues in the banking sector, this article highlights the unauthorized use of SWIFT codes and the implications of rising frauds on India's economic growth.

22. **The Impact of Social Media on Mental Health: Voices from College Students:** This paper explores the relationship between social media use and mental health among young adults, shedding light on the mechanisms linking social media to mental health issues.

These chapters collectively offer a rich tapestry of insights into the multifaceted world of ethical marketing, data governance, and technology, providing valuable perspectives for researchers, educators, policymakers, and industry professionals alike.

IN CONCLUSION

In *Ethical Marketing Through Data Governance Standards and Effective Technology*, we have embarked on a journey through the dynamic landscape of modern marketing, where ethical considerations intersect with data governance and technological advancements. From analyzing frauds affecting financial security in the banking sector to exploring the impact of social media on mental health, each chapter offers unique insights into the challenges and opportunities facing marketers in today's digital age.

Throughout this edited reference book, we have witnessed the evolution of marketing practices, from traditional methods to the era of big data and artificial intelligence. We have examined the ethical dilemmas inherent in leveraging consumer data for targeted advertising and customer engagement, while also exploring innovative solutions to safeguard consumer privacy and trust.

As editors, our aim has been to shed light on the intricate complexities of ethical marketing and data governance, providing readers with a comprehensive understanding of the key issues at play. From the analysis of perception towards e-commerce platforms to the exploration of showrooming in retail, each chapter contributes to a deeper understanding of the ethical considerations that underpin modern marketing strategies.

Moving forward, it is imperative that marketers, policymakers, and industry stakeholders continue to prioritize ethical practices and responsible data governance. By embracing transparency, accountability, and consumer-centric approaches, we can foster a marketing landscape that not only drives economic growth but also upholds ethical standards and respects individual rights.

We hope that the insights presented in this book will inspire further research, dialogue, and action in the pursuit of ethical marketing practices and effective data governance standards. Together, let us navigate the ever-changing terrain of digital marketing with integrity, innovation, and a commitment to ethical principles.

Shefali Saluja
Chitkara Business School, Chitkara University, India

Varun Nayyar
Chitkara University, India

Kuleep Rojhe
Chitkara University, India

Sandhir Sharma
Chitkara Business School, Chitkara University, India

Chapter 1
An Empirical Study of Online and Offline Way of Disclosure of Corporate Environmental Material:
A Contrast

Annumeet Nagra
GNA University, India

Shefali Saluja
(iD) https://orcid.org/0000-0002-8560-5150
Chitkara Business School, Chitkara University, India

ABSTRACT

The growth of the internet and other IT has altered global ease of necessary material outside of national boundaries. Due to the internet's capacity to disseminate information at a rapid pace, most businesses today are taking advantage of the opportunity to reveal financial as well as nonfinancial material to their stakeholders, such as environmental related content. The sample used in the current study consisted of 100 businesses that are listed on the BSE-500 Index Stock. T-test was utilised as the statistical method in the current study to compare the online and offline modes of disseminating environmental information by Indian businesses and MNCs. MS-Excel Analysis Tool Pack was used as the study's software. Analysis of it has shown that it is a sad situation when some of the top executives of major corporations are found to be withholding any type of information about their environmental performance. In India, online environmental reporting is still in its infancy. Large business houses and markets with high market capitalization do not give much thought to their surroundings.

DOI: 10.4018/979-8-3693-2215-4.ch001

INTRODUCTION

Nowadays, it is common for corporate entities to use the internet for a variety of commercial goals (Scott and Jackson, 2002; Coupland, 2006; Jenkins and Yakovleva, 2006). The internet can be used for conducting business or transferring business-related materials. The internet also contributes to a global meeting field for those interested in environmental content (Jenkins and Yakovleva, 2006). Given the cost accumulation and the substance of approach for an increasing number of people, the appeal of such internet environmental reporting (IER) is evident (Gray and Bebbington, 2001). The Internet Environmental Reporting (IER) programme aims to reduce corporate spending while also attempting to improve public access to information about business practises and to provide a massive amount of content.

Environmental Reporting on the Internet: A Developing Stage

According to (Perera et al 2003), internet is a new intermediate which is adequate to diminish the exaggeration in transmission means and curtail the deal between prosperous and abundance of material. The OECD (2004, 2005) states that the application of the internet and other IT upgrade material promulgation deriving in more balanced; cost valuable and convenient approach to pertinent material by investors. The expansion in internet and other IT has changed universal convenience of requisite material beyond national confines. Indeed, with the help of internet transmission of material is more valuable and malleable as compared to other medium of transmission. Another probable aspect of the internet in developing countries it is comparably unique medium transmitting material to public providing volume of material in a greater speed and in more and in better adequate ways to various stakeholders (Aly et al 2010). In the words of (Debreceny et al 2002), today most of the companies are taking benefits to unveil financial as well as non-financial material like environmental related material to their stakeholders because of internet's capacity in dispersing material at a high speed.

As (Line et al 2002), states that now several corporate introduce social reporting in their environmental statement; some of the companies provide a fully unified corporate sustainability report, while some of the corporate define their statement as environment, health and safety (EHS) reports. Particularly, firms have their own way of environmental reporting on the internet, some corporate form their statement confers to distinct stakeholders; some disclose confer to segment of their business or environmental and social matters. According to (Gray et al 2001), the feasible research related to the environmental reporting conduct has patented on developed nations and limited consideration has been provided to the case of environmental reporting of developing nations. In spite the speedy rise of web utilization in the financial market, in this field the scholastic research is still in its inception phase. Therefore, this investigation grants to the actual group of research by concentrating on the convenience of environmental material on company's websites. Still only a few of environmental statement on the corporate websites; for instance, (Ahmed and Sulaiman 2004), have asserted the importance of research beyond ARs to analyse the amount of environmental reporting by companies.

LITERATURE REVIEW

Adams and Frost (2004), the researchers have taken a study of sample of top 100 firms of Australia, UK and Germany. The aim of the entire study was to gather an extensive explanation of corporate responsibility to and use of web technologies. The conclusion has been drawn by the authors that for most of the firm's web-site is recognize as an essential intermediate for the communication of environmental and societal data, still the transmission of environmental and social information is recognize as a comparatively unnecessary operation of the corporate web-site, in spite of that customers and shareholders actually the most necessary stakeholders effecting web-site design and the NGOs and government bodies were found to be the main users of environmental and social information.

Chatterjee and Mir (2008) have used a sample for the study consists of the top 38 Indian listed companies and this selection depends on the market capitalisation of the corporate. The authors have assessed the deliberate environmental data revelation by the Indian firms on their ARs and online, the authors have stated that there is a decline of environmental revelation as 15 out of 38 companies mentioning no environmental data online.

Bhasin (2012), the author has elected 39 Indian firms as sample of study during the year 2005 to 2006 and the author has inspected the websites of all the selected firms that is 39 from time to time. The author has found that companies present more environment related matters on their sites, in sharp comparison, to detailing made inside their ARs but lamentably, environment related matters in ARs is general, vast, and historical in nature, without precisely explaining the environment administration strategy pursued by the presentation of assertion from the company executives regarding conformity with the external norms.

Uwalomwa UWUIGBE (2012), the author has taken the sample for the study which includes 30 companies of Nigeria who are listed at the NSE and the purpose of the study was to investigate in Nigeria either there is an important distinction between the financial and non-financial companies in the degree of web-based CED and the conclusion has been drawn by the author that there is no important or significant distinction between the financial and non-financial organisations in the level of web-based CED.

Anastácia Rosa Portellaa and José Alonso Borba (2020), the authors have taken the sample of the study are divided into 12 sectors. Of the 117 companies, 57 are from Brazil and 60 from the USA. The purpose of this paper is to contribute to the area of environmental accounting, as it investigates whether the companies located in different countries, from different sectors, in different stages of development and regulatory environments present different levels of environmental disclosure and to explain the environmental disclosure extension on corporate websites of companies in Brazil and the USA through corporate characteristics. To achieve such purpose, an environmental disclosure index (EDI) was created, and a model was used to investigate whether the variables environmental performance, size, profitability, debt, sector and country explain the disclosure on the website. The conclusion has been drawn that the US companies stood out compared to Brazilian companies throughout the EDI

RESEARCH METHODOLOGY

The present study presents a comparative study of websites and annual reports of disclosure of environmental related data in selected manufacturing companies. In this research, need an analysis of official websites of 100 selected manufacturing companies which are divided into Indian and MNC's corporations. Firstly, the official websites of all these 100 corporations were inspected and to analyse the convenience and the amount of environment related material administer on their official websites. Then, content analysis has been applied to inspect the amount of environment related material in the company's ARs. Thirdly, to make comparison of websites and ARs of Indian companies and MNC's in respect to dispersing of environment related information and to achieve the results t-test has been utilized. In the present study, the data has been examined by using MS-Excel tool pack.

The main reason to use a sample of large companies was that these companies are globally recognized and more likely to have a web page that provides corporate environmental reporting (CER) and these companies or sectors have great impact on the environment due to their processing techniques so excluded the non-financial sector as this sector has no negative effect on the environment (Fortes 2002).

HYPOTHESIS DEVELOPMENT

Ho1: There is no significant distinction between the environmental data revealed in the annual reports of Indian companies and annual reports of MNC's.

Ha1: There is a significant difference between the environmental data disclosed in the annual reports of Indian companies and annual reports of MNC's.

Ho2: There is no significant distinction between the environmental data disclosed on the websites of Indian companies and websites of MNC's.

Ha2: There is a significant distinction between the environmental data revealed on the websites of Indian companies and websites of MNC's.

RESULTS AND DISCUSSION

Percentage of Companies Disclosing Environmental Information

The companies which have selected for the aim of this study, it is supposed that in their work performance they should be immensely virtuous, and they should also contribute the information about their business activities whether ethical or unethical regarding these business practices influencing the environmental surrounding and natural reserves. In the below table no 1 detailed description has been mentioned in respect of the percentage of companies unveiling their environmental data in their ARs and on their websites.

Table 1. Percentage of companies disclosing of environmental information

Status of company's environmental disclosure material in the Ars	Company's not disclose environmental material in the annual report	Company's disclose environmental material on the websites	Company's not disclose environmental material on the websites
77%	23%	68%	32%

Source: By the author's analysis

Interpretation

After analysing the above table, it has been found that some prestigious companies who did not provide any single word regarding environmental protection on their websites and even in their ARs. It was found that out of 100 selected companies as the sample of study 77% companies reveal their environmental activities in their ARs and 23% companies didn't unveil any environmental information in their ARs. Whereas, in case of websites or online 68% companies disclose their environment related information on their websites and 32% companies did not disclose any single word regarding sustainability or environment on their websites. It is a melancholy state of incident when some of the leaders of the huge corporate world are not contributing any kind of information regarding their environmental performance. The outcomes are persistent with the results of other studies Bhasin (2012), Naser et al (2006), Zhang et al (2007) and Boliver and Garcia (2004).

Indian Companies and MNC's Disclosing Environmental Information

The details of disclosure of environmental performance regarding Indian companies and MNC's in respect of ARs and websites have been shown in the below table.

Table 2. Percentage of Indian companies and MNC's disclosing of environmental information

Indian companies disclose environmental Information in ARs and websites		MNC's disclose environmental information in ARs and websites	
Annual reports (48%)	Websites (43%)	Annual reports (29%)	Websites (25%)

Source: AR's of companies and websites

Interpretation

From the above table it has been found that in case of Indian company's the scores are 48% and 43% regarding annual reports and websites, respectively. On the other context, in case of MNC's, 29% companies reveal their environmental information in their ARs, and 25% companies disclose their environmental related activities in their websites. After all these analyses, it has been found that still in India environmental reporting on the web is at its infancy stage. In India, there must be some mandatory guidelines regarding the protection of environment which must be lying on all the corporate sectors whether it is small, medium, or large. The Indian government must impose penalty if any of the corporate associate does not follow the environment related guidelines.

Position of Disclosure of Environmental Material

In the absence of important guidelines and rules, it has been found from the study that the position of revelation of environmental data on the website diversifies from firm to firm. The detailed position of revelation of environmental data has been depicted in the below table:

Table 3. Position of environmental disclosure (ED) in the ARs and the websites

Position of ED	Board's report	Sustainability report	BRR	CSR section	Sustainability action	EHS policy	Others	Multiple segment	About us
Annual reports	25	-	30	-	18	15	5	6	-
Websites	-	35	-	15	14	11	8	8	7

Source: Author's detailed analysis
*BRR stands for business responsibility report, EHS stands for environment, health and safety.
*Others segment covers like environmental performance, environmental protection and conservation, natural capital, environment management and Swachh Bharat Abhiyaan.
*Multiple segments cover sections under various sub sections.

Interpretation

In the above table, it has been seen that in case of annual reports the most selected position for disclosure of environmental material is the BRR section where 30 out of 100 companies provided information regarding environment in this section following by board's report section as 25 companies provided environmental information in different headings like in the form of sustainability and environment information, environmental performance and energy conservation, environment sustainability, environment management etc. In case of websites, the favourite place was found in the sustainability report as 35 companies disclosed information directly on the sustainability report section. In the rest of the section 15 companies disclosed information in CSR segment, in case of sustainability action segment 14 companies disclosed the segments like EHS (11), others (8), about us (7) and multiple segments (8) companies reveal environmental data. After studying the various annual reports and websites, we have found that it become trouble for some of the customers and users to restore any effective meaning from the different places as the environment related information is dispersed at different places.

Comparative Study of Environmental Information Disclosure in Companies ARs and Websites

This section of the examination analysed whether the material disclosed on the firm's website and in the company's ARs are identical or distinct. The t-test has been applied in the below tables to examine the difference. The detailed explanation of variance in disclosure of the Indian companies (annual reports) and MNC's (annual reports) has been given in the table no 4:

Table 4. Variance in disclosure of the Indian companies (annual reports) and MNC's (annual reports)

	Indian companies (annual reports)	MNC's (annual reports)
Mean	16.31	9.40
Variance	187.77	69.99
Observation	32	32
Hypothesized mean difference	0	-
Df	31	-
t-stat	2.43	-
P(T<=t) one-tail	0.00	-
t critical one-tail	1.67	-
P(T<=t) two-tail	0.01*	-
t critical two-tail	2.00	-

Note- *Level of significant at 0.05 or 5%

Interpretation

In the above table, it has been found that p-value is (0.01) which is below than 5% level of significance (0.01<0.05) indicates that a statistically significant distinction exists between the position of environmental disclosure in the (ARs) of Indian firms and (annual reports) of MNC's. Hence the null hypothesis (H01) stands rejected.

The detailed explanation of variance in disclosure of the Indian companies (websites) and MNC's (websites) has been mentioned in the below table:

Table 5. Variance in disclosure of the Indian companies (websites) and MNC's (websites)

	Indian companies (websites)	MNC's (websites)
Mean	17.75	8.87
Variance	141.54	56.30
Observation	32	32
Hypothesized mean difference	0	-
Df	31	-
t-stat	3.56	-
P(T<=t) one-tail	0.00	-
t critical one-tail	1.67	-
P(T<=t) two-tail	0.00*	-
t critical two-tail	2.00	-

Note- *Level of significant at 0.05 or 5%

Interpretation

In the above table, it has been seen that the p value is (0.00) that is statistically significant at the 5% level of significance (0.00<0.05) imply that a significant distinction exists between the status of environmental revelation in the Indian company's (websites) and MNC's (websites), so the null hypothesis (H02) stands rejected.

CONCLUSION

From the detailed analysis, it has been concluded that the difference between the annual reports and websites in both the context of Indian co and MNC's but the condition of MNC's websites and annual reports regarding disclosure of environmental items in contrast to Indian company's annual reports and websites was not very bad their percentage level was satisfactory and shows their concern regarding environmental surroundings and their behavior. In the entire above study, it has been noticed that some of the important rules and regulations regarding environment protection has been implemented in the MNC's annual reports or websites instead of Indian company's annual reports or websites.

REFERENCES

Ahmed, K., & Courtis, J. K. (1999). Associations between corporate characteristics and disclosure levels in annual reports: A meta-analysis. *The British Accounting Review*, *31*(1), 35–36. doi:10.1006/bare.1998.0082

Ahmed, K., & Nicholls, D. (1994). The impact of non-financial company characteristics on mandatory compliance in developing countries: The case of Bangladesh. *The International Journal of Accounting*, *29*(1), 60–77.

Ajinkya, B., Bhojraj, S., & Sengupta, P. (2005). The Association Between Outside Directors, Institutional Investors, and the Properties of Management Earnings Forecasts. *Journal of Accounting Research*, *43*(3), 343–376. doi:10.1111/j.1475-679x.2005.00174.x

Akbas, H.E. (2014). Company characteristics and environmental disclosure: An empirical investigation on companies listed on Borsa Istanbul 100 Index. *Journal of Accounting and Finance,* 145-163.

Aktas, R., Kayalidere, K., & Kargin, M. (2013). "CSR and analysis of sustainability reports in Turkey," *International Journal of Economics and Finance*, 5(3), ● Bhasin, M.L. (2012), "Corporate environmental reporting on the internet: An exploratory study', *International. Journal of. Managerial and Financial Accounting*, *4*(1), 78–103.

Bhuiyan, M. H. U., Pallab, K. B., & Suman, P. C. (2007). Corporate Internet Reporting Practice in Developing Economies: Evidence from Bangladesh'. *Cost and Management*, *35*(5).

Bora, B. J., & Das, T. C. (2013). Corporate environmental reporting in the context of recent changes in regulatory framework with special reference to India.

Chambers, R. J. (1966). *Accounting, evaluation and economic behaviour*. Prentice Hall.

Chatterjee, B., & Mir, M. Z. (2008). The current status of environmental reporting by Indian corporations. *Managerial Auditing Journal, 23*(6), 609–629. doi:10.1108/02686900810882138

Chaudhary, A. (2011). Changing structure of Indian textiles industry after MFA (MultiFibre Agreement) phase out: A global perspective'. *Far East Journal of Psychology and Business, 2*(2), 1–23.

Hossain, M., & Reaz, M. (2007). The determinants and characteristics of voluntary disclosure by Indian banking companies. *Corporate Social Responsibility and Environmental Management, 14*(5), 274–288. doi:10.1002/csr.154

Hossain, M., Tan, M. L., & Adams, M. (1994). Voluntary disclosure in an emerging capital market: Some empirical evidence from companies listed on Kuala Lumpur Stock exchange. *The International Journal of Accounting, 29*(4), 334–351.

Suchman, C. M. (1995). Managing legitimacy: Strategic and Institutional approaches. *Academy of Management Review, 20*(3), 571–61. doi:10.2307/258788

Sumaiani, Y., Haslinda, Y., & Lehman, G. (2007). Environmental reporting in a developing country: A case study on status and implementation in Malaysia. *Journal of Cleaner Production, 15*(10), 895–901. doi:10.1016/j.jclepro.2006.01.012

Suttipun, M., & Stanton, P. (2012). A study of Environmental Disclosures by Thai listed Companies on Websites. *Procedia Economics and Finance, 2*, 9–15. doi:10.1016/S2212-5671(12)00059-7

Uwuigbe, U., & Jimoh, J. (2012). Corporate environmental disclosure in the Nigerian manufacturing industry: A study of selected firms. *African Research Review, 6*(3), 71–83. doi:10.4314/afrrev.v6i3.5

Van Marrewijk, M., & Werre, M. (2003). Multiple levels of corporate sustainability. *Journal of Business Ethics, 44*(2-3), 107–119. doi:10.1023/A:1023383229086

Zhang, T., Gao, S. S., & Zhang, J. J. (2007). Corporate Environmental Reporting on the Web – An Exploratory Study of Chinese Listed Companies. *Issues in Social and Environmental Accounting, 1*(1), 91–108. doi:10.22164/isea.v1i1.10

Chapter 2
Artificial Intelligence in Forensic Accounting

Shefali Saluja
🆔 https://orcid.org/0000-0002-8560-5150
Chitkara Business School, Chitkara University, India

Varun Nayyar
Chitkara University, India

Shuchi Dawra
🆔 https://orcid.org/0000-0001-9296-6838
Chitkara Business School, Chitkara University, India

Mansi Jain
Chitkara Business School, Chitkara University, India

Rishi Prakash Shukla
🆔 https://orcid.org/0000-0003-0854-7302
Chandigarh University, India

ABSTRACT

The artificial intelligence technological revolution is sweeping across the globe; audit is no exception. The dimension of auditing is about to get revolutionized with not just automation, but intelligence-based automation; the future of traditional auditing, especially manual one, is being redesigned. IAA, or intelligent audit automation, is the next generation of auditing services that encapsulates new auditing business models, new auditing professionals, and new ways of looking at the data creation. With the increase in accounting frauds in the current economic scenario, the discovery of financial accounting fraud detection (FAFD) has become a prominent topic in the field of education, research and industry. The chapter investigates the current economic fraud detection issues and proposes an accounting framework using business intelligence as a viable way to address them. The chapter adopts an exemplary research approach to present how business intelligence can be used in detecting accounting fraud.

DOI: 10.4018/979-8-3693-2215-4.ch002

INTRODUCTION

Today many industries are turning to Artificial Intelligence (AI) to perform tasks that were previously performed by humans. (Omoteso, 2012) When it comes to processing large amount of data, detecting fraud by identifying unusual patterns, communicating with customers online, and performing other important tasks, the financial service industry has embraced AI. For example, in facial reorganization, voice recognition, or Machine Learning (ML), there are a few excellent use cases. In addition to improving customer value propositions, new technologies also improve the efficiency and effectiveness of the organization.It has been a hot topic in recent years to predict AI applications that will be available in the financial services sector soon. Especially as blockchains and cryptocurrency acceptance increase, there is a high chance that transaction security and account security will improve. Due to reduced or eliminated transaction costs, the need for a intermediary is eliminated. All types of digital assistants and applications will continue to improve themselves using a cognitive computing. From debt repayment to tax adjustment, smart machines can plan and perform both short-term and long-term tasks (Sandhu and Saluja, 2023). A greater degree of transparency will result in more detailed, accurate and complete customer reporting, which can take hours to complete by humans. During Artificial Intelligence, general accounting officers left the accounting system to complete a few more complex tasks (Saluja et al.,2021). This will significantly improve job performance, reduce errors, increase corporate productivity, and allow the accounting industry to continue to transform the accounting field. The accounting industry has a long history of applying artificial intelligence (AI) applications, especially financial reporting and auditing. The recent development of AI products has contributed to the development of robots and robust infrastructure of experts in accounting software. So, this emerging technology has made a huge difference in the market environment and affected the business activity. (Berdiyeva et al, 2021) The advent of accounting software and the new AI developments have completely transformed accounting systems. Highly intelligent Artificial Intelligence Algorithms can meet the need for new power in the financial sector as computer computing power grows. (Kokina & Davenport, 2017) AI is widely used in investment management, algorithm trading, fraud detection, lending, and underwriting, to name just a few. Administrators will be able to determine illegal compliance using AI. This is the emergence of experience based on supervision of transaction and analysis of large amounts of data, while the required skills and knowledge of regulators will be discussed. Artificial intelligence depends on understanding the nature of human intelligence by creating computer programs capable of simulating human behavior and provide participants with the information they need to help them perform various decisions quickly and timely. This has led to the development of the concept of accounting in many areas, most notably the integration of accounting with the law, which has led to the emergence of what is known as Forensic Accounting, which crystallized in two terms (Accounting; Forensics); thus, the term accounting means the identification, recording, classification and summarizing of economic events in a logical manner (Wong & Venkatraman, 2015). The organization provides financial information to make economic decisions; with regard to the term Forensic, it is a term associated with the courts of law. A forensic accountant needs such technology-based programs and mimics the human mind. It also has great speed in providing the necessary information and power beyond human capabilities in terms of speed and accuracy. Therefore, this study has been helpful in showcasing the impact of artificial intelligence in the performance of a forensic accountant.

Objectives of the Paper

1. To outline the structures which are followed by the Artificial intelligence system to detect the anomalies and fraud patterns.
2. To focus on the relevance of big data and data mining is facilitating the process of Forensic accounting.
3. To identify how specialized skills and specific knowledge of the Artificial Intelligence system can help in the field of forensic accounting.

LITERATURE REVIEW

The business of the future in general, and especially in the field of accounting, may have a broad and clear understanding of the 21st century of governance, awareness and accountability created by the environment. Therefore, accountants and auditors working in markets and corporations should have a clear understanding of how to deal with fraudulent transactions and forensic accounting calculations. The concept of forensic accounting is new, leading to a lack of education. Similarly, a study conducted by McMullen and Sanchez (2010) found that the demand for forensic accountants may be increased in the future, especially in the area of fraudulent financial reporting. At present, the impact of AI on auditing is particularly evident in the data acquisition area (data extraction, comparison, and verification) (Wong & Venkatraman, 2015). This means that AI-enabled technology can find relevant information, extract it from documents, and make it available to human auditors, allowing them to devote more time to areas requiring higher-level judgement. Modern artificial intelligence (AI) tools are increasingly capable of scanning keywords and patterns into complex electronic documents in order to identify and extract relevant accounting information from a variety of sources, such as sales, contracts, and invoices (Ryman-Tubb et al, 2018). There is a growing demand for Big Data knowledge and skills, especially among business and accounting professionals.

Russom (2011) predicts the increasing use of Big Data, especially in the areas of predictable analytics, machine learning, practical intelligence, visual effects (dashboards), data storage systems, database management systems and big data technologies. A study by Charted Global Management Accountant (2014) suggests that the use of cloud-based solutions in accounting information systems encourages professional accountants to know more about Big Data capabilities, such as cyber security / information. Traditionally, forensic accountants rely on domain knowledge driven approach, which includes information on specific fraud / crime schemes and the expert opinions expressed by red flags on detection and discovery of fraud (Berdiyeva et al, 2021). Progressive forensic accountants use unstructured data statistics and machine learning to "discover hidden patterns within the data themselves, thus exposing the unknown" in order to improve their chances of finding unexpected fraud. Chen and Storey (2012) argue that Big Data analytics can improve the performance of financial fraud detection. Cao, Chychyla, and Stewart (2015) suggest that Big Data / analytics can improve the efficiency and effectiveness of financial statement audits. Auditors may use statistics to analyze more information on clients' past transactions or the results of previous audits in order to identify fraudulent risks and to pave the audit efforts in detecting fraud. For example, auditors including accountants may use statistical relationships between business items and processes to detect unusual events or fraud. On the other hand, insignificant information can limit the amount of Big Data usage and data analysis to auditors. Auditors, on the other hand, need knowledge and skills to clearly understand the quality and relevance of data in order to make informed decisions.

RESEARCH METHODOLOGY

1. Data Collection
2. Data Analysis
3. Data Presentation
4. Data summary
5. Conclusion and

Limitations

Figure 1. Research methodology

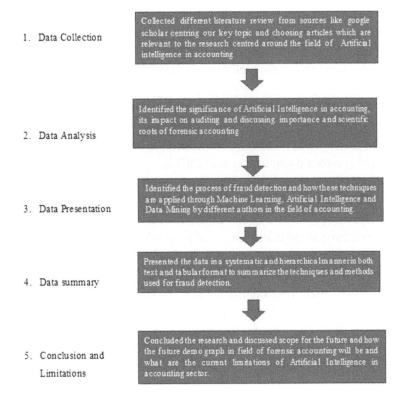

The research carried out by the authors were in reference to the topic of Artificial Intelligence in accounting along with the discussing about machine learning and data mining which are closely linked to artificial intelligence and the proposed techniques and methods of fraud detection by various authors.

Impact of Artificial Intelligence on Accounting and Auditing

The field of general accounting and auditing in particular has undergone significant changes due to advances in data analytics and artificial intelligence (AI). This paper encourages the need to critically evaluate the use of artificial intelligence in accounting. Although the concept of using accounting and auditing skills is certainly not new, there is reason to expect that their impact on the sector will be significant in the coming years due to the latest technological advances (Baldwin et al, 2006). Artificial intelligence requires both big data and processing power, and both are widely available today. The auditing is particularly relevant to the use of data analytics and artificial intelligence because it has been challenging to enter a large amount of formal and informal data to gain an understanding of the financial and non-financial performance of companies. Also, most of the audit activities are organized and repetitive, and therefore, can be done automatically. In other words, accounting and auditing have not been left behind in the recent spring of AI. (Bell & Carcello, 2000) The focus of AI skills in auditing is basically on the automation of labor-intensive work. At present, the impact of AI on auditing is particularly evident in the area of data acquisition, data mining (data extraction). This means that AI-enabled technology can retrieve relevant data, extract it from documents, and create it helpful for a human auditor, who can devote most of his time to areas that need high judgment. For example, AI tools can detect if a company records unusually high sales just before the end of the reporting period, or releases unusually high payments immediately after the end of the reporting period. AI tools can also detect anomalies in data, such as an unexpected increase in orders somewhere, unusually high expense items sent by one person.

Trend-Enablers of AI in Accounting

For AI to get a solid foundation in today's world rather than come out several times over the past few decades, it relies heavily on four potential trends: ABCD.

Availability of affordable and powerful equipment. The rapid technological advancement has opened the door to the powerful growth of computing power. This goes hand in hand with tumbling cost of computing. Improved computing power also comes in the form of highly improved processing speed. These days technology experts have noted that what could have taken weeks to process in the last ten years, has taken just a few hours in the last five years and can now be done in minutes. Accessibility, portability and speed is why AI is now readily available in businesses for use, adoption and implementation.

Better algorithms will be used. Like computing power, AI techniques and algorithms have also seen significant improvements in recent times. With a lot of research poured into changing and developing the basic algorithms behind AI, there is now a complete series of AI strategies that can be used to solve various problems. A growing community of developers are constantly updating and refining these algorithms while also integrating them into free accessible packages in open-source programming languages such as R and Python.

Cloud-computing has provided AI a platform to shine by providing advanced access beyond hardware and device storage. Companies have begun moving to cloud-based platforms to run operations from the cloud without being pressured by physical limitations. Cloud providers like Google Cloud integrate AI and ML services into an application programming interface (API) that allows businesses to create customized solutions for their own or their clients' problems. Cloud platforms also enable data storage, computer capabilities and image processing units (GPU) scalable, thus enabling AI and ML algorithms to work efficiently without the limitations of on-site computer hardware. Advanced learning using Neural

Networks has proven to work at least 10 times faster with cloud-based GPU speeds compared to standard computer processing units (CPUs).

Data is everywhere. Traditionally, data collected for analysis were primarily numerical and structured. The growth and flow of Big Data, in addition to the growing number of social media platforms, has led to an unprecedented "hunger" for data of all kinds, including images, text and videos. Previously These types of data were not considered useful in analytics or AI and ML. However, Big Data storage systems, whether virtual or cloud-based, have now allowed for random data storage and processing of this data. A good example is Apache Hadoop, a powerful Big Data analytics engine.

Forensic Accounting and Its Scientific Rooting

The main purpose of auditing is not to detect fraud or fraudulent practices. Instead, the auditors are intended to determine whether the information in the financial statements is presented in accordance with GAAP. While one of their responsibilities includes informing managers about the existence of significant differences or fraud, the primary responsibility for preventing fraud and detection lies with the management. Here comes forensic accounting (also called forensic auditing) into the picture. Forensic Auditors go beyond the financial statements and collect data from various internal and external sources to identify anomalies and gather the audit evidence. They look at financial data and statistics and conduct inquiries and interviews with company officials and employees to detect fraud and other illegal business activities. Whenever a scandal of accounting or fraud is exposed, the need and importance of forensic auditors intensifies. (Omoteso, 2012) With the advancement of technology, the importance of AI software and products has become increasingly important in auditing and investigative firms to expose fraud and address advanced issues. Forensic accounting is a practice of accounting that involves the investigation of organizational records to obtain evidence of financial crime. While forensic investigators do go over bookkeeping records, similar to an auditor, the objectives and scope of a forensic investigation are vastly different and require a different form of training. Forensic investigators also examine non-financial records such as management records, minutes of meeting, or even the access records maintained at the guard house. Forensic investigation focusses on the company's internal control system but also aimed at understanding their potential weakness to identify possible exploitation, usually in the form of complex fraud schemes or alternatives to theft methods (Saluja,2022). In addition, forensic accounting can also be used to check compliance with company rules as well as the overall structure of the organization to manage both current and future risks. These advisory services often see forensic accountants providing expert opinions or advice to help the company manage its uncertainties. Forensic investigators often consider situations where existing controls are broken, or there may be fraud, or where there are instances of non-compliance the company has never experienced (Bell & Carcello, 2000).

Figure 2. Forensic accounting framework using artificial intelligence
(Authors)

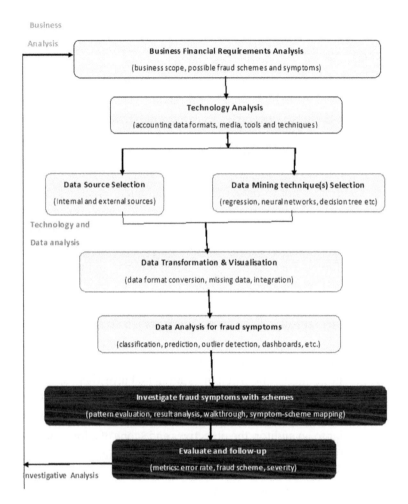

Use of AI and Machine Learning in Forensic Accounting

AI has emerged as a useful tool for classifying financial data over many years in order to identify patterns of spending and risky transactions. (Kokina & Davenport, 2017) The use of these AI platforms greatly improves the efficiency of forensic auditing and reduces the timeline of work performed. New fraud schemes appear every year and fraudsters are becoming increasingly complex due to advances in information technology (IT). It is important for organizations and financial firms to use new software and AI platforms to improve the effectiveness of their research and investigations in order to detect fraudulent activity where internal controls fail or fall short (Baldwin et al, 2006).

Now let's just discuss how Artificial intelligence (AI) and its subset of Machine Learning (ML) can empower the forensic auditors:

1)   BIG DATA TECHNOLOGY

Big data can generate a link between both financial and non-financial information in order to detect potential patterns. Includes data extraction in informal genres such as texts, social media content, conference reports and discussions.

2) NEURAL NETWORKS

Neural networks can show complex and indirect relationships in data to detect financial fraud. They see trends and complex relationships that cannot be seen with other methods of computational methods.

3) MATCH BETWEEN TWO UNRELATED PARTIES

AI compares data on websites with various systems - especially those where data has never been compared. For example, it will check supplier payments to check for cases where the provider's name, address or bank account matches employee details. Comparing between different or unrelated databases in a limited time is almost impossible for humans. AI gives them an extra chance to look at the matters in depth.

4) VARIETY OF DATA SYSTEMS AND TOOLS

Financial Auditors must audit the books of accounts and other financial records held by management. However, for forensic auditors, the most difficult task is to deal with a number of data systems such as back-office programs, customer relationship management systems (CRMs), communication platforms, emails and mobile messaging applications for data collection and retrieval patterns (Baldwin et al, 2006).

In addition to analyzing systematic data, which can be found in the accounting system or Enterprise Resource Planning (ERP), forensic auditors should obtain informal information available via email, WhatsApp and other communication channels. AI can capture information, identify patterns and organize data into manageable groups for human analysis - less than one-tenth of the time a team can take.

Forensic and Big Data Analytics Tool for Fraud Detection

1) THE MEANING OF BIG DATA

The most common definition of Big Data identifies itself as "high volume, high speed and versatile information assets requiring inexpensive, innovative forms of information processing for enhanced insight and decision making". This definition emphasizes certain aspects of Big Data. In particular, while the "high volume" of data is related to its maximum size, the high velocity corresponds to the speed at which the data is given and the "high variety" refers to the greater number of sources from which it is derived (Sharma & Panigrahi, 2012).Big data is powerful for businesses. It provides important insights and potential opportunities for these companies to get the information they need to transform their business course to meet customer needs. Big data offers the opportunity for a modern business owner. By analyzing big data, companies can better focus on resources, for example, in segments that best fit consumer needs. In the simplest examples, big data can help a company predicting buying trends, allowing the company to store the right products on the shelves, before they run out

2) THE ADOPTION OF BIG DATA: CHALLENGES AND OPPORTUNITIES FOR THE AUDITORS

One of the major risks this benefits of big data face is the increased risk of fraud. It's hard to identify, it's hard to follow, and it's hard to stop. A fraudulent employee or transaction is easily created. Detecting fraud and working to detect criminal activities has become a major part of the job. The use of Big Data analysis in the auditing field is important. First, some Authors highlight the fact that Big Data will drastically change accounting with particular reference to accounting quality and appropriateness of accounting information. In particular, Big Data, in terms of financial statements, can improve transparency and useful decision-making. Someone has suggested the use of Big Data as "audit evidence". Audit evidence is the entire set of information that an auditor needs to obtain in order to determine whether the financial statements are kept in accordance with accounting principles. In this case, Big Data represents basic audit evidence due to its relevance and reliability. The use of Big Data enables auditors to analyze large population of data for financial and non-financial information.

3) THE USE OF BIG DATA IN FRAUD AUDITING

Big data analysis can be used effectively when there is lack of "traditional" audit evidence collected mainly through financial information, in the case of fraud detection. Acquiring evidence of an existing fraud can be difficult considering that great part of this evidence is related to management's lifestyle, ethics and moral value (Sharma & Panigrahi, 2012). In addition, fraud represents a very small percentage of transactions. Big data represent rich data sources useful to identify potentially fraudulent activities rendering too difficult for fraudster to cover the fraud committed in the financial statements. In these respects, thanks to the analytic nonfinancial data and nonfinancial measures can be use as variables to develop predictive tools able to aid auditors in detecting fraud (Wong & Venkatraman, 2015). A possible use of Big Data to prevent fraud, for example, deals with money laundering operations. Big data analytics can be used also in order to obtain evidence about fraud using financial information.

BENFORD'S LAW

The technique of detecting the anomalies in the data which is commonly used on a pattern based is Benford's law. According to this law, when one looks at a large set of number, it is expected that the probability of each number occurring from 1 to 9 is likely and roughly to be equal but according to Benford, the probability of occurrence of 1 is 30% and it keeps on reducing for the subsequent numbers and for 9 it is as low as 5% (Cho & Gaines, 2007). It is supported by the Newcomb's observation that "the law of probability of the occurrence of numbers is such that all man Tissa's of their logarithms is equally probable," The expression that can conveniently explain this observation is

$$P(d) = Log10\left(\frac{1+d}{d}\right) for\ d\epsilon\ \{1,.....,9\}$$

The rough probability of each number is for 2 it is 17.6%, 3(12.5%), 4(9.7%), 5(7.9%), 6(6.7%), 7(5.8%), 8(5.1%) (Cho & Gaines, 2007). By application of this law, if data is fabricated, this law can be applied to check whether the probability roughly matches with the given data and if it doesn't, data is deemed fabricated and checked further. The success rate of Benford's law is not very high when applied to data which is corelated as data independence is the fundamental characteristic for the application of Benford's law.

Mark Nigrini an author most promoting Benford's Law came up with three fraud detection techniques, which are:

1. Same-Same-Same
2. Same-Same-Different
3. Relative Size Factor

Definition

Measure: Set of values or data on which the process being is carried out.

Level: Step organization of data that will allows the checking on different levels of data representation.

Same-Same-Same

The formula definition of Same-Same-Same operator can be given as *SSS(Measure, Levels_of_Selection, Same_Level)*.

Where measure and level have the same definition that has been defined previously, so when the SSS operator is applied on the data, it will return the values when measure comes same for the given level of selection corresponding to the same level defined in the data (Moreno et al., 2018). For example, we can say that if this operator is applied to a supermarket data, it will present the data which indicates same product of same quantity bought by the same customer.

Same-Same-Different

The formula definition of Same-Same-Different operator can be given as *SSD(Measure, Levels_of_Selection, Same_Level, Different_Level)*.

Where measure and level have the same definition that has been defined previously, so when the SSD operator is applied on the data, it will return the values where the measures come same for the given level of selection corresponding to same level for different levels defined in the data (Moreno et al., 2018). Taking the same situation as example from above when the SSD is applied to the data of a supermarket, it will return the data which indicates that the same product is bought of the same quantity by different customers.

Relative Size Factor

The formula definition of Relative Size Factor operator can be given as *RSF(Measure, Levels_of_Selection)*.

Where measure and level have the same definition that has been defined previously, so when the RSF operator is applied on the data, it will return the highest value of measure corresponding to the level of selection and the second highest value in the data (Moreno et al., 2018). Again, applying this on the above discussed situation, when the RSF is applied on the data of a supermarket, it will return the highest amount value for the given product and the second highest amount value bought by any customer.

Table 1. Representation of fraud detection techniques researched

S NO.	NAME OF THE AUTHORS	YEAR	TECHNIQUES DISCUSSED	DESCRIPTION OF TECHNIQUE
1.	Boris Kovalerchuk, Evgenii Vityaev, Robert Holtfreter	2007	Hybrid Evidence Correlation (HEC) Method	The HEC method comprises of 5 major steps which include the collection of data and forming a single data base from different databases, then applying simple fraud detection rules to the database and if all conditions are true, then the single condition is negated, then all the negated conditions are collected under a single database and are analyzed by the auditor and the whole process is discussed in the detail in further part of the paper.
2.	Wendy K. Tam Cho and Brian J. Gaines	2007	Benford Law	According to Benford Law, all the single digit numbers in the number system ranging from 0-9 doesn't have equal probability of appearing in database, it has decreasing probability as the value increases so the number 1 has the most probability of appearing while number 9 has the least.
3.	E.W.T. Ngai, Yong Hu, Y.H. Wong, Yijun Chen, Xin Sun	2011	Regression Model, Naive Bayes, CART, Bayesian Belief Network	Regression Model- The method which is used to define the relationship between a series of independent variables with a single dependent variable is known as regression modelling. Naive Bayes- It is a probability prediction method which takes different attributes into account while calculating the probability. The primary base which is used for calculating is Bayes Theorem. CART- CART stands for Classification and Regression Tree, it is method or algorithm which helps in calculating target value based on machine learning and either dependent, independent or both values are involved this is hierarchal in nature and is in the form of decision tree structure. Bayesian Belief Network- It is the graphical representation of the variables and their condition dependencies and is acyclic in nature, which is when no defined cyclic process is followed.
4.	John Akhilomen	2013	Pattern detection using Decision tree and Neural Networks	Decision Tree- It follows top-down approach in which different conditions are tested whether they are true or not and the following condition which is being selected is based on the previous response. Neural Networks- a sequence of artificially crested hardware and software where the relationship between output and input are continuously changing based upon the conditions is known as an artificial neuron. So, the work of these neurons is to test then conditions and present the output accordingly.
5.	Roger A. Leite, Theresia Gschwandtner, Silvia Miksch, Erich Gstrein, and Johannes Kuntner	2015	Node Link Diagrams	Node Link Diagram- Node Link Diagram comprises of two major parts, Node and Link, A node is represented by a point whereas the link between them is represented by a line, and based on the diagrams, a fraud visual signature is generated on study of past fraud cases and the whole data is cross verified where signatures and the patterns similar to the past findings are analyzed.
6.	Farzaneh A. Amani, Adam M. Fadlalla	2017	Predictive, Descriptive and Prescriptive Data Mining	Predictive data mining is used to predict the future or future values in the case of data. Descriptive data mining is used to describe the anomaly or change in data patterns Prescriptive data mining to get the proposed solution to the problems and anomalies encountered.

Continued on following page

Table 1. Continued

S NO.	NAME OF THE AUTHORS	YEAR	TECHNIQUES DISCUSSED	DESCRIPTION OF TECHNIQUE
7.	Dahee Choi, Kyungho Lee	2018	SMOTE, RUS, Feature Selection, ANN, F-Measure	SMOTE- It is a method in which arbitrary values are being generated for over sampling which makes the data much more diverse and less prone to errors as duplication of same values is not being done. RUS-. This method of under sampling randomly extracts sample data from the database reducing the number of normal transactions which helps in the class imbalance problem. Feature Selection- It is the process of selecting features which are much more appropriate for the given model as selecting all the features can reduce the accuracy and it also increases the processing time of data. ANN- Artificial Intelligence works like a human brain where pattern creation and data processing are carried out and decisions are made on the basis of these data processing and patterns, it follows statistics and predictive modelling. F-Measure- It is a method to measure the accuracy of the predicted value. $$Precision = \frac{True\ Positive}{(True\ Positive + False\ Positive)}$$ $$Recall = \frac{True\ Positive}{(True\ Positive + False\ Negative)}$$ $$F - Measure = \frac{2*Precision*Recall}{(Precision + Recall)}$$
8.	Francisco Javier Moreno Arboleda, Jaime Alberto Guzman-Luna, Ingrid-Durley Torres	2018	Benford Law	Under Benford Law here three major techniques are used which are Same-Same-Same, Same-Same-Different and Relative Size Factor, these techniques not only helps in the pattern recognition but it also presents the recognized data in a summarized manner.
9.	Zabihollah Rezaee, Jim Wang	2018	Data Warehousing, Expert System, Digital Investigation	Data Warehousing- The Process of constructing a unified data system in this the data is cleaned, sorted and integrated to form a single database is known as data ware housing. It helps in reducing ambiguity in data and increases the overall consistency of data. Expert System- It is system which is designed to take decisions based on if-else ladder and act as an expert in the field, of expertise sit takes decisions based on the vast knowledge in the field of expertise. This system is made in reference of expert in real life. Digital Investigation- The process of investigating any digital event in reference to the patterns and anomalies which were previously observed.

Continued on following page

Table 1. Continued

S NO.	NAME OF THE AUTHORS	YEAR	TECHNIQUES DISCUSSED	DESCRIPTION OF TECHNIQUE
10.	Nick F. Ryman-Tubb, Paul Krause, Wolfgang Garn	2018	K-Folded Cross validation approach, F-Score, ROC Curve, MCC Method	K-Folded Cross Validation Approach- It is method in which the machine learning model is evaluated based on a single basis of evaluation which is K, it is the number of groups in which data is divided into. F-Score- This method has been discussed before in which we calculate the accuracy in reference to the predicted value. ROC Curve- ROC stands for Receiver Operating Characteristic Curve, which is used to measure the performance of a model based on the classification thresholds and has two parameters which are plotted $$TPR = \frac{TP}{(TP + FN)} \qquad FPR = \frac{FP}{(FP + TN)}$$ MCC Method – It is a method which is used to evaluate the models which work on binary classification and is used to measure the difference between actual and predicted value $$MCC = \frac{\left((TN*TP) - (FN*FP)\right)}{\sqrt{(TP+FP)(TP+FN)(TN+FP)(TN+FN)}}$$

The table has been sourced from: (Kovalerchuk et al., 2007) (Cho & Gaines, 2007)(Ngai et al., 2011) (Akhilomen, 2013)(Leite et al., 2015) (Amani & Fadlalla, 2017) (Choi & Lee, 2018)(Moreno et al., 2018) (Rezaee & Wang, 2018)(Ryman et al., 2018)

INFERENCE FROM MODEL PROPOSED BY DAHEE CHOI AND KYUNGHO LEE

The model proposed by Dahee Choi and Kyungho Lee has high efficiency in fraud detecting as it is tested on the real-time financial data in Korea. According to the experiment it was found that the machine learning based model is much more effective than neural network-based model. Neural networks take longer to implement as compared to machine learning model. Also, the model which was based on machine learning presented a best suited combination of both clustering and classification algorithms.

Figure 3. Working of fraud detection model
(Author)

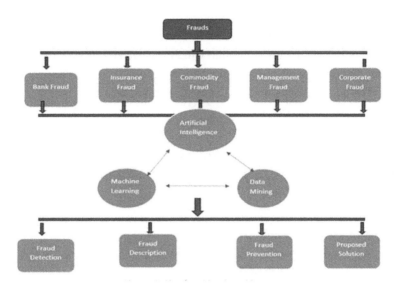

Data Mining in the Field of Accounting

Data Mining has been identified as a part of top emerging technologies of future and has been ranked among top ten in the field by American Institute of Certified Public Accountants (AICPA) (Amani & Fadlalla, 2017). It is an algorithm-based approach which works on the pattern extraction from the given data. The key objective of data mining is helping an organization in decision making, future evaluation and data interpretation (Rezaee & Wang, 2018). Data Mining has three key objectives to play in an organization, which are:

Description

Its key focus is to find the patterns which can be easily interpreted by humans which are used to describe the data. These patterns can be easily understandable and can be interpret to make sense of the given data.

Prediction

It focuses on predicting the behavior of how the future data will behave based on predefined models and algorithms which in turns helps in the decision making and future planning.

Prescription

The Prescription involves the solution to the proposed problem which is based on the model which is taken as the reference point of all internal and external processing of data.

In the field of forensic accounting, the role of data mining is important both on macro and micro level, on macro-Level we can consider data mining to be working on the Audit Engagement level while on micro level data mining also helps in fraud detection on basic business transaction level (Amani & Fadlalla, 2017). The technique which is majorly used in data mining of forensic accounting is descriptive data. As the way in which frauds are being committed are evolving, the key objective of data mining is not to focus on a particular transaction but to focus on a group of transaction which in turn leads to fraud, and to detect such type of behavior, new technique which involve advance method-based algorithms are implemented. So, the authors are discussing about the method developed known as Hybrid Evidence Correlation (HEC) Method. The steps involved in HEC method are:

Step One

Combining all databases that the company has into a single database. These small databases may include all the internal and external transaction of the company (Kovalerchuk et al., 2007).

Step Two

Frequent data correlations pattern should be discovered in this step and no help of fraud training data should be taken but fraud ontology which can be defined as the characteristic that define a fraud can be used to perform such task (Kovalerchuk et al., 2007).

Step Three

For the third step, we negate the conclusion of the process based on the outcome of second step. For instance, If the pattern followed is up to n-1 places, we form conditions around it from A_1 to A_{n-1} and the general pattern is

If conditions $A1,A1,...,AN-1$ are true, Then conclusion AN is true

But for the above step, we will negate the conclusion of all the condition which satisfy the if then condition

If conditions $A1,A1,...,AN-1$ are true, Then conclusion AN is false

(Kovalerchuk et al., 2007)

Step Four

Prepare a different set of all the condition which satisfy the if then condition (Kovalerchuk et al., 2007)

Step Five

Analyse the conditions which are prepared in step forth for a potential fraud detection and the transactions should be analysed by an auditor to differentiate it from the general errors (Kovalerchuk et al., 2007).

For both of the first two step, the fraudulent patters will be provided to the algorithm and it has to only match it with the subsequent data. The HEC Method uses easily understandable patterns which can be interpreted by any auditor. It takes help of standard clustering, so that data can be grouped into meaningful clusters and auditor can make some sense of the presented clusters.

CONCLUSION

Techno-literacy will be Tailwinds that will empower new generation of Financial Practitioners to switch to new orbits as professionals. Audit will improve with the use of AI. AI is not the technology of the future, but a reality. Contrary to popular belief that "AI will take over the mankind", this article reinforces the truth - forensic auditors will get empowered, not replaced. AI will provide additional capacity and time for auditors to focus on areas that need their consideration and focus. With benefits such as the ability to extract data from variety of formal and informal formats, identify unusual patterns, focus on data processing, and improvement in audit quality, forensic accounting will thrive (Akhilomen, 2013). This paper contradicts the need for rapid detection of accounting fraud in response to the recent rise in high-profile financial fraud by large corporations in both developed and developing countries. To close the gap, the authors have raised the forensic accounting framework using business intelligence in the form of three-dimensional analysis from business, technology and data, and investigative research ideas of organization. In this paper, the authors have introduced a number of strategies to detect fraud especially from the financial and forensic accounting sectors. Based on these strategies, the authors have identified specialized operators who specialize in detecting fraud in the data warehouse.AI and machine learning will stay here - while technology creates a lot of data issue, and it also provides a solution. As the authors have seen over time with our growing confidence in technology, AI will become a necessity instead of a luxury, and the data volume of corporates will increase the need for an effective investigative tool. In order to maximize the benefits of AI in research, investigators and compliance professionals will need to be flexible in adapting their approach to deal with the large amount of data. In addition, with the increase in cross-border investigations, the relevant data privacy rules should be taken into consideration during the design phase of the AI process before they can be deployed to the investigation. AI also recognizes the need for close collaboration between data professionals, lawyers, forensic accountants, investigators and law enforcement professionals to ensure the effective and successful integration of AI into investigations and law enforcement systems. AI is unlikely to replace human evaluation and critical thinking, but machine learning should stay close and improve the process of human decision-making (Choi & Lee, 2018). Survey report that respondents believe the use of Big Data analytics improves forensic accounting processes, but data security threats limit the use of Big Data statistics. This is consistent with the fact that the use of Big Data analytics has increased dramatically, but cybersecurity is still an important issue in the use of big data analytics. With regard to forensic accounting processes, the survey finds that Big Data strategies include descriptive and decisive analysis, data capture and Big Data attributes such as accuracy, reliability, accessibility and consistency are important in forensic accounting practices.

Implication of the Study

Industry Perspective- In financial sector, a single fraud can disrupt the whole financial ecosystem. This disturbance often can be so significant that it can affect a nation's economy to a greater magnitude. So, fraud detection had become an integral part of financial sector in present scenario and the technology is playing key role in this endeavour. The most significant growth had been seen in Artificial intelligence which is becoming an integral part in forensic accounting. In the following study, the discussion of various fraud detection techniques can help the industry to get a deeper knowledge of how frauds are detected with the use of modern tools which will in turn helps in the smooth integration of financial and technological sector.

Academic Perspective- The research was carried out using a variety of literature reviews and was backed up by evidence focusing on presenting the topic in much broader light, defining the relationship between the AI and forensic accounting, presenting the findings in theoretical and technical viewpoint and how the scenario has changed over past decade in the field. In addition, some of the techniques of fraud detection are also discussed in detail for better understanding of the process.

Scope for Future Research

Though the artificial intelligence has been present for few decades now, it is still a new topic in the field of accounting. Topics such as machine learning and data mining are very much in their early stages when accounting is concerned. Fraud detection and many other applications of artificial intelligence have seen the light of the day in past decade itself and there is a long way ahead. But due to vigorous growth of artificial intelligence in every sector present in the market, most of the financial activities from book keeping to transaction statements are prepared on digital platforms itself which made the relation between the two deeper. In future, the advancement of Artificial intelligence will not only be limited to fraud detection but will also help in fraud prevention and working on a very autonomous level without the need for any human assistance. With the further development of technology, anomalies patterns will not only be recognized but also, they can be recorded and can be used as a point of reference in future. The paper has discussed the techniques used and how the demo graph has started to change but has kept in mind the newly formed clear linkage between the two. The paper also focuses on how all the applications of artificial intelligence from basic to advance can be seen in accounting.

The above discussed advancement will need some time to reach the execution phase, but the paper is written in hopes to summarize how the artificial intelligence has set its roots in the field of forensic accounting and how the technical aspect of artificial intelligence can be applied in real world accounting for fraud detection.

REFERENCES

Akhilomen, J. (2013). *Data Mining Application for Cyber Credit-Card Fraud Detection System*. Advances in Data Mining, Applications and Theoritical Aspects. doi:10.1007/978-3-642-39736-3_17

Amani, F. A., & Fadlalla, A. M. (2017). Data mining applications in accounting: A review of the literature and organizing framework. *International Journal of Accounting Information Systems*, *24*, 32–58. doi:10.1016/j.accinf.2016.12.004

Amelia, A., & Baldwin, C. E. (2006). *Opportunities for Artificial Intelligence development in the Accounting domain: The case for auditing*. Wiley Interscience.

Baldwin, A. A., Brown, C. E., & Trinkle, B. S. (2006). Opportunities for Artificial Intelligence Development in Accounint Domain: The Case for Auditing. *Intelligent systems in Accounting, Finance and Management*.

Bell, T. B., & Carcello, J. V. (2000). A Decision Aid for accesing the Likelihood of fraudulent Financial Reporting. *A Jouranal of Practice and Theory*.

Berdiyeva, O., Islam, M. U., & Saeedi, M. (2021). Artificial Intelligence in Accounting and Finance: Meta-Analysis. *International Business Review*.

Cho, W. K., & Gaines, B. J. (2007). Breaking the (Benford) Law. *The american statisticians*.

Choi, D., & Lee, K. (2018). An Artificial Intelligence Approach to Financial Fraud Detection. *Security and Communication Networks*, *2018*, 1–15. doi:10.1155/2018/5483472

Kokina, J., & Davenport, T. M. (2017). The Emergence of Artificial Intelligence: How Automation is Changing Auditing. *Journal of Emerging Technologies in Accounting*, *14*(1), 115–122. doi:10.2308/jeta-51730

Kovalerchuk, B., Vityaev, E., & Holtfreter, R. (2007). Correlation of Complex Evidence in Forensic Accounting using Data Mining. *Journal of Forensic Accounting*.

Leite, R. A., Gschwandtner, T., Miksch, S., Gstrein, E., & Kuntner, J. (2015). Visual Analytics for Fraud Detection and Monitoring. *2015 IEEE Conference on Visual Analytics Science and Technology (VAST)*. IEEE. 10.1109/VAST.2015.7347678

Moreno, F. J., Luna, J. A., & Torres, I. D. (2018). Fraud detection-oriented operators in a data warehouse based on forensic accounting techniques. *Computer Fraud & Security*.

Ngai, E., Hu, Y., Wong, Y., Chen, Y., & Sun, X. (2011). The application of data mining techniques in financial fraud detection: A classification framework and an academic review of literature. *Decision Support Systems*, *50*(3), 559–569. doi:10.1016/j.dss.2010.08.006

Omoteso, K. (2012). The application of artificial intelligence in auditing: Looking back to the future. *Expert Systems with Applications*, *39*(9), 8490–8495. doi:10.1016/j.eswa.2012.01.098

Rezaee, Z., & Wang, J. (2018). Relevance of big data to forensic. *Managerial Auditing Journal*.

Ryman-Tubb, N. F., Krause, P., & Garn, W. (2018). How Artificial Intelligence and machine learning research impacts payment card fraud detection: A survey and industry benchmark. *Engineering Applications of Artificial Intelligence*, *76*, 130–157. doi:10.1016/j.engappai.2018.07.008

Saluja, S. (2022). Identity theft fraud- major loophole for FinTech industry in India. *Journal of Financial Crime*. doi:10.1108/JFC-08-2022-0211

Saluja, S., Aggarwal, A., & Mittal, A. (2021). Understanding the fraud theories and advancing with integrity model, *Journal of Financial Crime*. doi:10.1108/JFC-07-2021-0163

Saluja, S., & Sandhu, N. (2023). Whistle blowing of corporate frauds in India. *International Journal of Business and Globalisation*, *35*(3), 277–287. doi:10.1504/IJBG.2023.134940

Sandhu, N., & Saluja, S. (2023). Fraud Triangle as an Audit Tool. *Management and Labour Studies*, *48*(3), 418–443. doi:10.1177/0258042X231160970

Sharma, A., & Panigrahi, P. K. (2012). A Review of Financial Accounting Fraud Detection based on Data Mining Techniques. *International Journal of Computer Application*.

Wong, S., & Venkatraman, S. (2015). Financial accounting fraud detection using business intelligence. *Asian Economic and Financial Review*, *5*(11), 1187–1207. doi:10.18488/journal. aefr/2015.5.11/102.11.1187.1207

Chapter 3
Balancing Ethics and Economics:
Navigating Data Governance in India's Marketing World

Divya Dang
Chandigarh University, India

Sahil Kohli
https://orcid.org/0000-0002-3792-988X
Chandigarh University, India

ABSTRACT

In this chapter, the authors unravel the intricate dance between ethics, data governance, and economics in India's vibrant digital marketing sphere. It's a deep dive into how India, a burgeoning digital power-house, grapples with the challenges of protecting consumer data while fostering ethical marketing. The authors shed light on the crucial role data plays in today's marketing strategies in India and ponder the repercussions for consumer privacy. By critically examining India's current data protection laws and stacking them up against global benchmarks, the authors pinpoint areas ripe for innovation. The unique hurdles Indian marketers face in the big data era are laid bare, and the authors explore cutting-edge tech solutions that promise to guide ethical choices and policy shaping. Wrapping up, the chapter casts an eye to the future, envisioning a balanced path for India's economic growth that doesn't lose sight of ethical marketing and robust data governance. It's about charting a course for an economy that's digital-first but ethics-forward.

INTRODUCTION

The rapid digitization of the Indian economy over the past decade has transformed the country into one of the largest and fastest-growing digital markets globally. With over 500 million internet users and boasting the world's second-highest number of smartphone users, India has embraced the power of digital platforms for communication, commerce, and more (IAMAI-Kantar ICUBE 2020). This proliferation

DOI: 10.4018/979-8-3693-2215-4.ch003

of technology and data has disrupted traditional marketing approaches and created both opportunities and ethical challenges for businesses operating in the Indian marketplace.

This chapter examines the complex interplay between ethics and economics within India's digital marketing ecosystem. It traces the evolution of the country's data-driven marketing strategies and analyses the current standards and regulations around ethical marketing practices and data governance. Core issues such as balancing consumer protection with business interests, the role of regulatory bodies, and the need for transparency in data management are discussed. The unique challenges inherent in the Indian context, ranging from digital literacy gaps to infrastructural limitations, provide the backdrop for evaluating pragmatic solutions to democratize ethical and responsible marketing.

By highlighting examples of technologies and innovations that can enhance transparency, enforce compliance, and safeguard consumer rights, this chapter provides perspectives on how marketers in India can leverage data responsibly. It concludes with policy recommendations centred on industry self-regulation, public-private partnerships, and consumer education to create a robust framework for ethical marketing aligned with India's development needs.

The Evolution of India's Digital Economy

Beginning in the early 2000s, India's digital revolution was sparked by the proliferation of internet-enabled services, increased tech investments, and supportive governmental policies for digital adoption. Consumer demand for online services also rose rapidly, accelerated by factors like affordable smartphones, inexpensive mobile data, and an increasingly youthful population. By 2005, the number of internet users in India had crossed 50 million, growing eight-fold in five years (Malik et al., 2019).

E-commerce emerged as a particularly thriving sector, with companies like Flipkart, Snapdeal, and Amazon capturing the e-retail market. As per IBEF (2022), the Indian e-commerce market stood at $43.7 billion in 2019 and is projected to grow to $111.40 billion by 2025. Online retailers have also fuelled demand by offering deep discounts and cashback offers, using investment capital to acquire customers (Chakravorti & Sharma, 2020). The e-commerce boom has transformed online shopping from a niche activity to a mainstream habit for middle class consumers.

India's digital payments ecosystem has also evolved exponentially, enabled by government efforts like demonetization, Unified Payments Interface (UPI), and tax incentives for digital transactions. From just 343.07 million digital transactions in 2015-16, the volume grew to 5591.07 million transactions by 2019-20 (MeitY, 2021). Payment apps like Paytm, PhonePe, Google Pay dominate, while payment gateway firms like Razorpay enable online merchant transactions. The entry of neobanks offering digital banking solutions will further transform online financial services.

The country also boasts the world's second-largest internet user base at 483 million, growing at 20% annually (NASSCOM, 2020). This expanding digital footprint has created a thriving online media and entertainment industry, with over-the-top (OTT) video streaming services like Netflix, Amazon Prime Video, Disney+ Hotstar seeing massive growth since 2016. Other online content sectors like news, music streaming, podcasts, and gaming have also taken off.

Edtech platforms like Byju's, upGrad, and Unacademy are capitalizing on India's vast education market through offerings like online courses, test prep, and K12 learning apps. Telemedicine providers like Practo are also gaining traction for online doctor consultations and e-pharmacies. This rising user base across sectors has positioned India as an attractive testing ground for global tech firms' new products and business models tailored for developing economies.

The rapid adoption of digital services transformed marketing strategies, with companies increasingly using technology for segmentation, targeting, customer engagement and analytics. As Subramanian (2018) highlights, the proliferation of digital marketing in India has been underpinned by the availability of granular customer data that enables hyper-personalization. Location-based marketing, social media advertising, influencer marketing, and other data-driven approaches have become ubiquitous.

However, the opaque and poorly regulated nature of data collection practices raises ethical red flags. Instances like Cambridge Analytica's misuse of Facebook user data highlight how the absence of data protection norms can enable unethical profiling and micro-targeting by marketers, compromising consumer privacy (Chakraborty et al., 2018). Thus, while digital marketing strategies have fuelled business growth, they necessitate governance frameworks to ensure ethical balance.

Ethical Marketing: Principles and Practices in India

Ethical marketing refers to practices guided by honesty, fairness, and societal well-being considerations that avoid harm to consumers and the community (Murphy et al., 2005). It stands in contrast to solely profit-driven marketing done through misleading claims, subliminal messaging, and other tactics that adversely impact consumers.

Operating ethically has tangible benefits for brands beyond goodwill, including higher customer retention, loyalty, and ROI (Brigger et al., 2014). Hence, ethical marketing is increasingly being integrated into corporate philosophy, positioning brands as responsible actors who follow regulations, self-imposed codes of conduct, and societal norms. However, research on ethical marketing practices in India indicates certain gaps.

A study by Upadhyay and Singh (2017) shows the prevalence of misleading content, pressures sales tactics, limited transparency around pricing and personal data usage, and inadequate redressal mechanisms across sectors like healthcare, education and financial services. Chhonker et al. (2017) highlight how majority of ethical lapses relate to deception, privacy infringement, targeting vulnerable groups, and promotion of harmful products - all enabled by poor enforcement.

Several Cases Showcase Such Unethical Practices Across Industries

Healthcare

- In 2016, Coca-Cola was forced to pull down an online campaign for Maaza mango drink accused of falsely claiming it had "no added preservatives or artificial flavors" by India's advertising watchdog ASCI (Bhatia, 2016).
- Pharmaceutical companies have often faced charges of surrogate advertising to promote banned drugs. For example, pharmaceutical firm Morepen was indicted in 2015 for using a cosmetic brand to promote its glucose powder illegally as a drug for diabetes (Singh, 2015).
- 80% of online pharmacies operate illegally without licenses and enable easy access to prescription medicines without requisite safeguards, raising ethical concerns (Ranganathan et al., 2020).

Edtech

- In 2022, an Indian government probe found edtech firms like Byju's subsidiary WhiteHat Jr had misled parents and students with dubious marketing claims and hard-sell tactics (Press Trust of India, 2022).
- Other edtech platforms like upGrad have faced criticism for exaggerated claims around job placements used aggressively in sales pitches to students (Press Trust of India, 2022).

E-Commerce

- In 2018, e-commerce major Flipkart was forced to withdraw assertions that its products were available at the "lowest prices" after complaints (Shenoy, 2018).
- Critics have accused e-retailers like Amazon of exploiting loopholes to offer deep discounts and preferential treatment to certain sellers (Reuters, 2019). This skews competition.

Financial Services

- In 2018, Airtel Payments Bank was found to be opening accounts without consent, enabled by linking with mobile SIM for subsidies (ET Bureau, 2018).
- Instances of fraud by Ponzi schemes and illegal investment operators using digital platforms are frequent, aided by false promotions and allure of quick profits (Bloomberg, 2018).

These examples highlight the prevalence of deception, lack of transparency, and exploitation of consumers across major sectors. While India has basic consumer protection regulations, their enforcement has been inadequate to curb such unethical marketing especially on digital platforms.

Regulatory Shortcomings Enabling Unethical Marketing

Several factors underlie the regulatory gaps that allow misleading and fraudulent practices to persist in Indian marketing:

1. **Ambiguity in Existing Laws:** Laws like the Consumer Protection Act 1986 and Cable TV Network Rules 1994 contain provisions to prevent false advertising and protect consumers. However, lack of clarity on key definitions and applicability to digital media enables unethical marketers to exploit loopholes (Upadhyay, 2017).
2. **Poor Enforcement Mechanisms:** Regulators like the Central Consumer Protection Authority lack resources to effectively monitor and penalize unfair marketing. Self-regulation by industry bodies like ASCI remains non-binding and poorly enforced (ASCI, 2018).
3. **Inadequate Grievance Redressal:** Consumers find it difficult to report grievances related to misleading ads or fraudulent schemes, especially those promoted online. Lack of channels for redressal allows marketers to act with impunity (Dey et al., 2018).

4. **Limitations on Digital Oversight:** The IT Act 2000 does not adequately cover data protection, privacy and consent issues that underpin contemporary digital marketing. Data-driven targeting, ad auctions, and profiling fall through regulatory cracks (Nair, 2020).

5. **Jurisdictional Constraints:** E-commerce entities, social media platforms and other digital marketplaces operate across borders. Enforcing regulations on such intermediaries not based in India poses challenges (Bhattacharjee et al., 2020).

This lack of stringent deterrence encourages marketers to prioritize profits over ethics. However, greater public scrutiny is compelling gradual improvements on self-regulation.

Efforts Towards Ethical Self-Regulation

Some positive initiatives indicate growing self-awareness around ethical marketing among Indian businesses:

- Industry associations like ASCI, DLAI and NASSCOM have framed voluntary codes and standards to promote transparency and address common malpractices. However, ensuring compliance remains a challenge.
- Large e-commerce firms and edtech startups have enhanced disclosure protocols and communication practices in response to criticisms of misleading claims. But systemic issues of deep discounting and exploitation persist.
- Digital platforms like Facebook, Twitter and Google have expanded grievance mechanisms for reporting problematic content, as mandated by the IT Rules 2021. But enforcement continues to be an issue.
- Fintech firms are collaborating with regulators on sanitizing their app ecosystem after concerns over predatory lending apps. Policy recommendations have emerged but translating these into practice will require collective commitment.
- Businesses are deploying technology solutions like blockchain, data anonymization and platform audits to address data privacy, security and ethics concerns. However, adoption remains limited thus far.
- Some companies are proactively investing in training programs on digital ethics for their marketing and product teams. However, impact depends on integrating ethical thinking into organizational culture.

These piecemeal efforts indicate increasing recognition of the need for ethical marketing standards and practices aligned with India's digital growth. But change cannot arise from legislation alone. Cultural shifts towards greater skepticism of marketing claims, demanding transparency and accountability, and balancing business goals with social welfare are essential.

Framework for Ethical Marketing

Scholars have proposed integrating the following pillars into a normative framework to enable ethical marketing in the Indian context (Chatterjee, 2021; Murphy 1998):

1. **Truthfulness:** All claims and representations made in promotions must be factual, verifiable and not misleading. Data to substantiate claims should be disclosed proactively.
2. **Authenticity:** Marketing communication should not manipulate perceptions insidiously but appeal to consumers' rational abilities.
3. **Privacy:** Collection and use of personal data must respect individual privacy rights and norms. Consumers' informed consent must guide analytics-driven targeting and segmentation.
4. **Transparency:** Disclosure norms around paid or sponsored content, advertiser-platform relationships, data collection and profiling algorithms should be strengthened to enable informed choices.
5. **Fairness:** Marketing practices must not exploit vulnerabilities or inequalities. Discrimination and exclusion must be avoided. Reasonable access to redressal is vital.
6. **Societal Well-being:** Beyond legal compliance, marketers must evaluate the ethical implications of their activities, products and messaging on social norms, environmental sustainability and economic development.

Operationalizing this requires both regulatory oversight and voluntary initiatives by industry and civil society stakeholders. Some key measures include:

- Enacting a strong data protection law covering aspects like privacy, consent and data localization critical for the digital economy.
- Establishing an independent regulator to monitor marketing practices across offline, print, TV and online media.
- Mandating increased disclosures on targeting, ad frequency, content modifications, and data collection.
- Creating efficient grievance redressal systems especially for financial frauds.
- Rethinking incentive structures within organizations that promote hard-sell tactics, such as sales commission targets.
- Investing in regular training programs and impact assessment exercises for marketing teams on ethical practices.
- Incentivizing development of privacy-enhancing technologies and transparent AI systems through competitions and incubator initiatives.
- Undertaking national multi-media campaigns to spread awareness on consumer rights and avenues for redressal.
- Setting up dedicated helpline numbers and online portals to report misleading ads or unethical conduct across languages.
- Enhancing coordination between policy bodies, financial regulators, industry associations and law enforcement agencies.
- Promoting academic research on ethical marketing issues relevant for contemporary Indian business.

Marketing is crucial for business success, but economic objectives need not compromise consumer welfare and rights. Unethical marketing that erodes public trust will prove self-defeating in the long run. India must proactively shape its digital future by pioneering ethical innovation. The collaborative efforts of policymakers, businesses and civil society will determine this journey.

Challenges in Implementing Ethical Marketing

While the imperative for ethical marketing is clear, translating principles to practice faces complex roadblocks:

1. **Monitoring Limitations:** The scale and complexity of India's marketing ecosystem poses challenges in monitoring ethics compliance across traditional and digital media. Enforcement capacities need urgent strengthening.
2. **Cultural Relativism:** Varying cultural attitudes towards issues like privacy, communal rights over individual rights, tolerance for paternalism and skepticism of business claims underpin the Indian context. These shape perceptions of ethical breaches.
3. **Resource Constraints:** Small businesses and startups with limited resources may find investments in self-regulation burdensome. Building capabilities requires patient engagement and incentives.
4. **Economic Pressures:** Focus on growth targets, investor pressures and competitive dynamics incentivize unethical practices. Changing organizational culture takes time.
5. **Regulatory Arbitrage:** When laws differ across geographies, global entities tap jurisdictions with weaker regulations. Harmonization of marketing rules across markets will curb this venue shopping.
6. **Lack of Global Coordination:** Transnational digital platforms do not fall under national policy mandates. Cooperating to enforce standards within their ecosystem needs multilateral efforts.
7. **Consumer Demand:** Desire for low prices and deep discounts drive demand for platforms that gain advantage through opaque practices. Altering such expectations calls for persistent public engagement.
8. **Data Complexities:** The scale and intricacy of data collection, analysis and application in digital marketing pose novel governance challenges with no clear precedents.
9. **Rapid Innovation:** Technological innovations enable new forms of segmentation, targeting and engagement outpacing policy. Responsible innovation policies are critical.
10. **Short-term Thinking:** Focus on immediate growth incentives marketers to disregard long-term reputation damage from unethical conduct. Farsighted mindsets are essential.

Bridging these challenges requires harmonizing the interests of diverse stakeholders. Balancing business objectives, consumer rights, cultural nuances and social welfare is key to sustaining an equitable digital economy. India must shape its regulatory approach based on transparent public discussions and primacy to citizen well-being. The risks of unchecked unethical marketing outweigh short-term gains.

Guiding this transition will need a spirit of open collaboration between policymakers, industry, academia and civil society. Some pragmatic steps can catalyse momentum:

1. Undertake multi-stakeholder consultations on ethical marketing issues and policy solutions.
2. Commission an expert panel to design sector-specific codes of conduct and compliance mechanisms.
3. Launch competitive funds to support startups addressing digital ethics-related themes.
4. Introduce mandatory ethics modules in marketing and technology academic programs.
5. Recognize leaders pioneering ethical practices through high-visibility annual awards.
6. Leverage cultural touchpoints like religious festivals to spread awareness.
7. Promote grassroots consumer collectives to advocate for ethical business standards.

India's policy choices today will sculpt digital development outcomes for generations. Prioritizing transparent, fair and truthful marketing practices can nurture an equitable marketplace. The time for collaborative action is now.

Data Governance in India: Laws and Regulations

Robust data governance frameworks are crucial for enabling ethical marketing practices, especially in light of the pervasive use of customer data and analytics. India's approach to data regulation has evolved considerably, though gaps persist.

The Information Technology Act (IT Act) 2000 laid the early foundation for cyber laws pertaining to data security, privacy and electronic transactions. However, its limited applicability to marketing practices meant growing data collection by private companies occurred in a regulatory vacuum until the 2010s. Two significant developments helped address this - the framing of privacy as a fundamental right by the Supreme Court in 2017, and the subsequent proposal of a comprehensive data protection law.

The Personal Data Protection Bill 2019 (PDPB), built on the recommendations of the Justice Srikrishna Committee, aims to regulate processing of personal data by government and private entities (Chhaparia, 2019). Its key provisions relevant to digital marketing ethics include necessitating consent for data collection, constraints on sensitive data usage, mandatory reporting of data breaches, and penalties for non-compliance.

However, the bill has faced criticisms around ambiguities in definitions, broad exceptions to government authorities, and lack of redressal mechanisms (Kaur, 2020). For instance, while prohibiting processing of sensitive personal data like health or sexual orientation, it allows such processing for "reasonable purposes" without clarity on what constitutes reasonability. Its vague provisions for cross-border data flows, which are critical in digital services, have also raised business concerns.

In contrast, frameworks like EU's General Data Protection Regulation (GDPR) adopted in 2016 have more well-defined consent requirements, individual rights and restrictions around using sensitive data like political opinions or ethnic origin that can enable unethical profiling (Tikkinen-Piri et al., 2018). Scholars have recommended clarifying PDPB provisions around consent, purpose limitation, and rights to object in line with GDPR (Rahman, 2018).

Table 1. Comparing India's personal data protection bill 2019 and EU's GDPR on key provisions

Provision	India's Personal Data Protection Bill, 2019	EU's General Data Protection Regulation (GDPR)
Consent	Consent required but exceptions made for purposes like fraud detection, debt recovery, whistleblowing etc. which may enable data use without consent.	Explicit, informed, clear consent required for data processing. Must be as easy to withdraw consent as to give it.
Purpose Limitation	Personal data can be processed only for purposes consented to by data principal originally. However, exemptions dilute this.	Data collected only for specified, explicit and legitimate purposes. Not permitted beyond that.
Rights to Object	Can object to processing for specific purposes. But right itself is unclear.	Right to object to processing, including for purposes like profiling, is clearly specified.
Sensitive Personal Data	Prohibits processing but provides exceptions for "reasonable purposes". Ambiguity in defining such purposes.	Sensitive data like racial/ethnic origin, religious beliefs, health etc. subject to much stronger protection and restrictions.
Cross-Border Data Transfer	Provisions are vague, no clarity on data localization requirements.	Data transfer outside EU allowed only to countries with adequate protection standards.
Regulator	Central Data Protection Authority has broad powers including audits, inquiries, and imposing penalties.	Independent supervisory authorities in each EU state to monitor and enforce GDPR.

Passage of a comprehensive data protection law (see Table 1) like PDPB would significantly strengthen India's data governance. However, effective implementation requires investing in regulatory capacity for enforcement and nudging businesses towards voluntary adherence. Absent robust ethics-driven self-regulation, provisions to safeguard consumer rights may exist only on paper.

Challenges in Balancing Ethics and Economics

Despite growing awareness and enabling regulations, balancing ethical priorities with commercial growth imperatives poses multifaceted hurdles in the Indian context.

Low Digital Literacy

Firstly, low digital literacy, especially among rural communities and economically marginalized groups, reduces understanding of data-related rights and redressal avenues. For instance, a 2021 study of rural internet users in an Indian state found 71% had no knowledge of privacy policies, while only 9% reviewed terms and conditions before downloading apps (Mali et al., 2021).

Such knowledge gaps are exploited by marketers for opaque data collection and profiling, which can perpetrate exclusion and discrimination (Muralidharan et al., 2014). Raising awareness thus faces infrastructural barriers limiting reach. Even among literate users, ability to interpret tech jargon and identify potential consent issues remains limited.

Cultural Perceptions of Privacy

Secondly, cultural perceptions of concepts like privacy differ, with community interests often superseding individual rights (Kshetri, 2014). Normative judgements on issues like targeted advertising thus show greater tolerance in India versus Western notions valuing information privacy (Jai & King, 2016). Consequently, unethical practices by marketers receive limited pushback.

For example, Facebook's Free Basics program that offered limited free internet access was opposed in many countries for restricting user choice. However, Indian policymakers faced public criticism for denying this access on net neutrality grounds, overriding privacy concerns (Gupta, 2020). Such varied attitudes lead to justifying data collection practices that seem intrusive from individualistic privacy perspectives.

Compliance and Enforcement Hurdles

Lastly, poor self-regulatory standards within industries, lack of transparency from data aggregators like social media platforms, and inadequate grievance mechanisms impede ethical marketing (Udupa, 2020). While laws like the PDPB would strengthen data governance, effective implementation requires investing in state capacity.

Absent enforcement reforms, unethical excesses damaging consumer trust may continue despite regulations. A 2021 investigation of online lending apps in India revealed use of unethical algorithms and data collection practices violating user privacy (Jagadish et al., 2021). Despite RBI restrictions on such apps, over 50 loan providers were found flouting norms due to lack of compliance mechanisms.

Such cases highlight that voluntary self-correction by businesses is critical alongside policy interventions. However, ensuring compliance across a vast, complex country with over half a billion internet users poses systemic enforcement challenges. Beyond drafting legislation, strengthening regulatory capacity to monitor wrongdoing, investigate complaints, and impose penalties is essential.

Balancing Innovation and Regulation

Rapid digital innovation also complicates regulation. marketing techniques evolve quickly, enabling new forms of segmentation, targeting and consumer engagement based on data analytics. Policies formulated today risk becoming outdated or circumvented by next-generation technologies tomorrow.

But premature overregulation also risks stifling innovation in India's thriving digital economy. Fostering responsible self-regulation without compromising flexibility calls for nuanced policy approaches. Promoting ethics literacy among developers and product managers, incentives for human-centric tech innovation, and public-private collaboration are imperative.

India must avoid heavy-handed state intervention in digital spaces but exercise oversight to protect consumer rights. Navigating this balance remains an ongoing challenge.

Case Studies Highlighting Dilemmas

Some case studies showcase the specific tensions between ethical marketing practices and commercial growth priorities in the contemporary Indian context:

Online Pharmacy Regulation

The rise of e-pharmacies like Netmeds, PharmEasy and Medlife revolutionized access to medicines in India. However, studies show over 80% of such platforms operated illegally without mandated licenses

(Ranganathan et al., 2020). Lax oversight enabled sale of prescription drugs without requiring prescriptions or verification.

While shutting down such apps can safeguard against misuse, it reduces healthcare access for underserved communities relying on them. However, continuing opaque practices risks consumer harm. Reconciling ethical imperatives of safety with the convenience e-pharmacies provide remains contested, underscoring regulatory dilemmas.

Edtech Advertising Practices

Edtech firms like Byju's and Unacademy have been investigated for questionable advertising tactics like false claims or high-pressure sales to parents and students. But tightening guidelines on marketing pitches might disadvantage startups competing with established players.

Here balancing a level-playing field to nurture innovation versus protecting end-users from exploitation poses ethical and economic trade-offs. Light-touch regulation risks unethical practices, but heavy-handed restrictions may curb sector growth, denying educational opportunities.

Data Sharing by Digital Platforms

Global platforms like Amazon, Microsoft and Google accumulating vast user data are critical for India's digital economy. Mandating local storage and access to data can aid law enforcement. However, enforcing data localization erodes efficiency gains from globalized data flows, hurting innovation and growth.

This dilemma between societal interests and business competitiveness recurs across domains like taxation, market access, content regulation and privacy protection. Reconciling nationalist priorities with global business models continues to challenge regulators.

Influencer Marketing on Social Media

Social media influencers are increasingly leveraged for product promotions given their sway over certain demographic segments. But lack of transparency regarding paid or sponsored content masquerading as objective advice risks misleading consumers.

However, enforcing stringent disclosures and restrictions may impose entry barriers for upcoming influencers. Social media platforms are also averse to content interventions that undermine user experience. Fighting deception without compromising economic opportunities is the key tension here.

E-commerce Deep Discounting

The massive discounts and cashback offers that enabled India's e-commerce boom have been criticized as anti-competitive practices of platforms like Amazon and Flipkart. But prohibiting such discounts can slow overall sectoral growth.

Here the dilemma is between unethical market distortion versus fueling digital adoption and MSME access. Policy choices involve trade-offs between fair competition and innovation incentives.

These examples reflect the multifaceted balancing challenges between ethical imperatives and commercial interests in India's complex digital transition. Navigating these while fostering inclusive growth calls for nuanced public debate and consultative policymaking.

Key Factors Underlying Challenges

Several interlinked factors underlie the challenges in balancing ethics and economics for Indian marketers and regulators:

1. **Digital Literacy Gaps:** Low awareness of data rights and adequate grievance mechanisms allows unethical practices targeting less informed groups. Fixing this entrenched gap requires long-term investment.
2. **Infrastructural Constraints:** India's sheer population scale and multilayered socioeconomic diversity poses hurdles in equitable enforcement of regulations across urban and rural areas.
3. **Resource Limitations:** Budget, manpower and technical capabilities of regulators limit effective monitoring of digital spaces. Voluntary compliance is thus essential.
4. **Cultural Perceptions:** Varying cultural attitudes to privacy, paternalism and mistrust of commerce shape Indian consumer responses to marketing practices.
5. **Rapid Innovation:** The complexity and scale of India's digital economy enables innovative promotion tactics outpacing policy. Light-touch regulation balances flexibility and oversight.
6. **Economic Pressures:** Competitive intensity incentivizes market distortion by platforms despite reputational risks. Mature self-regulation takes time to crystallize.
7. **Weak Enforcement:** Despite stringent policies, India's state capacity limitations hinders compliance. But heavy-handed restrictions also risk stifling innovation.
8. **Transnational Operations:** Regulation and monitoring of global digital intermediaries like Facebook and Amazon exceeds national jurisdiction. Multilateral cooperation is essential.
9. **Consumer Demand:** Price-sensitive Indian consumers fuel demand for deep discounts despite criticisms. Altering such expectations requires persistent engagement.
10. **Lack of Consultation:** Absence of substantive public consultations in policymaking leads to missteps, delays and confusions hampering ethical orientation of businesses.

These limitations underscore that effective change requires a collaborative ethos and pragmatic policy calibration centred on citizens' rights. Neither state diktats nor industry self-regulation alone can enable ethical marketing in India's complex transition.

Potential Solutions and Interventions

Scholars and practitioners have proposed several potential measures to address the multifaceted challenges:

1. **Foster Proactive Self-Regulation:** Incentivize businesses to formulate voluntary codes of conduct, transparency reports, auditing mechanisms and grievance redressal systems.
2. **Leverage Technology for Oversight:** Deploy solutions like AI, blockchain and crowdsourced audits for real-time monitoring of online marketing platforms.
3. **Invest in State Capacity:** Expand manpower, resources and training programs for bodies like CCPA to strengthen enforcement of consumer protection laws.
4. **Public-Private Cooperation:** Platforms should proactively coordinate with policymakers on issues like content moderation, competition and data access through defined processes.

5. **Incentivize Responsible Innovation:** Provide funding, tax incentives and recognition to start-ups deploying privacy-enhancing technologies and ethical AI systems.
6. **Raise Consumer Awareness:** Undertake multimedia literacy campaigns for data rights.
7. **Promote Industry Standards:** Industry associations should recognize organizations pioneering ethical practices through certifications and annual awards.
8. **Leverage Cultural Values:** Appeal to community-oriented sensibilities and wisdom traditions that prize transparency, accountability and social welfare.
9. **Cross-Border Coordination:** Partner with global forums like the UN, OECD and G20 to shape codes of conduct for transnational digital intermediaries.
10. **Consultative Policymaking:** Actively engage diverse stakeholders through public consultations and expert working groups for major digital economy regulations.
11. **Foster Academic Research:** Fund interdisciplinary scholarship on digital ethics issues relevant for contemporary Indian business and policymaking.
12. **Emphasize Long-term Thinking:** Boards and shareholders should focus on long-term brand reputation and strategic value over short-term growth incentives alone.
13. **Review Organizational Cultures:** Assess internal structures that inadvertently promote unethical practices through narrow metric-based evaluations and incentives.
14. **Ethics by Design:** Build organizational capacity to integrate ethical thinking and impact assessments into product development and marketing.
15. **Global Best Practice Sharing:** Enable exchanges between policymakers and businesses to learn from ethical marketing solutions implemented globally.

A multifaceted approach harnessing India's cultural wisdom, governance capabilities and entrepreneurial dynamism can enable responsible digital growth. The challenges are complex but the opportunities are profound.

Key Takeaways

Some key insights emerge from analysing India's challenges in balancing marketing ethics and business growth:

- Achieving an optimal balance requires consistent effort by all stakeholders rather than piecemeal initiatives. Helping consumers make informed choices should be the priority.
- Nuanced regulation aligned with ground realities is vital, neither stifling innovation with over-regulation nor permitting exploitation due to weak oversight.
- Voluntary self-regulation guided by codes of conduct and community accountability will complement laws in shaping ethical practices.
- Investing in awareness, redressal mechanisms, and inclusive capacity building across languages and geographies will improve outcomes.
- Leveraging India's technology prowess and cultural wisdom can promote transparent, fair digital platforms.
- Fostering cooperation between policymakers, businesses and civil society is key to balancing diverse priorities. Holistic development should guide policy.

- Nurturing ethics-driven leadership and long-term thinking across public and private institutions will positively influence organizational cultures over time.
- Promoting academic research and global collaboration on digital ethics can inform India's policy choices on balancing economic and social welfare.
- Reform must be accompanied by cultural change towards greater scepticism of marketing claims and balancing individual and community rights.

With foresight and collective endeavour, India can pragmatically optimize both innovation and ethics. The digital economy's next chapter will be defined by the priorities set today.

Technological Innovations and Solutions

Advances in digital technologies can potentially address some key ethical challenges in marketing practices and data governance. However, a nuanced approach is needed to ensure solutions align with social realities. Expanding digital literacy, fostering responsible innovation mindsets, and multistakeholder coordination will complement technological interventions for balanced outcomes.

Blockchain for Transparent and Auditable Data Sharing

Blockchain-based decentralized ledgers allow secure sharing of verified information between multiple entities, while protecting user privacy. Individuals retain greater control over how personal data is accessed and utilized across platforms. Consumers can track data flows through immutable records to ensure ethical collection and use (Raman et al., 2020).

For example, startups like DataEmber are using blockchain to develop personal data accounts where users can grant limited access to third parties. All data transactions are logged providing full audit trails. Users retain visibility and control over how their data is monetized. Such solutions can make digital marketing more transparent and consensual.

Blockchain also enables smart contracts that programmatically encode consent requirements, permissions, sharing restrictions and machine-readable privacy policies. This facilitates transparent auditing and compliance. Some startups are already developing blockchain-based data sharing networks for sectors like healthcare.

However, most marketing-related data collection currently happens without explicit consent. Mandating blockchain protocols through regulation may curb innovation in emergent technologies. Encouraging voluntary adoption by platforms through incentives and spreading awareness, while thoughtfully designing compliant systems, will be important.

Federated Learning for Ethical and Private Analytics

Federated Learning (FL) techniques enable collaborative analytics and machine learning model development without requiring central aggregation of actual user data. Data stays decentralized on user devices while model insights are collated in a privacy-preserving manner (Lyu et al., 2020). This allows deriving collective wisdom from large datasets distributively while protecting sensitive personal information.

For instance, Swarm Learning is an Indian startup using FL for predictive analytics by organizations without compromising customer data privacy. Marketers can employ such solutions cooperatively to gather valuable insights from consumer data across companies without needing direct data transfer or exposure. However, promoting awareness and building capabilities will be essential for wide adoption.

Differential Privacy and Anonymization Techniques

India must also incentivize development of privacy-enhancing technologies like differential privacy, homomorphic encryption, zero knowledge proofs and synthetic data generation that allow complex computation on masked datasets (Jain et al., 2021). Techniques like AI-based data anonymization and federated analytics further help securely perform profiling or ad targeting without compromising sensitive personal information.

Start-ups like ANSR and Elemential Labs provide customized data anonymization and encryption solutions for Indian enterprises to improve compliance. Platforms like Atlan employ differential privacy to derived insights from data without leakage. However, small businesses may need support in adoption. Clear guidelines on anonymization standards for ethical personalization and segmentation must complement integration of privacy-preserving tools. Ensuring solutions align with human values through impact assessments is also vital.

Transparent and Accountable AI Systems

Integrating human-centric design in marketing tech, promoting algorithmic transparency, instituting audits and fostering data ethics literacy among product teams will drive accountability. Techniques like ethics boards, external audits, algorithmic bias testing and participatory design can embed oversight and assessment in technology development lifecycles.

Independent ratings and due diligence certification for AI systems by standards bodies can guide adoption. Promoting open source marketing technologies like AdScala and transparent AI will improve trust and agility in self-correction. Focus must shift from opaque profit-driven systems towards collaborative innovation centred on human welfare.

Data Cooperatives and Trusts

Data trusts and platform cooperatives are decentralized data sharing models that preserve user agency through collective consent and democratic control. They uphold consent, purpose restrictions and collective data rights - countering the data monopolies of global corporations (Chatterjee, 2021).

For example, India Stack allows paperless KYC by individuals and aggregates payments data through consent. Extending its approach to cover marketing data could improve portability and reduce misuse. Global non-profits like data.org promote data trusts for social benefit. Their potential to ensure ethical data-driven marketing should be explored.

However, voluntary membership and complex coordination across fragmented platforms and marketers may hinder scale initially. Interoperability standards and incentives for data collectors to participate could help by improving cost-benefit attractiveness. But avoiding excessive state interference that stifles innovation will need careful policy design.

Multistakeholder Literacy, Skilling and Inclusion

Expanding digital literacy programs, nurturing responsible innovation mindsets within companies, and instituting policies mandating algorithmic transparency and ethics review boards are vital to harness technology's potential while mitigating risks.

Initiatives to provide internet access, vernacular language interfaces and digital skilling for marginalized communities can also counter exclusion. But addressing root inequities in access will require multifaceted digital capacity building across India's socioeconomic landscape. Persistent engagement, insights from field experiments and fostering localized innovation will be key.

Coordination Challenges

Realizing these solutions at scale faces coordination hurdles. Marketing practices span diverse sectors and platforms. Orchestrating collective action is complex across fragmented players. India should leverage forums like NASSCOM, ASSOCHAM and CII to drive convergence.

Regulatory mandates also risk promoting checkbox compliance that fails to change organizational cultures fundamentally. Sustained outcomes require fostering internal buy-in and capabilities within companies through training, impact assessments and improved incentive structures.

No Perfect Technological Fix in Isolation

Importantly, no perfect technological fix exists in isolation. Solutions must be grounded in public deliberation, align with people's values and accompany broader reforms in policies, business models and social attitudes. Technology is an enabler, not an outcome.

With foresight and collective endeavour, India can harmonize economic and social good by co-creating transparent, fair and empowering marketing technologies that protect consumer rights while also furthering prosperity. Some pragmatic pathways for progress include:

Policy and Governance Interventions

- Formulate nuanced guidelines and standards for ethical usage of emerging tools like AI, blockchain etc. in marketing
- Strengthen capabilities of regulatory bodies like CCPA to monitor technology deployments and compliance
- Mandate external audits and impact assessments for platforms and high-risk systems
- Create outcomes-based policies that allow flexibility in technology choices by businesses Business and Technology Actions
- Adopt human-centric design practices that consider social impacts early in product development
- Implement training programs on responsible innovation and ethics-by-design for product teams
- Participate in multistakeholder forums for developing voluntary codes of conduct and transparency standards
- Contribute to open datasets and benchmarks for AI accountability in marketing tech

Societal and Multilateral Measures

- Raise public discourse through consultations on balancing economic growth with ethics
- Partner with global bodies like IEEE, WEF and UN to shape technology governance norms with consensus
- Create multilingual interfaces, vernacular data literacy programs and inclusive digital infrastructure
- Incentivize startups developing low-cost privacy enhancing solutions for small businesses
- Enable grassroots consumer collectives to assess technology impacts and give feedback

By combining its profound humanistic sensibilities and innovation capabilities, India can shape global dialogues on ethical technology for sustainable prosperity. With collaborative endeavour, a brighter equitable digital future beckons. In summary, India must leverage its profound humanistic tradition and digital capabilities to shape an ethically oriented, digitally empowered future. With pragmatic collaborative effort focused on equity and transparency, we can build marketing technologies that create value responsibly for all.

Future Directions and Policy Recommendations

The path ahead for nurturing ethical marketing aligned with India's development priorities requires a multi-pronged strategy combining policy reforms, public awareness campaigns, enforcement mechanisms, and thought leadership.

On the policy front, self-regulation within industries relying extensively on customer data must be encouraged. Industry bodies like CII, FICCI and NASSCOM can play a key role by bringing member companies together to co-create robust codes of conduct, transparency standards, and consequence frameworks applicable across sectors. Voluntary adherence to such ethical codes, with peer accountability, can complement top-down regulation.

Secondly, raising public consciousness of data rights and grievance redressal avenues is essential. Here, public-private partnerships can undertake nationwide digital literacy initiatives in regional languages, leveraging civil society partnerships. Empowering disadvantaged communities through access to knowledge and tools for data privacy can counter exploitation.

Thirdly, capacities for monitoring compliance and enforcement require strengthening. Expanding the mandate, manpower and technological resources available to bodies like the Central Consumer Protection Authority would bolster oversight. Steeper fines and penalties for violations can also serve as deterrence. However, excessive punitiveness may not suffice without fundamental cultural shifts towards integrity and ethics-driven self-regulation.

Lastly, India can Aim to emerge as a thought leader and ethical role model for innovation in the digital economy. Increased funding for academic research on ethical technologies, data governance models and responsible marketing practices can inform policymaking. Supporting start-ups pioneering privacy-enhancing and transparent AI solutions through competitions and incubators can also catalyse responsible innovation. At the diplomatic level, India can champion principles of equity and accountability in global governance conversations on regulating digital platforms and data flows.

In summary, the suggested combination of voluntary industry codes, nationwide literacy drives, stringent but balanced enforcement, and signalling thought leadership can enable India to leverage its digital dividends equitably and responsibly. But this evolution requires patient collaborative work across government, businesses and civil society.

CONCLUSION

This chapter has analysed India's evolving digital marketing landscape and the associated interplay between ethics and economic priorities. While data-driven marketing has fuelled competitive advantage, absence of robust governance risks consumer rights and trust. Tackling challenges around awareness, attitudes, and state capacity requires a collaborative approach prioritizing transparency, choice, and accountability.

India's youthful demography and tech-savvy consumer base provide the foundation for such an ethics-driven, human-centric vision of marketing. Technological solutions can be harnessed to enforce compliance even as self-regulation gathers momentum. Ultimately, balancing business interests with social welfare will determine if India propagates digital inequalities or emerges as a leader in ethical innovation. This evolution rests on collaborative action between policymakers, industry, academia and civil society.

REFERENCES

Bhatia, S. (2016, August 11). ASCI upholds complaints against Coca Cola, Patanjali, Vivel and others. *The Economic Times*. https://economictimes.indiatimes.com/industry/cons-products/fmcg/asci-upholds-complaints-against-coca-cola-patanjali-vivel-and-others/articleshow/53679318.cms

Bhattacharjee, S., Agarwal, A., Malhotra, P., Bahl, S., Sharma, A., & Bir, A. (2020). *The Road Ahead: Digital Challenges for the Indian Economy*. Carnegie India. https://carnegieindia.org/2020/10/15/road-ahead-digital-challenges-for-indian-economy-pub-82924

Bloomberg. (2018, December 13). Ponzi schemes thrive in Indian e-commerce boom. *Livemint*. https://www.livemint.com/Money/J5stT8m5VjhXeSZk9ZcHTO/Ponzi-schemes-thrive-in-Indian-ecommerce-boom.html

Brigger, D., Bronkar, S., & Dearing, C. (2014). The Value of Ethical Marketing. *Ubiquity*, *2014*(February), 1–8.

Bruner, J. S. (1975). The Ontogenesis of Speech Acts. *Journal of Child Language*, *2*(1), 1–19. doi:10.1017/S0305000900000866

Bureau, E. T. (2018, January 11). Without consent: Airtel Payments Bank opens accounts of subscribers. *The Economic Times*. https://economictimes.indiatimes.com/industry/banking/finance/banking/without-consent-airtel-payments-bank-opens-accounts-of-subscribers/articleshow/62483222.cms?from=mdr

Chakraborty, I., Paranjape, B., Kakarla, S., & Ganguly, N. (2018). Stop Clickbait: Detecting and preventing clickbaits in online news media. *2016 IEEE/ACM International Conference on Advances in Social Networks Analysis and Mining (ASONAM)*. IEEE. 10.1109/ASONAM.2016.7752207

Chakravorti, B., & Sharma, S. (2020). *Digital planet 2020: How competitiveness and trust in digital economies vary across the world.* The Fletcher School, Tufts University. https://sites.tufts.edu/digital-planet/digital-planet-report/

Chatterjee, D. (2021). Emerging Data Governance Issues. In *India*. Data Governance Network.

Chhonker, M. S., Verma, D., & Kar, D. (2017). *Ethics in Digital Marketing: Illusion or Reality. Journal of Information.* Communication and Ethics in Society. doi:10.1108/JICES-10-2016-0036

Dey, B. L., Mohanty, S., Rao, U. H., Ghose, A., & Swain, P. (2018). *Regulating digital financial services in India: A policy discussion.* Digital Asia Hub.

Gupta, P. (2020). *Digital sovereignty and the conundrum of rules: Should India ban TikTok? 3ie Working paper; 34.* New Delhi: International Initiative for Impact Evaluation (3ie). doi:10.23846/WP0034

IAMAI-Kantar ICUBE. (2020). *ICUBE 2020 Report.* https://cms.iamai.in/Content/ResearchPapers/d3654bcc-002f-4fc7-ab39-e1fbeb00005d.pdf

Jagadish, H. V., Jain, S., Kasturi, R., Verma, Y., & Viswanathan, R. (2021). *Harms of predatory digital lending in India.* INAFI India.

Jai, T. M., & King, N. J. (2016). Privacy issues on the internet. In S. Simpson & H. Weisburd (Eds.), *The Criminology of White-Collar Crime* (pp. 245–265). Springer.

Jain, P., Gyanchandani, M., & Khare, N. (2021). Big data privacy: A technological perspective and review. *Journal of Big Data, 8*(1). Advance online publication. doi:10.1186/s40537-020-00359-2

Kaur, P. (2020). Analysing India's Personal Data Protection Bill, 2019. *The Dialogue, 15*(1), 94–111.

Kshetri, N. (2014). Big data's impact on privacy, security and consumer welfare. *Telecommunications Policy, 38*(11), 1134–1145. doi:10.1016/j.telpol.2014.10.002

Lyu, L., Yu, L., Yang, Q., Fu, X., Yue, X., Wang, H., & Ren, K. (2020, May). Differentially Private Federated Learning for Mobile Crowdsensing. *IEEE Transactions on Mobile Computing, 20*(10), 2957–2970.

Mali, S. V., Nikam, K., Gopal, C. V., & Phursule, R. N. (2021). A study on awareness about data privacy among users of digital services in rural area. *Materials Today: Proceedings.* doi:10.1016/j.matpr.2020.11.067

Malik, P., Sareen, P., & Dhir, A. (2019). Factors affecting adoption of digital payment systems in the era of demonetization in India. *Global Business Review, 20*(3), 706–720. doi:10.1177/0972150919832044

Meit, Y. (2021). *Digital payments transactions maintained robust growth momentum in FY 2020-21.* Ministry of Electronics and Information Technology. https://pib.gov.in/PressReleasePage.aspx?PRID=1712859

Muralidharan, S., Rasmussen, L., Patterson, D., & Shin, J. H. (2014). Speaking justice to power: Ethical alternatives and moral critiques in a data-driven society. *Popular Communication, 12*(4), 244–255. doi:10.1080/15405702.2014.969839

Murphy, P. E. (Ed.). (1998). *Ethics in marketing: International cases and perspectives.* Psychology Press.

Balancing Ethics and Economics

Murphy, P. E., Laczniak, G. R., Bowie, N. E., & Klein, T. A. (2005). *Ethical marketing: Basic ethics in action*. Pearson/Prentice Hall.

Nair, S. (2020). *The Personal Data Protection Bill, 2019: An Analysis of Compliance Requirements for Businesses. Global Community of Practice on Privacy, Anonymization, Respect for Data Subjects & Ethics (PRADE)*. United Nations Development Programme, Asia-Pacific.

NASSCOM. (2020). *India: $1 Trillion Digital Economy by 2025*. NASSCOM. https://nasscom.in/knowledge-center/publications/india-1-trillion-digital-economy-2025

Press Trust of India. (2022, January 5). Education Ministry finds serious irregularities in WhiteHat Jr's offerings. *ThePrint*. https://theprint.in/india/education-ministry-finds-serious-irregularities-in-whitehat-jrs-offerings/799127/

Rahman, M. S. (2018). The Advantages and Disadvantages of Using GDPR as a Model Law on Data Privacy in India. *National Law School of India Review*, *30*, 99–122.

Raman, M., Bhatt, S., Chaliganti, S., Mital, M., Omolara, O., Satyavolu, J., & Viswanathan, R. (2020). *Blockchain Explained*. USAID-FHI 360. https://www.findevgateway.org/paper/2020/09/blockchain-explained

Ranganathan, N., Nagappa, A. N., & Dominic, P. (2020, September). A study of online pharmacies in India. *Research in Social & Administrative Pharmacy*, *16*(9), 1218–1224. doi:10.1016/j.sapharm.2019.12.021

Reuters. (2019, January 31). Some of Amazon's sellers are faking authority for electronics. *Business Insider*. https://www.businessinsider.in/some-of-amazons-third-party-sellers-are-faking-their-authority-to-sell-electronics/articleshow/67760843.cms

Shenoy, J. (2018, December 20). Flipkart withdraws 'Lowest Price' Commitment as Epic Price War with Amazon Cools Off. *News18*. https://www.news18.com/news/business/flipkart-withdraws-lowest-price-commitment-as-epic-price-war-with-amazon

Singh, S. (2015, September 2). Pharma firm in dock for surrogate ads. *The Hindu*. https://www.thehindu.com/news/cities/Delhi/pharma-firm-in-dock-for-surrogate-ads/article7616663.ece

Subramanian, S. (2018). The Rise of Hyper-Personalized Marketing Experiences Across Channels. *Martech Advisor*. https://www.martechadvisor.com/articles/customer-experience-2/the-rise-of-hyper-personalized-marketing-experiences-across-channels/

Tikkinen-Piri, C., Rohunen, A., & Markkula, J. (2018). EU General Data Protection Regulation: Changes and implications for personal data collecting companies. *Computer Law & Security Report*, *34*(1), 134–153. doi:10.1016/j.clsr.2017.05.015

Udupa, S. (2020). Ethics and ethos of digital governance in India. *Ethics and Information Technology*, *22*(2), 117–128.

Upadhyay, P. (2017). Effectiveness of Regulations in India with Regard to Unethical Marketing Practices. *Procedia Computer Science*, *122*, 487–494. doi:10.1016/j.procs.2017.11.396

48

Upadhyay, P., & Singh, S. (2017). Ethical issues in the practices of Indian corporate sectors. *Journal of Indian Business Research*. doi:10.1108/JIBR-02-2017-0025

Chapter 4
Balancing the Scale:
Ethical Marketing in the Age of Big Data – A Comprehensive Analysis of Data Governance Standards and the Role of Effective Technology

Sayani Das

https://orcid.org/0000-0003-0076-7466

Institute of Mass Communication, Film, and Television Studies, India

Archan Mitra

https://orcid.org/0000-0002-1419-3558

Presidency University, India

ABSTRACT

This chapter explores the integration of ethical marketing practices, data governance standards, and technology. Highlighting the importance of transparency, consumer control, accountability, and benefi-cence, it examines data protection regulations like GDPR and CCPA, and the role of AI and blockchain in promoting ethical practices. Case studies of Patagonia and Unilever demonstrate ethical marketing's potential, while the Cambridge Analytica scandal underscores the consequences of neglect. A compre-hensive framework for ethical marketing is proposed, offering guidelines for businesses and policy-makers. The chapter concludes with future directions, emphasizing the need for regulatory evolution, technological advancements, consumer empowerment, and cross-disciplinary collaboration to achieve ethical marketing that respects consumer privacy and fosters trust.

DOI: 10.4018/979-8-3693-2215-4.ch004

INTRODUCTION

The convergence of ethical marketing, data governance, and technology in the digital era is a crucial subject of study for both academics and professionals. Ethical marketing include strategies that uphold consumer rights and privacy, placing a strong emphasis on transparency and fairness in the gathering and utilisation of data. The widespread adoption of digital technology has granted organisations unparalleled access to enormous quantities of personal data, hence intensifying issues over privacy and the ethical utilisation of information. To navigate this intricate terrain, it is imperative to possess a thorough comprehension of data governance standards, which encompass established protocols and rules aimed at guaranteeing the reliability, protection, and confidentiality of data. This chapter seeks to examine the ways in which ethical marketing practices can be strengthened by rigorous data governance rules and the efficient utilisation of technology. It offers a comprehensive study of the impact of these practices on consumers, businesses, and legislators.

Ethical marketing serves as both a legal requirement and a moral guide for organisations in their dealings with consumers. According to Smith (2020), ethical marketing strategies are crucial for establishing trust and enduring relationships with consumers, which are vital for achieving sustainable corporate success. The incorporation of customer data into marketing methods, while providing the opportunity for customised experiences, raises substantial ethical concerns. The need for a framework that upholds consumer autonomy and permission becomes crucial in addressing the delicate balance between personalisation and privacy (Jones, 2019).

Data governance refers to the systematic implementation of processes, policies, and standards to efficiently manage and safeguard data. Within the realm of marketing, it is crucial to employ a fundamental mechanism to ensure responsible and ethical utilisation of consumer information. The General Data Protection Regulation (GDPR) in the European Union and the California Consumer Privacy Act (CCPA) in the United States are significant legal frameworks designed to improve data protection and privacy (European Commission, 2016; State of California, 2018). These regulations establish requirements for the collection, storage, and utilisation of data, while also granting customers more authority over their personal information. This sets a worldwide standard for data management.

Technology has a double impact on ethical marketing and data governance. Technological breakthroughs, such as artificial intelligence (AI) and blockchain, provide chances to improve data security, transparency, and user involvement (Harris & Dennis, 2020). However, the fast rate at which technology is advancing poses persistent difficulties for safeguarding privacy and data security, necessitating the constant adjustment of governance frameworks (Kumar et al., 2019). Hence, comprehending the significance of technology is crucial for effectively addressing the ethical problems in marketing.

The objective of this chapter is to offer a thorough examination of ethical marketing by considering data governance principles and technology. The chapter will provide insights into the development of ethical marketing techniques that uphold consumer privacy and foster trust by analysing the theoretical foundations, legislative framework, and technological progress. By doing this, it aims to contribute to the wider discussion on ethical practices in marketing, the management of data, and the influence of technology on the future of interactions between consumers and businesses.

Section 1: Introduction to Ethical Marketing and Data Governance

Ethical marketing entails the implementation of moral principles in marketing activities. It encompasses the values of truthfulness, impartiality, and accountability in all forms of advertising. Moreover, it demonstrates consideration and regard for the intended audience and the impact it may have on them (Smith, 2020). The significance of ethical marketing is amplified in the digital era, as firms have greater capacity to gather, scrutinise, and exploit extensive quantities of personal data. The digital landscape, distinguished by internet-based transactions, social media engagements, and digital promotions, presents distinct difficulties and possibilities for ethical marketing. Consumers in the present era possess a higher level of knowledge and connectivity, hence expecting brands to exhibit transparency, authenticity, and regard for their privacy (Jones, 2019). Ethical marketing is not only a legal and moral duty, but also a strategic benefit that promotes trust and fosters long-term commitment among consumers. Trust is crucial in consumer connections, as it forms the foundation. By fostering trust through ethical practices, businesses can enhance customer loyalty and promote brand advocacy (Harris & Dennis, 2020).

Data Governance Standards: GDPR, CCPA, and Beyond

Data governance rules, such as the General Data Protection Regulation (GDPR) and the California Consumer Privacy Act (CCPA), are important landmarks in the development of data protection and privacy legislation. The General Data Protection Regulation (GDPR), implemented by the European Union in 2018, establishes a stringent benchmark for safeguarding data, empowering individuals to exercise authority over their personal information, and putting stringent responsibilities on data processors and controllers (European Commission, 2016). The General Data Protection Regulation (GDPR) places significant emphasis on concepts such as obtaining consent, ensuring the right to access personal data, and implementing the right to be forgotten. As a result, it brings about substantial changes in the methods by which organisations gather, retain, and handle personal data.

In a similar vein, the CCPA, enacted in 2020, grants California residents unparalleled control over their personal information. This includes the rights to be informed, to have their data deleted, and to choose not to have their personal data sold (State of California, 2018). These policies emphasise an increasing worldwide agreement on the significance of safeguarding consumer privacy and setting forth explicit principles for data management.

The Intersection of Ethical Marketing and Data Governance

Businesses in the digital age must prioritise the convergence of ethical marketing and data stewardship. The relationship between ethical marketing practices and data governance standards is closely connected, since both strive to uphold consumer rights and promote responsible utilisation of information. The enforcement of GDPR, CCPA, and analogous rules has immediate ramifications for marketing efforts, necessitating organisations to embrace transparent methodologies in data acquisition, consent, and manipulation.

The junction emphasises the necessity of aligning marketing ethics and data governance standards in a strategic manner. Businesses are required to comply with these requirements while also ensuring their marketing practices are effective. This requires a thorough awareness of both legal obligations and ethical issues. Integrating ethical marketing with data governance principles not only ensures compliance but also improves brand reputation, cultivates consumer trust, and promotes a culture of accountability towards consumer data (Kumar et al., 2019).

Business strategies have been significantly impacted by the digital age, with ethical marketing and data governance taking front stage. Ethical marketing, characterised by its dedication to integrity, equity, and accountability, plays a vital role in fostering trust and loyalty in the digital marketplace. Data governance guidelines, such as the General Data Protection Regulation (GDPR) and the California customer Privacy Act (CCPA), establish the regulatory structure for safeguarding customer privacy and guaranteeing ethical data use. The convergence of these areas emphasises the significance of harmonising marketing strategies with legal and ethical norms, providing a route for enterprises to interact with consumers in a clear, considerate, and significant way.

Section 2: The Ethical Implications of Data Use in Marketing

Analysis of How Consumer Data is Used in Marketing

Consumer data plays a crucial role in marketing tactics in the digital era, allowing businesses to customise their advertising efforts, personalise customer experiences, and ultimately, boost sales. The application of consumer data encompasses a spectrum of information, from fundamental demographic data to more intricate behavioural data, such as web surfing patterns, purchase records, and interactions on social media (Kotler & Keller, 2016). The utilisation of advanced analytics and artificial intelligence technologies has significantly improved marketers' capacity to forecast customer behaviour, accurately divide markets into segments, and provide highly focused advertising (Chaffey & Ellis-Chadwick, 2019).

Data-driven marketing strategies, such as personalised suggestions, targeted email campaigns, and customised advertising on social media platforms, significantly depend on the analysis of customer data. These approaches are not only efficient in attracting customers but also in maximising marketing budgets by allocating resources to the segments with the highest likelihood of conversion (Homburg, Jozić, & Kuehnl, 2017). Nevertheless, the comprehensive accumulation and use of consumer data give rise to noteworthy ethical concerns, demanding a meticulous equilibrium between marketing efficacy and regard for customer privacy.

Ethical Concerns Arising From Data Use in Marketing

The ethical ramifications of utilising customer data in marketing are complex, encompassing issues pertaining to privacy, permission, transparency, and data security. An important ethical consideration revolves around privacy and the degree to which consumers are informed about and have authority over the gathering and utilisation of their personal data (Martin & Murphy, 2017). Oftentimes, customers may lack a comprehensive understanding of the extent of data being gathered or its use, resulting in sentiments of intrusion and exploitation.

Consent is a fundamental ethical factor. The adoption of express consent as required by rules such as GDPR represents a shift towards granting customers more authority and control. Nevertheless, the execution of consent mechanisms typically remains intricate and obscure, with customers commonly consenting to conditions without fully comprehending the consequences (Boerman, Kruikemeier, & Zuiderveen Borgesius, 2018).

Ensuring clear and open communication on data collecting procedures and the use of consumer data in marketing campaigns is crucial for maintaining ethical standards in marketing. However, the intricate nature of data ecosystems, which involve numerous third parties and technological processes, can pose difficulties in attaining transparency (Couldry & Mejias, 2019).

Ultimately, ensuring the protection of data is a paramount ethical consideration. Given the rise in data breaches and cyberattacks, it is crucial to prioritise the protection of consumer data. Failure to safeguard consumer data not only infringes against privacy rights but also undermines consumer confidence and tarnishes company reputation (Martin & Murphy, 2017).

Therefore, the utilisation of customer data in marketing offers potential advantages as well as ethical dilemmas. Data-driven marketing methods have the potential to enhance customer experiences and improve marketing efficiency. However, they also give rise to significant ethical concerns including privacy, permission, transparency, and data security. To tackle these concerns, it is essential to demonstrate a dedication to ethical practices, which entails transparent communication with consumers, ensuring the secure management of data, and complying with regulatory norms. As the digital environment progresses, the ethical principles that govern the utilisation of consumer data in marketing must also advance.

Case Studies Highlighting Ethical and Unethical Marketing Practices

Case Study 1: Patagonia - A Model of Ethical Marketing

Patagonia, a firm specialising in outdoor clothes and gear, has gained recognition for its enduring dedication to environmental sustainability and ethical business principles. An exemplary instance of its ethical marketing is the "Don't Buy This Jacket" campaign, initiated to persuade customers to reconsider their purchases by emphasising the environmental consequences of consumerism (Chouinard, Ellison, & Ridgeway, 2011). This campaign demonstrates ethical marketing by being transparent and dedicated to sustainability, directly challenging the traditional consumer culture. Patagonia's strategy not only corresponds with its brand principles but also cultivates confidence and devotion among its client base, showcasing how ethical marketing can also contribute to a robust brand image and enduring corporate prosperity.

Case Study 2: Cambridge Analytica and Facebook - A Breach of Ethical Marketing

The Cambridge Analytica controversy exemplifies egregious instances of unscrupulous marketing strategies. The incident involved the unauthorised collection of personal information from millions of Facebook users, which was then utilised for political advertising. This incident brings attention to important concerns regarding privacy, permission, and openness (Cadwalladr & Graham-Harrison, 2018). The controversy not only prompted inquiries into Facebook's data governance processes but also sparked concerns about the ethical ramifications of utilising consumer data for personalised advertising without clear user agreement. This case study highlights the significance of ethical considerations in data utilisation, the requirement for explicit consent methods, and the possible consequences for corporations who neglect ethical norms in their marketing strategies.

These case studies exemplify the divergent results of ethical and unethical marketing techniques. Patagonia's advertising demonstrates a dedication to moral values, which strengthens customer loyalty and fosters consumer confidence. Conversely, the Cambridge Analytica incident exemplifies the possible outcomes of unethical marketing strategies, such as the erosion of consumer confidence and legal implications. These instances highlight the significance of following ethical principles in marketing, placing emphasis on openness, permission, and the preservation of consumer privacy.

Section 3: Current Data Governance Frameworks and Their Impact

Detailed Examination of Various Data Governance Frameworks

Data governance frameworks are crucial for overseeing the acquisition, retention, and use of data, guaranteeing that these activities are carried out with ethical considerations and adherence to legal requirements. In this analysis, we explore some pivotal frameworks that have had a substantial influence on marketing strategies worldwide.

General Data Protection Regulation (GDPR): The General Data Protection Regulation (GDPR), implemented by the European Union in 2018, is considered one of the most rigorous data protection laws worldwide. It grants individuals enhanced authority over their personal data, encompassing the entitlements to access, rectify, erase, and limit the processing of their data. The GDPR also mandates the implementation of data protection measures from the beginning of system architecture, known as "data protection by design and by default" (European Commission, 2016).

California Consumer Privacy Act (CCPA): The CCPA, the most comprehensive state data privacy law in the United States, goes into effect in 2020 and gives California residents the right to know what personal data is collected about them, why it is collected, and whether it is sold or disclosed, and to whom. Additionally, it provides customers with the option to decline the sale of their personal data (State of California, 2018).

Personal Data Protection Act (PDPA): The PDPA in Singapore is a data protection law that regulates how organisations gather, utilise, and disclose personal data. The objective is to safeguard individuals' personal data from unauthorised use and encourage effective handling of personal data within organisations (Personal Data Protection Commission, 2012).

The Effectiveness of These Frameworks in Regulating Marketing Practices

The efficacy of data governance frameworks such as GDPR, CCPA, and PDPA in overseeing marketing tactics is apparent through many means:

- **Augmented Consumer Confidence:** By guaranteeing openness and authority over personal data, these policies facilitate the establishment of consumer confidence, which is vital for customer retention and brand allegiance.
- **Compliance and Legal Risk Mitigation:** By adhering to these guidelines, organisations safeguard their financial stability and reputation by lowering the possibility of incurring heavy penalties and legal ramifications from non-compliance.
- **Advancement of Ethical Marketing:** These policies promote the use of ethical marketing strategies that uphold customer privacy and data security, in line with wider corporate social responsibility objectives.

International Differences and Challenges in Data Governance

Global organisations face issues due to the divergent data governance regimes between countries, despite the shared objective of safeguarding personal data. These disparities can be ascribed to divergent cultural perspectives on privacy, legal customs, and degrees of enforcement.

- **Divergent Criteria:** The General Data Protection Regulation (GDPR) is widely regarded as the benchmark for safeguarding data, although not all nations have enacted rules that match its stringent requirements. This disparity is a challenge for international corporations that need to navigate through a fragmented set of regulations.
- **Cross-Border Data Transfers:** The conditions for cross-border data transfers differ depending on the rules. The General Data Protection Regulation (GDPR) imposes limitations on the transfer of data to countries outside the European Union (EU), unless those countries can guarantee a sufficient degree of data protection. This presents difficulties for international operations (European Commission, 2016).
- **Compliance Expenses:** Adapting to the data protection regulations of each jurisdiction can incur significant expenses and require substantial allocation of resources, particularly for SMEs.

Data governance frameworks are essential in influencing ethical marketing practices by setting explicit criteria for safeguarding data and ensuring consumer privacy. Although these frameworks have successfully facilitated the promotion of transparency and consumer autonomy around personal data, substantial obstacles persist due to worldwide disparities and the difficulties of ensuring compliance across various jurisdictions. In order to effectively tackle these difficulties and establish consistent worldwide data protection standards, it is crucial to maintain an ongoing conversation and collaboration at the international level as the digital landscape progresses.

Section 4: The Role of Technology in Ethical Marketing

Exploration of Technologies Aiding in Ethical Marketing (AI, Blockchain, etc.)

The incorporation of sophisticated technologies into marketing strategies has created fresh opportunities for ethical marketing. Artificial Intelligence (AI) and blockchain technologies are leading the way in this shift, providing solutions to ethical challenges encountered by marketers.

Artificial Intelligence (AI): AI and machine learning algorithms provide the capability to accurately analyse consumer behaviour and preferences, facilitating personalised marketing that upholds consumer privacy. AI-powered technologies can guarantee that marketing methods are respectful and founded on consumers' authorised data, thereby adhering to ethical marketing norms. Furthermore, AI can assist in the detection and removal of prejudices in marketing initiatives, guaranteeing impartiality and parity (Kaplan & Haenlein, 2020).

Blockchain: Blockchain technology is a vital tool for ethical marketing since it provides unmatched transaction security and transparency. Blockchain technology can establish a decentralised and unchangeable record of transactions, which can effectively verify the accuracy of promises made by marketers and thereby eliminate deceptive ads. In addition, blockchain technology has the capability to safeguard consumers' data, offering a heightened level of security and transparency in managing personal information (Tapscott & Tapscott, 2016).

Case Studies of Technology Applications in Ethical Marketing

Case Study 1: Unilever and Blockchain for Supply Chain Transparency

Unilever has employed blockchain technology to improve transparency in its supply chain, specifically in the acquisition of sustainable palm oil. Unilever utilises blockchain technology to offer consumers easily verifiable and transparent information about the source of their products and the sustainability measures implemented during manufacture. This strategy not only boosts consumer confidence but also promotes ethical buying choices (Unilever, 2020).

Case Study 2: Stitch Fix and AI for Personalized Fashion Recommendations

Stitch Fix, an internet-based service for personalised garment styling, using artificial intelligence (AI) to provide individualised fashion suggestions to its clientele. The company's utilisation of AI upholds client preferences and privacy by relying on data directly supplied by customers and their feedback on prior choices to provide recommendations. The personalised service provided by Stitch Fix demonstrates ethical marketing principles by utilising customer data in a respectful and useful manner to improve the consumer experience.

Future Trends and Potential Technologies in This Area

The trajectory of ethical marketing is expected to be influenced by emerging technologies that augment transparency, personalisation, and security. Several prospective future trends encompass:

Internet of Things (IoT): By giving marketers access to real-time information about customer behaviour and preferences, IoT devices can enable more ethical and accurate personalisation. However, this also requires strict data protection and privacy protocols.

Quantum computing: With the ability to process enormous volumes of data at previously unheard-of rates, quantum computing may provide new avenues for the moral analysis of consumer data, guaranteeing that personalisation and targeting are carried out without violating privacy.

Virtual Reality (VR) and Augmented Reality (AR): These technologies can produce immersive experiences that let customers engage transparently and engagingly with companies and products, opening the door for more moral marketing strategies that put the needs and preferences of the customer first.

AI and blockchain technologies play a crucial role in promoting ethical marketing practices by providing solutions that effectively combine personalised experiences with privacy and transparency. The case studies of Unilever and Stitch Fix exemplify the practical utilisation of these technologies in advancing ethical marketing. As we anticipate the future, the ongoing development of technology holds the potential to significantly augment marketers' ability to communicate with consumers in an ethical and responsible manner.

Section 5: Developing a Framework for Ethical Marketing in the Digital Era

Proposing a Comprehensive Framework for Ethical Marketing

Ethical marketing is a framework that places importance on transparency, consumer respect, and integrity in all marketing activities. An all-encompassing structure for ethical marketing necessitates a multifaceted strategy that incorporates ethical principles, data governance rules, and the judicious use of technology. This framework is specifically crafted to provide firms and governments with guidance in developing marketing tactics that not only adhere to legal obligations but also surpass them to achieve elevated ethical benchmarks.

Core Principles of the Ethical Marketing Framework

Transparency: Companies must to provide explicit information regarding their methods of collecting, using, and disseminating consumer data. This entails obtaining express agreement from consumers and offering easily comprehensible privacy policies (Martin & Murphy, 2017).

Consumer Autonomy: Consumers should own autonomy over their personal data, encompassing the right to view, rectify inaccuracies, delete, or opt-out of data gathering (Boerman, Kruikemeier, & Zuiderveen Borgesius, 2018).

Integrity and Accountability: Businesses need to be responsible for safeguarding customer information and making sure that their marketing strategies don't deceive or take advantage of customers.

Beneficence: Marketing tactics should strive to maximise consumer welfare while refraining from engaging in behaviours that may result in damage. This encompasses safeguarding consumer privacy and preventing manipulation (Kaplan & Haenlein, 2020).

Integration of Data Governance Standards and Technology in This Framework

In order to successfully adopt this ethical marketing strategy, firms need to incorporate strong data governance norms and ethically utilise technology.

Compliance with Data Protection legislation: Businesses must adhere to data protection laws, including GDPR, CCPA, and other applicable legislation, to ensure that their marketing operations satisfy the most stringent standards of data privacy and security.

Application of Ethical AI and Machine Learning: Without sacrificing privacy, technology should be leveraged to improve customer experiences. AI systems should be engineered to mitigate bias and uphold equity in targeted marketing strategies (Kaplan & Haenlein, 2020).

Blockchain for Transparency: By using blockchain technology to produce unchangeable, transparent records of how customer data is used, marketing techniques can become more trustworthy and accountable (Tapscott & Tapscott, 2016).

Guidelines for Businesses and Policymakers

For businesses:

- **Incorporate Privacy-by-Design:** Embed privacy and data protection measures into the creation stage of all marketing technologies and initiatives.
- **Inform customers:** Offer transparent details regarding data practices and equip customers with awareness about their rights and ability to manage their data.
- **Perform Routine Ethical Audits:** Consistently assess marketing practices to verify their compliance with ethical standards and regulatory mandates.

For policymakers:

- **Establish unambiguous regulatory guidelines:** Furnish businesses with explicit and practicable directives about ethical marketing and data protection activities.
- **Facilitate Global Collaboration:** Strive to achieve uniformity in data protection regulations across different regions, thereby streamlining adherence for multinational enterprises.
- **Promote Innovation in Ethical Marketing:** Promote the creation and uptake of technologies, including blockchain and ethical AI, that improve ethical marketing techniques.

An all-encompassing structure for ethical marketing necessitates the incorporation of ethical principles, data governance norms, and responsible utilisation of technology. By following this approach, firms may cultivate trust and loyalty among consumers, while legislators can ensure that regulations endorse ethical and innovative marketing methods. The overarching objective is to establish a marketing ecosystem that upholds consumer rights and fosters transparency, accountability, and integrity.

CONCLUSION

This comprehensive study has clarified the complex and diverse field of ethical marketing, emphasising the crucial importance of data governance rules and the use of innovative technology. The fundamental concepts of ethical marketing are transparency, customer control, accountability and integrity, and beneficence. These principles are essential for establishing trust and cultivating enduring connections with consumers. An analysis of data governance frameworks, such as GDPR, CCPA, and PDPA, has demonstrated their crucial function in overseeing marketing practices and guaranteeing the privacy and safeguarding of customer data. AI and blockchain technologies have become influential instruments in advancing ethical marketing by providing solutions that improve transparency, security, and personalisation.

The examination of Patagonia and Unilever's case studies, in conjunction with the scrutiny of the Cambridge Analytica incident, have emphasised the significance of ethical norms in the field of marketing and the potential repercussions of disregarding such issues. These conversations have resulted in the proposal of a complete framework for ethical marketing. This framework highlights the importance of including data governance norms and responsible technology use. It also offers practical instructions for firms and regulators to follow.

Future Research Directions in Ethical Marketing and Data Governance

Regulatory Evolution: With the ongoing advancement of digital technologies, it is crucial to have regulatory frameworks that can adapt accordingly. Future endeavours should prioritise the establishment of universal data protection norms that tackle the advancements in technology and data handling methods, thereby promoting a more unified regulatory framework.

Technological Advancements: More research is needed to determine the ethical implications of cutting-edge technologies like virtual reality (VR), augmented reality (AR), the Internet of Things (IoT), and quantum computing. The objective of research should be to comprehend the ethical use of these technologies in marketing strategies, with a specific emphasis on improving consumer experiences while ensuring the protection of privacy and data security.

Consumer Empowerment: Future endeavours should prioritise equipping customers with enhanced information and resources to effectively control their data and privacy preferences. Advancements in digital literacy and technology that enhance privacy can have a substantial impact on accomplishing this objective.

Sustainability and Ethical Consumption: Future research should focus on the crucial junction of sustainability and ethical marketing. Marketers can promote sustainable consumption behaviours by employing ethical marketing methods that support environmental sustainability and social responsibility, in line with wider societal objectives.

Cross-Disciplinary Collaboration: Cross-disciplinary collaboration is necessary to address the complex issues that arise when marketing, technology, and ethics come together. Future research and practice should engage professionals from disciplines such as data science, law, ethics, and consumer psychology, promoting a comprehensive approach to ethical marketing.

Overall, the pursuit of fully harnessing the potential of ethical marketing is ongoing. By following to the principles specified in this framework and consistently adjusting to technology improvements and legislative changes, businesses can not only comply with legal requirements but also enhance their processes to reach the utmost ethical standards. Policymakers should persist in refining and adjusting legislation to safeguard consumers in a constantly evolving digital environment. The primary objective is to establish a marketing ecology that is both efficient and maintains the dignity and privacy of consumers.

REFERENCES

Boerman, S. C., Kruikemeier, S., & Zuiderveen Borgesius, F. J. (2018). Online behavioral advertising: A literature review and research agenda. *Journal of Advertising, 47*(1), 33–63.

Cadwalladr, C., & Graham-Harrison, E. (2018). Revealed: 50 million Facebook profiles harvested for Cambridge Analytica in major data breach. *The Guardian.*

Chaffey, D., & Ellis-Chadwick, F. (2019). *Digital Marketing.* Pearson Education.

Chouinard, Y., Ellison, J., & Ridgeway, R. (2011). *The Responsible Company: What We've Learned From Patagonia's First 40 Years*. Patagonia.

Couldry, N., & Mejias, U. A. (2019). *The Costs of Connection: How Data Is Colonizing Human Life and Appropriating It for Capitalism*. Stanford University Press.

European Commission. (2016). *Regulation (EU) 2016/679 of the European Parliament and of the Council of 27 April 2016 on the protection of natural persons with regard to the processing of personal data and on the free movement of such data (General Data Protection Regulation)*. Official Journal of the European Union.

Harris, L., & Dennis, C. (2020). *Marketing the e-Business*. Routledge.

Homburg, C., Jozić, D., & Kuehnl, C. (2017). Customer experience management: Toward implementing an evolving marketing concept. *Journal of the Academy of Marketing Science, 45*(3), 377–401. doi:10.1007/s11747-015-0460-7

Jones, R. (2019). Ethical issues in digital marketing and social media marketing. *Journal of Direct, Data and Digital Marketing Practice, 20*(1), 37–45.

Kaplan, A., & Haenlein, M. (2020). Artificial intelligence in marketing: A review and future research agenda. *Journal of the Academy of Marketing Science, 48*, 120–135.

Kotler, P., & Keller, K. L. (2016). *Marketing Management*. Pearson.

Kumar, V., Rajan, B., Gupta, S., & Pozza, I. D. (2019). Customer engagement in service. *Journal of the Academy of Marketing Science, 47*(1), 138–160. doi:10.1007/s11747-017-0565-2

Martin, K. D., & Murphy, P. E. (2017). The role of data privacy in marketing. *Journal of Marketing, 81*(2), 36–57. doi:10.1509/jm.15.0497

Martin, K. D., & Murphy, P. E. (2017). The role of data privacy in marketing. *Journal of Marketing, 81*(2), 36–57. doi:10.1509/jm.15.0497

Personal Data Protection Commission. (2012). *Personal Data Protection Act 2012*. Singapore Statutes Online.

Smith, T. J. (2020). *Ethical marketing and the new consumer*. John Wiley & Sons.

State of California. (2018). *California Consumer Privacy Act (CCPA)*. California Legislative Information.

State of California. (2018). *California Consumer Privacy Act (CCPA)*. California Legislative Information.

Stitch Fix. (2019). *How Stitch Fix Uses AI to Personalize Fashion*. Stitch Fix.

Tapscott, D., & Tapscott, A. (2016). *Blockchain Revolution: How the Technology Behind Bitcoin Is Changing Money, Business, and the World*. Penguin.

Unilever. (2020). *Unilever achieves 100% traceability for palm oil through blockchain technology*. Unilever.

Chapter 5
Customer Engagement in Metaverse Using Big Data

Devesh Bathla
 https://orcid.org/0000-0003-3990-5934
Chitkara Business School, Chitkara University, India

Raina Ahuja
Kurukshetra University, Kurukshetra, India

ABSTRACT

Customer engagement and customer retention are closely linked, and the metaverse offers a unique opportunity for brands to build lasting relationships with their customers. Metaverse allows brands to create a virtual representation of their stores and to interact with customers in that space. The metaverse offers a platform for community building, where brands can create a sense of belonging and connection among their customers. Brands can create virtual events, social spaces, or games that bring their customers together and foster a sense of community. By building a community around their brand, customers are more likely to feel connected to the brand and to each other, which can increase the likelihood of repeat purchases and brand advocacy. The metaverse concept has been popularised in science fiction and video games but has gained momentum in recent years as a potential next step for the internet.

INTRODUCTION TO METAVERSE

The term "metaverse" refers to a hypothetical future state of the internet, where virtual and physical worlds merge to create a shared, immersive space. In this world, people can interact with each other and digital objects in real time, using avatars to represent themselves (Stokel-Walker, 2022). The metaverse concept has been popularised in science fiction and video games but has gained momentum in recent years as a potential next step for the internet.

The term "metaverse" was coined by science fiction author Neal Stephenson in his 1992 novel "Snow Crash." In the book, the metaverse is a fully immersive virtual world where people can interact with

DOI: 10.4018/979-8-3693-2215-4.ch005

each other and digital objects in real time. While Stephenson's vision of the metaverse was fictional, it inspired real-world efforts to create similar virtual worlds.

In the years since "Snow Crash," the metaverse concept has been popularised in video games, such as World of Warcraft, Second Life, and Minecraft. These games allow players to create avatars and interact with other players in a shared digital space. While these games are not a true metaverse, they represent early examples of the technology that could enable a metaverse in the future.

The idea of a true metaverse has gained momentum in recent years, driven by advances in virtual reality (VR), augmented reality (AR), and blockchain technology. VR and AR enable immersive, three-dimensional experiences that could make a metaverse feel more realistic and immersive than ever before. Blockchain technology, the underlying technology of cryptocurrencies like Bitcoin, could enable decentralised ownership and governance of digital assets in a metaverse (Murray et al., 2022).

In a true metaverse, people could use avatars to represent themselves and interact with each other and digital objects in real-time (Mozumder et al., 2022). They could explore virtual worlds, participate in events, and even conduct business. For example, a musician could perform a virtual concert in a metaverse, and fans worldwide could attend using their avatars. A businessperson could attend a virtual conference and meet with other attendees to discuss business opportunities. The possibilities for a metaverse are limited only by our imaginations.

While the metaverse is still a hypothetical future state of the internet, many companies are working to make it a reality. Facebook has announced plans to create a metaverse and is investing heavily in VR and AR technology to make it happen. Epic Games, the company behind the popular video game Fortnite, is also exploring the potential of a metaverse and has created a virtual concert venue that can host events with millions of attendees.

The potential benefits of a metaverse are significant. A metaverse could create new opportunities for social interaction, entertainment, and commerce. It could enable people to connect with each other in new and meaningful ways and create new business opportunities that were previously impossible. It could also enable new forms of art and expression, allowing people to explore new worlds and experiences currently beyond our reach.

INTRODUCTION TO BIG DATA

Big data refers to large and complex data sets that are difficult to process using traditional data processing techniques (Elgendy & Elragal, 2014). Various sources, such as social media, e-commerce transactions, and customer interactions, typically generate these data sets. Big data has become an increasingly important tool for businesses, as it can provide valuable insights into customer behaviour and preferences.

Brands can use big data for customer personalisation in a number of ways. By analysing large data sets, brands can better understand their customers' needs and preferences and use this information to create personalised experiences that better meet their customers' expectations. One of the key ways that brands use big data for customer personalisation is by analysing customer behaviour. By tracking customer interactions and purchase history, brands can identify patterns and trends in their customers' behaviour (Campbell et al., 2020). This information can be used to create personalised recommendations and offers tailored to each customer's interests and preferences.

For example, Amazon is known for its personalised product recommendations. By analysing customer behaviour and purchase history, Amazon is able to suggest products that customers are likely to be interested in. This helps customers find what they are looking for more quickly and increases the likelihood of purchasing.

Another way brands use big data for customer personalisation is by analysing customer feedback. By gathering customer feedback through surveys, social media, and other channels, brands can gain valuable insights into what customers like and dislike about their products and services (Elena, 2016). This information can be used to improve products and services and create personalised experiences that better meet customers' needs.

For example, Starbucks uses customer feedback to create personalised offers for its loyalty program members. By analysing customer feedback and purchase history, Starbucks can offer personalised promotions tailored to each customer's preferences. This not only increases customer loyalty but also helps to improve the overall customer experience.

In addition to analysing customer behaviour and feedback, brands can also use big data for customer segmentation. By segmenting customers into different groups based on factors such as age, gender, and location, brands can create personalised experiences that are tailored to each group's needs and preferences (Cook et al., 2003).

For example, Netflix uses customer segmentation to personalise its content recommendations. By analysing viewing history and customer feedback, Netflix can recommend content tailored to each customer's preferences. This not only helps to improve the overall customer experience but also helps to retain customers and increase customer loyalty.

Another way that brands use big data for customer personalisation is by leveraging real-time data. By collecting and analysing data in real time, brands can respond quickly to changes in customer behaviour and preferences and create personalised experiences that are tailored to each customer's needs (Buhalis & Sinarta, 2019).

For example, Uber uses real-time data to create personalised experiences for its customers. By tracking customer location and ride history, Uber can offer personalised promotions and discounts tailored to each customer's needs. This not only helps to improve the overall customer experience but also helps to retain customers and increase customer loyalty.

There are many benefits to using big data for customer personalisation. By creating personalised experiences that are tailored to each customer's needs and preferences, brands can improve the overall customer experience, increase customer loyalty, and drive revenue.

While the use of big data for customer personalisation offers many benefits for brands, it also presents some challenges. As brands collect and use more data about their customers, there are growing concerns about data privacy. Customers may be uncomfortable with how much data brands collect about them and may be wary of sharing their personal information.

Another challenge brands face when using big data for customer personalisation is ensuring that the data they use is accurate and high-quality. Inaccurate or incomplete data can lead to incorrect insights and ineffective personalisation strategies.

Further, brands may also struggle to integrate data from multiple sources, such as social media, CRM systems, and website analytics tools. This can make it difficult to create a complete picture of the customer journey and personalise experiences effectively.

Big data offers brands an opportunity to collect, analyse, and use data to understand their customers better and personalise their experiences. By analysing customer data, creating targeted marketing campaigns, recommending products, improving customer service, and enhancing the overall customer experience, brands can build stronger relationships with customers, increase loyalty, and ultimately drive more sales and revenue.

However, brands must also be mindful of the challenges of using big data for customer personalisation, including data privacy concerns, data quality, and integration issues. By addressing these challenges and developing a comprehensive data strategy, brands can harness the power of big data to create more personalised and engaging experiences for their customers.

CUSTOMER ENGAGEMENT IN METAVERSE

Customer engagement and customer retention are closely linked, and the metaverse offers a unique opportunity for brands to build lasting relationships with their customers. Metaverse allows brands to create a virtual representation of their stores and to interact with customers in that space.

Here are some ways in which customer engagement in the metaverse can lead to customer retention:

Personalised Experiences

By offering personalised experiences in the metaverse, brands can connect with their customers more deeply. This could include personalised virtual try-ons, customised avatars, or virtual events tailored to a specific audience. By providing a personalised experience, customers are more likely to feel a sense of belonging and loyalty to the brand, which can increase the likelihood of repeat purchases.

Community Building

The metaverse offers a platform for community building, where brands can create a sense of belonging and connection among their customers. Brands can create virtual events, social spaces, or games that bring their customers together and foster a sense of community. By building a community around their brand, customers are more likely to feel connected to the brand and to each other, which can increase the likelihood of repeat purchases and brand advocacy (Turri et al., 2013).

Gamification

Gamification is the process of incorporating game elements into non-game contexts, such as shopping experiences. By using gamification in the metaverse, brands can create an engaging and interactive experience for their customers. This could include virtual scavenger hunts, challenges, or rewards for completing specific tasks. By making the shopping experience more fun and engaging, customers are more likely to return and make additional purchases.

Brand Storytelling

The metaverse provides an opportunity for brands to tell their story in a more immersive and interactive way. Brands can create virtual experiences that showcase their brand history, values, and mission. By creating a compelling narrative around their brand, customers are more likely to feel a sense of connection and loyalty to the brand, which can increase the likelihood of repeat purchases.

Customer Feedback

Engaging with customers in the metaverse also provides an opportunity for brands to receive direct feedback on their products and services. By creating virtual surveys, feedback forms, or interactive experiences that encourage customer feedback, brands can better understand their customers' needs and preferences. By listening to customer feedback, brands can improve their products and services, increasing customer satisfaction and loyalty.

By using personalised experiences, community building, gamification, brand storytelling, and customer feedback, brands can create a deeper connection with their customers, leading to increased customer retention and loyalty. As the metaverse continues to evolve, it is likely that more brands will experiment with these engagement strategies, leading to even more innovative and creative ways of building lasting relationships with customers.

BRANDS IN METAVERSE

With the rise of virtual reality and augmented reality, more and more brands are exploring the potential of the metaverse as a new platform for customer engagement. We will now look at some of the brands that use customer engagement in the metaverse and the strategies they use to connect with customers in this new medium.

Adidas

Adidas is a sportswear brand that has been exploring the potential of the metaverse for several years. In 2019, the company launched a virtual store in the game "Second Life," where players could purchase real-world Adidas products for their avatars.

Adidas has been experimenting with virtual try-on technology in the metaverse. The company has created virtual sneakers that players can try on and customise in games like "Roblox" and "Animal Crossing." By using virtual try-on technology, Adidas is able to offer a more engaging and interactive shopping experience for customers in the metaverse.

Gucci

Gucci is a luxury fashion brand that has been at the forefront of the metaverse trend. In 2020, the company launched its own virtual world, "Gucci Garden," which features a series of virtual rooms that customers can explore.

In Gucci Garden, customers can view and purchase the latest Gucci collections and participate in a range of virtual activities, including art exhibitions, games, and interactive experiences. The virtual world is designed to provide customers with a more immersive and engaging experience and to bring the brand to life in a new way.

Coca-Cola

Coca-Cola is a brand that has been experimenting with the metaverse for several years. In 2018, the company launched a virtual reality experience called "Coca-Cola Magic," which allowed customers to explore a virtual world and interact with Coke-themed objects and characters.

More recently, Coca-Cola has been exploring the potential of augmented reality in the metaverse. The company has created a series of AR filters and experiences that customers can use on social media platforms like Snapchat and Instagram. By using AR technology, Coca-Cola is able to offer a more interactive and engaging experience for customers and create a deeper connection between the brand and its audience.

Fortnite

Fortnite is a popular online game that has become a hub for virtual events and experiences. In 2020, the game hosted a virtual concert by rapper Travis Scott, which over 12 million players attended.

Since then, Fortnite has continued to host virtual events and collaborations with brands, including a partnership with Marvel that featured a series of virtual superhero outfits and items. By partnering with Fortnite, brands are able to reach a massive audience of engaged and enthusiastic players and connect with them in a more interactive and immersive way.

Nike

Nike is a sportswear brand that has been exploring the potential of the metaverse for several years. In 2019, the company launched a virtual store in the game "Roblox," where players could purchase virtual versions of real-world Nike products for their avatars.

Recently, Nike has been experimenting with virtual try-on technology in the metaverse. The company has created virtual sneakers that players can try on and customise in games like "Roblox" and "Fortnite." By using virtual try-on technology, Nike is able to offer a more engaging and interactive shopping experience for customers in the metaverse.

Burberry

Burberry is a luxury fashion brand that has been experimenting with the metaverse since 2019. That year, the company launched an AR-powered pop-up store in Tokyo, featuring a range of interactive and immersive experiences for customers.

More recently, Burberry has been exploring the potential of virtual try-on technology in the metaverse. The company has created a virtual showroom in the game "Bazaar," where customers can try on virtual versions of Burberry products and purchase them for their avatars. The virtual showroom is designed to provide customers with a more immersive and interactive shopping experience and to showcase the latest Burberry collections in a new and engaging way. Burberry has also created an exclusive virtual handbag collection on Roblox while a Roblox avatar carrying one of Burberry's exclusive bags.

American Eagle

American Eagle is a fashion brand that has been experimenting with the metaverse since 2020. The company launched a virtual store in the game "Animal Crossing," where players could purchase virtual versions of real-world American Eagle products for their avatars.

American Eagle has been exploring the potential of virtual events in the metaverse. The company hosted a virtual "Pride Prom" in the game "Roblox," which featured a range of interactive experiences and activities for players. By hosting virtual events, American Eagle is able to connect with its audience more engagingly and interactively and create a deeper connection with the brand.

Louis Vuitton

Louis Vuitton is a luxury fashion brand that has been exploring the potential of the metaverse since 2019. The company launched an AR-powered pop-up store in Los Angeles, which featured a range of interactive and immersive experiences for customers.

More recently, Louis Vuitton has been experimenting with virtual try-on technology in the metaverse. The company has created virtual versions of its latest collections, which customers can try on and purchase in games like "League of Legends" and "Honour of Kings." By using virtual try-on technology, Louis Vuitton is able to offer a more engaging and interactive shopping experience for customers in the metaverse.

Bmw

BMW is a car brand that has been exploring the potential of the metaverse since 2019. The company launched a virtual showroom in the game "Second Life," where players could view and purchase virtual versions of BMW cars for their avatars.

BMW has been experimenting with virtual test drives in the metaverse. The company has created a virtual driving experience in the game "Forza Horizon 4," which allows players to test drive virtual versions of BMW cars. By using virtual test drives, BMW is able to offer a more engaging and interactive experience for customers in the metaverse and showcase the latest BMW models in a new and innovative way.

Sephora

Sephora is a beauty brand that has been exploring the potential of the metaverse since 2019. The company launched a virtual store in the game "Second Life," where players could purchase virtual versions of real-world Sephora products for their avatars.

Sephora has been experimenting with virtual try-on technology in the metaverse. The company has created virtual versions of its latest makeup collections, which customers can try on and purchase in games like "Roblox" and "Animal Crossing." By using virtual try-on technology, Sephora is able to offer a more engaging and interactive shopping experience for customers in the metaverse.

The metaverse is a new platform for customer engagement that is being explored by a growing number of brands. By using virtual reality, augmented reality, and other technologies, these brands are able to offer a more immersive and engaging experience for customers in the metaverse and create a deeper connection with their audience. As the metaverse continues to evolve, it is likely that more brands will experiment with this new medium and that we will see even more innovative and creative uses of customer engagement in the virtual world.

USING BIG DATA IN METAVERSE FOR CUSTOMER ENGAGEMENT

In the metaverse, brands have access to vast customer data, which they can use to understand their customers better and create more personalised and engaging experiences. Big data plays a critical role in this process, as it allows brands to analyse and interpret customer data at scale, providing insights into customer behaviour, preferences, and trends.

Big data allows brands to collect and analyse data from customer interactions in the metaverse, such as the items they purchase, the virtual spaces they visit, and the activities they participate in. By analysing this data, brands can identify patterns and preferences that allow them to create more personalised experiences for their customers (Huang & Rust, 2021). For example, if a brand notices that a customer frequently visits a specific virtual space, they can offer promotions or experiences tailored to that space.

Personalisation is a critical factor in creating engaging experiences for customers in the metaverse. By analysing customer data, brands can gain insights into customer behaviour and preferences, allowing them to create personalised experiences that better resonate with their customers (Huang & Rust, 2021). For example, a virtual store could use data on a customer's previous purchases to make personalised product recommendations. This can lead to increased customer loyalty and retention, as customers are more likely to return to a brand that offers personalised experiences that cater to their individual preferences.

By analysing customer data, brands can use predictive analytics to anticipate customer needs and behaviour, allowing them to create more targeted and effective engagement strategies (Novak et al., 2000). For example, suppose a brand notices that a customer consistently purchases a certain type of product or service. In that case, it can anticipate the customer's needs and make recommendations or offers accordingly.

Predictive analytics is another important application of big data in the metaverse. By analysing customer data, brands can use machine learning algorithms to identify patterns and trends in customer behaviour, allowing them to make predictions about future behaviour. This can help brands to anticipate customer needs and offer personalised recommendations or promotions. For example, a virtual fashion brand could analyse a customer's past purchases and use predictive analytics to recommend new products that the customer will likely be interested in. This can help to improve customer retention and loyalty, as customers are more likely to return to a brand that offers personalised recommendations that cater to their individual preferences.

How predictive analytics model work and how the same can be deployed through big data in the metaverse.

Big data allows brands to segment their customers based on their preferences and behaviour, allowing them to create more targeted and effective engagement strategies. By segmenting customers based on data such as their location, age, and interests, brands can create tailored experiences that better resonate with their customers (Cook et al., 2003).

Customer segmentation is the process of dividing customers into groups based on shared characteristics or behaviour. By segmenting customers based on data such as their location, age, and interests, brands can create tailored experiences that better resonate with their customers. For example, a virtual music festival could use data on a customer's location and music preferences to offer personalised recommendations for acts to see at the festival. By tailoring the experience to the customer's individual preferences, brands can create more engaging experiences that are more likely to lead to customer retention and loyalty.

Big data also allows brands to track and measure the effectiveness of their engagement strategies, allowing them to make data-driven decisions for continuous improvement. By analysing customer data, brands can understand which engagement strategies are working well and which are not, allowing them to make changes and improvements to their strategy. For example, a virtual retailer could track the effectiveness of different promotions and offers and use this data to optimise their engagement strategy for maximum effectiveness. By continuously improving their engagement strategies, brands can create more engaging customer experiences that lead to higher retention and loyalty.

Advanced artificial intelligence and machine learning algorithms can also help brands better understand and engage with their customers (Kumar et al., 2019). These technologies can analyse vast amounts of data and identify patterns and trends that may be difficult or impossible to identify with traditional data analysis methods.

Finally, using advanced AI and machine learning algorithms can help brands better understand and engage with their customers. These technologies can analyse vast amounts of data and identify patterns and trends that may be difficult or impossible to identify with traditional data analysis methods. For example, a virtual retailer could use AI to analyse customer behaviour and preferences and use this data to create personalised product recommendations or promotions. By leveraging the power of AI, brands can create more engaging experiences for customers that lead to higher levels of retention and loyalty.

Big data plays a crucial role in helping brands achieve higher customer retention and engagement levels in the metaverse. By using data to personalise experiences, anticipate customer needs, segment customers, continuously improve engagement strategies, and leverage advanced AI, brands can create more effective and engaging experiences for their customers, ultimately leading to increased customer loyalty and retention.

CHALLENGES

As businesses try to leverage big data for customer retention in the metaverse, they may face several challenges. Here are some of the common challenges:

Integration of Big Data Tools: Integrating big data tools into existing metaverse platforms can be complex and time-consuming. This can pose a challenge for businesses that lack the technical expertise to manage and integrate these tools effectively.

Privacy and Security Concerns: Using big data in the metaverse raises concerns about privacy and security (Sun et al., 2022). Collecting and analysing customer data raises questions about who has access to it, how it is being used, and how it is protected.

Limited Customer Data: While big data has the potential to provide valuable insights into customer behaviour, some businesses may not have access to enough customer data to make informed decisions. In the metaverse, customer behaviour can differ from traditional e-commerce behaviour, and businesses may need to gather newdata typesa to make accurate predictions.

Fragmented Metaverse Landscape: The metaverse is a fragmented landscape with many different platforms, protocols, and technologies. This can make it difficult for businesses to develop a cohesive strategy that works across all platforms (Bathla & Awasthi, 2021).

Technical Limitations: Some metaverse platforms may have technical limitations that make it difficult to collect and analyse customer data. For example, some platforms may not support data tracking or may not provide access to data in a standardised format.

High Investment Costs: Adopting big data tools for the metaverse can require significant time and resources. Businesses may need to hire specialised staff, invest in new technology, and undergo extensive training to leverage big data for customer retention effectively.

Lack of Understanding of Metaverse: The concept of the metaverse is still new and relatively unknown to many businesses. As a result, there may be a lack of understanding of how big data can be used in the metaverse and what kind of data is most helpful in driving customer retention.

The challenges of leveraging big data for customer retention in the metaverse require businesses to carefully consider the technical, organisational, and ethical implications of integrating these tools into their operations. The process may require a significant investment of time and resources, and businesses must remain vigilant in their efforts to protect customer privacy and security.

SHAPE OF THINGS TO COME

The future for brands using big data in the metaverse for customer retention and engagement is promising. As the metaverse continues to grow and expand, so will the opportunities for businesses to leverage big data to drive customer loyalty and engagement. With access to more customer behaviour data, brands can provide even more personalised experiences for their customers in the metaverse. By using predictive analytics and machine learning algorithms, brands can anticipate customer needs and provide tailored recommendations (Bathla et al., 2021).

As the metaverse continues to grow, there will be more standardisation and integration of data and platforms (Rawal et al., 2022). This will make it easier for businesses to use big data to drive customer retention and engagement across multiple platforms. Real-time data analytics will become more common in the metaverse, allowing brands to track and respond to customer behaviour in real time. This will enable brands to identify trends and adjust their strategies accordingly quickly.

As privacy and data usage concerns continue to grow, brands will need to be more transparent in their use of customer data. Brands that are transparent and ethical in their data usage are likely to be more successful in building customer trust and loyalty.

Artificial intelligence (AI) and virtual reality (VR) technologies which are continuously advancing, will become more integrated into the metaverse. This will provide even more opportunities for brands to leverage big data to drive customer engagement and retention.

With technological advancements and increased standardisation of data and platforms, businesses can use big data to provide even more personalised customer experiences in the metaverse. As long as brands are transparent and ethical in their data usage, they are likely to successfully build customer trust and loyalty.

REFERENCES

Bathla, D., & Awasthi, S. (2021). Analytical Impact of Technology on the COVID-19 Pandemic. In Blockchain Technology and Applications for Digital Marketing (pp. 236-249). IGI Global.

Bathla, D., Awasthi, S., & Singh, K. (2021). Enriching User Experience by Transforming Consumer Data Into Deeper Insights. In Big Data Analytics for Improved Accuracy, Efficiency, and Decision Making in Digital Marketing (pp. 1-18). IGI Global. doi:10.4018/978-1-7998-7231-3.ch001

Buhalis, D., & Sinarta, Y. (2019). Real-time co-creation and nowness service: Lessons from tourism and hospitality. *Journal of Travel & Tourism Marketing*, *36*(5), 563–582. doi:10.1080/10548408.2019.1592059

Campbell, C., Sands, S., Ferraro, C., Tsao, H., & Mavrommatis, A. (2020). From data to action: How marketers can leverage AI. *Business Horizons*, *63*(2), 227–243. doi:10.1016/j.bushor.2019.12.002

Cook, B. I., Wayne, G. F., Keithly, L., & Connolly, G. N. (2003). One size does not fit all: How the tobacco industry has altered cigarette design to target consumer groups with specific psychological and psychosocial needs. *Addiction (Abingdon, England)*, *98*(11), 1547–1561. doi:10.1046/j.1360-0443.2003.00563.x PMID:14616181

Elena, C. A. (2016). Social Media – A Strategy in Developing Customer Relationship Management. *Procedia Economics and Finance*, *39*, 785–790. doi:10.1016/S2212-5671(16)30266-0

Elgendy, N., & Elragal, A. (2014). Big Data Analytics: A Literature Review Paper. *Lecture Notes in Computer Science*, *8557*, 214–227. doi:10.1007/978-3-319-08976-8_16

Huang, M., & Rust, R. T. (2021). A strategic framework for artificial intelligence in marketing. *Journal of the Academy of Marketing Science*, *49*(1), 30–50. doi:10.1007/s11747-020-00749-9

Kumar, V., Rajan, B., Venkatesan, R., & Lecinski, J. (2019). Understanding the Role of Artificial Intelligence in Personalized Engagement Marketing. *California Management Review*, *61*(4), 135–155. doi:10.1177/0008125619859317

Mozumder, M. I., Sheeraz, M., Athar, A., Aich, S., & Kim, H. (2022). Overview: Technology Roadmap of the Future Trend of Metaverse based on IoT, Blockchain, AI Technique, and Medical Domain Metaverse Activity. *2022 24th International Conference on Advanced Communication Technology (ICACT)*. 10.23919/ICACT53585.2022.9728808

Murray, A., Kim, D., & Combs, J. (2022). The promise of a decentralised Internet: What is web 3.0 and HOW can firms prepare? *Business Horizons*. doi:10.1016/j.bushor.2022.06.002

Novak, T. P., Hoffman, D. L., & Yung, Y. (2000). Measuring the Customer Experience in Online Environments: A Structural Modeling Approach. *Marketing Science*, *19*(1), 22–42. doi:10.1287/mksc.19.1.22.15184

Rawal, B. S., Mentges, A., & Ahmad, S. (2022). The Rise of Metaverse and Interoperability with Split-Protocol. *2022 IEEE 23rd International Conference on Information Reuse and Integration for Data Science (IRI)*. IEEE. 10.1109/IRI54793.2022.00051

Stokel-Walker, C. (2022). Welcome to the metaverse. *New Scientist*, *253*(3368), 39–43. doi:10.1016/S0262-4079(22)00018-5

Sun, J., Gan, W., Chao, H., & Yu, P. S. (2022). Metaverse: Survey, Applications, Security, and Opportunities. ArXiv (Cornell University). https://doi.org//arxiv.2210.07990 doi:10.48550

Turri, A. M., Smith, K., & Kemp, E. (2013). Developing Affective Brand Commitment through Social Media. *Journal of Electronic Commerce Research*, *14*(3), 201. https://web.csulb.edu/journals/jecr/issues/20133/Paper1.pdf

Chapter 6
Ethical Marketing:
A Systematic Literature Review

Nibedita Gogoi
St. Xavier's College, Kolkata, India

Rounak Agarwal
St. Xavier's College, Kolkata, India

Sumanta Dutta
St. Xavier's College, Kolkata, India

ABSTRACT

This chapter used a bibliometric analysis to assess the leading authors, countries, organisation, and journals in the domain of ethical marketing research while identifying prevailing research trends. Influential authors in ethical marketing research are Gene R. Laczniak and Patrick E. Murphy. United Kingdom leads in terms of ethical marketing research, followed by the findings of this research, which identify influential authors, countries, organizations, journals, and trends in the field of ethical marketing, can inform policy makers, educators, and researchers in India and globally about the importance of ethical marketing to promote transparency and sustainability to build trust and long-term customer loyalty which will help a business to survive in the market and achieve the organisational goals.

INTRODUCTION

In today's environment doing business and sustaining in the long run is a very crucial task as it possesses both opportunities and challenges that need to be overcome. Nowadays consumers have their ongoing changing variability in their demands and are becoming more informed and educated day by day. Therefore, a business now cannot focus on the purpose of production only, but they need to be duly ethical in their practices and processes of doing the business to sustain.

Sustainability goals should be set in all countries and societal stakeholders should be involved. However, this leads to challenges in different environments, marketing systems, and corporate goals.

DOI: 10.4018/979-8-3693-2215-4.ch006

The conceptualization of sustainable marketing and sustainability marketing are different and reflect the evolution of sustainability in marketing (Tian & Kamran (2023)). A business can adopt its ethical practices by providing good packaging of the products. Packaging for goods needs to meet different requirements for consumers, society, producers, and trade. Ukraine's development prompts socially responsible consumption and ethical marketing. 70% of purchasing decisions are made by consumers, making package design important. It is a profitable way of investing. Packaging should neutralize harmful effects on the environment Lialiuk et al. (2019). Contemporary society expects ethical and sustainable conduct from companies, and consumers value an organization's social responsibility. Cause-related marketing (CRM) is a manifestation of corporate responses to stakeholder expectations and has become increasingly popular among organizations over the last three decades. CRM campaigns contribute to product value creation through active customer participation, lending a participative attribute to CRM (Shanbhag et al. (2023)).

LITERATURE REVIEW

Przhedetsky *et al.* **(2018)**[1] in their article critically discuss social-ethical marketing in business and how the public and the medical community are involved in communication on social network platforms. Social networks and ICTs can be used to address oncological disease challenges in Russia. The economic response to oncology challenges is presented as a model. Large companies who are producing medicines for cancer treatment and provide healthcare services are involved in corresponding communication with the population in need of this help are analyzed here. **Clark (2014)** in her article discusses how marketing practitioners and academics can work together to overcome ethical objections to standard market research practices in the digital world. Digital technologies have transformed research, providing wider access to participants and quicker results, but also posing ethical challenges such as privacy, confidentiality, and data reliability. Legal and regulatory bodies, such as the Cookie Law, require explicit consent from users before storing or retrieving information. Academic researchers are also under pressure to ensure ethical compliance through the Ethical Review process. The article highlights the importance of sharing education and expertise to address ethical challenges inherent in online market research. **Tan & Salo (2021)** in their paper are trying to create a link between Block Chain Technology and ethical marketing practices. For this they have analyzed a literature review of 163 articles and a co-citation analysis identified key elements of Block Chain capabilities, attributes, and underlying economic theories of Block Chain. They propose a shift of ethical marketing logic in the blockchain-based sharing economy that delineates principles of stakeholder capitalism. **Shanbhag** *et al.* **(2023)** try to create and validate belief-based formative indicators to assess purchase intent towards products related to CRM campaigns in South Asia. These scales have robust internal consistency, robustness, and continuity. Behavioral beliefs, norm beliefs, and control beliefs significantly influence attitude, subjective norms, and perception of behavioral control. Furthermore, purchase intention strongly influences purchase behavior. This supports the concept of planned behavior in CRM campaigns and is consistent with the wider field of ethical consumption. **Lialiuk et al. (2019)** discuss the importance of producing comprehensive consumer packaging that meets modern requirements and meets the needs of consumers, manufacturers, and society. The transition from classical marketing to social and ethical marketing is important for producers. The article defines consumer packaging as a marketing tool and presents options for packaging recycling, including returnable packaging and appropriate materials. The researcher found that introducing marketing experts to local government institutions that specialize in environmental matters and solving the problem of interaction and responsibility of all packaging recycling participants can improve the overall environmental health and welfare of society.

Tian & Kamran (2023) examine the relationship between marketing, social and environmental issues, culture, consumers, and sustainability in strategic management. It uses a network technique to examine research clusters and analyze relationships among sustainability theories in marketing practice. Six cluster groups emerged, reflecting the important role of marketing in linking sustainability, society, the environment, and consumers. The study categorizes the intellectual structure of journal publications and suggests the influence of social and cultural notions on consumer-focused sustainable marketing. **Laczniak et al. (1981).** Ethics of marketing can be divided into process and product-based issues. Social marketing can influence the acceptance of socially relevant ideas. The concept of consumers objecting to a product being marketed has not been systematically studied. The vignette technique in experimental social psychology has been developed to overcome this problem. The authors selected four products that were perceived as having different ethical propriety in the minds of the public. **Peattie & Samuel (2021)** discuss the potential of Fairtrade Towns (FTT) to ethically enhance their branding. It presents insights from a qualitative study of marketing practices across eleven UK FTTs. FTT accreditation can work symbiotically with a place brand through connections to other fundamental aspects of a place's identity and character. This research shows that FTT status, and its associated ethical consumption, hospitality, and retailing practices, are being actively integrated into the branding of places for both residents and visitor audiences. This approach helps to reimagine places to which tourists go and within which residents live, as interconnected and part of an ethical agenda.

METHODOLOGY

To understand which countries and journals have the biggest impact on the study of Ethical Marketing and to know the trends in this research area, we conducted a systematic Bibliometric analysis of the research literature. A methodology of three stages was carried out for the bibliometric analysis: definition of search criteria and selection of databases, adjustment of research criteria and export of final data, and analysis and discussion of results. As "Ethical Marketing" is the topic analysed in this research, articles containing "Ethical Marketing" were searched in title, abstract or keywords, from the published documents in the databases till 2023. To gather the data, we have used Scopus database. There was total "192" documents and after applying the filter of English only "183" documents were found useful for our purpose.

Figure 1. Phases

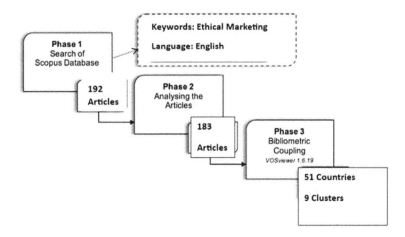

OBJECTIVES

1. To identify the most prominent organisation in the field of Ethical Marketing.
2. To examine the top journals on Ethical Marketing and trends in this field.

RESULTS AND DISCUSSION

Most Influential Organisation

Through this research we tried to analyse which organisations have the most impact on the study of Ethical Marketing. The ranking of most influential organization is led by "University of Birmingham, Department of Commerce, Birmingham, United Kingdom" with 984 citations.

The next position is occupied by "Vienna University of Economics and Business Administration, Vienna, Austria" with 219 citations, followed by "Department Of Marketing, College of Business Administration, Marquette University, United States" and "Institute of Ethical Business Worldwide, Mendoza College of Business, United States "with 203 citations, "Nanyang Business School, Singapore" led the fourth position with 186 citations and the fifth position is occupied by "Auburn University, United States" with 147 citations.

Figure 2. Ranking of organisation in relation to number of citations

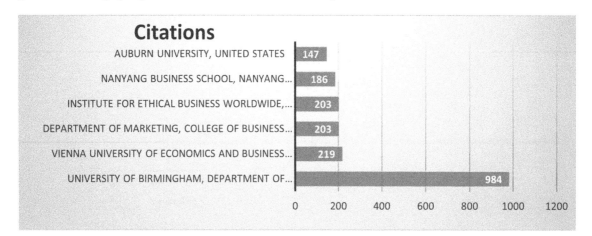

In case of number of documents "Centre of Commerce and Management, Rmit University, Vietnam" and "East China University of Science and Technology, Shanghai, China" with 5 documents. The second position is led by "Cass Business School, United Kingdom" with 3 documents and "Cardiff Business School, United Kingdom", "Maquette University, United States" with 2 documents.

Figure 3. Ranking of organisation in relation to number of documents published

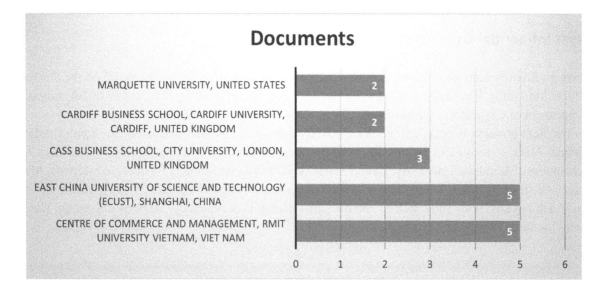

Most Influential Journal

Ethical Marketing is a topic that has gained significance in the recent years due to growing awareness among consumers widely. The "Journal of Consumer Marketing" leads in terms of number of citations with 1077, followed by "Journal of Business Ethics" with 879 citations and "Journal of Macromarketing" with 381 citations, "Psychology and Marketing" with 147 citations and "Journal of Public Policy and Marketing" with 120 citations.

Figure 4. Ranking of journals in relation to number of citations

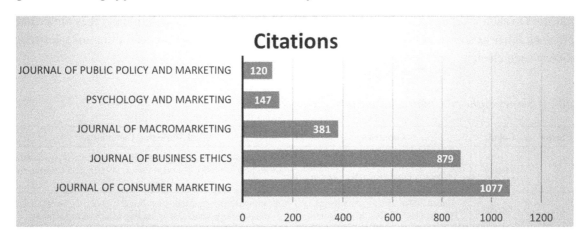

"Journal of Business ethics" has the highest number of documents published with 15 documents followed by "Developments in Marketing Science: Proceedings of the Academy of Marketing Science" and "Ethical and Social Marketing in Asia: Incorporating Fairness Management" with 7 documents. The third position is led by "Dental Update" and "Journal of Macromarketing" with 6 documents followed by "Sustainability (Switzerland)" with 5 documents.

Figure 5. Ranking of journals in relation to number of documents published

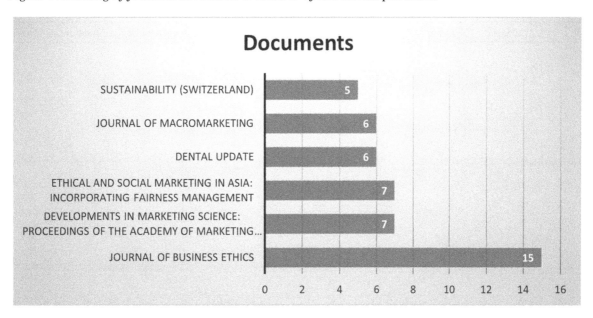

Countries' Network Forming Clusters

Out of 51 countries, 32 countries form a network with 9 different colours clusters and each clusters have different countries with common area of research in the domain of "Ethical Marketing" and form an individual colour network with minimum one document. In some way or the other these 9 clusters are connected to each other regarding the concept of "Ethical Marketing" but individually they are different from each other as shown in Figure 5. Each colour and node of connection detect the linkage strength between each cluster.

Table 1. Shows authors' country cluster on ethical marketing

Cluster	Colour	Countries	Ethical Marketing Components
1	Red	India, Russian Federation, Bangladesh, Indonesia, Puerto Rico, Kyrgyzstan	Green Marketing, Green Products, ESG Management, Corporate Social Responsibility, Business Ethics, Social Effect Concern for Society.
2	Green	United States, Japan, South Korea, Florida, Saudi Arabia, Hilton Hotels	Consumer Behaviour, Marketing, Brand Loyalty, Consumer Brand Relationships, Extended Marketing Mix, Macromarketing.
3	Blue	Iran, Germany, Netherland, Thailand	Social media, Sustainable Marketing, Neuromarketing, Advertising, Purchasing Intention, Moral Identity.
4	Pink	China, Vietnam	Country Branding, Cross- Country Studies, Fair Trade, Fairness Management, Reputation Management, Consumer Perception.
5	Yellow	Malaysia, Pakistan, Algeria	Moral and Ethical Behaviour, Marketing Norms, Relationship Quality, Cause Driven Advertising, Consumerism, Product Fairness.
6	Orange	Austria, Brunei Darussalam, Hong Kong	International Marketing, Religion, Consumer Behaviour, Marketing Ethics, Consumer Ethic, Business Ethic.
7	Brown	Canada, United Arab Emirates	Ethics, Meta-Data, Self-Brand Connection, Sharing Economy, Co-Creation.
8	Light Blue	United Kingdom, Columbia, Cyprus	Social Marketing, Unethical, Ethical Issues, Discrimination.
9	Purple	Australia, Nigeria, Singapore	Ethical Behaviour, International Marketing, Consumer Confidence.

Figure 6. Authors country network

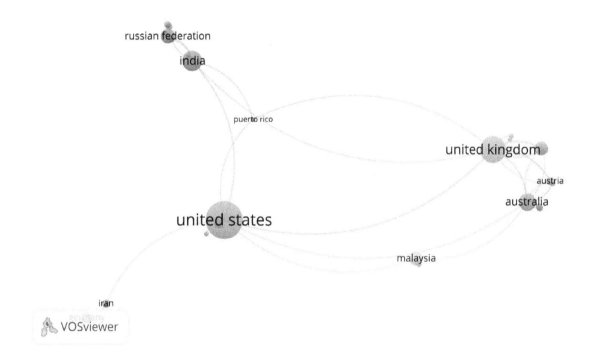

CONCLUSION

The shift from traditional marketing to social and ethical marketing is evident as businesses nowadays give more focus on consumer expectations. Ethical marketing is gaining importance in recent times because consumers are becoming more and more aware. The finings of this bibliometric analysis help us to know the most influential organisations in the field of Ethical marketing. It also enabled us to know which journals are influential. We can also see that out of 51 countries, 32 countries form a network with 9 different clusters. These findings would help in providing valuable insights for policymakers, academicians and practitioners interested in Ethical Marketing.

REFERENCES

Clark, L. (2014). Ethical marketing research in the digital age—How can academics and practitioners work together? *Journal of Direct, Data and Digital Marketing Practice*, *15*(4), 258–259. doi:10.1057/dddmp.2014.17

Laczniak, G. R., Lusch, R. F., & Strang, W. A. (1981). Ethical marketing: Perceptions of economic goods and social problems. *Journal of Macromarketing*, *1*(1), 49–57. doi:10.1177/027614678100100109

Lialiuk, A., Kolosok, A., Skoruk, O., Hromko, L., & Hrytsiuk, N. (2019). Consumer packaging as a tool for social and ethical marketing. *Innovative Marketing*, *15*(1), 76–88. doi:10.21511/im.15(1).2019.07

Lialiuk, A., Kolosok, A., Skoruk, O., Hromko, L., & Hrytsiuk, N. (2019). Consumer packaging as a tool for social and ethical marketing. *Innovative Marketing*, *15*(1), 76–88. doi:10.21511/im.15(1).2019.07

Peattie, K., & Samuel, A. (2021). Placing an ethical brand: The Fairtrade Towns movement. *Journal of Marketing Management*, *37*(15-16), 1490–1513. doi:10.1080/0267257X.2021.1913215

Przhedetskiy, Y. V., Przhedetskaya, N. V., Przhedetskaya, V. Y., Bondarenko, V. A., & Borzenko, K. V. (2018). *The role of social-ethical marketing and information and communication technologies in response to challenges of oncology.*

Shanbhag, P. R., Pai, Y. P., Kidiyoor, G., & Prabhu, N. (2023). Development and initial validation of a theory of planned behavior questionnaire: Assessment of purchase intentions towards products associated with CRM campaigns. *Cogent Business & Management*, *10*(2), 2229528. doi:10.1080/23311975.2023.2229528

Shanbhag, P. R., Pai, Y. P., Kidiyoor, G., & Prabhu, N. (2023). Development and initial validation of a theory of planned behavior questionnaire: Assessment of purchase intentions towards products associated with CRM campaigns. *Cogent Business & Management*, *10*(2), 2229528. doi:10.1080/23311975.2023.2229528

Tan, T. M., & Salo, J. (2023). Ethical marketing in the blockchain-based sharing economy: Theoretical integration and guiding insights. *Journal of Business Ethics*, *183*(4), 1113–1140. doi:10.1007/s10551-021-05015-8

Tian, Y., & Kamran, Q. (2023). Mapping the intellectual linkage of sustainability in marketing. *Business and Society Review*, *128*(2), 251–274. doi:10.1111/basr.12313

Tian, Y., & Kamran, Q. (2023). Mapping the intellectual linkage of sustainability in marketing. *Business and Society Review*, *128*(2), 251–274. doi:10.1111/basr.12313

Chapter 7
Ethical Marketing and Sustainable Development Goals

Ankita Sharma
🆔 https://orcid.org/0000-0002-7432-9488
Navrachana University, India

Varun Nayyar
🆔 https://orcid.org/0000-0001-5609-9327
Chitkara University, India

ABSTRACT

The chapter focuses on social and ethical concept of marketing, which appeared in connection with the need to bring the business into line with the requirements of both modern market economy and the principles of social responsibility to individual consumers and society. Most modern enterprises recognize the need to implement tools for social and ethical marketing, increasing awareness and consumer protection. The studies suggest that ethical marketing, particularly through the incorporation of corporate social responsibility (CSR) and sustainable development goals (SDGs), can positively impact brand loyalty and promote ethical consumer behavior Social and ethical marketing at its core implements the principles of consumer orientation, innovation, increasing the value of goods, awareness of the social mission, and social responsibility of the enterprise. Increasingly, enterprises are willing to be guided by marketing ethics, such as limiting potential damage, meeting basic needs, economic efficiency, innovation, consumer education and awareness, and consumer protection.

INTRODUCTION

Businesses are encountering significant obstacles in the pursuit of sustainable development and expansion (Hunt, 2010). Companies must adhere to escalating environmental and social laws and regulations, adjust to mounting apprehension regarding the limited availability of natural resources, take into account shareholders' perspectives on socially responsible business practices, and align with the changing social attitudes and values in capitalist societies (Jones et al., 2016). Companies have started incorporating

DOI: 10.4018/979-8-3693-2215-4.ch007

sustainability indicators into their corporate social responsibility (CSR) programs in response to these trends and the recognition of their social obligations (Borin & Metcalf, 2010). The United Nations heavily depends on corporations to effectively accomplish the Sustainable Development Goals (SDGs). "Jones et al. (2016b)". Moreover, marketing endeavors aimed at social engagement frequently encounter skepticism and mistrust. Marketing is seen to have caused harm to society in various ways, one of which is by promoting an unsustainable increase in demand and consumption. (Jahdi and Açikdilli, 2009). With "planned obsolescence," a deliberate strategy by businesses to create goods and services that purposefully degrade over a brief period of time, marketing has also influenced consumption patterns. This compels consumers to buy new products. However, marketing can still be employed in methods that lead to the attainment of sustainability. (Peattie & Crane, 2005) Several companies have already devised effective methods for creating sustainable products and services, spreading environmental information, monitoring the sustainability of their supply chains, and informing consumers about the sustainability implications of their product choices (Peattie & Belz, 2010). It is imperative to acknowledge that in today's business landscape, companies must implement a system for assessing the social consequences of their business choices. Failure to do so puts them at risk of falling behind rival businesses that have already implemented sustainable growth strategies (Strategy and Society: The Link Between Competitive Advantage and Corporate Social Responsibility, 2007).

This chapter attempts to explain how the use of ethical marketing strategies might contribute to the achievement of the Sustainable Development Goals (SDGs) by businesses.

THE EVOLUTION OF MARKETING SCHOOLS OF THOUGHT

An analysis of the evolution of marketing across the years can be conducted using many frameworks. In this chapter, we will discuss the marketing theories and concepts that have been established in academia and have shaped marketing practices throughout history.

The initial marketing school of thought recognized in academics is the management school, which held a prominent position from 1950 to 1960. This school of thought prioritized the seller or manufacturer in the marketing process, neglecting the involvement of dealers, suppliers, or other sorts of enterprises. During the period from 1970 to 1980, the activist school became more prominent, with a primary concentration on the consumer's market perspective, neglecting any consideration of institutional or macro viewpoints. Simultaneously, in 1970, a rival ideology known as the macromarketing school developed and has since been the dominant school of thinking. The macromarketing school emphasizes the interdependent connection between organizations, society, and all stakeholders in the organization's surroundings (Sanclemente-Téllez, 2017). Before 1969, marketing concepts were based on the presence of financial transactions, with marketing being seen solely as a tool to facilitate these transactions. As a result, marketing theory primarily focused on explaining and examining the pricing, promotion, and distribution of goods and services exclusively in commercial markets. However, beginning in 1969, the "broadening movement," which believed that confining marketing to a commercial context was constraining, promoted the idea that marketing might be implemented on a broader scale beyond merely commercial operations (Kotler, 2005).

In the realm of marketing activities, a succession of five primary concepts has emerged over time. The initial step was the production concept, which focused on meeting unfulfilled demand by increasing production volumes while reducing costs. Subsequently, the product concept emerged, prioritizing the enhancement of quality and the incorporation of pioneering attributes to align with consumer preferences. Subsequently, the selling concept emerged, employing assertive selling techniques and promotional efforts to stimulate consumer demand for products. During the mid-twentieth century, there was a notable transition towards a consumer-centric approach, with the main objective of providing exceptional value to specific clients. Subsequently, the idea of societal marketing emerged, highlighting the importance of conducting marketing activities while taking into account social and ethical factors (Kumar et al., 2012). The United Nations Conference on Environment and Development, held in 1992, emphasized the responsibility of enterprises to contribute to the attainment of sustainable development (Kinoti, 2011), so laying the foundation for sustainability marketing. Presently, there is a strong emphasis on integrating sustainability into marketing efforts as a pivotal element in attaining a competitive edge. Sustainability marketing stands out by addressing not only immediate individual and social requirements, but also by striving to meet the needs of future generations. In order to be considered a part of sustainable marketing, firms must adopt a marketing plan that meets the demands of customers while also maintaining profitability, public interest, and ecological balance (Kumar et al., 2012).

ETHICS AND MARKETING RESPONSIBILITY

For the past sixty years, academics have extensively studied marketing ethics. Prior to approximately 1970, the marketing ethics literature was predominantly considered as such (Hunt & Vitell, 1986). The current state of study and analysis of marketing ethics remains robust. In 2012, a compilation of 90 previously published journal papers on marketing ethics was assembled into a five-volume anthology (Murphy, 2017). The prevailing academic research on marketing ethics is predominantly characterized as "positive" and empirical. This is due to the fact that the majority of the study was conducted in the past. This type of study reveals empirical consistency and statistical trends among fundamental variables. This is a crucial strategy. Academics studying marketing and aiming to enhance ethical standards require dependable data. Morality is the pragmatic implementation of ethics, since it converts the theoretical notion of ethics into a tangible and beneficial entity for society. Morality encompasses the establishment of practical expectations for behavior and ethical guidelines. Ultimately, it presents a collection of ethical principles upheld by society (Yeh et al., 2020). By examining the concepts of ethics and morality, it becomes clear that, although they are interconnected, their definitions only partially overlap. Literature often examines the necessity of more precise definitions of terminology, as this can result in misconceptions or erroneous conclusions (Vadera & Pathki, 2021). Nevertheless, due to their frequent interchangeable usage, it has been observed that differentiating between ethics and morality can be a difficult task. It is essential to differentiate between the words from a scientific standpoint, as it enables a comprehensive examination of ethics as a whole and a more targeted explanatory approach that takes into account various levels and viewpoints (Blumenthal-Barby & Burroughs, 2012). While significant scientific advancements have been achieved through focused problem-solving, it is imperative to address the establishment, regulation, and evaluation of ethics and marketing responsibility in the future.

SUSTAINABLE DEVELOPMENT AND MARKETING

Sustainability elucidates the correlation between marketing and sustainability by highlighting their shared fundamental element, which is "values." Marketing aims to generate value for stakeholders (Sanclemente-Téllez, 2017b), while the formula for sustainable development includes value as one of the four elements that impact sustainability.

Sanclemente states that the formula dictates that S is equal to the product of D, T, V, and G, represented as $S = D \times T \times V \times G$.

where S (sustainability) denotes the state of environmental equilibrium and D (demography) pertains to human capacity, influenced by demographic factors such as population structure and migratory patterns. T, or technology, encompasses the advancement of technology through the introduction of new products, processes, and organizational innovations. V, or values, pertains to a set of agreed-upon and accepted values that guide social and market activities among businesses, authorities, consumers, employees, and others. G (government) denotes the stance of central and local authorities towards the economy and society.

Peattie and Belz (2010b) contend that conventional marketing fails to incorporate social and ecological concerns into its framework, as it primarily focuses on the customer's viewpoint. In this traditional framework, social and ecological issues are regarded as limitations to the expansion of the economy. Kilbourne (2004) argues that this perspective on marketing originates from the prevailing societal framework that is founded on the principles of economic and political liberalism. A dominant social paradigm refers to the prevailing set of conventions, beliefs, values, and behaviors that collectively shape the most generally shared worldview within a given community. The author argues that this worldview seems to contradict sustainable development by promoting heightened consumption. Moreover, the absence of agreement over the approach to addressing climate change while simultaneously sustaining economic growth suggests that efforts to address environmental issues are perceived as conflicting with the fundamental principles of capitalism, economics, and consumerism. Margolis et al. (2009) stated that this perspective is deeply rooted to the point that they argue that anyone who questions the idea that a company's primary goal is more than just maximizing shareholder value must acknowledge the prevailing social belief. Compounding the gravity of the situation, the notion that the sole objective of a company is to enhance shareholder value has firmly permeated the mindset of aspiring managers through the educational programs offered by business schools. Proponents of this paradigm argue that it is illogical to enhance the performance of several variables since it becomes impossible to calculate opportunity costs and make decisions on courses of action when there are more than one variable present (Margolis & Walsh, 2003). Within this framework, marketing prioritizes immediate economic benefits while neglecting the long-term ecological consequences that contribute to environmental issues (Mitchell et al., 2010).

SUSTAINABILITY AND ETHICS

The term "sustainability" is currently prevalent in policy contexts, corporations, and third-sector organizations (Torelli, 2020). Companies in various industries globally must incorporate sustainability measures into their operations (Walsh & Dodds, 2017). The environmental discourse within both the governmental and business spheres traces its origins to the publication of the study "Limits to Growth" in 1972. This discourse has since evolved to encompass the notions of sustainable development, corporate social responsibility (CSR), and the triple bottom line. The current proposal of the environmental, social, and corporate governance (ESG) paradigm has superseded prior ones and encompasses both the evolution of sustainability and corporate sustainability. Throughout history, crises have been catalysts for societal transformation, encompassing social, political, and economic shifts that can be either beneficial or detrimental. The global crises serve as evidence of the interconnectedness and interdependence of the various elements of sustainable development (Nayyar, 2022; Priyadarshini, 2022). The COVID-19 epidemic serves as an illustration of this phenomenon. Amidst this crisis, certain authors concur that society has developed a heightened consciousness regarding sustainability concerns. Companies have actively pursued the acceleration of their sustainable practices, while investors have shifted their investments towards companies that prioritize environmental, social, and governance (ESG) practices. Additionally, more environmentally conscious consumers have demonstrated a greater inclination towards consuming from and working for sustainable companies. This aligns with a worldview that is more attuned to human values and awareness, as well as with improved socio-environmental and economic outcomes (Yu et al., 2020). At both the individual and organizational levels, ethics can have an impact on the implementation of sustainability (Nayyar and Batra, 2020; Wesarat et al., 2017). De Paula and Cavalcanti (2000) argue that ethics is a fundamental component of sustainability. Furthermore, ethics concerns the contemplation of the inherent significance of all human endeavors, and it exerts an impact on both individuals. Since ethics can provide clarity on matters of morality, ethical principles serve as guides for business activities and aid organizations in making moral decisions (Smith et al., 2014). Hence, the primary objective of business ethics is to guarantee that managers incorporate an ethical aspect into their decision-making process and carefully consider the ethical consequences of their strategic choices prior to taking action. Enterprises must demonstrate responsibility and sustainability, since they have the potential to make a substantial contribution to the advancement of sustainable development (Bredillet, 2014). According to Wahab (2021), companies play a significant role in promoting environmental unsustainability. This may be attributed to ethical transgressions if the issue of environmental unsustainability is examined from an ethical and moral standpoint. By using sustainability strategies to mitigate its environmental impact, an organization will embrace sustainable behaviour, which is both ethically and morally commendable (Torelli, 2020). Hence, contemplating the principles of ethical conduct in business is crucial for attaining sustainability in a dynamic environment (Cassar, 2019). Given that the primary objective of organizations is to generate profit, it is worth considering how to establish a connection between ethics, socio-environmental responsibility, and business goals. Engaging in a business endeavour that is associated with ethical principles and environmental concerns allows for the harmonization of economic, social, and environmental duties. Companies that prioritize ethics are in a favourable position to attain sustainability. The reference is from De Lange et al. (2012). Moreover, the implementation of business ethics can contribute to the attainment of sustained economic prosperity (Nayyar, 2018; Wesarat et al., 2017). Ethics, sustainability, sustainable development, CSR, and ESG are distinct concepts that are frequently employed with varying definitions to describe a unified trajectory. Nevertheless, it is crucial to acknowledge that these words are interconnected in both theoretical and practical aspects (Torelli, 2020). Companies must consider these links in their operations to prevent corporate social responsibility and unethical conduct (Lin-Hi & Müller, 2013). Ambiguity exists in distinguishing between responsible and irresponsible acts (Nayyar, 2023; Clark et al., 2021). Thus, it is comparatively simpler to discern the factors that hinder sustainable development as opposed to those that promote it. In addition to recognizing corporate social responsibility (CSR) policies in large firms, it is also beneficial to uncover unethical and irresponsible practices. Stakeholders can utilize this to exert influence and diminish motivations for engaging in greenwashing and other unethical behaviours (Yue et al., 2022).

CONCLUSION

With the rising public concern and pressure regarding problems facing the world today, such as environmental deterioration, poverty, hunger, disease, and a lack of education (Jones et al., 2016a), it is anticipated that sustainable marketing will become the norm just as the internet and e-commerce did before it. However, in order to bring about this change willingly and gradually instead of by force, businesses need to make advancements on the sustainable marketing front as quickly as possible (Peattie & Crane, 2005b). It has also become apparent that a new corporate philosophy has worked around the dominant social paradigm and emerged over the years (Kinoti, 2011b). Businesses are now expected to integrate corporate strategy with sustainability to be able to compete in the long run (Öberseder et al., 2011). It is acknowledged that businesses must work towards achieving the triple bottom line (Borin & Metcalf, 2010), and several frameworks have been developed to this end. While changes will need to be made to the traditional marketing mix to achieve sustainability, marketing remains integral to achieving sustainability through the design of sustainable products and services and influencing consumers' product choices in favor of sustainability (Peattie & Belz, 2010b). While several frameworks have been developed for sustainable marketing, such as the integration of green marketing, social marketing, and critical marketing ("Shaping a Sustainable Future," 2022), there is still a lack of a specific and practical framework for accomplishing the Sustainable Development Goals (SDGs). The SDGs, or Sustainable Development Goals, set forth by the United Nations serve as a blueprint for organizations aiming to adopt sustainable practices. However, the business community must still determine the most effective approach to addressing the Sustainable Development Goals (SDGs).

In summary, this chapter has presented various proposals that seek to facilitate additional investigation and examination of how companies might contribute to the accomplishment of the Sustainable Development Goals (SDGs). The propositions primarily concern the correlation between Corporate Social Responsibility (CSR) and the Sustainable Development Goals (SDGs). They also address the alignment of business objectives with the SDGs, the need for businesses to prioritize specific SDGs without compromising others, the reporting of business outcomes in relation to sustainability impact, the exploration of novel approaches to combat unsustainable consumption patterns, the engagement of employees in the sustainability agenda, and the importance of adaptability. and agile in adjusting to fluctuations in sustainability's ever-changing data and statistics.

REFERENCES

Blumenthal-Barby, J., & Burroughs, H. (2012). Seeking better health care outcomes: The ethics of using the "Nudge.". *The American Journal of Bioethics*, *12*(2), 1–10. doi:10.1080/15265161.2011.634481 PMID:22304506

Borin, N., & Metcalf, L. E. (2010). Integrating Sustainability into the marketing Curriculum: Learning activities that facilitate sustainable marketing practices. *Journal of Marketing Education*, *32*(2), 140–154. doi:10.1177/0273475309360156

Bredillet, C. (2014). Ethics in project management: Some Aristotelian insights. *International Journal of Managing Projects in Business*, *7*(4), 548–565. doi:10.1108/IJMPB-08-2013-0041

Cassar, C. (2019). Business ethics and sustainable development. In Springer eBooks (pp. 139–150). doi:10.1007/978-3-030-11352-0_39

Clark, C. E., Riera, M., & Iborra, M. (2021). Toward a theoretical framework of corporate social irresponsibility: Clarifying the gray zones between responsibility and irresponsibility. *Business & Society*, *61*(6), 1473–1511. doi:10.1177/00076503211015911

De Lange, D. E., Busch, T., & Delgado-Ceballos, J. (2012). Sustaining sustainability in organizations. *Journal of Business Ethics*, *110*(2), 151–156. doi:10.1007/s10551-012-1425-0

Hunt, S. D. (2010). Sustainable marketing, equity, and economic growth: A resource-advantage, economic freedom approach. *Journal of the Academy of Marketing Science*, *39*(1), 7–20. doi:10.1007/s11747-010-0196-3

Hunt, S. D., & Vitell, S. J. (1986). A General Theory of Marketing Ethics. *Journal of Macromarketing*, *6*(1), 5–16. doi:10.1177/027614678600600103

Jahdi, K., & Açikdilli, G. (2009). Marketing Communications and Corporate Social Responsibility (CSR): Marriage of convenience or shotgun wedding? *Journal of Business Ethics*, *88*(1), 103–113. doi:10.1007/s10551-009-0113-1

Jones, P., Comfort, D., & Hillier, D. (2016a). Common Ground: The sustainable development goals and the marketing and advertising industry. *Journal of Public Affairs*, *18*(2), e1619. doi:10.1002/pa.1619

Kilbourne, W. E. (2004). Sustainable communication and the dominant social paradigm: Can they be integrated? *Marketing Theory*, *4*(3), 187–208. doi:10.1177/1470593104045536

Kinoti, M. (2011a). *Green marketing Intervention Strategies and Sustainable Development: A Conceptual Paper*. http://www.ijbssnet.com/journals/Vol_2_No_23_Special_Issue_December_2011/32.pdf?update/journals/Vol_2_No_23_Special_Issue_December_2011/32.pdf

Kinoti, M. (2011b). *Green marketing Intervention Strategies and Sustainable Development: A Conceptual Paper*. http://www.ijbssnet.com/journals/Vol_2_No_23_Special_Issue_December_2011/32.pdf?update/journals/Vol_2_No_23_Special_Issue_December_2011/32.pdf

Kotler, P. (2005). The Role Played by the Broadening of Marketing Movement in the History of Marketing Thought. *Journal of Public Policy & Marketing*, *24*(1), 114–116. doi:10.1509/jppm.24.1.114.63903

Kumar, V., Rahman, Z., Kazmi, A. A., & Goyal, P. (2012). Evolution of Sustainability as Marketing Strategy: Beginning of new Era. *Procedia: Social and Behavioral Sciences*, *37*, 482–489. doi:10.1016/j.sbspro.2012.03.313

Lin-Hi, N., & Müller, K. (2013). The CSR bottom line: Preventing corporate social irresponsibility. *Journal of Business Research, 66*(10), 1928–1936. doi:10.1016/j.jbusres.2013.02.015

MargolisJ. D.ElfenbeinH. A.WalshJ. P. (2009). Does it Pay to Be Good. . .And Does it Matter? A Meta-Analysis of the Relationship between Corporate Social and Financial Performance. *Social Science Research Network*. doi:10.2139/ssrn.1866371

Margolis, J. D., & Walsh, J. P. (2003). Misery Loves Companies: Rethinking social initiatives by business. *Administrative Science Quarterly, 48*(2), 268–305. doi:10.2307/3556659

Mitchell, R. W., Wooliscroft, B., & Higham, J. (2010). Sustainable Market Orientation: A new approach to managing marketing strategy. *Journal of Macromarketing, 30*(2), 160–170. doi:10.1177/0276146710361928

Nayyar, V. (2018). 'My Mind Starts Craving'-Impact of Resealable Packages on the Consumption Behavior of Indian Consumers. *Indian Journal of Marketing, 48*(11), 56–63. doi:10.17010/ijom/2018/v48/i11/137986

Nayyar, V. (2022). Reviewing the impact of digital migration on the consumer buying journey with robust measurement of PLS-SEM and R Studio. *Systems Research and Behavioral Science, 39*(3), 542–556. doi:10.1002/sres.2857

Nayyar, V. (2023). The role of marketing analytics in the ethical consumption of online consumers. *Total Quality Management & Business Excellence, 34*(7-8), 1015–1031. doi:10.1080/14783363.2022.2139676

Nayyar, V., & Batra, R. (2020). Does online media self-regulate consumption behavior of INDIAN youth? *International Review on Public and Nonprofit Marketing, 17*(3), 277–288. doi:10.1007/s12208-020-00248-1

Öberseder, M., Schlegelmilch, B. B., & Gruber, V. (2011). "Why don't consumers care about CSR?": A qualitative study exploring the role of CSR in consumption decisions. *Journal of Business Ethics, 104*(4), 449–460. doi:10.1007/s10551-011-0925-7

Peattie, K. J., & Belz, F. (2010a). Sustainability marketing — An innovative conception of marketing. *Marketing Review St. Gallen, 27*(5), 8–15. doi:10.1007/s11621-010-0085-7

Peattie, K. J., & Belz, F. (2010b). Sustainability marketing — An innovative conception of marketing. *Marketing Review St. Gallen, 27*(5), 8–15. doi:10.1007/s11621-010-0085-7

Peattie, K. J., & Crane, A. (2005a). Green marketing: Legend, myth, farce or prophesy? *Qualitative Market Research, 8*(4), 357–370. doi:10.1108/13522750510619733

Priyadarshini, P. (2022). The COVID-19 Pandemic has Derailed the Progress of Sustainable Development Goals. *Anthropocene Science, 1*(3), 410–412. doi:10.1007/s44177-022-00032-2

Sanclemente-Téllez, J. C. (2017a). Marketing and Corporate Social Responsibility (CSR). Moving between broadening the concept of marketing and social factors as a marketing strategy. *Spanish Journal of Marketing - ESIC, 21*, 4–25. doi:10.1016/j.sjme.2017.05.001

Smith, G. E., Barnes, K. J., & Harris, C. (2014). A learning approach to the ethical organization. *The Learning Organization, 21*(2), 113–125. doi:10.1108/TLO-07-2011-0043

Strategy and society. (2007). Strategy and society: The link between competitive advantage and corporate social responsibility. *Strategic Direction*, *23*(5). doi:10.1108/sd.2007.05623ead.006

Torelli, R. (2020). Sustainability, responsibility and ethics: Different concepts for a single path. *Social Responsibility Journal*, *17*(5), 719–739. doi:10.1108/SRJ-03-2020-0081

Vadera, A. K., & Pathki, C. S. R. (2021). Competition and cheating: Investigating the role of moral awareness, moral identity, and moral elevation. *Journal of Organizational Behavior*, *42*(8), 1060–1081. doi:10.1002/job.2545

Wahab, M. A. (2021). Is an unsustainability environmentally unethical? Ethics orientation, environmental sustainability engagement and performance. *Journal of Cleaner Production*, *294*, 126240. doi:10.1016/j.jclepro.2021.126240

Walsh, P. R., & Dodds, R. (2017). Measuring the choice of environmental sustainability strategies in creating a competitive advantage. *Business Strategy and the Environment*, *26*(5), 672–687. doi:10.1002/bse.1949

Wesarat, P., Sharif, M. Y., & Majid, A. H. A. (2017). Role of Organizational Ethics in Sustainable Development: A Conceptual framework. *International Journal of Sustainable Future for Human Security*, *5*(1), 67–76. doi:10.24910/jsustain/5.1/6776

Yeh, C., Lin, F., Wang, T., & Wu, C. (2020). Does corporate social responsibility affect cost of capital in China? *Asia Pacific Management Review*, *25*(1), 1–12. doi:10.1016/j.apmrv.2019.04.001

Yu, E. P., Van Luu, B., & Chen, C. H. (2020). Greenwashing in environmental, social and governance disclosures. *Research in International Business and Finance*, *52*, 101192. doi:10.1016/j.ribaf.2020.101192

Chapter 8
Exploring Ethical Dimensions of Marketers' Influence on Electronic Word–of–Mouth and Its Effect on Customer Trust

Prachi Gupta
https://orcid.org/0009-0007-2757-7212
Chitkara Business School, Chitkara University, India

Rajni Bala
Chitkara Business School, Chitkara University, India

ABSTRACT

Electronic word-of-mouth, or e-WOM, has emerged due to the expanding trend of online transactions in every category. This change in consumer purchase behavior has led to the widespread presence of online reviews, which have become a significant reference source before purchases are made. Constant dependence of customers on these reviews has induced marketers to manipulate these to their benefit. They do so by offering discounts or incentivizing customers who readily agree to post false positive reviews of their products. All such fraudulent practices are termed "opinion spam," which undermines customers' trust. The study's objective is to look into the factors and practices that have led to the burgeoning issue of opinion spam and its impact on customer trust. The study also examines the different ethical norms and standards laid down by regulatory bodies and how marketers' actions align with those. The study is based on secondary data, mainly collected and compiled from academic articles, case studies, and industry reports on opinion spam, customer trust, and marketing ethics.

DOI: 10.4018/979-8-3693-2215-4.ch008

INTRODUCTION

Before purchasing, most consumers rely on word-of-mouth (WOM) from friends and acquaintances. Word-of-mouth is the finest source of information about products (WOM). As Internet technology evolves rapidly, people enjoy communicating their thoughts about products, brands, and enterprises over the Web. It is known as eWOM. eWOM is essential to consumers when deciding what to buy, and firms have recognized this. Over the past few years, eWOM's influence has progressively increased, offering multi-location business marketers many opportunities.

Marketing researchers and managers have taken notice of electronic word-of-mouth (eWOM) due to its unique features, such as its anonymity, ability to reach a large number of people, and availability for an unlimited period. These attributes have also contributed to eWOM's rapid adoption among customers. Roughly 90% of customers check internet reviews before visiting a store (Erskine's, 2017), and 84% place equal weight on internet reviews and personal recommendations (Bloem, 2021). 71% of buyers say they are more likely to buy something after seeing a recommendation on social media (Ewing, 2019). Brick-and-mortar businesses need to take notice of eWOM as it is increasingly becoming a significant source of revenue, as evidenced by the compelling data that supports it.

(Kavitha et al., 2008) Pointed out that eWOM and traditional WOM are quite comparable from many angles, especially when it comes to the fact that they both offer suggestions from person to person. However, electronic word-of-mouth (eWOM) is a more credible, clearly relevant, and effective means of evoking consumer empathy than material generated by marketers (Bickart and Schindler, 2002). When someone is trying to make a purchasing decision, the information-intensive, intangible, and impersonal features of eWOM settings can help to reduce uncertainty because people always look for information from a variety of sources to minimize uncertainty in the decision-making process (Kavitha et al., 2020). Undeniably, eWOM is a powerful tool for consumers to make informed decisions and for businesses to build their reputations. However, it can also be easily influenced and misused, resulting in fake reviews and deceptive practices known as opinion spam.

NEED OF THE STUDY

When making a purchase, about 64% of Indian shoppers consult e-commerce sites' product reviews and ratings (Khanna, 2021). These reviews greatly influence the reputation of online marketplaces, vendors, and service providers. Fake online reviews have a startling effect on e-commerce spending, impacting $791 billion in the US, $6.4 billion in Japan, $5 billion in the UK, $2.3 billion in Canada, and $900 million in Australia annually (World Economic Forum, 2022). Based on self-reporting by the top global e-commerce sites such as Trip Advisor, Yelp, TrustPilot, Amazon, and government statistics, 4% of all online reviews are fraudulent. When expressed in terms of financial impact, fraudulent internet reviews have a $152 billion direct impact on global online expenditure (World Economic Forum, 2022). As a result, there is a significant gap between users' online impressions gathered through electronic word-of-mouth, the company's website, and their offline experiences.

OPINION SPAM

Opinion spam is the unethical activity of fabricating or manipulating testimonials, reviews, comments, or opinions to mislead potential consumers or sway public opinion. Misleading customers entails forging favorable or unfavorable reviews for a good, service, or company. Positive opinions frequently translate into success and wealth for companies and individuals. Sadly, this incentivizes people to manipulate the system by posting fictitious comments or views to support or disparage specific target companies, products, services, or individuals. (Bing Liu, 2012). There are no venues or businesses where opinion spam is exclusive. This is common in companies where decision-making depends on consumer feedback as well as on a variety of internet review sites.

Due to the massive competition in the market, marketers generally use fake reviews to boost their sales on online platforms. Official statistics and self-reporting from major e-commerce sites such as Amazon, Yelp, Trustpilot, Tripadvisor, and Yelp indicate that, on average, 4% of online reviews are fraudulent (World Economic Forum, 2022). Fakespot, a company specializing in identifying fake reviews, conducted a study in 2021 estimating that around 42% of Amazon reviews might be unreliable or fake (Stieb, 2022). An investigation agency, CMA (Competition and Markets Authority), investigated counterfeit reviews in 2019 and found that some businesses paid for fake reviews to boost their ratings on platforms like Google, Amazon, and TripAdvisor (Authority, 2021). This investigation led to removing fake reviews and penalties for the businesses involved.

Marketers may pay people to post favorable reviews for goods or services (Gera et al., 2015). Customers may be led astray by these falsified reviews into believing that a product is superior to what it truly is. In 2020, Amazon came under fire for having phony reviews on its website. It was discovered that marketers were bribing consumers with cash or free merchandise in exchange for favorable evaluations, hence inflating the ratings of specific products (Business Standard, 2022). As a result, customers' views were distorted, and their buying decisions were influenced by false information. Astroturfing is another way that companies manipulate customers' opinions. Astroturfing is gaming the system to create fake or fraudulent reviews to post on the internet. This entails fabricating grassroots movements or campaigns to give the impression that a particular good, service, or concept is widely supported or opposed. Marketers may employ bots or phony social media profiles to spread their intended message. The tobacco industry has a long history of swaying public opinion. Historically, the tobacco industry has acted dishonestly by creating fake grassroots movements to oppose smoking legislation and regulations (Myers, 1998). They gave money to front groups or people to protest these policies, giving the impression that the public was genuinely concerned. Not only that, but some marketers also compensate influencers for promoting products, although they may not disclose this fact. This lack of openness can mislead followers who believe the influencer to be genuine. Companies can also manipulate customer ratings through selective disclosure. Marketers may present information selectively, highlighting a product or service's advantages while downplaying or concealing its drawbacks. This may skew the opinions of customers. By faking positive reviews or hiding bad ones, marketers can rig rankings and ratings in online marketplaces (Lim et al., 2021).

Marketers are also using paid surveys to increase their product sales. It has been discovered that several smartphone apps alter their ratings by purchasing favorable reviews. At least one review is read by 77% of users before downloading a free program (Alchemer.com, 2016). For a paid app, that figure rises to 80% (App Radar, 2020). 70% of people say that a four- or five-star app store rating for a brand's app leaves them with a more positive view of the brand (Alchemer.com, 2016). Businesses frequently provide in-app incentives or credits to customers who post excellent reviews or give high ratings. This distorts how good people think the app is and can confuse prospective users. Marketers can create false controversy around a product or service to garner attention and sway public opinion. In 2015, the brand Volkswagen was also involved in a dispute. This controversy featured purposeful manipulation of opinion through false marketing; however, it wasn't just a publicity stunt. By installing software to evade emissions tests, Volkswagen falsely advertised its diesel cars as environmentally benign (Russell, 2015). Until the controversy was made public, this deception shaped people's perceptions of the organization and its offerings.

These unethical practices have the potential to erode consumer and business trust. Although regulatory authorities frequently have policies to stop these manipulative techniques, they can nonetheless occur, particularly in less regulated settings or online.

FORMS OF OPINION SPAM

Opinion spam manifests in various forms, each with its deceptive tactics to influence consumer perceptions and decision-making processes. Fake reviews are the most egregious form. Fake reviews are wholly deceptive and false. Usually, those who have yet to use the product or service submit them. These evaluations are illegal and shouldn't even be permitted. There have been cases when businesses have created false Google profiles to give negative or positive reviews to competitors. Opinion spam also has another sneaky side: sponsored reviews. Paying people to post positive reviews of a product or service even when they have not used it themselves is known as an incentive review. The assessments need more authenticity. They are not always illegal, even though they could be against the platform's terms of service. There have been reports that Amazon sellers give out free or heavily reduced items to consumers who write positive reviews. Companies have attempted to manipulate Yelp ratings by posting fake reviews or offering incentives for positive comments. Review manipulation adopts a different tack by using incentives or prizes to pressure clients into providing unfavorable reviews. It entails bribing customers with gifts or incentives to write unfavorable reviews. Trip Advisor is a travel and restaurant website founded in the United States. It has been discovered that certain hotels and restaurants have been using Trip Advisor to manipulate their rankings or publish fictitious positive reviews to harm the reputations of their rivals.

IMPACT OF ONLINE SPAM ON CONSUMER TRUST

A person's or company's reputation is damaged when linked to fraud. For example, tens of millions of users' private Facebook data were compromised in 2014 by Cambridge Analytica contractors and staff, who were keen to sell psychological profiles of American voters to political campaigns (Confessore, 2018). It was the most significant known leak in Facebook history. The Cambridge Analytica controversy negatively impacted user confidence in Facebook and its reputation. The platform's credibility was damaged by the improper use of user information for political ends. Numerous phony employment portals and recruitment firms in India trick job seekers by presenting attractive prospects; nevertheless, they ultimately extract money or pilfer personal data. Online job marketplaces lose credibility when people are solicited to pay for fictitious interviews or provide personal information that might be used to commit identity theft.

Fraud incidents have increased in tandem with India's explosive rise in digital payment systems. Consumer trust in digital payment platforms such as Paytm, PhonePe, and Google Pay has been damaged by cases of fraudulent transactions, whereby fraudsters pose as customer support agents or employ phishing techniques to get payment credentials. Scams such as fake initial coin offers (ICOs) and Ponzi schemes have surfaced in India as bitcoin has gained popularity. One instance of a Ponzi scheme where investors lost money was the BitConnect scam, which offered huge profits through a lending program (Reiff, 2023). The Ponzi scheme run by Bernie Madoff is one instance. Investors lost billions of dollars due to this investment hoax, which promised huge returns and damaged public confidence in financial institutions and investment prospects (Hayes, 2023).

On e-commerce sites, fake reviews and ratings can deceive customers. Phony reviews impacted the credibility of Amazon's products. Customers' trust has decreased due to sellers' fraudulent reviews to promote their products. The burgeoning e-commerce sector in India has encountered difficulties due to phony merchandise, counterfeit items, and untrustworthy vendors. Customers now need clarification on the legitimacy of things purchased online due to instances of fake goods being offered on websites like Flipkart and Amazon. Companies also sell customer data that breaches customer privacy. A significant incident data breach happened in 2017 at Equifax, one of the largest credit reporting agencies in the United States. It exposed the susceptible personal data of hundreds of millions of people, thus causing people to lose complete trust in its security system (Fruhlinger, 2020). A phishing scam in 2016 impacted Gmail users when messages received in Google Docs were clicked, enabling the hacker to access the user's complete email account and manipulate information and emails. Users fell into the trap of phishing emails as the sender appeared to be someone from their address book. Such scams shake up users' faith in internet services (Townsend, 2017).

The widespread occurrence of SIM card cloning, SMS phishing attacks, and phone frauds, where crucial information relating to bank accounts and finances is requested by people posing as bank officials, is damaging the integrity of telecom and banking services. During elections, the spread of false information and the floating of provocative material on social media sites gain prominence, hurting the trust and emotions of the general population. Unethical practices for selfish gains further boost the objectives of fraudsters and increase the number of scams around, resulting in mistrust.

MARKETERS INVOLVEMENT IN OPINION SPAM

Yelp, a popular review website, has been charged with review fraud and extortion. Allegations have been made that Yelp sales representatives have offered to delete or remove negative reviews in exchange for payment from businesses to promote their products (Harris, 2015). The legitimacy and accuracy of Yelp's reviews strted to cause users and businesses to lose faith in the platform. Comparably, Samsung's reputation took a hit after it was revealed that the business had planned a phony online campaign to undermine rival HTC by using fictitious favorable ratings to erode customer confidence. In 2013, Samsung was fined by the Taiwanese fair Trade Commission for launching a fraudulent online campaign targeting its competitor, HTC. Samsung hired advertising agencies to write favourable evaluations of HTC's products and promote their devices with high ratings (Souppouris, 2013). When this deceptive tactic was discovered, Samsung's reputation and customer confidence were damaged. In 2009, the electronic manufacturer Belkin came under fire for bribing people to write positive reviews of its products on Amazon (Baker, 2009). It was noticed that Belkin employees were paying writers to generate positive reviews. This incident severely tarnished the reputation of Belkin's products and online reviews. The travel review website TripAdvisor has addressed problems with fraudulent reviews. TripAdvisor had failed to adopt controls to prevent false reviews, while at the same time promoting the sites's content as authentic and genuine (The associated Press CNBC, 2014). An Italian business was penalized in 2018 for creating ficitious positive evaluations to raise the ratings of lodging facilities and dining establishments. Such incidents have caused customers to lose faith in the validity of the platform's reviews. Volkawagen engaged in a dishonest marketing strategy when it purposefully manipulated emissions tests for its diesel vehicles, but this went beyond a simple opinion trick. The company represented their cars as ecologically friendly even though it was aware that they produced pollutants far beyond the allowed limits (Hotten, 2015). This problem damaged Volkswagen's trust and reputation with customers' throught the globe. A few companies that sell health supplements have been exposed for fabricating blogs or webpages including fictitious endorsements or testimonials from medical professionals. Customers are tricked by these dishonest marketing strategies into thinking that the supplements work by using fictitious claims and endorsements. In 2019, Skin care brand Sunday Riley settled with the Federal Trade Commission after the company was accused of posting fake reviews of their products on Sephora's website for two years. According to the FTC, employees of the company were ordered to write fake reviews and dislike negative ones in order to boost sales. (Elassar, 2019). In recent years, media outlets worldwide have raised concerns about the reliability of popular consumer-generated media (CGM), citing instances where hotel managers pose as customers or prompt staff to write fake positive reviews about their own businesses or negative reviews about competitors. In one notable case, a British entrepreneur created a fake restaurant to demonstrate Trip Advisor's failure in addressing fake reviews, which garnered positive feedback (Smith, 2013). This highlights the widespread presence of fake and promotional content on CGM platforms, leading users to question the authenticity of reviews and emphasizing the importance of trust in such platforms (Jindal & Liu, 2008).

ETHICAL DIMENSIONS

Ethical marketing practices have been found to have a significant impact on consumer trust, loyalty, and commitment. Studies have shown that ethical behavior by sellers leads to increased trust and satisfaction among customers, which in turn influences their loyalty towards the brand. Ethical marketing practices also contribute to the sustainability of value-adding products and customer-brand relationships, which positively affect brand loyalty.

The Department of Consumer Affairs has recently announced new regulations aimed at curbing fraudulent reviews and ratings on e-commerce websites. These regulations apply to websites that sell consumer durables, restaurants, and tour and travel services. The new standard, named "ISO 19000:2022" Principles and Requirement for their Collection, Moderation and Publication," under the Bureau of Indian Standards (BIS), requires platforms to have review administrators moderate reviews in order to filter out biased or fraudulent reviews. Additionally, it mandates that reviews include posting dates and ratings at the time of platform publication.

As per the new rules, Customers will noit be able to change their reviews after they have been submitted. Consumers must provide their contact information and consent to the items and conditions in order to post reviews. Furthermore, if it is discovered that a website has published fake reviews, it will be penalized for unfair business practices. Zomato, Swiggy, tata sons, reliance Retail, meta and numerous other platform are among those that fall under the purview of the new standard (staff, 2023).

A few corporations, including Amazon, Trip Advisor, and Booking.com, sent representatives to the first fake reviews conference, which TripAdvisor organised in san Francisco in October 2022. During the conference, businesses discusses prevalent problems and possible solutions related to the issue of fake reviews. In 2022, Amazon brought legal action against more than 10,000 facebook group administrators who attempted to submit false reviews in our stores in exchange for money or free items. Additionally, the company sued more than 90 dishonest people globally who allowed false reviews. Additionally, It blocked more than 2022 million purportedly false reviews using machine learning. Amazon is using artificial intelligence to look for indicators of fraud in the reviews. When Amazon discoverd that a review is fake, They take immediate action to delete or block it, and if necessary, they also revoke a customer's review permissions, ban accounts belonging to bad actors, and take further legal action against the individuals implicated. Before taking action, Amazon's professional investigators—who have received specialized training in recognizing abusive behaviour search for further indications if a review raises red flags but more proof is required (Woollacott, 2023; Times of India, 2023).

CONCLUSION

Maintaining customer trust while identifying and eliminating bogus reviews is an ongoing challenge. False reviews may bring in customers for a short period but it's the ethical practices followed by a business that will provide a positive buying experience and result in building long-term trusting relationship. Strategy to grow and win over more customers definitely requires a continual assessment of the user reviews and their impact. With the growing trend of opinion spam, it becomes essentials for the companies following ethical standards to keep a check on the fraudulent practices of its offenders and employ strategies to counter those. Healthy business environment can get built when e-commerce platforms give utmost importance to transparency, wherein date and ratings of all reviews posted get visible, with no right to any individual to edit them once posted. Those engaging in wrong behaviors of fabricating the reviews should be punished under the law. Also some advance technology with machine learning algorithms should get developed to effectively identify and eliminate fake reviews. A widespread menace of opinion spam cannot get curtailed by any single entity but required collaborative efforts by government, regulatory bodies, e-commerce platforms and all different stakeholders. Awareness and proper knowledge need to be given to customers so that they do not fall prey to frauds and fake online reviews. Well informed and aware customer, raising voice against unethical practices can bring down the rate at which wrong tactics are employed by business to trap them. Customers' reviews are very impactful, but important is to move that impact in a positive direction, which benefits both the business and customers in the long run.

REFERENCES

Alchemer.com. (2016). *Mobile Ratings: The Good, The Bad & The Ugly*. Alchemer. https://www.alchemer.com/resources/blog/mobile-ratings-good-bad-ugly

App Radar. (2020). *How ratings and reviews affect consumers' decision to download apps.* Business of Apps.https://www.businessofapps.com/insights/ratings-reviews-affect-consumer-decision-download-apps

Authority, C. a. M. (2021). *CMA to investigate Amazon and Google over fake reviews.* GOV.UK. https://www.gov.uk/government/news/cma-to-investigate-amazon-and-google-over-fake-reviews

Baker, L. (2009). Belkin caught buying fake consumer reviews. *Search Engine Journal.* https://www.searchenginejournal.com/belkin-caught-buying-fake-consumer-reviews/8325/

Bickart, B., & Schindler, R. M. (2002). Internet forums as influential sources of consumer information. *Journal of Interactive Marketing, 15*(3), 31–40. doi:10.1002/dir.1014

Bloem, C. (2021). *Eighty-four percent of people trust online reviews as much as friends. Here is how to manage what they see.* Inc.com. https://www.inc.com/craig-bloem/84-percent-of-people-trust-online-reviews-as-much-.html

Business Standard. (2022). *Amazon sues admins of over 10,000 Facebook groups over fake reviews.* Business Standard. https://www.business-standard.com/article/companies/amazon-sues-admins-of-over-10-000-facebook-groups-over-fake-reviews-122072000043_1.html

Confessore, N. (2018). Cambridge Analytica and Facebook: the scandal and the fallout so far. *The New York Times.* https://www.nytimes.com/2018/04/04/us/politics/cambridge-analytica-scandal-fallout.html

Elassar, A. (2019). *Skin care brand Sunday Riley wrote fake Sephora reviews for almost two years, FTC says.* CNN. https://edition.cnn.com/2019/10/22/us/sunday-riley-fake-reviews-trnd/index.html

Erskine, R. (2017). 20 Online reputation statistics that every business owner needs to know. *Forbes.* https://www.forbes.com/sites/ryanerskine/2017/09/19/20-online-reputation-statistics-that-every-business-owner-needs-to-know/?sh=5647de13cc5c

Ewing, M. (2019). *71% More Likely to Purchase Based on Social Media Referrals.* Hubspot. https://blog.hubspot.com/blog/tabid/6307/bid/30239/71-More-Likely-to-Purchase-Based-on-Social-Media-Referrals-Infographic.aspx

Fruhlinger, J. (2023). *Equifax data breach FAQ: What happened, who was affected, what was the impact?* CSO Online. https://www.csoonline.com/article/567833/equifax-data-breach-faq-what-happened-who-was-affected-what-was-the-impact.html

Gera, T., Thakur, D., & Singh, J. (2015, February). Identifying deceptive reviews using networking parameters. In *2015 International Conference on Computing and Communications Technologies (ICCCT)* (pp. 322-327). IEEE. 10.1109/ICCCT2.2015.7292769

Harris, S. (2015). *Yelp accused of bullying businesses into paying for better reviews. (2015, January 14).* CBC. https://www.cbc.ca/news/business/yelp-accused-of-bullying-businesses-into-paying-for-better-reviews-1.2899308

Hayes, A. (2023). *Bernie Madoff: Who he was, how his ponzi scheme worked.* Investopedia. https://www.investopedia.com/terms/b/bernard-madoff.asp

Hotten, B. R. (2015). *Volkswagen: The scandal explained.* BBC News. https://www.bbc.com/news/business-34324772

IEEE. (2014). *Understanding the process of writing fake online reviews.* IEEE Xplore. https://ieeexplore.ieee.org/abstract/document/6991395

Imbler, S. (2018). *Can you trust Amazon vine reviews?* Wirecutter: Reviews for the Real World. https://www.nytimes.com/wirecutter/blog/amazon-vine-reviews/

Kavitha, C., & Varadharaj, B. (2020). Role of Electronic Word of Mouth in Online Booking. *Journal of XI An University of Architecture & Technology., 12*(2), 534–542.

Khanna, A. (2021). Reviews and ratings drive Indian online shoppers to 'Buy Now' button [REPORT]. Dazeinfo. https://dazeinfo.com/2021/03/16/online-shopping-india-reveiws-ratings

Lim, W. M., Gupta, S., Aggarwal, A., Paul, J., & Sadhna, P. (2021). How do digital natives perceive and react toward online advertising? Implications for SMEs. *Journal of Strategic Marketing*, 1–35. doi:10.1080/0965254X.2021.1941204

Liu, B. (2012). Opinion spam detection. In Synthesis lectures on human language technologies (pp. 113–125). doi:10.1007/978-3-031-02145-9_10

Myers, E. (1998). *The manipulation of public opinion by the tobacco industry: past, present, and future.* DigitalCommons@UM Carey Law. https://digitalcommons.law.umaryland.edu/jhclp/vol2/iss1/7

Rastogi, A. & Mehrotra, M. (2017). Opinion Spam Detection in Online Reviews. *Journal of Information & Knowledge Management, 16*(4), pp.

Reiff, N. (2023). *How to identify cryptocurrency and ICO scams.* Investopedia. https://www.investopedia.com/tech/how-identify-cryptocurrency-and-ico-scams/

Russell, H. (2015). *Volkswagen: The Scandal.* BBC. https://www.bbc.com/news/business-34324772

Souppouris, A. (2013). Samsung fined $340,000 for faking online comments. *The Verge.* https://www.theverge.com/2013/10/24/5023658/samsung-fined-340000-for-posting-negative-htc-reviews

Staff, A. (2023a). *Amazon's blueprint for private & public sector partnership to combat fake reviews.* IN About Amazon. https://www.aboutamazon.in/news/amazon-india-news/a-blueprint-for-private-and-public-sector-partnership-to-stop-fake-reviews

Staff, A. (2023b). *Amazon detects fake reviews using Artificial Intelligence.* IN About Amazon. https://www.aboutamazon.in/news/retail/detecting-fake-reviews-with-advanced-ai

Stieb, M. (2022). *Amazon fake reviews: Can they be stopped?* Intelligencer. https://nymag.com/intelligencer/2022/07/amazon-fake-reviews-can-they-be-stopped.html

The Associated Press. (2014). *TripAdvisor fined $600,000 for fake reviews.* CNBC. https://www.cnbc.com/2014/12/23/tripadvisor-fined-600000-for-fake-reviews.html

Times Of India. (2023). How Amazon, Booking.com, Tripadvisor and others aim to reduce fake reviews. *The Times of India*. https://timesofindia.indiatimes.com/articleshow/104503422.cms?utm_source=contentofinterest&utm_medium=text&utm_campaign=cppst

Townsend, T. (2017). More than a million people were affected by the Google Docs phishing attack. *Vox*. https://www.vox.com/2017/5/4/15545138/million-people-targeted-google-docs-gmail-phishing-hack

Woollacott, E. (2023). Amazon calls on governments to help crack down on fake reviews. *Forbes*. https://www.forbes.com/sites/emmawoollacott/2023/06/13/amazon-calls-on-governments-to-help-crack-down-on-fake-reviews/?sh=2239b80e40e0

World Economic Forum. (2022). *Fake online reviews cost $152 billion a year. Here's how e-commerce sites can stop them*. WEF. https://www.weforum.org/agenda/2021/08/fake-online-reviews-are-a-152-billion-problem-heres-how-to-silence-them

Yoon, S. N. (2008). *The effects of electronic word -of -mouth systems (EWOMS) on the acceptance of recommendation*. Research Gate. https://www.researchgate.net/publication/280148041_The_effects_of_electronic_word_-of_-mouth_systems_EWOMS_on_the_acceptance_of_recommendation/citations

Chapter 9
Exploring Market Knowledge Dimensions and Knowledge Integration Mechanisms in Automotive Cybersecurity and IoT

Priya Jindal
Chitkara Business School, Chitkara University, India

Lochan Chavan
Chitkara Business School, Chitkara University, India

ABSTRACT

There has been a wide range of technological improvements and breakthroughs, allowing new vehicles to evolve and adapt to changes to obtain a competitive advantage. Consumers' lives have been made easier by autonomous vehicles, such as cybersecurity, the internet of things (IoT), 5G technology, V2X communication, etc. These autonomous vehicles may examine system weaknesses and threats with the use of the market knowledge dimension and the knowledge integration mechanism, and they can then collaborate to reduce all potential risks and vulnerabilities. By concentrating on potential flaws and risks in automotive vehicles, cyber security, and IoT play important roles in advancing the physical world.

INTRODUCTION

Our Automobiles have begun to function, feel, and appear more and more like computers. They assist us with navigation, communication, entertainment, braking, and even steering by using a variety of sensors and screens. The concepts of linked and autonomous driving fall within the wide category of "intelligent vehicles," which encompasses two distinct but related technologies (Watney & Draffin, 2017). The term "Internet of Things" (IoT) refers to a network of connected objects with sensors that may be accessed by

DOI: 10.4018/979-8-3693-2215-4.ch009

computers or smartphones for monitoring or control. These gadgets can exchange data as well as collect it. The IoT concept's key strength is the significant impact it will have on a variety of facets of daily life and the behavior of potential users. The main goal is to provide the reader with the chance to comprehend what has been done (protocols, algorithms, proposed solutions), what needs to be addressed, which are the enabling factors of this evolutionary process, and which are its weaknesses and risk factors (Atzori et al., 2010). The Market Knowledge Dimension and Knowledge Market Integration will support the analysis, evaluation, implementation, design, and development of the IoT and cyber security system to protect smart drives and deliver technological advancement to address risks and vulnerabilities in the automotive industry.

A. Internet of Things and Cybersecurity in the Automobile Industry

IoT is an emerging technology that enhances the performance of the vehicle, helps the driver, increases the comfort for the passenger, rescues the passenger in case of accidents, in providing secured parking, avoids road rule violations, etc. It is a promising technology to leave a secure and comfortable life. Auto-makers can now produce more vehicles, optimize maintenance procedures, enhance safety features, and gather and analyze real-time data to assure predictive maintenance, lower downtime, and boost overall efficiency. The connectivity, credibility, availability, flexibility, confidentiality, and compatibility of the globe can all be improved by IoT (Jeong et al., 2018). Managing risks, repairing holes in systems, and enhancing system resilience are all aspects of cybersecurity strategies. The National Highway Traffic Safety Administration (NHTSA) of the United States defines automotive cybersecurity as "the protection of automotive electronic systems, communication networks, control algorithms, software, users, and underlying data from malicious attacks, damage, unauthorized access, or manipulation" (Morris et al., 2018). With the aid of a variety of hardware and software solutions, cyber-security safeguards data and systems for processing or storing it (Juneja et al., 2020). Without cyber security, businesses are helpless against hacking and data breaches and turn into easy targets for attackers (Alhayani et al., 2021).

I. Automotive Industry

Modern automobiles are increasingly interconnected. Electronic control units (ECUs) are used to regulate and monitor the internal vehicle network and its related subsystems to achieve internal connection (Loukas, 2015). Computer applications encourage improved production procedures, develop new business models, lower costs and risks, enable real-time data collection, integrate a rapidly growing number of software-based applications, and enhance product performance (Liu et al., 2012). The adoption of the Internet of Things (IoT) in design, development, and manufacturing processes has enhanced the performance of products (Aris et al., 2015), but it has also increased reliance on design, engineering, manufacturing, and component outsourcing, which in turn depends on establishing trust with suppliers through increased knowledge-sharing.

II. Smart Drive Security

Assessing potential vulnerabilities, identifying common cyber threats, evaluating the security of the smart drives, and tracking down and identifying threats and assaults against targeted targets are all made easier with the help of smart drive security as shown in Figure 1. Additionally, it reveals how consumers feel about the company and how much they believe in its cybersecurity for connected vehicles. A precise security framework for the smart drive is developed based on cybersecurity and IoT.

Figure 1. Factors affect the automobile sector
(Author's compilation)

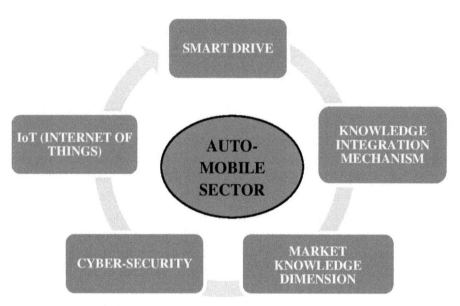

B.   Exploring Market Knowledge Dimensions and Knowledge Integration Techniques within the Context of Automotive Cybersecurity and IoT can have Substantial Effects across a Variety of Domains.

1.   **Improved Automotive Cybersecurity:** The first and most important impact is to increase the potential of automotive cyber security. To provide more efficient security measures and spot new trends in vehicles, market notice timings are used to analyze customer demand, industry practices, and market trends. To increase the safety and dependability of automobiles, some security frameworks are designed expressly for smart driving.

2.   **Increased Consumer Confidence:** Smart drives are crucial for establishing and preserving consumer confidence. If smart vehicles lack the security measures put in place for them, customers welcome IoT-enabled features and technology in the vehicle. The consumer's growing confidence in smart drive automobiles will likely fuel market expansion.

3.   **Regulatory Compliance and Standards:** Stakeholders' specialists must adhere to cyber security standards and regulations to guarantee the safety and security measures used in smart drives by automotive manufacturers. The implementation of regulatory requirements and assistance to businesses in achieving compliance with pertinent standards are equally vital. Achieving regulatory compliance prevents legal problems and increases the reputation of secure and reliable smart drives.

4.   **Innovation and Market Positioning:** The organization is better equipped to develop the product following consumer tastes and expectations by assessing chances for innovation in

automobile security with the help of the market knowledge dimension. Modern security features will provide the product with a distinctness that will make it stand out from competitors. Innovation in smart drive security will affect how companies are positioned in the market. To get a competitive advantage, the market position will make it possible to focus on specific automotive industry segments.

5. **Interdisciplinary Collaboration:** The market knowledge dimension and knowledge integration mechanism underline the importance of multidisciplinary cooperation in addressing cyber security issues. By incorporating knowledge from a variety of industries, including automobile manufacturing, the field of cybersecurity, IoT technologies, and more, this collaborative *approach* may produce security solutions that are both completer and more effective.

6. **Industry Expansion and Economic Impact:** The smart drive contributes to the expansion and sustainability of the automobile sector by ensuring customer safety measures. The necessity for reliable cybersecurity solutions will need to increase as smart drives become more widely used. Companies who invest in R&D to develop smart drives benefit from growth potential by introducing innovation to the automotive industry that will boost the sector's overall economic impact.

Overall, securing smart drives in terms of automotive cyber security and IoT has extensive ramifications for the industry, its customers, and the government, resulting in a wider economic impact. The stakeholders in the automotive industry may work together to build a safer and more secure environment for the future of connected vehicles by addressing the dangers, possibilities, and difficulties through research.

I.   Market Knowledge Dimension

The market knowledge dimension investigates the potential areas by identifying the key players in the automobile cyber security and IoT market. It also helps check the market growth, market potential, competitor offerings, and different opportunities for innovation by analyzing current market trends and consumer demands for vehicles. It also mentions regular compliance standards in the automobile industry and examines the regulator requirement for the automobile industry. Helps the company in making informed decisions regarding product development, investment strategies, and Market positioning.

II. Knowledge Integration Mechanism

Knowledge integration mechanisms look for information from sources like academic studies, industry reports, cyber security professionals, and user feedback to assist design thorough and efficient cyber security solutions. Knowledge integration mechanisms determine and analyze how various stakeholders, such as researchers, experts, and manufacturers, contribute to knowledge integration. They also identify the knowledge sources that are used in the creation of automotive cyber security solutions. The automotive cyber security area identifies and implements best practices for combining knowledge from several fields. Collaboration and data exchange are important factors in enhancing security measures. Fig. 2. depicts that in the context of automotive cybersecurity and IoT (Internet of Things), securing the smart drive serves several crucial functions.

Figure 2. Functions of cyber-security & IoT
(Author's compilation)

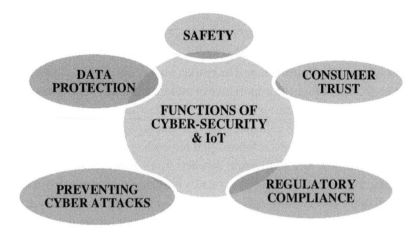

1. **Safety:** Ensuring the safety of the driver, passengers, pedestrians, and other road users is one of the main goals of security smart drives. Cyber-attacks that could compromise the control systems of vehicles and cause accidents and injuries must be avoided and secured against by various sensors, communication networks, and software components.

2. **Data Protection:** Data created and gathered by smart vehicles, including sensitive data on the performance and location of the vehicle as well as private information about the driver and passengers, must be safeguarded to avoid unauthorized access and misuse. The smart drive's key goals are to safeguard user privacy and personal information while preserving the accuracy of information searches.

3. **Preventing Cyberattacks:** As a vehicle's connectivity increases, so does the possibility of cyberattacks. Hackers and other bad actors will try to take advantage of weaknesses in network infrastructure, communication protocols, and smart drives to access steel data without authorization or take control of the vehicle. Such attacks are prevented by the implementation of strong cybersecurity measures.

4. **Regulatory Compliance:** Businesses that adopt IoT technology and protected smart drives place a high value on regulatory compliance, which ensures the security and safety of corresponding vehicles. Automakers must adhere to the laws and regulations governing cyber security to continuously manufacture goods with the required safety and security characteristics.

5. **Consumer Trust:** Ensuring security precautions in the deployment of smart drives will encourage consumers to accept IoT features and technology in vehicles. Potential market growth will result from establishing and sustaining consumer confidence in connected vehicles through secure smart drives. Consumers are more likely to approach vehicles with connected features once they have more confidence in smart drive technologies.

In conclusion, securing the smart drive is crucial for safety, data protection, preventing cyberattacks, regulatory compliance, and fostering customer trust in the area of automotive cyber security and IoT.

Effective knowledge integration processes are essential for maintaining competition, satisfying consumer expectations, and continuously improving in the fast-developing vehicle business.

III. Threats & Vulnerabilities

The terms "threats & vulnerabilities" in cybersecurity and IoT are used to help and recognize the deficiencies and weaknesses in the system which are easily traceable and exploited by hackers, and cyber attackers, which disturbs the privacy of both users and the safety of car occupants and distracts the operation of connected vehicles. Some typical vulnerabilities are as follows:

A) **Inadequate Encryption:** If encryption standards are not followed this will rise unethical access to crucial data transmitted between IoT devices and automobile systems

B) **Inadequate Secure Authentication:** If the authentication protocols are not secured it will give access to important data and automobile functionality.

C) **Hacking and remote control:** Hackers may get unauthorized access to the vehicle's connected systems, allowing them to influence crucial operations like brakes or acceleration.

D) **Data breaches:** If sensitive data, such as private and vehicle data, is not properly kept, it may be harmed, posing privacy concerns and opening the door to data exploitation.

E) **Denial of Service (DoS) Attacks:** Cybercriminals might obstruct the operation of vital systems, which could lead to accidents or other security issues.

F) **Outdated software:** If the software is not updated often, connected components may be vulnerable to known vulnerabilities and cyberattacks.

G) **Insecure Communication Protocols:** Hackers can pick up information on and alter communication channels between IoT devices and automotive systems.

H) **Physical Access:** Physical access to the systems of a vehicle might lead to unauthorized use and manipulation of critical functions.

I) **Inadequate Access Control:** Poorly maintained access controls may allow unauthorized individuals to access personal vehicle data and systems.

J) **Over-the-Air (OTA) Update Vulnerabilities:** To install malicious software upgrades on the target vehicle, attackers may target OTA update techniques.

K) **Supply Chain Weaknesses:** Components and software for vehicles may be affected as a result of vulnerabilities introduced during the production process or inside the supply chain.

    C. Market Knowledge Dimension and Knowledge Market Integration can help address these vulnerabilities & threats in the following ways:

        I. Market Knowledge Dimension

To prevent existing vulnerabilities in the automobile industries the manufacturers' stakeholders' experts have to focus on the most critical and sensitive areas for improvement and also invest in adopting secure and safety measures. The types of threats faced by the automobile company. The types of threats faced by the automobile industry where immediate attention/ action in the required areas is identified with further investment in cyber security measures are carried out by understanding the current state of the market.

II. Knowledge Market Integration

Knowledge market integration helps in sharing and collaborating the cyber security knowledge among various departments in the industry such as securities researchers, and regulatory bodies manufacturers, and facilitates the exchange of data, threat intelligence, and best practices. This integration allows for the dissemination of best practices, threat intelligence, and innovative technologies to improve the overall security posture of connected vehicles, leading to better security solutions. Fig. 3. Shows the insights from Market Knowledge Dimension combined with Knowledge Market Integration can help the automotive industry.

1. Recognize risks and vulnerabilities and take measures to control, so they won't harm privacy. Learn from prior experiences, obtain knowledge, and develop crisis management skills.
2. Creating awareness among the customer against threats and attacks and educating them to recognize the attacks in order to take immediate security measures.
3. Having timely software updates, evaluating vulnerability, and security updates are some preventions to be undertaken for safeguarding the data which helps in reducing vulnerabilities.
4. Adopting the best practices and having knowledge of current cybersecurity development helps to take necessary measures against cyberattacks.

In general, the combination of Market Knowledge Dimension and Knowledge Market Integration enables the automotive industry to develop a stronger cybersecurity position, lowering the probability of successful cyber-attacks and maintaining the safety and integrity of connected vehicles and their occupants. Additionally contributes to the development of an automotive ecosystem that is more reliable and flexible, giving consumers trust and guaranteeing the secure and efficient operation of connected vehicles.

III. Risk Management

The number and diversity of connected devices entering IoT networks increase at an exponential rate, which increases the risk of security exposures. Because IoT systems lack security, hackers and intruders have easier access to sensitive data and essential infrastructure. By adding system redundancy and restricting the amount of connectivity, several businesses are attempting to reduce the cyber threats that their automobiles face (Bathla et al., 2022). Fig. 3. depicts a four-layer IoT cyber risk management framework is suggested to help identify the key elements affecting cyber security risk and design a cost-effective cyber security risk management strategy. The four layers of the IoT cybersecurity risk management framework are the IoT cybersecurity ecosystem layer, IoT cybersecurity infrastructure layer, IoT cybersecurity risk assessment layer, and IoT cybersecurity performance layer. Due to their interdependence, these layers are put on, in order.

Figure 3. Four layers of the IoT cybersecurity risk management framework (Lee, 2020)

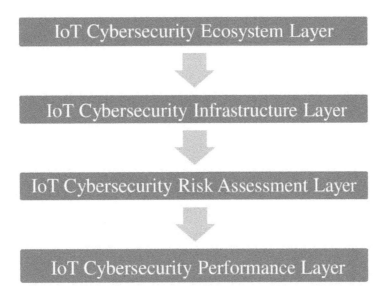

The IoT cyber ecosystem layer consists of standardization organizations, government agencies, external users, opponents, and IoT cyber security solution developers. To secure IoT systems, security managers must develop appropriate security responses. Due to a lack of knowledge, the organization is unable to create IoT cybersecurity solutions that are in line with market trends and market growth. IoT service security technology developers create solutions using the most up-to-date tools to secure data transfer, prevent hacking, and maintain privacy standards. The IoT cyber infrastructure layer helps with evaluating the importance of the IoT cyber infrastructure from both a technological and management standpoint. Organizations of employees or internal users, along with technology departments, make up this layer. They allocate resources here to maximize the likelihood that threats and vulnerabilities will be defended against (Aggarwal et al., 2019). Cybersecurity changes in technology are taken into account for risk management to safeguard its resources and services. The third layer of IoT cyber risk assessment examines and monitors present and potential threats, as well as identifying and comprehending the methods used by hackers to launch cyberattacks. The fourth and last layer is IoT cyber performance is based on deployment, monitoring, and continual cyber security enhancement. It assists in restoring lost data as well as stopping and detecting cyberattack activity. To track cyberattacks and retaliate in real-time, real-time data is gathered. Performance targets are set for ongoing improvement.

CONCLUSION

In terms of safety on the roads, environmental, sociological, and moral challenges, cybersecurity safety, competitiveness, and jobs, connected vehicles provide new problems for authorities and lawmakers. Instead of being isolated areas of concern, these domains are connected. One of the main difficulties in creating a cooperative approach to managing cybersecurity in the business and public interest is the conflict between the need for knowledge sharing among many different actors and the disincentives to disclose vulnerabilities and cybersecurity breaches. Despite the scope and possible consequences of cybersecurity challenges, the topic has received very few contributions that concentrate on the broader social, economic, and behavioral dimensions rather than the technological before the IoT concept is widely embraced, many difficult issues still need to be addressed and both technological and social problems must be ironed out.

REFERENCES

Aggarwal, A., Mittal, R., Gupta, S., & Mittal, A. (2019). Internet of things driven perceived value co-creation in smart cities of the future: A PLS-SEM based predictive model. *Journal of Computational and Theoretical Nanoscience*, *16*(9), 4053–4058. doi:10.1166/jctn.2019.8292

Alhayani, B., Mohammed, H. J., Chaloob, I. Z., & Ahmed, J. S. (2021). Effectiveness of artificial intelligence techniques against cyber security risks apply of IT industry. *Materials Today: Proceedings*, 531. doi:10.1016/j.matpr.2021.02.531

Aris, I. B., Sahbusdin, R. K. Z., & Amin, A. F. M. (2015, May). Impacts of IoT and big data to automotive industry. In *2015 10th Asian control conference (ASCC)* (pp. 1-5). IEEE.

Atzori, L., Iera, A., & Morabito, G. (2010). The internet of things: A survey. *Computer Networks*, *54*(15), 2787–2805. doi:10.1016/j.comnet.2010.05.010

Bathla, D., Awasthi, S., & Ahuja, R. (2022). PESTEL Analysis of the Automotive Industry. In Applying Metalytics to Measure Customer Experience in the Metaverse (pp. 143-160). IGI Global. doi:10.4018/978-1-6684-6133-4.ch013

Jeong, Y., Son, S., Jeong, E., & Lee, B. (2018). An integrated self-diagnosis system for an autonomous vehicle based on an IoT gateway and deep learning. *Applied Sciences (Basel, Switzerland)*, *8*(7), 1164. doi:10.3390/app8071164

Juneja, S., Sharma, R., & Hsiung, P. A. (2020, February). Proceedings of international conference on contemporary technologies of computing, analytics and networks–Editorial. In *2020 Indo–Taiwan 2nd International Conference on Computing, Analytics and Networks (Indo-Taiwan ICAN)* (pp. i-viii). IEEE.

Lee, I. (2020). Internet of Things (IoT) cybersecurity: Literature review and IoT cyber risk management. *Future Internet*, *12*(9), 157. doi:10.3390/fi12090157

Liu, T., Yuan, R., & Chang, H. (2012, October). Research on the Internet of Things in the Automotive Industry. In *2012 International Conference on Management of e-Commerce and e-Government* (pp. 230-233). IEEE. 10.1109/ICMeCG.2012.80

Loukas, G. (2015). Cyber-physical attacks on implants and vehicles. *Cyber-Physical Attacks*, 59-104.

Morris, D., Madzudzo, G., & Garcia-Perez, A. (2018). Cybersecurity and the auto industry: The growing challenges presented by connected cars. *International Journal of Automotive Technology and Management*, *18*(2), 105–118. doi:10.1504/IJATM.2018.092187

Watney, C., & Draffin, C. (2017). *Addressing new challenges in automotive cybersecurity*. R Street Institute.

Chapter 10
Industry Development at COIR:
Trade Reforms and India's Export Outcomes

Dharmesh Dhabliya
https://orcid.org/0000-0002-6340-2993
Vishwakarma Institute of Information Technology, India

M. N. Nachappa
Jain University, India

Ritu Rani
Vivekananda Global University, India

Neha Nitin Karnik
ATLAS SkillTech University, India

Anishkumar Dhablia
Altimetrik India Pvt. Ltd., India

Jambi Ratna Raja Kumar
https://orcid.org/0000-0002-9870-7076
Genba Sopanrao Moze College of Engineering, India

Ankur Gupta
https://orcid.org/0000-0002-4651-5830
Vaish College of Engineering, India

Sabyasachi Pramanik
https://orcid.org/0000-0002-9431-8751
Haldia Institute of Technology, India

ABSTRACT

In developing India, the traditional coir industry employs 0.55 million people. Production of coconuts and coir is dominated by Kerala. Karnataka and Tamilnadu afterwards provide good coir. India is benefiting from the manufacturing of coir. This is having an impact on the coir sector due to commercial enterprises. This research looked at the effects of two trade reforms on the development, performance, and solution of India's coir sector. Trade influences trade volume and propels growth. Trade growth and volume are impacted by trade liberalization. Two significant trade agreements that had an impact on the coir business were the WTO Agreement on Textiles and Clothing (ATC) and the GATT Multi-Fiber Agreement (MFA). Data for the study came from the Coir Board's annual reports as well as websites belonging to the Reserve Bank of India, Ministry of External Affairs, Ministry of Commerce and Industry, and Coir Board.

DOI: 10.4018/979-8-3693-2215-4.ch010

INTRODUCTION

India's economy was mostly rural and industrially underdeveloped when it gained its freedom for a variety of reasons. Despite the nation's repeated deliberate endeavors to boost industrialization, this sector's percentage of GDP hasn't improved. Because of the agricultural sector's prominence, there were many conventional and agro-based businesses that were present and continuously expanded. We had strong trade connections with other nations, especially the Arab world, prior to gaining our formal independence. These ties drive these agro-based and traditional businesses. But British dominance changed the industrial pattern to their advantage. Either way, after Independence, there was purposeful meddling so that five-year plans could be used to establish a strong industrial base for the country. India created and advanced a few key and significant industries as a consequence. But the importance of small, traditional agro-businesses never goes away.

Trade promotes the growth of industries as it is a progress engine. International and domestic trade is both possible. However, the influence of global commerce on industrial performance is stronger due to technical transfer. But trade volume is also influenced by other factors. Changes in both domestic and foreign commerce have a significant and enduring impact on a nation's export performance and, in turn, its development. This essay aims to investigate how different trade reforms have affected the export performance of the coir industry, a prominent and long-standing industry in India, especially in Kerala.

The Committee on Commodity Problems (FAO, UN, 2011) looked at export patterns for Jute and Hard Fibers (JHFs) between 1996 and 2010. They concluded that two major turning events for the worldwide trade in JHFs were the adoption of the WTO Uruguay Round accords since 1996 and the Multi-Fibre Agreement (MFA) phase-out in 2004. Therefore, this MFA, its phase-out, and its elimination as a consequence of the adoption of ATC under WTO have a greater impact on the production and exports of fiber and fiber-related goods. For that reason, I tried to look at trends in India's coir exports over those years. This performance was compared to India's total exports in order to ascertain the effect of trade reforms on the export performance of coir and coir products. Owing to these changes, Kerala, where the industry was established and has had a long-standing monopoly, is also included in the research.

Coir Industry Growth

The production of coir was among the first industries in India. The most important coconut-producing states in the nation are Maharashtra, Karnataka, Andhra Pradesh, Kerala, and Tamil Nadu, in addition to Goa, Assam, Orissa, Andaman & Nicobar, Pondicherry, and Lakshadweep. The states of Andaman & Nicobar, Goa, and Goa are also coconut-producing states. India is the world's biggest producer of coconuts, accounting for almost two thirds of global production of coir and products produced from it. It is this country, together with its neighbor Sri Lanka, that produces over 90 percent of the coir fiber used worldwide. The yearly output of coir fiber in India is around 280000 metric tons (MT).

The coir industry in the country employs more than 5.5 lakh people (0.55 million). Kerala produces the majority of coir and coir-derived goods in India, making up over 61% of the country's total coconut output. In the country's rural economy, the sector offers a steady source of employment, especially for women.

The goals

- To research how India's coir industry has developed

- To research trade liberalization and the coir industry's export performance
- Examine the Coir Industry Agreement on Textiles and Apparel.

Source of Data and Methods

In order to do research on the present situation, data was gathered from a wide range of secondary sources. These secondary sources included the Government of India's and the Coir Board's annual reports, together with the export figures available on the Coir Board's official website. Data on India's total exports was gathered by using the official websites of the Reserve Bank of India, the Ministries of External Affairs, and the Ministries of Commerce and Industry, all of which are under the jurisdiction of the Government of India. It was vital to include both the periodic growth rates and the compound annual growth rate (CAGR) while doing research on the efficacy of coir exports. While the second approach calculates growth over a defined length of time, the first method computes growth on an annual basis. To calculate the periodical growth rates, semi-log regression models were used instead of the more traditional linear models. This action was taken as a result of the export data's exponential pattern. To get a better idea of how the aforementioned changes may impact the market, we compared the overall export of the Indian economy to the total export of coir and other commodities associated with coir. This was carried out to provide a more accurate understanding of the impact on the market.

Reforms in Trade

Significant economic changes were implemented by the Indian government in 1991. These included proposals for tax cuts, banking liberalization, foreign investment, and the opening of the nation's markets to outside commerce. The two major trade reforms that affected the exports of coir and coir-related goods addressed in this article were the Multi-Fiber Agreement (MFA) under the GATT Regime and the Agreement on Textiles and Clothing (ATC) under the WTO Regime. Part of the shift from the GATT framework to the WTO system is the phase-out of the Multi Fiber Agreement, another period of changes. To help in understanding the study, a brief synopsis of the main trade changes was required first.

Multifiber Contract (MFA)

Initiated in 1974, the Multi-Fiber Agreement served as a temporary measure to help developed countries cope with the growing influx of fiber and fiber-related goods from developing countries. The usage of quotas enabled this to be done. The capacity of local businesses to compete with overseas rivals is somewhat hampered by this kind of defense. The goal was to provide industrialized nations enough time to develop their own fiber businesses [Alberto Portugal-Perez and John S. Wilson, 2010]. This would assist in lowering the quantity of fiber and fiber-related items that are imported from emerging nations. This is true for fibers that are firm or soft. Both exporting and developing nations opposed it and persisted in demanding the liberalization of the textile and clothing trade. This directly led to the presentation of draughts of the Agreement on Textiles and Clothing (ATC), which was negotiated during the GATT's Uruguay Round of trade negotiations, in 1991. When the ATC was finally implemented on January 1, 1995, it cleared the path for the transparent and orderly elimination of quantitative limits. It provided a clear structure, which made this feasible.

The Consent to Remove MFA Quotas

Article 2 of the Agreement outlines the four-stage schedule for quota liberalization that the ATC set. Each phase required the integration of a certain proportion of textile categories, as per the 1990 levels. Table 3.1 shows the timeline for the elimination of MFA quotas in accordance with the WTO Agreement on Textiles from 1995 to 2005.

Table 1. Removal of Quota under ATC

Removal of Quota (%)	Date of Implementation
16	1st January 1995
17	1st January 1998
18	1st January 2002
49	1st January 2005

The Agreement on Apparel and Textiles (ATC)

The Uruguay Round resulted in the Agreement on Textiles and Clothing (ATC), which is being implemented over a ten-year period. It represents the integration of the textile sector into the mainstream of WTO standards. This integration is happening because of the ATC. The two most significant features of the ATC are thought to be the gradual removal of restraints over a period of ten years in accordance with a predetermined schedule and the phased-out of additional restraints and other measures during the phase-out period through the proposed Textile Monitoring Body (TMB) of the ATC. While each of these aspects is important in and of itself, the progressive relaxation of constraints is more important than the other.

Findings and Conversations

Under this subject is a study of how different trade changes have affected the export performance of the Indian coir sector. The impacts were analyzed using two variables the amount, caliber, and export trend.

Quantity of Exports

Analysis was done on the volume and value of exports from the coir business throughout different reform eras. For analytical reasons, the different reform periods are characterized as follows:

ATC Period: 2015–16 to 2019–20; MFA Period: 1995–96 to 2003–04; Phase-out of MFA: 2005–06 to 2010–11;

Table 2. The compound annual growth rates of India's coir and coir product exports relative to the country's overall exports throughout these time periods.

Periods		CAGR [Quality of coir and coir product's exports (%)]	CAGR [Value of coir and coir product's exports (%)]	CADR [overall exports (%)]
MFA	1995-96 to 2003-04	0.77	13.88	19.42*
Phase out of MFA	2005-06 to 2010-11	9.9	9.76	15.56
ATC	2015-16 to 2019-20	18.93	15.25	12.95

Table No. 2 shows that throughout the period of quantitative constraints on fibre goods (MFA), the export of coir and coir derivatives from India only increases marginally. Overall exports climbed from 43834 tons in 1995–1996 to 48286 tons in 2003–2004. On the other hand, during the years that the MFA restriction was being phased down, the exports of coir and coir products rose annually. Over the course of these 10 years, there was an increase in exports of 75650 tons. The volume of coir exported rose significantly by 16.73 present between 2015–2016 and 2019–2020, another ATC period, going from 137026.97 tons in 2015–2016 to 1036564 tons in 2019–2020. The value of coir exports increased at a strong pace throughout each of these reform phases, reaching a high under ATC. In contrast to the growth rates of coir and coir products, the CAGR of India's overall exports revealed a negative trend in growth rate when we analyzed throughout different reform periods. To have a better understanding of the growth rates throughout these eras, we depend on the growth rates broken down by period. To calculate the export growth rates throughout different trade liberalization periods, regression analysis was used. To build a regression model, the export patterns across different time periods were first looked at. The fitted trend forms made it clear that both the overall amount of India's exports and the exports of coir and coir products followed an exponential pattern. A compound growth model was fitted to ascertain the growth rates shown by equation 1.

$$Y_t = Y_0(1+r)t\dots\dots\dots\dots\dots\dots \tag{1}$$

Where, Y_t = quantity of coir exports or value of coir exports or total exports
r = compound growth rate
t = time period
For the purpose of estimation, the model (1) was transformed to a semi- log regression model as equation 2.

$$Ln\ Y_t = + \beta t + u_t\dots\dots\dots\dots\dots\dots \tag{2}$$

Where, Y_t = quantity of coir exports or value of coir exports or total exports
t = time period,
β = parameters
u_t = random error term Run the regression, and from these regression results, we have our compound growth rates using the following equation.

$$r = AL \, (\beta) - 1 \ldots\ldots\ldots\ldots \tag{3}$$

By using this equation number 4.3, the compound growth rates were calculated and were shown in table number 3.

Table 3. Growth rates under various trade reforms

Periods	Growth rate of Quality of coir exports	Growth rate of value of coir exports	Growth rate of total exports from India
MFA	-0.2935	1.456	1.6718*
Phase out of MFA	1.6579	1.6647	1.68985
ATC	1.7174	1.6932	1.5879

Table 3 makes clear that, over the reform periods, the export of coir and coir products has grown positively in terms of export value; nevertheless, due to quantitative limits under the MFA, the export has grown negatively in terms of export volume. But throughout the past two reform periods (phasing out the MFA and ATC), the export had positive growth rates when these limitations were removed. Comparing the growth rates, we can see that they increase with more trade liberalization.

Comparing the export of coir and coir products to the overall export from India, it was evident that the total exports increased faster than the export of coir and coir products during the MFA's installation and phase-out, when there were quantitative restrictions on the export of fiber. Nonetheless, exports of coir and coir-derived products grow faster than total exports throughout ATC. Stated differently, the export performance was negatively impacted by trade regulations that were too restrictive.

Exportation Trends

Previous research has shown that the coir industry does better when trade obstacles are removed. New industrial technologies brought forth by expanded free trade raised productivity and creation of cutting-edge items. The coir industry's performance was enhanced by all of these. But if we focus on Kerala's coir industry, we see that it cannot benefit from trade liberalization or knowledge transfer. This is due to the fact that it is a State industry that has historically found it challenging to adopt modern production technologies for a number of reasons. Consequently, adjacent States such as Tamil Nadu and Karnataka seized upon these technical innovations and began the coir industry. New items powered by technology therefore entered the market and took the lead in the export basket. Kerala's proportion of the total coir export falls as a consequence, while the other states' portion rises.

Table 4. The composition of Indian coir export during each reform period can be examined to analyze this

MFA period				Phase out of MFA				ATC period			
1995-1996		2003-2004		2005-2006		2010-2011		2015-2016		2019-2020	
Q	V	Q	V	Q	V	Q	V	Q	V	Q	V
Coir Yarn (56.72)	Coir Yarn (50.25)	Handloom mats (46.02)	Handloom mats (56.35)	Handloom mats (45.42)	Handloom mats (50.99)	Handloom mats (40.29)	Handloom mats (60.75)	Coir pith (40.32)	Handloom mats (55.58)	Coir pith (57)	Coir pith (43.6)
Handloom mats (29.08)	Handloom mats (39.91)	Coir yarn (38.63)	Coir yarn (24.38)	Coir yarn (32.78)	Handloom matting (27.54)	Coir pith (27.05)	Tufted mats (10.89)	Handloom mats (33.56)	Tufted mats (23.85)	Coir fibre (38.73)	Coir fibre (29.8)
Handloom mating (9.78)	Handloom mating (12.05)	Handloom matting (16.78)	Handloom matting (19.81)	Handloom matting (17.85)	Coir yarn (18.7)	Coir yarn (14.64)	Handloom matting (11.26)	Tufted mats (16.53)	Coir pith (8.65)	Tufted mats (6.7)	Tufted mats (21.5)
Coir rugs and carpets (5.89)	Coir rugs and carpets (7.86)	Coir rugs and carpets (6.41)	Coir rugs and carpets (8.45)	Coir rugs and carpets (6.45)	Coir rugs and carpets (11.04)	Tufted mats (8.65)	Coir yarn (9.6)	Coir yarn (8.05)	Coir yarn (7.56)	Handloom mats (2.9)	Handloom mats (9.5)
Curled coir (3.96)	Curled coir (1.69)	Curled coir (2.87)	Rubberised coir (1.88)	Curled coir (4.67)	Coir other sorts (1.86)	Handloom matting (7.68)	Coir pith (6.53)	Handloom matting (3.15)	Handloom matting (5.78)	Geo-textioles (1.7)	Geo-textioles (2.5)

The distribution of the different products produced by the coir industry in terms of overall exports is shown by the export pattern. This was also investigated in different reform times. Table No. 4.2 lists the top five items by value and quantity of all coir product exports over different trade liberalization periods. The table displaying the top five coir export commodities illustrates how different trade reforms have affected the composition of coir exports. During the early phases of the MFA, handloom mats trailed in second place in terms of value (50.25) and quantity (56.72) of coir yarn exports. This has just reversed throughout the most recent MFA eras. Handloom mats are the most popular product at this moment, ranking first in terms of quantity (46.02) and price (56.35), followed by coir yarn. This explains the increase in export value during this period of quantitative restrictions. Stated differently, the mix of exports changed as a consequence of quantitative constraints, favoring a greater number of completed goods with value addition.

Handloom mat exports have outpaced coir exports over the whole MFA phase-out. At the outset, handloom mats accounted for 50.99 percent of the overall value and 45.42 percent of the entire quantity. During the MFA phase-out periods, the ratio of handloom mats to all coir exports rises to 40.29% and 60.75% in terms of value. Value-added goods also prevailed at this time due to numerous quantitative restrictions to preserve our export profits expansion. It should be mentioned, nonetheless, that coir pith, a product with superior technology, comes in second place in terms of quantity and fifth place in terms of value. Due to the usage of traditional manufacturing techniques that resulted in serious environmental problems, this product only passes through one stage of manufacture and is handled as garbage. When we include the ATC, coir pith ranks first in terms of quantity and third in terms of value in the early eras. However, the fact that coir pith has become the most valuable and abundant product in the last year is a significant development. It should be noted that the primary raw material for coir products, coir fiber, ranks second in terms of both quantity and value. Since Kerala is primarily focused on the product sector and direct exports of raw materials, it does not profit from this change in the export pattern. Consequently, raw resources are expensive and in short supply. This has led to worse conditions for Kerala's coir industry.

CONCLUSION

Any nation's export performance is influenced, either directly or indirectly, by a wide range of national and international variables. The worldwide export of fiber and items connected to fiber is impacted by the aforementioned trade changes. An empirical analysis of export data for the chosen sector may indicate that export performance is enhanced by more liberal trade regulations. The above claim was supported by a comparison of India's exports. Because of the transfer of technologies, it also led to a rise in product diversity. The majority of those who stand to gain from these developments do so. When Kerala controlled this field, it accomplished significantly more.

REFERENCES

Indu, K. (2015). An Inquiry in to the Changing Market Conditions for Coir Products. *Proceedings of Development Seminar, IV International Kerala Studies Congress 2015*. Research Gate.

Issac, T. (2017). *Kerala Coir: The Agenda for Modernisation*, National Coir Research and Management Institute, Thiruvananthapuram.

Kumaraswamy, P. M. (2015). Marketing of Traditional Coir Products- Problems and Prospects. *Proceedings of Development Seminar, IV International Kerala Studies Congress 2015*. Research Gate.

Portugal-Perez, A. & Wilson, J. (2010). *Export Performance and Trade Facilitation Reform: Hard and Soft Infrastructure*. (Policy Research working paper No. 5261). World Bank.

Sahni, P. (2014). Trends in Indias Exports: A comparative Study of Pre and Post Reform Period. *IOSR Journal of Economics and Finance, 3*.

Chapter 11
Instagram and Body Dysmorphia

Lakshmy Ravindran
Amrita Vishwa Vidyapeetham, Kochi, India

P. Ravindranath
Amrita Vishwa Vidyapeetham, Kochi, India

ABSTRACT

Studies have shown that excessive use of Instagram can lead to feelings of inadequacy and low self- esteem as individuals compare themselves to the carefully curated and edited lives of others. Additionally, the constant exposure to unrealistic beauty standards and idealised lifestyles on Instagram can contribute to body dissatisfaction and distort one's perception of reality, creating unrealistic beauty standards, unattainable for most people. This can further fuel feelings of inadequacy and self-doubt, impacting mental health and overall well-being. Negative ideas and perceptions of our physical bodies, as well as issues with body image, can cause significant distress and have serious psychological and medical effects. Body dysmorphia and eating disorders were linked to a high level of social media addiction. Educating users about the importance of setting boundaries and practicing self-care while using Instagram can help mitigate its negative effects on mental well-being.

INTRODUCTION

Over the past few years, Instagram has become popular among Indian social media users. It is the second platform in the market after Facebook. Many statistics from numerous sources show that Instagram is the most used in India. As of May 2023, Instagram accounts for over 38% of all social messaging in India. This is a marked increase from the previous year. Indian users spend an average of 2.4 hours a day on social media; This is below the global average of 2.5 hours per day. Today, due to the increase in mobile phone sales and usage, most social media channels are accessed via mobile phones. Today, there are 290 million social media users in India who spend most of their screen time on various social networking sites. Interestingly, the main age group on these platforms are teenagers. 31% of all social

DOI: 10.4018/979-8-3693-2215-4.ch011

media users in India are young people aged 13-19 (Statista, 2021). The main users of Facebook and Instagram in India are between the ages of 18-24. This shows that these platforms are designed to suit the needs of young people. Facebook has 97.2 million users among this group of young people. There are 69 million Instagram users from India alone, most of whom are Millennials and Generation Z users (Chakola, A, 2022).

As we all know, social media affects many things, both good and bad, especially the Indian youth. While social media usage increased by 70% in the first five months of the epidemic, the news shared by users on various platforms such as Instagram, Facebook and Twitter increased by 45% during this period. Therefore, it is clear that this dependence has increased considerably in a short time at the time of the pandemic.

Pooja (not her real name) started using Instagram at a young age and found it useful. She used the photo-sharing app as a powerful influencer, but her relationship with the platform turned into an issue with body image. She was diagnosed with an eating disorder when she was 19 years old. "I feel like my body is not good enough because even though I go to the gym regularly, my body is still not as good as influencers," says Pooja, who is now 20 years old and recovering.

Recent research shows that social media such as Instagram and Facebook intentionally create psychological and body image issues for young users, especially teenagers. Many of these physical problems can develop into eating disorders such as anorexia nervosa, bulimia nervosa, and binge eating disorder. Young people are more at risk of getting affected. Physical change makes young people less likely to participate, which has many health effects: They are stressed and often compete with other friends who do it for 'keeping up with the joneses.

This is probably not surprising considering how many people there are. Social media users choose a "perfect" version of their lives to which everyone can compare themselves. Teens on Instagram are constantly bombarded with images of the "perfect" body. These images are everywhere, from Instagram feeds to ads to Search pages, and they create unrealistic and often impossible ideas. It is not surprising that young people use these terms to the extent that they struggle with body dissatisfaction, frustration, lack of self-confidence, depression, stress and many other problems.

Body Dysmorphic Disorder

According to the Mayo Clinic, body dysmorphic disorder (also known as body dysmorphia) is a psychological disorder in which a person becomes obsessed with one or more body features, or lack thereof. These shortcomings are minor differences that mostly happen to people with a not so-perfect body, or they are "disadvantages" that cannot be accepted by others. It is important to remember that body dysmorphic disorder cannot be easily prevented by other people telling the affected person that they are beautiful or that they do not see their flaws as seriously as they think. While there are many factors, such as family history or a person's brain structure, social and aesthetic expectations can aggravate, according to the Mayo Clinic. Now let's go to the most popular photo platform: Instagram.

Negative Effects of Instagram on Teenagers

Instagram is a mobile photo sharing site that allows users to edit and share photos and videos. Instagram users often post photos as content and can like, comment or repost other users' photos. In recent years, research has increasingly focused on the impact of social media on women's body image. These studies show that participation in social media can lead to negative health effects for young female users, such as poor sleep, lack of self-confidence, increased anxiety and depression, lack of interest and negative emotions, and increased risk of body dissatisfaction and underweight. Many believe that these problems are just faced by females. Because of this thought, male users of social media may not be aware of the impact of social media on them, because men see body image as a women's problem and therefore reject their physical concerns because they do not want to share them in public as it may make them appear tender, or weak.

A 2019 report found that almost half of Instagram influencers surveyed said their work as influencers affected their health, and 32% reported negative body image. In another study conducted in 2017, Instagram was evaluated as the most dangerous social media for young people's health. Instagram (and other photo- and video-based apps like Snapchat and TikTok) offer filters and lenses that can change a person's appearance. Instagram's filters, along with other apps that make it easier to remove blemishes and alter body image, have made it easier for users to view the photos flowing through their feeds as true to reality. Additionally, Instagram is often seen as a place to show off your "essence" when you look your best and do fun things. Although there are some accounts and models that try to balance this out, when viewers see that the reality of what they see on the screen is up to the person behind the account, it gives them the impression of life – with all its ups, downs and not just perfect skin and body.

The negative impact of image changes does not only come from other people. If you frequently see edited photos of yourself, this may also make you feel like there's something wrong with your face and body. A study by psychologist Phillippa Diedrichs and the Dove Self-Esteem Project found that 60% of girls feel insecure because their appearance doesn't match their online photos.

The ease with which people can see slightly "better" versions of themselves and the culture that places positive value on physical features have real consequences in the world: The rise of face filters has led to an increase in the number of searchers, assisted plastic surgery, where people ask plastic surgeons to match their face to their filter.

What is often missing from the discussion of body dysmorphia and ideas of beauty is awareness of how the body can support these ideas and how these ideas endow the body with capabilities. If you have a visual impairment that makes you look different from what Western culture considers beautiful, it can be difficult to feel physically at home. This also has a negative impact on many marginalized people. Beauty standards generally look at the colour white and the features of white people as the best standard and do not view dark complexion as desirable.

In addition to body dysmorphia, Instagram perpetuates fatphobia (discrimination or hatred of body fat) by focusing on women with slim "Instagram bodies" altered by cosmetic exercises and technology. These "Instagram bodies" are mostly women with a balanced body, such as the difference between small hips, big hips, thin legs and thighs. The app has been criticized for censoring or "shadowbanning" content from fat people or plus creators (especially people of colour or other races), while also allowing these designers to share similar content without interruption.

Yes, behaviour that makes people - especially women - feel like there's something wrong with their body and needs treatment, that makes us cry, that causes acne or a growing waistline, is perpetuated and fuelled by consumer businesses that make money by exploiting insecure people. The Indian cosmetics market is expected to be $1.35 billion by 2023 and reach $2.27 million by 2028, growing at a compound annual growth rate (CAGR) of 10.91% during the forecast period (2023-2028), according to marketing intelligence platform, Mordor intelligence. Recognizing that the pressures of social relationships create great results for these businesses can help us understand that our bodies are okay, as we see in the disability model.

There are many (similar) real photos on Instagram, many of which represent the ideal body. In fact, this phenomenon plays an important role on Instagram; Research suggests that teens and young adults may feel anxious, dissatisfied with their bodies, and openly pressured to look good in a relationship, especially in the face of differing opinions. Since Instagram gives users the opportunity to edit their content before publishing it on their profiles, users tend to engage in self-disclosing behaviour. In their interviews with 24 young women in Singapore, researchers Chua and Chang found that in order to please their fans, social media users will satisfy expectations and be preferred by presenting options on their own. Self-expression among young women focuses on many aspects of the body and ideas of beauty. The main reason for self-promotion is the desire to attract attention with your words, especially from friends. But advertising isn't the most popular activity on Instagram. In fact, teenagers and young Instagram users often see and "like" content on other people's profiles. A long-term study found that looking at other users' best photos led to more depression over time.

A Facebook survey of young Instagram users in the US and UK found that more than 40 percent of those who said they felt "unattractive" said the feeling started while using Instagram. A study by Facebook executives concluded that Instagram was designed to be more "social" than rival apps such as TikTok and Snapchat. While TikTok focused more on business, Snapchat focused on fun filters that "focused on the face." In contrast, Instagram focuses mainly on the bodies and lifestyles of its users.

Teens told Facebook researchers they felt "harmed" by Instagram and wanted to control it less, but didn't have the self-control to control their use. An internal study published by Facebook in 2019 stated that "young people blame Instagram for increasing the rate of anxiety and depression" and that "this response is personal and consistent across all groups." It found that young people were persuaded to commit suicide.

Body concerns and unhealthy eating habits are on the rise for both women and men in many developing countries. Eating disorders are the leading cause of death in men due to mental illness, with 400,000 men suffering from them in the UK alone. Eating disorders will affect 10 million men in the United States at some point in their lives.

The media is often accused of making young men feel bad about their bodies. On image-based social media such as Instagram, consumers' bodies are constantly seen and scrutinized. Given the popularity of social media among young people and the power of image-based content shared by users, it is important to examine how these new channels affect body emotions and behaviours, especially for emotional users and healthy.

The Role of Upward Comparison

Viewing, commenting, and sharing on Instagram may not be directly related to body dissatisfaction, but it is, as evidenced by comparing teens in the Facebook data report. According to the tripartite model of body dissatisfaction and eating disorders, adolescents are influenced by three elements: parents, friends, and the media. As primary social caregivers, parents have an impact on their daughters' body image and self-esteem, which may result from direct or indirect comments about weight or appearance. As children grow and enter adolescence, friends become more important than physical issues, especially when relationships and adjustment are still held ransom by fear of approval from others. Teens learn from their peers what body image is associated with popularity and attractiveness. Finally, the media plays an important role because in the media, women are often shown as attractive and having the perfect body, which can lead to body anxiety in people who see them.

Previous research has shown that some social networks, such as Instagram, can lead to emotional deficits due to social comparisons. From the perspective of comparison theory, in the absence of objective self-evaluation, people will evaluate themselves by comparing themselves to others. You can do this by comparing upward and downward. Higher comparison occurs when people compare themselves to those who are better. The word "better" can refer to different characteristics, including appearance. The huge collection of photos, videos and stories on Instagram gives users many opportunities to compare themselves with others. Research shows that social comparisons directly lead to more comparisons of "opinions" and negative thoughts about one's body image. In the study, Brown and Tiggemann found that viewing photos on Instagram showing attractive and thin celebrities and friends was associated with greater body dissatisfaction, mediated by social comparison. Similarly, Kleman et al. Research has shown that doctored Instagram photos may have a negative impact on young women's body image; This is an effect that contradicts the comparison. The number of followers, the number of "likes" and the number of comments on photos or videos provide useful information about other people's interests and will therefore lead to the formation of values for evaluating oneself in comparison with others. In fact, a study has shown that the more "likes" there are, the more people want to be attractive to that person, and the more comparison and body dissatisfaction there is. Finally, while comparison with the ideal image leads to higher levels of body dissatisfaction, comparison of the ideal image with the real image leads to a decrease in body dissatisfaction. The best Instagram photos are often associated with positive emotions, which are characteristic of negative relationships.

Friends as Targets of Comparison

Many photos and stories on Instagram are posted by friends. Research shows that women tend to imitate their peers better to feel part of the group. Participants said they were more likely to follow friends who rated them positively and had the most "likes" on social media. When talking about friends, it is important to distinguish between close and distant friends. In fact, previous research has shown that the interaction between attractive distant friends is more dangerous than interaction with close friends; The main reason for this is that young women are attracted to having relationships with unknown perfect faces.

Social Media Influencers for Comparison

Like Friends, Instagram allows users to connect directly with people they wouldn't normally know, such as social media influencers. Influencers are individuals who have been able to establish a strong presence online through the use of regular posts and the ability to create communities on their social media accounts. An example of this is Kim Kardashian, one of the most respected women on Instagram. As of September 2023, she has 369 million followers on Instagram. Kardashian's photo always made her look "perfect" and very attractive. For this reason, she was criticized because the high self-confidence she expressed could harm young women who felt they were not that strong.

Although social media, and Instagram in particular, are often accused of voluntarily or involuntarily disseminating attractive body images, little research to date has examined the relationship between female influencers' views on Instagram and female body image. Brown and Tiggemann conducted the first study of this kind and showed that women appearing in photos shared by the most popular people on Instagram were associated with greater body dissatisfaction. Similar results were found in a recent study by Lowe-Calverley and Grieve, who compared Instagram influencers' top photos in terms of high and low ratings (i.e., likes, number of followers). The authors found that ideal image led to greater body dissatisfaction, regardless of the value of the popularity factor. But the best visuals are accompanied not only by these indicators, but also by words that represent the viewer's interest. Hu points out that image-related comments like "success" or "body goals" can directly affect women's self-esteem. Sad Emotions about the actual body, cause one to experience negative feelings about one's own body.

Eating Disorders

Eating Disorder (ED) is associated with a heavy burden of treatment worldwide for a variety of mental illnesses that affect the quality of life of patients and their families and cause high mortality rates. This disease is generally described as occurring in young women, but in recent years male patients have also developed symptoms of ED. Overestimation of thinness is common in Western countries and is considered an important factor contributing to the onset of ED. The consequences of urbanization and globalization have slowed the spread of these diseases in India due to cultural changes.

Eating disorders will increase with the use of social media. Study after study shows that social media use is linked to an increased risk of eating disorders. Since there has been research on the relationship between body image and eating disorders, a review of this research was also conducted. A review of 67 studies on the subject was published in 2015. What were the results? Internet use, especially social media, is associated with increased body image and eating disorders. Developmental characteristics may make young people particularly vulnerable to these effects.

Mental Health/Mood

Depression, low self-esteem, feeling anxious, and body dissatisfaction are all linked to Instagram use. One study examined frequency of Instagram use and found that it was associated with all negative outcomes. Sharing selfies can be emotionally draining. A study published in 2018 found that college-aged women who took and shared selfies had lower self-esteem and felt less attractive. Interestingly, these negative results occurred even when participants were allowed to remember and recall the images.

Cosmetic Surgery on the Rise

A survey conducted by the American Society of Plastic Surgeons in 2021 found that almost half of patients reported that social media played a role in their decision to seek plastic surgery. To improve psychological body image, people try different diets, exercises, or plastic surgery. Dissatisfaction with the outcome can persuade people to seek interventions such as plastic surgery to improve their appearance. Selfies are frequently used in advertising, and their popularity has led to increased awareness of people's appearance. This has led to an increased demand for plastic surgery to enhance content such as future selfies. Cosmetic surgery is a professional profession that focuses on improving or altering a person's face through surgery and treatment. The global demand for cosmetic surgery has increased significantly over the last few years. According to the American Society of Plastic Surgeons (ASPS), approximately 17 million plastic surgeries were performed in 2016.

The total annual cost of these surgeries is approximately 16.4 billion dollars. In a study conducted by the International Society of Aesthetic Plastic Surgery (ISAPS), it was stated that Saudi Arabia ranked 29th among the 30 countries with the highest plastic surgery costs in the world. From 2012 to 2016, cosmetic procedures for men and women increased by 58%. Most of these surgeries (92%) were performed on women; Rhinoplasty (nose aesthetic surgery) was one of the top five surgeries between 2015 and 2016. There is a growth in facial surgery trends and advertising. intervention, treatment progression, and patient characteristics. Media exposure, particularly through satellite television, has been influenced by the prevalence of rhinoplasty surgery. Research shows that increased media exposure, low self-esteem, and dissatisfaction with life can lead to plastic surgery.

According to ISAPS, India ranks fourth with plastic surgery accounting for 4.3% of all surgeries worldwide! According to research volume data, the most popular type of cosmetic surgery in India as of January 2021 is hair transplantation, with over 30,000 cases per month. Liposuction and rhinoplasty followed, with more than 20,000 and 19,000 results.

Anxious Brain Activity

The brain changes with "likes". One study examined brain activity associated with Instagram "likes" in young adults using fMRI brain imaging. fMRI is an imaging technique that can detect changes in blood flow in different parts of the brain and show areas of brain activity. When participants saw more attractive pictures, their brain activity increased. When one's self-image is liked, the brain's reward center is activated.

The search for sophistication increases with Instagram use. In particular, one study found that looking at articles focusing on likes (models, bloggers) led to a greater desire to lose weight. Viewing other types of ads will not have the same effect.

Photo Manipulation

Photo manipulation can cause body image issues. A 2016 study titled "Best Picture: Direct Effects of Using Instagram Photos on Body Image in Teens" found that checking Instagram posts had a negative impact on young women. Since taking photos is so easy for doctors these days, this study examined the effects of looking at Instagram photos of friends who managed to get rid of eye bags, wrinkles and dirt and repair their legs to have slimmer legs and a slim waist. The results showed that exposure to doctored Instagram photos directly led to the loss of personal photos.

Suicidal Thoughts

A review of nine studies on relationships and suicide found that online relationships continue to increase self-harm because users participate in and receive negative messages that encourage self-harm and violent behavior towards others. Social networking sites are more associated with anxiety, less need for mental health support, less self-confidence and more suicidal thoughts.

Solutions

There are ways to protect your health and protect your mental health while still using Instagram and other social networking media.

1. Diversifying your feed is a good step: This not only helps you maintain your mental health, but also expands your horizons. This means deliberately targeting influencers who seek to challenge narrow aesthetic ideas. Many Indian influencers, models and celebrities support body positivity. They encourage inclusion and self-love by sharing their experiences and putting body shame aside. At the same time, social media influencers advocate for the representation of all body part in advertising and fashion. Dolly Singh is a popular media personality who started her career in film and fashion and soon stepped into showbiz. She has appeared in many online shows and even appeared in a commercial for the popular Colgate toothpaste. Despite this fame, Singh faced body shaming for being too thin. She often calls out bullying on Instagram, where she has 1.6 million followers. Dolly admits to being a fashionista, and her weight hasn't stopped her from wearing the things she loves.

   Tanvi, known as "Thechubbytwiler", has 199,000 followers on Instagram. She is a social media influencer on a mission to eliminate weight stigma. Tanvi is also a plus-size model and her fashion sense is evident on her Instagram page. Her bikini photos created quite a stir and went viral on the internet.

2. **The next step is information.** Being more mindful when using social media means paying more attention to your body and mind when you use social media, and how you feel when you consume content from people like you. If you're feeling stressed or depressed, give yourself a break from social media if necessary for your mental health.
3. **Social media literacy interventions**. This can help teenage girls avoid unhealthy consumption habits. The search for a connection between unhealthy eating habits and social media is so strong that scientists are working on a solution. One group found that an intervention that educates teenage girls about social media and its risks may reduce the risk of eating disorders.
4. **Reducing social media. Cutting down screen time** can reduce loneliness and depression. A group of researchers asked a group of undergraduate students to reduce their media use over three weeks. The group that reduced social media use reported less loneliness and depression than the control group.

CONCLUSION

According to the Wall Street Journal, 22 million young Americans use Instagram every day, and more than 40% of Instagram users are 22 years old and younger. It is important that we use all available resources to understand the impact of relationships on health.

Instagram's impact on issues like colourism is not widely discussed. In recent years, a worldwide effort has been made to eliminate these problems. Using Instagram should be seen as a pleasure, not a need. People should know that things on social media are often not about reality or just a representation and should not be used to compare with others. This year, Unilever decided to remove the word "Fair" from the "Fair & Lovely" brand (Odishatv Bureau, 2020). The Indian government has also made clear changes to the penalties to be imposed on any group that advertises or promotes counterfeit drugs or products under the Drugs and Substances Act, 1954.

Influencers are often viewed as role models especially by young people. They are often seen as the embodiment of success, fame and beauty. This has led to the rise of "desirable" content, in which celebrities present their lavish lifestyles and promote products that promise to make them popular.

But content promoted by influencers is not always good or healthy. Many influencers promote unrealistic body images, which can lead to body dissatisfaction and unhealthy eating habits among their followers. They also promote products and consumers, encouraging people to buy things they don't need or can't afford.

In addition to encouraging negative behaviour, influencers can also negatively impact young people's mental health. Social media platforms are designed to be defensive, and many teens spend hours scrolling through their feeds, comparing themselves to others and feeling inadequate. Content selected and edited by influencers can create a false impression of authenticity and leave young people feeling like they are not living up to the best version of themselves they see by their peers or online.

It is important to know that influencers are not bad or negative. Many use their platforms to promote positive messages such as body positivity, mental health awareness, and social justice. However, it is important to pay attention to the content we use and question the motivation behind it. We must not forget the fact that influencers are often paid to promote products and their content may not be accurate.

Parents and instructors are also responsible for assisting teenagers in navigating the world of social media. By educating young people media literacy skills, we can help them analyse the content they consume and make educated choices about what content to utilise.

Teens must strike a balance between social media and the rest of their lives. Help them make time for face-to-face interactions, outdoor activities, hobbies, and other vital endeavours. Encourage them to use social media as an addition to their offline life, rather as a replacement for it. The following are some useful reminders about how to use social media and technology properly in order to maximise the great benefits it may provide.

- Develop and manage your real-life relationships and experiences.
- Make an honest assessment of your usage. How much do you use social media, and why?
- Be yourself, and be friendly!
- Set limitations and take breaks. For example, no posting during school time, turning off the phone or keeping it in another room while sleeping, and establishing "technology-free" guidelines with friends and family members.
- Do not share your passwords with friends.
- Learn about privacy settings and check them frequently.
- Utilise social reporting policies and websites.
- Always think before posting.
- If you are a parent, monitor and limit your children's and teenagers' social media use, have open discussions about the benefits and risks, and model appropriate social media and technology use yourself.

Teenagers must learn to be accountable for their social media use because you cannot always monitor their social media accounts. You can't be there to tell them how much time to spend on social media, who they should interact with, and so on. Younger people sometimes struggle to appreciate long-term risks and rewards. This is not limited to social media. Many kids are unable to comprehend the negative aspects of social media due to the culture of rapid gratification. That is the bad news.

The good news is that you can use social media properly. Teenagers simply need to get accustomed to it. If utilised correctly, social media may be an effective learning tool. Consider consuming chocolate; there is a significant difference between the first delicious mouthful and diabetes. However, it is easy to start chewing and then forget to stop before it is too late.

Rules for Responsible Use of Social Media

Rules may differ in each household, based on your values and child. However, there are a few general guidelines to follow while teaching your child about social media responsibilities.

Controlling Time on the Screen

Children have the right to screen time, but you can limit it. The amount of screen time allowed might be determined by your teenager's level of responsibility. For example, if they do their homework, no limit is appropriate; however, if they are easily distracted, a screen time limit may be necessary.

Avoiding Sharing Personal Data

Teenagers' social concerns in the age of the internet can make sharing information with their friends simpler than with their relatives. However, kids may not always be aware of the risks of sharing personal information with others over the internet.

This personal information may be disclosed explicitly, such as telling strangers their entire name, or indirectly, such as uploading a picture of their home on Instagram. It is important to explain to your child what they should not post on Instagram or other social media platforms. It's not a bad idea to discuss how much privacy a teenager should have on the internet.

Bullying

It is not impossible for your youngster to bully someone. This can happen by accident. Teenagers are growing up in a digital world and are becoming accustomed to being anonymous. They may have un-intentionally damaged others' feelings. Or, worse, they may say hurtful things since they don't realise how much it will affect their peer. Check to see what their response is to how social media influences teenagers' self-esteem.

In summary, social media influencers can have a good or bad influence on the minds of young people. While we need to be aware of the risks that may arise, we must also recognize that influential people can be a source of inspiration and a good example. By promoting media literacy and positive thinking, we can help young people navigate the media world in a healthy and productive way.

REFERENCES

Ajayi, G. (2022). *Influence Of Instagram On Young Adults'perception Of Self: A Study Of Students Of Mountain Top University.*

Brown, Z., & Tiggemann, M. (2016). Attractive celebrity and peer images on Instagram: Effect on women's mood and body image. *Body Image*, *19*, 37–43. doi:10.1016/j.bodyim.2016.08.007 PMID:27598763

Chakola, A. (2022). *The Impact of Social Media Influencer on the Buying Behaviour of Gen Z in India* [Doctoral dissertation, Dublin, National College of Ireland].

Chang, L., Li, P., Loh, R. S. M., & Chua, T. H. H. (2019). A study of Singapore adolescent girls' selfie practices, peer appearance comparisons, and body esteem on Instagram. *Body Image*, *29*, 90–99. doi:10.1016/j.bodyim.2019.03.005 PMID:30884385

Dar, S. A., & Nagrath, D. (2023). The Impact That Social Media Has Had On Today's Generation Of Indian Youth: An Analytical Study. *Morfai Journal, 3*(2), 166-176.

Kleemans, M., Daalmans, S., Carbaat, I., & Anschütz, D. (2018). Picture perfect: The direct effect of manipulated Instagram photos on body image in adolescent girls. *Media Psychology*, *21*(1), 93–110. doi:10.1080/15213269.2016.1257392

Lowe-Calverley, E. (2019). *Picture perfect: a mixed-methods analysis of engagement with image-based social media content* [Doctoral dissertation, University Of Tasmania].

Rodgers, R. F., & Melioli, T. (2016). The relationship between body image concerns, eating disorders and internet use, part I: A review of empirical support. *Adolescent Research Review*, *1*(2), 95–119. doi:10.1007/s40894-015-0016-6

Sharma, A., Sanghvi, K., & Churi, P. (2022). The impact of Instagram on young Adult's social comparison, colourism and mental health: Indian perspective. *International Journal of Information Management Data Insights*, *2*(1), 100057. doi:10.1016/j.jjimei.2022.100057

Van den Berg, P., Thompson, J. K., Obremski-Brandon, K., & Coovert, M. (2002). The tripartite influence model of body image and eating disturbance: A covariance structure modeling investigation testing the mediational role of appearance comparison. *Journal of Psychosomatic Research*, *53*(5), 1007–1020. doi:10.1016/S0022-3999(02)00499-3 PMID:12445590

Weinstein, E., & James, C. (2022). *Behind their screens: What teens are facing (and adults are missing).* MIT Press. doi:10.7551/mitpress/14088.001.0001

Chapter 12
Marketing 5.0 and the Role of Mind Mapping in Content Advertising:
An Analysis

Navreet Kaur
Chitkara Business School, Chitkara University, India

Preeti Kaushal
School of Business Studies, Chitkara University, India

ABSTRACT

Two factors viz. technology and consumer needs are the main drivers of the marketing evolution referred to as Marketing 5.0. The business philosophy in the present phase of marketing is about a confluence between technology and humanity. The chapter entails a focus on how technology aids human marketers and advertisers to create content and the subsequent emotional experience of consumers. The emphasis primarily is on mind mapping – a dynamic visual representation of a group of ideas clustered around and linked to a single central topic; a tool to unleash creative impulses. The main themes are high-level ideas that radiate from the central image as 'branches' and result in content creation such as slogans and taglines, formulating of marketing strategies, and building of a brand identity. A discussion on transformation in the field of content marketing over the years, the benefits and drawbacks of AI-assisted content creation and the ethical challenges in AI-powered marketing is an integral part of the chapter.

INTRODUCTION

Content marketing as a marketing strategy is an integral part of content advertising (Team, 2015). Content marketing became popular after the advent of the internet and today, it is primarily on digital platforms. It is the practice of creating and disseminating valuable, authentic and relevant content to attract and engage a target audience. The ultimate goal is to generate gainful consumer action. According to Carmicheal

DOI: 10.4018/979-8-3693-2215-4.ch012

(2021), the goal of content marketing is to provide value to the audience by educating, entertaining, or inspiring them, rather than directly promoting a product or service. It is similar to "pull marketing" or inbound marketing where the customer is attracted to the product or service. "Push marketing" is a strategy focused on "pushing" products to a specific audience and is similar to content advertising. Also called "organic marketing", content marketing uses non-paid marketing tactics to reach an online audience. For example, a marketing professional at a travel company may write travel blogs to generate interest of prospective customers in the services offered by the enterprise and to motivate them to embark upon an exciting journey. On the other hand, paid marketing or content advertising requires the company to spend money to promote their brand or message. One way of Content advertising is Pay-Per-Click (PPC) where advertisers pay a fee to the search engine or website owner whenever an advertisement is clicked. It is a targeted reach for immediate visibility. Sales may be low despite high Click-Through Rate (CTR) because of poorly designed landing page or people clicking out of curiosity. Content marketing is a low cost solution that helps build visibility but takes time. Organic search results in higher quality leads and better conversions than those bought with PPC.

Inbound marketing, branded content, and storytelling are some of the strategies associated with content marketing. The techniques primarily involve luring potential customers, influencing and inspiring them with useful material rather than annoying them with unwelcome advertisements. Storytelling, an impactful marketing strategy, is based on the premise that brands that tell more sell more. Stories contain a larger narrative that can be communicated through films, pictures, verbally or in written form. Shirmohammadi (2023) talks about the power of storytelling – a marketing tool leaving a lasting emotional impact and fostering customer loyalty. Visual elements, in particular, enrich a narrative that aligns with brand values leading to a strong CTA (Call to Action) and consequently a deeper engagement of the audience with the brand. Few examples are Nike's 'Just Do It' campaign aimed at sports enthusiasts by featuring inspiring stories of athletes; Dove's field experiment serving as a campaign focussed on breaking the traditional beliefs held by women about beauty. Through the "Real Sketches" video, Dove promoted body image positivity and the customer segment connected to the statement: "You are more beautiful than you think."

EVOLUTION OF CONTENT MARKETING

Old methods of content marketing and advertising were primarily offline and did not employ social media or complex IT main frames. Television advertisements, radio advertising, print advertising, direct mail advertisements, billboards and off-site signs, cold calling, door-to-door sales, and banner ads are a few examples of traditional media. Forsey (2022) giving a detailed account of the evolution of content marketing in the past decade observes that content marketing is not static and will continue to transform. The paradigm shift in the nature of content marketing was the Zero Moment of Truth (ZMOT) study conducted by Google in 2011 which brought about the significance of how and why businesses need to focus on impactful, engaging and authentic marketing content. As per the study, 88% of shoppers at the outset of the buying cycle indulge in a thorough research about the product or service they need and word of mouth is a definitive factor at this stage. This led to the necessity of Search Engine Optimization (SEO) for a company's online presence and brand image.

The advancement of Web 2.0 led to the rise of social media marked by user-generated content and a two-way flow of information. Rise of the social media that involves a different kind of content consumption than a search engine is a disruptive trend in marketing and other areas of business. The primary difference is in terms of the mechanism by which the content reached the target audience. Search engine enables the consumer to find content more pointedly viz. by seeking specific information to particular keywords while social media allows users to consume content more passively. Facebook feed, for example, brings content to the doorstep of the consumer and also contains subconscious subliminal influences. In the era of Marketing 5.0, along with other trends, there is a change in the nature of the content: sharable, attention grabbing and spreading across fast through the digital medium. Videos are in vogue since these are easier to follow as compared to blog posts, email newsletters or ebooks. Content marketing came into existence much before modern advertising and it is the changing cultural and consumer mindset coupled with technological advances that have led to its evolution in terms of new formats and platforms (Burt, 2023). Modern day examples of content marketing include:

i.   Blogging: A company may create a blog that provides informative articles on a specific topic that its target audience is interested in.
ii.   Video marketing: A company may create educational or entertaining videos to showcase its products or services, or to engage with its audience.
iii. Social media: A company may use social media platforms to share interesting and relevant content, such as news articles, blog posts, infographics, and videos that its followers would find valuable.
iv.   E-books and whitepapers: A company may create in-depth guides or reports that provide valuable information to its target audience.
v.   Podcasting: A company may create a podcast series that discusses industry news, provides expert insights, or offers tips and advice on a particular topic.
vi.   Infographics: A company may create infographics that visually represent data or information in an easily understandable and shareable format.
vii. Email marketing: A company may send out newsletters or promotional emails that provide valuable information or offer to its subscribers.

A study by Conductor – a reputed technology company – revealed that when deciding between 4 brands, 83.6% of consumers who read a piece of educational content chose the brand to purchase. AI in content creation can be used for generating ideas and analyzing audience engagement. AI tools use natural language processing (NLP) and natural language generation (NLG) techniques to learn from existing data and produce content that matches user preferences. Artificial intelligence, including generative AI, is used in advertising today to do everything from generating ad creative to optimizing ad budgets and predicting advertising campaign performance. Sentiment analysis is the process of analyzing digital text to determine if the emotional tone of the message is positive, negative, or neutral. Today, companies have large volumes of text data like emails, customer support chat transcripts, social media comments, and reviews.

The significance of content creation, to a large extent, depends on the business strategy and consequently the marketing strategy. Branding, for instance, is an inseparable part of the differentiation business strategy which is based on the premise of 'brand loyalty'. Logos and taglines are a type of content that plays a critical role in helping the company not only to market its products but also in communicating its ethos and character. The impact of logos and taglines created through an AI generated mind map is much greater. There are four stages of the marketing funnel: 1) awareness, 2) consideration, 3) conversion, and 4) loyalty. A brand's goal in each stage is to 1) attract, 2) inform, 3) convert, and 4) engage customers. An appropriate logo helps fulfil these goals. AI has also been instrumental in disruptive advertising in this age of competition.

THE ORIGINATORS OF CONTENT MARKETING

Burt (2023) and <u>Walters</u> (2023) have given a detailed account of the historical landmarks in content marketing beginning with Benjamin Franklin (1732) who published Poor Richard's Almanack – a handbook essentially launched to promote his printing business. The alamanac – a precursor of modern content marketing – included calendars, weather forecasts, and astronomical data along with promotional content to generate interest of the readers in his business. In 1814 Galignani – publisher and owner of Librairie Galignani launched a newspaper <u>Galignani's Messenger</u>, containing articles by influential authors. This strategic move helped build the bookstore's reputation among the intellectual community and expanded their business coverage. Johnson & Johnson (1888) published industry-specific content by launching a manual entitled 'Modern Methods of Antiseptic Wound Treatment.' This was not only a first aid kit that educated doctors and patients alike but also a tool to help build the company's image.

In the 1920s, Procter & Gamble created radio content in an attempt to advertise their soap products. They sponsored daytime serials or radio dramas that integrated soap products into captivating storylines later known as "soap operas." The initiative entertained the listeners, familiarized them with P&G products and paved the way for future forms of content marketing. Mid-20th century saw the invention of television – a medium that enabled businesses to show their market presence. An example of this transformation is when Xerox in the 1960s utilized the television to introduce its innovative photocopier technology to a broad audience. Digital revolution ushered in with the emergence of Archie – the first search engine – in the 1990s which allowed users to search files on FTP (File Transfer Protocol) servers. Other technological breakthroughs that followed were advanced search engines like Google, 'banner advertising' marked by clickable creative ads on websites, and platforms like LinkedIn, MySpace, and Facebook. These platforms allowed businesses to connect with a broader user base on a relatively personal level leading to a social media explosion. The 'mobile era' began in early 2000s and mobile marketing emerged as a powerful force. Increasing popularity of mobile devices transformed the way people consumed digital media. BlogAds were a significant development in 2002 which was followed by podcasting which involved audio content in 2004. The global pandemic in 2020 accelerated the adoption of digital tools and strategies making it more critical than ever for businesses to stay connected with their customers.

MIND MAPPING

The mind map – a modern day content creation strategy – helps streamline and simplify the content creation process. It involves the linking of ideas and concepts leading to formation of relevant content. It is a diagrammatic representation typically showing the central concept, say marketing strategies, linked to sub concepts in the form of main strategies (viral marketing, branding, and content marketing) and specific strategies (event promotion, sponsorships, etc.). A mind map is a tree-like structure representing non-linear relationships between ideas and concepts which are not arranged by order or hierarchy.

Each idea is equally important and information is organized in a non linear fashion like in the brain (Cabrera, 2024).

Content creation through a mind map involved 4 steps:

i.   Choosing the main idea of interest or the starting point from where other ideas will branch out, for e.g. company strategy.
ii. Generating sub ideas associated with the central idea. Three ideas related to company strategy are marketing strategies, customer service strategies, and productivity strategies.
iii. Creating more sub-topics or elaborating the existing sub-topics. For example, three main strategies that are aspects of the company strategy lead to second order strategies such as trade shows, customer reviews and project management. Each of the ideas represents a node connected to other nodes through lines or branches.
iv. Including visual cues such as images, icons, graphics and colour-matching similar ideas to make the mind map comprehensible and attractive to the audience.

The role of a mind map in marketing is to plan and organize content planning through brainstorming. It involves idea generation to build brand identity, devise marketing strategies, define the target customer, and streamline the process of project management. A mind map is a kind of 'stream of consciousness' and a 'free association' of ideas that take the shape of words painted on a canvas to make a meaningful picture. People think as a team, thus, accelerating the ideation process; teams can be delegated tasks for project management. Visual thinking helps structure thoughts converting them into workable ideas that can be communicated effectively to various stakeholders. For example, website development includes presentation of ideas; content planning includes arriving at effective forms of media content and their merits as per needs. For building a brand identity, the mind map would include the following:

i.   Differentiation of the company from competitors
ii. Company image and reputation in the market
iii. Brand marketing strategies
iv. Measuring brand awareness
v.   Brand distribution

With regard to AI-powered content creation using a mind map, York (2024) has enlisted 10 AI tools used in 2024 to facilitate mind mapping; Coggle, Boardmix, Whimsical AI, GitMind, Lucidchart to name a few. He considers AI as 'a creative partner' of teams which helps find unique relationships and insights that the human eye might fail to detect, thus, going beyond human imagination and reshaping the creative process. A sound AI tool as per York (2024) must include the following features:

i.   Intuitive and easy to use interface
ii. Smart AI suggestions enabling gap-identification, connecting of ideas and a supply of keywords.
iii. Compatibility of the software with other digital platforms
iv. Features enabling robust collaboration with other team members
v.   Fair pricing

ETHICAL CHALLENGES IN AI-POWERED MARKETING

Marketing gurus define the fifth generation of marketing or Marketing 5.0 (M 5.0) as involving the use of technologies mimicking the human brain to create and communicate the value of products, services, and community upliftment to the target audience. According to Kotler et al. (2021) there are five components of marketing 5.0: it is data-driven, predictive, contextual, augmented, and agile.

Based on market research, Huang and Rust (2021b) developed a three-tiered classification of AI as deployed in marketing:

i. Mechanical AI entailing automation of repetitive and routine tasks and used for data collection (marketing research), segmentation (marketing strategy), and standardization (marketing action).
ii. Thinking AI for processing of data for new insights and decision-making as required in market analysis (marketing research), targeting (marketing strategy), and personalization (marketing action).
iii. Feeling AI referring to interactions with humans or analyzing human feelings and emotions employed for customer understanding (marketing research), positioning (marketing strategy), and relationization (marketing action).

Kaplan and Haenlein (2019) categorized AI applications according to the level of intelligence thus:

i. Analytical AI (cognitive intelligence)
ii. Human-inspired AI (cognitive and emotional intelligence)
iii. Humanized AI (cognitive, emotional, and social intelligence)

Empirical evidence (e.g., Belk, 2020; De Bruyn et al., 2020) shows that AI systems that are humanized or emotionally intelligent do not come without ethical controversies. In fact, ethics is a key issue that comes up when technology is used to solve human problems. There are certain crucial aspects for marketers to pay attention to while creating content through AI. The most important component in the marketing and advertising process is the customer; hence all questions of ethics revolve around him right from market research to formulating a strategy such as branding. The experience economy is marked by an era of the knowledge customer. Forrester researchers published two studies regarding technology management and competitive strategy in what they called, "The Age of the Customer." The Age of the Customer is a concept that states that modern consumers have significantly more influence over their purchasing behavior and the overall buying process than ever before. The term was also used by Blasingame (2014).

AI in marketing is not just a technology but it is about re-defining strategy, re-engineering activities and relationships. Ethical controversies are serious fallout of the applications of AI systems to business. Hermann (2022) has taken a multi-stakeholder perspective to study the ethical challenges of deploying AI in marketing and has discussed about how it can be used to promote social and environmental well being. Given the all encompassing impact of AI, the discourse around ethical values in regard to both AI development and use has gained momentum (e.g., Cowls et al., 2021; Stahl et al., 2021). According to researchers (e.g., Floridi et al., 2020), the primary objective of AI, like any other invention should be to promote social good (beneficence) and to prevent any harm (non-maleficence).

Hermann (2022) says that the moralistic deontological approach to AI ethics needs to be replaced by the utilitarian perspective marked by a cost-benefit analysis across stakeholders. AI in marketing should be for social good and sustainable consumption. AI-based solutions lead to sustainability and AI in marketing can contribute to sustainable development. This can result in a win-win-win situation for companies, customers, and society at large (Vlačić et al., 2021). Hermann (2022) gives a multi-stakeholder model of AI ethics in marketing which comprises of four ethical variables viz. beneficence, non-maleficence, justice, and autonomy connected to the principle of explicability as a central enabling ethical principle. Beneficence refers to well-being, common good, sustainability of energy and resources and dignity; non-maleficence is about security and privacy of personal information; justice is defined in terms of fairness, inclusion, non-discrimination and solidarity; autonomy broadly means freedom of choice and informed consent; explicability is about transparency, responsibility, and acting with integrity. The latter forms the basis of all ethics in technology.

Each of these principles when not applied to AI models result in unethical marketing. The doctrines form the basis of 'social marketing' which entails promoting a cause for community upliftment and not for personal benefit. Information on available resources and services may be provided to refugees through AI-enabled chatbots; social media data may be analysed by organizations through Natural Language Processing (NLP) to understand the needs and sentiment of affected communities; AI-driven mental health apps are being used to provide mental health support (Majzumdar, 2023) and for medical diagnosis (Mittal et al., 2024; Singh and Sharma, 2023).

Digital customer data obtained through user-generated content helps identify customer needs by means of automatic technology. AI can collect a wide range of data from customers, which can be categorized into several types:

i. Demographic data: This kind of data consists of details on an individual's age, gender, location, level of education, and employment. Utilizing this data will allow you to customize the customer experience by grouping your consumers into several categories.

ii. Behavioural data: This category of data includes specifics on how clients use a business's goods and services, like past purchases and browsing activities, search terms, and website clicks. By using this data, products and services can be improved, patterns and trends can be found, and personalized recommendations can be made.

iii. Feedback data: This kind of data consists of details that consumers have submitted via forms, surveys, and other channels for providing feedback. Measurements of customer satisfaction and opportunities for improvement can be made with this data.

iv. Transactional data: This kind of data consists of details regarding customer transactions, including past purchases, payment details, and shipment details. By using this data, customized suggestions can be made to enhance the customer's checkout process.

v. Interaction data: This kind of data comprises details on how clients communicate with the AI systems of a business, including voice commands, chatbot or virtual assistant discussions, and other interactions. This data can be utilized to enhance AI system performance and customize the user experience for customers.

In general, this information is utilized to detect trends and patterns, enhance products and services, tailor the customer's experience, and provide recommendations. It also aids in better decision-making by forecasting the behaviour of customers.

Machine intelligence software helps customize the marketing mix, persuade customers, and aids in customer satisfaction. Psychological traits can be deciphered by looking at digital footprints and smart phone data; predictions about income can be made through FB likes and status updates. AI-powered recommender systems, if properly trained, can benefit both customer and company in terms of serving both cognitive and affective needs along with contributing to resource efficiency and predicting sales behaviour after studying customer preferences. AI models help e commerce companies and online retailers to turn browsers into buyers and foster cross-selling. Ethical considerations in AI based marketing can be met only by balancing profit and consumer trust. Unlike social marketing examples of unethical use of AI can be seen in commercial marketing which has profit as the primary motive and uses tools to influence emotions, thoughts and purchase decisions of consumers. For example, the ethical principle of privacy may be at risk if the company uses targeted advertisements that may harm vulnerable customers. Gambling-related products could be marketed to a consumer whose personal data indicates a gambling addiction. Similarly bias inherent in AI software may flout the principle of justice and solidarity artificial intelligence. For instance, motion-activated soap dispensers were less likely to recognize the hands of people of colour than the hands of white people; Bots can also engage in hate speech and harassment, and breed discord in particular groups or organizations. An AI algorithm sending information on a tech job opening to men and not women is another example of a discriminatory outcome due to bias in AI.

To reiterate, while using AI in marketing technology, companies should be mindful of the consequences of losing consumer trust. Research shows that on average, 25% of a company's market value depends on its reputation. A 2022 Cisco survey indicates that 81% of the customers believed that the way organizations treat their personal data was directly proportional to the respect they had for their customer. Unethical digital marketing practices can be curtailed if marketers abide by the following guidelines (Nakka, 2020):

i.   Truthful product Information: provide complete and truthful product information
ii. Avoiding false claims in advertisements
iii. Refraining from adverse comments on sensitive topics
iv. Cultural sensitivity
v.   Privacy by avoiding wrongful data mining and data extraction to create marketing campaigns

CONCLUSION

Traditional marketing as a promotional strategy targets audiences using offline materials. Marketers may use traditional marketing to interact with consumers in physical locations. They typically insert these marketing materials in places where their audience is more likely to see, hear or interact with them. Examples of traditional marketing are radio and television commercials, billboards and direct mail campaigns. Traditional marketing is important because it reaches audiences who spend time away from their computers and smartphones. It can also reach a wider audience if you place your advertisements in public areas many people regularly visit, connect you with a local audience and make you more recognizable to members of the community. Eight types of traditional marketing methods include: Handouts (flyers), Billboards, direct mail, print ads, event marketing, broadcasting over radio and television, cold calling, product placement (embedded marketing). However, as new trends in technology are coming up, both content marketing and content advertising have transformed. Content is still the king and is presented in new formats to suit modern customers. Since marketers are dealing with humans and not robots, it is crucial to remember the human touch in all domains of AI-assisted business. AI is all about intelligent machines especially computer programs that can mimic the problem solving and decision making capabilities of the human mind.

Companies need to ensure that the utilization of technology for creation of marketing content must be in alignment with customer needs, have an emotional appeal, and must aim at trust and long term association with customers enabling them to make informed buying decisions. It must be kept in mind that content creation is virtually not possible without 'content collection'. AI-based technologies collect marketing-related data to make informed decisions that have an impact on the success of marketing efforts and business efficiency. Customer profiles are analysed for sending tailored/ customized messages to particular segments.

With the increasing sophistication and accessibility of technologies such as virtual and augmented reality, business-to-business (B2B) marketers will be able to provide their target audiences with immersive, interactive experiences. Those who remain at the forefront of innovation in content marketing will be best positioned to drive development and success in the B2B space as it continues to expand. Therefore, increasing brand recognition and putting your brand on the map are the main goals of content marketing. Potential clients are unable to make knowledgeable selections regarding goods or services in the absence of awareness. It offers a venue for brands to express their identities and cultivate ties with consumers. Content marketing is a strategic marketing method that aims to shape and continuously strengthen a brand's identity, rather than just communicating a brand's story.

REFERENCES

Belk, R. (2020). Ethical issues in service robotics and artifcial intelligence. *Service Industries Journal*. doi:10.1080/02642069.2020.1727892

Blasingame, J. (2014). *The age of the customer: Prepare for the Moment of Relevance*. SBN Books.

Burt, T. (2023, December 22). *The History of Content Marketing*. LinkedIn. https://www.linkedin.com/business/marketing/blog/linkedin-ads/our-infographic-of-the-week-a-brief-history-of-content-marketing

Cabrera, I. (2024, March 12). *How mind mapping helps marketers create Better content - Venngage*. Venngage. https://venngage.com/blog/mind-mapping/

Carmicheal, K. (2021, August 9). *Push vs. Pull Marketing: Top Differences & How to Use Them*. Hubspot..https://blog.hubspot.com/marketing/push-vs-pull-marketing

Competitive strategy in the age of the customer. (n.d.). Forrester. https://www.forrester.com/report/Competitive-Strategy-In-The-Age-Of-The-Customer/RES59159?docid=59159

Conductor. (n.d.). *Conductor — Enterprise SEO & content marketing platform*. Conductor. https://www.conductor.com/

Consumers want more transparency on how businesses handle their data, new Cisco survey shows. (n.d.). Investor. https://investor.cisco.com/news/news-details/2022/Consumers-want-more-transparency-on-how-businesses-handle-their-data-new-Cisco-survey-shows/default.aspx

Cowls, J., Tsamados, A., Taddeo, M., & Floridi, L. (2021). A definition, benchmark and database of AI for social good initiatives. *Nature Machine Intelligence*, *3*(2), 111–115. doi:10.1038/s42256-021-00296-0

De Bruyn, A., Viswanathan, V., Beh, Y. S., Brock, J. K.-U., & von Wangenheim, F. (2020). Artifcial intelligence and marketing: Pitfalls and opportunities. *Journal of Interactive Marketing*, *51*, 91–105. doi:10.1016/j.intmar.2020.04.007

Floridi, L., Cowls, J., King, T. C., & Taddeo, M. (2020). How to design AI for social good: Seven essential factors. *Science and Engineering Ethics*, *26*(3), 1771–1796. doi:10.1007/s11948-020-00213-5 PMID:32246245

Forsey, C. (2022, April 12). *The Evolution of Content Marketing: How It's Changed and Where It's Going in the Next Decade*. Hubspot. https://blog.hubspot.com/marketing/future-content-marketing

Hermann, E. (2022). Leveraging artificial intelligence in marketing for social good - An ethical perspective. *Journal of Business Ethics*, *179*(1), 43–16. doi:10.1007/s10551-021-04843-y PMID:34054170

Huang, M. H., & Rust, R. T. (2021b). A strategic framework for artifcial intelligence in marketing. *Journal of the Academy of Marketing Science*, *49*(1), 30–50. doi:10.1007/s11747-020-00749-9

Kaplan, A., & Haenlein, M. (2019). Siri, Siri, in my hand: Who's the fairest in the land? On the interpretations, illustrations, and implications of artifcial intelligence. *Business Horizons*, *62*(1), 15–25. doi:10.1016/j.bushor.2018.08.004

Kotler, P., Kartajaya, H., & Setiawan, I. (2021). *Marketing 5.0: Technology for Humanity*. John Willey & Sons.

Mazumdar, R. (2023, October 8). *AI for Social Good: How AI is Being Used to Solve Real-World Problems*. LinkedIn. https://www.linkedin.com/pulse/ai-social-good-how-being-used-solve-real-world-rana-mazumdar/

Mittal, R., Jeribi, F., Martin, R. J., Malik, V., Menachery, S. J., & Singh, J. (2024). DermCDSM: Clinical Decision Support Model for Dermatosis using Systematic Approaches of Machine Learning and Deep Learning. *IEEE Access : Practical Innovations, Open Solutions*, *1*, 47319–47337. doi:10.1109/ACCESS.2024.3373539

Nakka, S. (2020, November 22). *Concerns about unethical practices in digital marketing*. https://www.linkedin.com/pulse/concerns-unethical-practices-digital-marketing-sanket-nakka/

Shirmohammadi, S. (2023, October 19). *The Power of Storytelling in Marketing: Lessons from Nike, Dove, and Patagonia*. LinkedIn. https://www.linkedin.com/pulse/power-storytelling-marketing-lessons-from-nike-dove-shirmohammadi-xsjac/

Singh, J., & Sharma, D. (2023). Automated detection of mental disorders using physiological signals and machine learning: A systematic review and scientometric analysis. *Multimedia Tools and Applications*. doi:10.1007/s11042-023-17504-1

Stahl, B. C., Andreou, A., Brey, P., Hatzakis, T., Kirichenko, A., Macnish, K., Laulhé Shaelou, S., Patel, A., Ryan, M., & Wright, D. (2021). Artifcial intelligence for human fourishing—Beyond principles for machine learning. *Journal of Business Research*, *124*, 374–388. doi:10.1016/j.jbusres.2020.11.030

Vlačić, B., Corbo, L., Costa e Silva, S., & Dabić, M. (2021). The evolving role of artificial intelligence in marketing: A review and research agenda. *Journal of Business Research*, *128*, 187–203. doi:10.1016/j.jbusres.2021.01.055

Walters, C. (2023, May 4). *The history of content marketing*. Content Marketing Agency | Content Marketing Services by CopyPress. https://www.copypress.com/blog/history-content-marketing/

York, A. (2024, March 20). *10 AI tools for mind mapping and brainstorming in 2024*. ClickUp. https://clickup.com/blog/ai-tools-for-mind mapping/#:~:text=AI%20can%20help%20transform%20thoughts,mind%2Dmapping%20and%20brainstorming%20sessions%3F

Chapter 13
Navigating the Digital Frontier:
An In-Depth Analysis of the Evolving Marketing Mix and the PPACE Acceleration Factor

Ashutosh D. Gaur

(iD) https://orcid.org/0000-0003-4322-5747

Mangalmay Institution of Management and Technology, India

ABSTRACT

This chapter delves into the changing landscape of marketing in the digital age. It examines the evolution of the traditional marketing mix, the proliferation of digital media platforms, the rise of MarTech, and the emergence of P-PACE as an eighth element in the marketing mix. This research highlights the profound impact of technology and the internet on the marketing mix and the emergence of new dimensions such as participation, public opinion, physical proof, process, personalization, and political power. It also explores the acceleration factor, encapsulated in the concept of P-PACE, and how it has become a fundamental element in the marketing mix. The implications and applications of P-PACE and its significance in contemporary marketing are discussed, emphasizing the advantages of harnessing the power of acceleration for businesses.

INTRODUCTION

The contemporary landscape of marketing is in a state of perpetual transformation, characterized by the incessant march of technological progress and the ubiquitous presence of the Internet. The marketing mix, a fundamental concept in the field of marketing, has been a guiding framework for businesses and marketers to address consumer needs and wants. Developed by Jerome McCarthy in 1964, the traditional marketing mix consists of four core elements: Product, Price, Place, and Promotion (McCarthy, 1964). However, the past two decades have witnessed an unparalleled revolution in the way businesses approach marketing. Advancements in technology and the proliferation of digital platforms have led to

DOI: 10.4018/979-8-3693-2215-4.ch013

significant alterations in the marketing mix and have prompted scholars and practitioners to reevaluate and expand upon its foundational principles.

This paper embarks on a scholarly exploration of the evolving terrain of marketing, with a particular emphasis on the impact of the Internet and digital technologies on the marketing mix. The objective is to discern the underlying shifts and disruptions that have led to the reconfiguration of marketing strategies and the emergence of new dimensions in the marketing mix. Additionally, this research seeks to illuminate the pivotal role of a novel addition to the marketing mix, denoted as "P-PACE," as it reflects the acceleration factor that reverberates through all other elements. This innovative framework reflects the dynamic and fast-paced nature of contemporary marketing, where speed is often the essence of competitiveness and customer satisfaction.

Technology as a Transformative Catalyst

The marketing arena, like many other domains, has felt the transformative force of technology. The impact of digitalization, enabled by the Internet, has been pervasive, altering the way businesses interact with their customers, execute marketing campaigns, and conduct market research. In the era of information technology, customers have become more connected, empowered, and informed, challenging businesses to adapt to their evolving needs (Kalyanam & McIntyre, 2002).

The proliferation of digital media platforms has ushered in a new era of marketing. It has not only provided novel channels for communication and interaction with consumers but has also redefined how information is disseminated and products are marketed. In the pre-digital era, marketing was primarily one-directional, with companies pushing messages to passive audiences through traditional media. However, the advent of the Internet has transformed consumers into active participants who engage with brands, share their experiences, and influence the perceptions of others (Sharma & Sheth, 2004). This shift from a one-way communication model to a two-way, interactive dialogue has compelled marketers to rethink their strategies and embrace the digital revolution.

One of the key developments in this context is the rise of digital and social media marketing (DSMM). Social media platforms, such as Facebook, Twitter, and Instagram, have become central to the marketing strategies of many businesses. These platforms provide a space where consumers not only search for products, read reviews, and compare prices but also share their experiences and opinions, amplifying the reach and impact of marketing campaigns (Kalyanam & McIntyre, 2002).

Furthermore, the ubiquity of "smart" mobile devices and the seamless integration of technology into everyday life have redefined the consumer's path to purchase. Consumers can now seamlessly transition from researching a product on their smartphone to making a purchase on a tablet or laptop, or even in a physical store. This omni-channel experience has compelled businesses to adopt multi-platform marketing strategies to ensure a consistent and engaging customer experience (Lamberton, 2016).

Reimagining the Traditional 4Ps

The traditional marketing mix, characterized by the 4Ps—Product, Price, Place, and Promotion—has been a cornerstone of marketing strategies for decades. It provided a structured approach to understanding and addressing customer needs and wants. However, the digital age has introduced new complexities, leading to a reevaluation of this framework.

A seminal contribution to the reimagining of the marketing mix came from Booms and Bitner in 1980 when they proposed adding three new Ps: Participation, Physical Proof, and Process (Booms & Bitner, 1980). These additional elements aimed to make the marketing mix more applicable to the service industry, where intangibles and customer experience play a crucial role. The service sector has witnessed profound changes with the advent of technology, and these additional Ps sought to address the unique challenges and opportunities presented in this sector.

Kotler, a luminary in the field of marketing, argued for the inclusion of Political Power and Public Opinion, recognizing the influence of public sentiment and regulatory forces on marketing strategies (Kotler, 1986). In the age of social media and information sharing, public opinion can significantly impact a brand's reputation and bottom line.

Another dimension introduced to the marketing mix is Personalization (Goldsmith, 1999). Personalization recognizes that in the digital era, customers expect tailored experiences and products that cater to their individual preferences. The ability to gather and analyze data about consumers' behavior and preferences has enabled businesses to create personalized marketing campaigns and product recommendations.

In the wake of these additions to the marketing mix, the traditional 4Ps have been met with skepticism by academics, marketers, and researchers (Lauterborn, 1990). The traditional emphasis on products has evolved into a customer-centric approach, where businesses are encouraged to consider products as solutions, prices as consumer expenses, locations as a matter of convenience, and marketing as a form of communication (Lauterborn, 1990). This paradigm shift reflects the changing dynamics of the market, where the customer's perspective takes center stage.

Incorporating P-PACE: The Acceleration Factor

One of the most remarkable changes that technology and the Internet have brought to marketing is the acceleration of every aspect of business operations. The pace at which organizations can innovate, develop products, set prices, market their offerings, and professionalize their various functions is now heavily influenced by technology. This acceleration factor has a profound impact on decision-making processes and corporate strategies.

The dot-com boom and the subsequent proliferation of Internet marketing marked a pivotal moment in this acceleration. The Internet provided a unique bridge between the virtual and physical worlds, enabling businesses to expand their reach and connect with customers beyond their local borders. This led to the emergence of a new category known as E-marketing, where digital possibilities complement the predominantly offline marketing environment and add significant value (Lauterborn, 1990).

As a result, the rate at which technology can progress in all aspects has become a critical driver of business success. The accelerated pace of technological development shapes a company's ability to create innovative products, set competitive prices, effectively market their offerings, and optimize various business processes. Moreover, this rapid progression affects the way organizations interact with customers, adapt to market changes, and stay ahead of competitors (Sawhney, Wolcott, & Arroniz, 2006).

The acceleration factor has prompted a closer examination of how businesses employ technology, the Internet, and digital possibilities to enhance various aspects of their operations. Factors such as perceived benefits, user readiness, and the level of value derived from technology are key considerations in understanding how organizations can harness the full potential of these innovations (Henfridsson & Bygstad, 2013).

In particular, businesses have harnessed Internet-based Information and Communication Technologies (ICTs) to sustain and enhance economic growth (Brynjolfsson & Kahin, 2000). These technologies have facilitated cost-effective and efficient internal management, operations, and coordination, both internally and externally. Similar to the impact of the Industrial Revolution, the Internet has dramatically reshaped business and consumer behavior (Sheth & Sharma, 2005). E-channels, made possible by ICTs, have opened up new avenues for businesses to serve their target customers more efficiently and cost-effectively compared to traditional physical channels. This shift has not only streamlined operations but has also paved the way for a more customer-centric approach, where businesses can respond more effectively to consumer demands and preferences (Brynjolfsson & Kahin, 2000).

The confluence of Internet, technology, and digital dynamics has also had a profound impact on how companies interact with their customers. Businesses now have access to a wealth of data, enabling them to gain deeper insights into customer behavior and preferences. This has transformed the customer journey, allowing for more personalized and targeted marketing strategies. Additionally, digital platforms have become integral to customer engagement, allowing for more effective communication and feedback mechanisms (Sharma & Sheth, 2004).

Moreover, the acceleration factor has driven significant changes in how technology-mediated selling is conducted. From the development of new products and services to the negotiation of prices through online auctions, technology has played a pivotal role in reshaping the sales process (Ferrell, Gonzalez-Padron, & Ferrell, 2010). The dynamics of online brand promotion have shifted from merely showcasing products to a more customer-centric approach that focuses on fulfilling customer desires and aligning with their preferences (Lamberton, 2016).

Marketing Technology (MarTech) has emerged as a critical driver of marketing effectiveness. It has enhanced the efficiency of marketing spending, measurement of marketing impact, dynamic pricing, and overall marketing operations (Sharma-Sheth, 2010). Interactive media has played a central role in reshaping the structure of Business-to-Consumer (B2C) channels, introducing a more direct and engaging means of connecting with consumers (Sharma & Sheth, 2005). The main elements that influence how technology is leveraged to enhance customer experiences and streamline processes are dynamic and multifaceted, reflecting the complex interplay between technology and marketing (Kalyanam & McIntyre, 2002).

The Expanding Marketing Mix: P-PACE

The unprecedented pace of change driven by technology and the Internet has given rise to the need for an updated and expanded marketing mix. In this context, the addition of the eighth "P" in the marketing mix, denoted as P-PACE, becomes both relevant and imperative. P-PACE represents the acceleration factor that underlies all other elements of the marketing mix. It embodies the idea that speed and agility are paramount in today's competitive marketplace.

P-PACE encompasses various aspects of marketing, reflecting the accelerated pace at which businesses must operate in the digital age. It affects product development, as businesses need to innovate rapidly to keep up with changing consumer preferences and technological advancements. Customer service must be swift and responsive to meet the demands of today's connected consumers. Pricing strategies should be agile, allowing businesses to adapt to changes in the market quickly. The distribution of products and reaching the target audience must be executed with efficiency and speed. Communication and advertising campaigns should be timely and responsive to market dynamics. Employee and customer participation should be encouraged and facilitated in real time. Physical and virtual branding must be aligned with the fast-paced digital landscape (Lauterborn, 1990).

P-PACE is not just a response to the challenges of a rapidly changing market; it is also a reflection of the opportunities that technology and the Internet present. Businesses that can harness the power of acceleration can gain a competitive edge, respond to customer needs more effectively, and drive innovation. P-PACE is not simply about speed but about using that speed strategically to gain a competitive advantage (Sheth & Sharma, 2005).

As businesses and marketers navigate this new landscape, they are increasingly recognizing the value of P-PACE in shaping their marketing strategies. This research aims to delve into the implications of P-PACE and how it has become a fundamental element in the marketing mix. The concept of P-PACE invites us to consider not only what products and services we offer but also how quickly we can adapt and respond to a rapidly evolving market.

In summary, the evolution of the marketing mix, driven by technology and the Internet, has given rise to the recognition of the acceleration factor, encapsulated in the concept of P-PACE. Businesses that can adapt to the rapid changes and harness the power of acceleration are poised to thrive in the digital age. This research will delve deeper into the implications and applications of P-PACE and its significance in contemporary marketing.

Marketing Alters

The realm of marketing has undergone profound transformations in recent years, primarily fueled by the pervasive influence of technology and the omnipresence of the Internet. These alterations have had a profound impact on how businesses engage with their customers, the strategies they employ, and the fundamental concepts that guide their operations. This section explores the significant changes that have shaped the contemporary marketing landscape and the underlying factors that have driven these alterations.

Digital Media Platforms and Consumer Engagement

One of the most notable changes in marketing has been the transformation brought about by digital media platforms. These platforms have not only created new channels for interaction with consumers but have also redefined the way businesses inform, engage, and sell to their target audiences. Technology advancements and the proliferation of the Internet have played a pivotal role in this shift (Sharma & Sheth, 2004).

With the rise of social media and e-commerce platforms, consumers now have the ability to search for products, assess their suitability, compare prices, make purchases, and even provide reviews and feedback in a seamless and interconnected manner (Kalyanam & McIntyre, 2002). This has disrupted the traditional one-way communication model of marketing, where businesses pushed messages to passive audiences. Instead, consumers have become active participants in the marketing process, sharing their experiences, influencing the perceptions of others, and having a direct impact on a brand's reputation (Sharma & Sheth, 2004).

Digital and Social Media Marketing (DSMM)

The expansion of digital marketing has closely mirrored the progress of technology. Facebook and the widespread adoption of "smart" mobile devices serve as emblematic examples of technological advancements that have reshaped marketing strategies (Sharma-Sheth, 2010). DSMM has become a central component of contemporary marketing strategies, offering businesses new tools for data processing, performance measurement, and decision-making (Sharma-Sheth, 2010).

Businesses are no longer restricted to traditional advertising methods. They can harness the power of search engine optimization (SEO), pay-per-click (PPC) advertising, content marketing, and even artificial intelligence to reach their target audiences (Sharma & Sheth, 2004). The marketing landscape has expanded beyond recognition, providing businesses with a wealth of options and approaches to engage customers.

The Expanding Marketing Mix

The traditional marketing mix, characterized by the classic 4Ps—Product, Price, Place, and Promotion—has been a foundational framework for businesses and marketers (McCarthy, 1964). However, the advent of digital technologies and the ever-increasing influence of the Internet have necessitated a reimagining of this framework.

Booms and Bitner (1980) were among the early proponents of expanding the marketing mix by introducing additional Ps, such as Participation, Physical Proof, and Process. These supplementary Ps were aimed at making the marketing mix more applicable to the service industry, where intangibles and customer experience play a central role (Booms & Bitner, 1980). The service sector has seen significant disruption due to technology, necessitating adaptations to the marketing mix.

Kotler (1986) further advocated for the inclusion of Political Power and Public Opinion in the marketing mix, recognizing the growing influence of public sentiment and regulatory forces on marketing strategies (Kotler, 1986). In the age of social media, public opinion can significantly impact a brand's reputation and customer loyalty.

Another dimension introduced to the marketing mix is Personalization (Goldsmith, 1999), acknowledging that in the digital era, consumers expect tailored experiences and products that align with their individual preferences (Goldsmith, 1999). Data analytics and digital technologies enable businesses to create personalized marketing campaigns and product recommendations, setting a new standard for customer-centric marketing.

The Changing Emphasis: Customer-Centricity

The original 4Ps of the marketing mix have faced criticism from academics, skeptics, and researchers who argue that the traditional framework places excessive emphasis on products, whereas the contemporary marketing approach is centered on customers (Lauterborn, 1990). This paradigm shift emphasizes the need for businesses to consider their products as solutions, prices as customer expenses, locations as a matter of convenience, and marketing as a form of communication (Lauterborn, 1990). The customer's perspective is now at the forefront of marketing strategies (Sheth & Sharma, 2005).

As technology enables businesses to gather and analyze vast amounts of data on consumer behavior and preferences, the marketing mix has evolved to better align with customer needs and expectations.

The focus has shifted from mass marketing to personalized marketing, where businesses aim to deliver tailored experiences that resonate with individual customers (Kalyanam & McIntyre, 2002).

Incorporating P-PACE: The Acceleration Factor

Perhaps the most significant alteration brought about by technology and the Internet is the acceleration factor. The pace at which organizations can innovate, develop products, set prices, market their offerings, and optimize various business functions is now heavily influenced by technology (Sawhney, Wolcott, & Arroniz, 2006).

The acceleration factor reflects the powerful driving force that shapes how businesses create, price, market, and professionalize various aspects of their operations. It has a profound impact on decision-making processes and corporate strategies (Sharma & Sheth, 2010). The dot-com boom and the subsequent expansion of Internet marketing marked a pivotal moment in this acceleration. The Internet became the bridge between the virtual and physical worlds, enabling businesses to expand their reach and connect with customers on a global scale (Sawhney, Wolcott, & Arroniz, 2006). This transformative period heralded the emergence of E-marketing, a category that complements the predominantly offline marketing environment and adds significant value (Lauterborn, 1990).

The rate at which technology progresses in all aspects has become a critical driver of business success (Sawhney, Wolcott, & Arroniz, 2006). The acceleration factor influences how organizations innovate, adapt to market changes, and stay ahead of competitors. Additionally, it affects how businesses interact with customers, respond to their needs, and create a seamless and efficient customer experience (Kalyanam & McIntyre, 2002).

Internet-based Information and Communication Technologies (ICTs) have become pivotal in enhancing economic growth and improving internal management, operations, and coordination (Brynjolfsson & Kahin, 2000). The Internet's impact on business and consumer behavior is often compared to the profound changes brought about by the Industrial Revolution (Brynjolfsson & Kahin, 2000). E-channels, facilitated by ICTs, have allowed businesses to serve their target customers more efficiently and cost-effectively than traditional physical channels (Brynjolfsson & Kahin, 2000).

The marketing landscape has been further reshaped by technology-mediated selling, with innovations extending beyond traditional product offerings. In this tech-driven society, consumers set prices on various platforms, and sellers negotiate through online auctions (Ferrell, Gonzalez-Padron, & Ferrell, 2010). Online brand promotion has shifted its focus from showcasing products to delivering what consumers desire rather than merely what marketers or competitors offer (Lamberton, 2016).

Marketing Technology (MarTech) has become instrumental in enhancing the quality and speed of marketing operations. It has improved the efficiency of marketing spending, measurement of marketing impact, dynamic pricing, and overall marketing processes (Sharma-Sheth, 2010). Digital platforms have created new value propositions and business models, impacting the structure of Business-to-Consumer (B2C) channels (Sharma & Sheth, 2005).

The evolution of marketing strategies and the expanded marketing mix have not only been influenced by technology but have also accelerated the adoption of new approaches and tools. Marketing practitioners are increasingly recognizing the need for agility and responsiveness to navigate the rapidly changing landscape (Lamberton, 2016).

Literature Review and Practice Insights

A comprehensive literature review and analysis of practical insights highlight the need to revise and adapt the marketing mix to the dynamics of the digital age. Speed, agility, and the acceleration factor have taken precedence over traditional marketing elements (Sharma & Sheth, 2004).

The digital revolution has precipitated the prioritization of velocity in marketing strategies, shifting the focus from the classic 4Ps to the new dynamic of P-PACE. The introduction of digital technologies and the internet has not only created new opportunities but has also necessitated a shift in how marketers approach their strategies and engage with customers (Sheth & Sharma, 2005).

The changing marketing landscape is prompting businesses to reconsider the components of the marketing mix. P-PACE, as a representation of the acceleration factor, has become a central element in contemporary marketing strategies. The emphasis is no longer solely on the product but on how quickly businesses can adapt to the rapidly evolving market, deliver personalized experiences, and respond to customer needs in real-time (Sharma & Sheth, 2005).

In conclusion, the alterations in the marketing landscape have been driven by the digital transformation and the accelerating pace of technology. The expansion of the marketing mix to accommodate P-PACE reflects the recognition that speed and agility are paramount in today's competitive marketplace. This alteration is not merely a response to the challenges posed by a rapidly changing market but also a recognition of the opportunities that technology and the Internet present. Businesses that can harness the power of acceleration are poised to thrive in the digital age, shaping the contemporary marketing landscape (Sharma & Sheth, 2005).

Constituents of the Marketing Mix

The traditional marketing mix, famously introduced by McCarthy in 1964, has long been the cornerstone of marketing strategies, encapsulating the essential elements that businesses manipulate to influence consumer behavior (McCarthy, 1964). The classic 4Ps—Product, Price, Place, and Promotion—have guided marketers and decision-makers in addressing consumer wants and needs, aiding both strategic and tactical planning. While these components have remained fundamental, the evolution of technology and the internet has prompted a reevaluation of the marketing mix, leading to the inclusion of new constituents (McCarthy, 1964).

Expanding on McCarthy's original framework, Booms and Bitner (1980) advocated the addition of three additional Ps, expanding the marketing mix to include Participation, Physical Proof, and Process, particularly relevant in the context of service-oriented industries (Booms & Bitner, 1980). The service sector, characterized by intangibles and customer experience, required a more comprehensive framework to address the unique aspects of service marketing.

Kotler (1986) further advanced the notion of an evolving marketing mix by emphasizing the inclusion of Political Power and Public Opinion, recognizing the increasing impact of public sentiment and regulatory forces on marketing strategies (Kotler, 1986). In today's digital age, where public opinion can significantly impact a brand's reputation, this addition has gained particular significance.

Goldsmith (1999) argued for the incorporation of Personalization into the marketing mix, acknowledging the rising consumer expectations for tailored experiences and products (Goldsmith, 1999). As businesses increasingly harness data analytics and digital technologies to create personalized marketing campaigns and product recommendations, the need for personalization in the marketing mix becomes evident.

The transition from the traditional 4Ps to the 7Ps is not without controversy, as it underscores the evolving focus of marketing from products to customers (Lauterborn, 1990). The 7Ps model requires businesses to view their products as solutions, prices as customer expenses, locations as a matter of convenience, and marketing as a form of communication (Lauterborn, 1990).

As we delve further into this paper, it becomes evident that these additional constituents in the marketing mix, born from the digital age, have set the stage for a comprehensive reevaluation of marketing strategies. The marketing mix, once a static framework, now requires adaptability and responsiveness to the fast-paced digital landscape.

Marketing Mix

The traditional marketing mix, originally formulated as the 4Ps by McCarthy in 1964, has long served as the foundation for marketing strategies in diverse industries (McCarthy, 1964). These core elements—Product, Price, Place, and Promotion—have guided businesses in addressing consumer needs, ensuring that their products or services meet market demands and wants, and facilitating strategic and tactical planning.

However, in the ever-evolving landscape of marketing, the introduction of technology and the omnipresence of the Internet have necessitated a reevaluation of the traditional marketing mix. In response to the dynamic and interconnected nature of the digital age, scholars and practitioners have advocated for the expansion of the marketing mix, introducing new elements to address the complexities of contemporary marketing (McCarthy, 1964).

Booms and Bitner (1980) proposed the addition of three more Ps, extending the marketing mix to encompass Participation, Physical Proof, and Process. This augmentation has proven particularly relevant in the context of service-oriented industries where intangibles and customer experience are central (Booms & Bitner, 1980). These additional Ps emphasize the significance of customer engagement, the tangible evidence of service quality, and the efficiency of underlying processes.

Kotler (1986) further emphasized the necessity of including Political Power and Public Opinion in the marketing mix, recognizing the growing influence of regulatory forces and public sentiment on marketing strategies (Kotler, 1986). In the digital era, where public opinion can rapidly shape brand perception, this addition is particularly salient.

Goldsmith (1999) argued for the incorporation of Personalization as a vital constituent of the marketing mix, acknowledging the rising consumer expectations for customized experiences and products (Goldsmith, 1999). As businesses increasingly employ data analytics and digital technologies to deliver personalized marketing campaigns and product recommendations, the concept of personalization becomes pivotal.

The transition from the traditional 4Ps to the contemporary 7Ps model has prompted a reorientation of marketing from a product-centric approach to a customer-centric one (Lauterborn, 1990). Under this paradigm, products are viewed as solutions, prices as customer expenses, locations as matters of convenience, and marketing as a means of communication (Lauterborn, 1990).

As the paper unfolds, it becomes evident that these supplementary components in the marketing mix, born out of the digital age, have set the stage for a comprehensive reevaluation of marketing strategies.

The marketing mix, once a static framework, now requires adaptability and responsiveness to thrive in the fast-paced digital realm.

Marketing Mix PACE Connect

The evolution of the marketing mix in response to the digital age and technological advancements has introduced a new dynamic, often referred to as the "PACE Connect." This element represents the interplay of various constituents of the marketing mix in a fast-paced and interconnected world, emphasizing the need for agility and responsiveness. PACE Connect is a conceptual framework that acknowledges the influence of technology and the Internet in shaping marketing strategies (Sharma & Sheth, 2004).

Internet, technology, and digital dynamics have converged to create a unique environment where businesses must navigate the challenges of an interconnected world while harnessing the opportunities presented by these advancements (Sheth & Sharma, 2005). PACE Connect embodies the idea that the speed of adaptation, innovation, and response to customer needs is a critical factor in achieving marketing success.

One key aspect of PACE Connect is the ability to harness technology to improve customer engagement. The rapid adoption of digital and social media platforms has transformed the way businesses connect with customers, enabling real-time interactions, personalized messaging, and instant feedback (Sharma-Sheth, 2010). Businesses must adapt their marketing strategies to leverage these technologies effectively.

Furthermore, technology-mediated selling has become a central component of PACE Connect. In this digital age, the process of selling goods and services has been fundamentally altered by technology and the Internet, impacting product development, customer service, pricing strategies, distribution, and audience engagement (Sheth & Sharma, 2005). The digital landscape has given rise to innovations such as dynamic pricing, online auctions, and customer-driven pricing platforms (Sheth & Sharma, 2004).

The marketing technology (MarTech) landscape plays a pivotal role within PACE Connect, enhancing the quality and speed of marketing operations (Sharma-Sheth, 2010). MarTech encompasses a wide array of tools and platforms designed to improve marketing effectiveness, measure impact, and streamline marketing processes (Sharma-Sheth, 2010). It empowers businesses to deliver targeted messages, optimize spending, and enhance customer experiences.

The interplay of these elements—Personalization, Agility, Connectivity, and Engagement—within PACE Connect reflects the intricate relationship between technology, the marketing mix, and the fast-paced nature of the digital age. Businesses that can successfully navigate this dynamic environment are poised to thrive in an era where the customer experience is paramount, and agility in responding to market changes is a competitive advantage.

PACE: A New "P" in Marketing

In the realm of contemporary marketing, the conventional 4Ps—Product, Price, Place, and Promotion—have long served as the pillars of marketing strategies. However, the advent of the digital age and the proliferation of technology and the Internet have given rise to a new "P" in marketing, known as PACE. PACE represents the essential dimension of speed and agility in marketing strategies, where responsiveness to market dynamics is of paramount importance (Sharma & Sheth, 2005).

The introduction of PACE into the marketing mix underscores the significance of agility and speed in adapting to the rapid changes brought about by technology and the interconnected world. In the digital age, businesses no longer have the luxury of time; they must respond quickly to consumer needs and market shifts (Sharma & Sheth, 2005).

The "P" in PACE stands for Personalization, a critical component in the modern marketing landscape. Consumers increasingly demand personalized experiences, and businesses are leveraging technology to deliver tailored content, product recommendations, and messaging (Goldsmith, 1999). Personalization is not merely a marketing strategy but a fundamental shift in how businesses interact with their customers.

Agility, the second component of PACE, recognizes the need for flexibility and responsiveness in marketing strategies. The digital age has introduced a level of unpredictability and constant change, requiring businesses to adapt swiftly to evolving consumer preferences and market conditions (Sharma & Sheth, 2005).

Connectivity is the third element of PACE, reflecting the interconnected nature of the digital world. Businesses must be adept at utilizing technology to connect with customers through various channels, from social media to e-commerce platforms, in real-time (Sharma & Sheth, 2005). This connectivity enables businesses to engage with their audience in a dynamic and immediate manner.

Engagement, the final component of PACE, is about creating meaningful interactions with customers. In the digital age, it's not enough to broadcast messages; businesses must engage in two-way conversations with their audience (Sharma & Sheth, 2005). Engagement fosters loyalty and brand advocacy.

The introduction of PACE as a new "P" in marketing signifies a shift from a static and product-centric approach to a dynamic and customer-centric one. Businesses that embrace PACE in their marketing strategies are better equipped to thrive in the fast-paced and ever-evolving digital landscape.

The Potential Challenges That Businesses May Face When Leveraging P-PACE, Such as the Need to Invest in Marketing Technology and the Challenge of Monitoring Public Sentiment

Leveraging P-PACE in contemporary marketing strategies brings about a host of opportunities but also presents several challenges that businesses must navigate. Two key challenges include the need to invest in marketing technology and the complexity of monitoring public sentiment and customer feedback.

Firstly, businesses seeking to embrace P-PACE must make substantial investments in marketing technology. Personalization, agility, connectivity, and engagement necessitate sophisticated tools and platforms. This investment includes adopting customer relationship management (CRM) systems, data analytics solutions, and marketing automation software to effectively deliver personalized content, respond swiftly to market changes, maintain an interconnected online presence, and engage with customers in real-time (Sharma-Sheth, 2010). This financial commitment can be a barrier for smaller businesses or those operating with limited resources.

Secondly, monitoring public sentiment and customer feedback is an intricate challenge in the digital age. With the advent of social media and online reviews, public sentiment can rapidly influence a brand's reputation. Businesses must not only track these sentiments but also respond in a timely and appropriate manner (Kotler, 1986). The challenge lies in managing the sheer volume of data generated by online conversations and reviews. Additionally, interpreting sentiment accurately and developing actionable strategies based on this data is a skill that many organizations are still working to perfect (Sharma & Sheth, 2005).

In conclusion, while P-PACE offers a pathway to success in the digital age, businesses must address these challenges effectively to fully harness its potential. The investment in marketing technology and the ability to monitor and respond to public sentiment and customer feedback are critical aspects of navigating the complex landscape of modern marketing.

Competitive Advantage

To best leverage P-PACE (Personalization, Agility, Connectivity, and Engagement) and gain a competitive advantage in the digital age, businesses can consider the following strategies:

1. **Invest in Marketing Technology:** Businesses should invest in advanced marketing technology, including CRM systems, data analytics tools, and marketing automation platforms. These technologies are essential for implementing personalization, streamlining processes, and effectively engaging with customers (Sharma-Sheth, 2010).
2. **Embrace Customer-Centricity:** Shift the focus from product-centricity to customer-centricity. Understand customer preferences, behaviors, and needs by analyzing data and use this information to deliver personalized experiences and content (Goldsmith, 1999).
3. **Real-Time Responsiveness:** Stay agile and responsive to market changes. Utilize real-time data analytics to adjust marketing campaigns, pricing, and product offerings swiftly (Sharma & Sheth, 2005).
4. **Multi-Channel Engagement:** Create an interconnected online presence across various digital channels, including social media, e-commerce platforms, and mobile apps. Consistent and meaningful engagement with customers across these channels is crucial (Sharma & Sheth, 2005).
5. Active Social Listening: Monitor public sentiment and customer feedback by employing social listening tools. Actively engage with customers in online conversations, addressing their concerns and feedback promptly (Kotler, 1986).
6. Employee Training: Train employees to understand and utilize marketing technology effectively. The success of P-PACE strategies often hinges on the skills and knowledge of the workforce.
7. Iterative Improvement: Continuously refine strategies based on data and feedback. P-PACE is about adapting to the dynamic digital landscape, and regular assessments and adjustments are essential (Sharma & Sheth, 2005).

By implementing these strategies, businesses can leverage P-PACE to create a competitive edge in the digital era, delivering personalized experiences, swiftly responding to market changes, and fostering deep customer engagement.

REFERENCES

Booms, B. H., & Bitner, M. J. (1980). Service firm marketing and organization. *Journal of Marketing*, 47–51.

Brynjolfsson, E., & Kahin, B. (2000). *Understanding digital economy*. MIT Press. doi:10.7551/mitpress/6986.001.0001

Ferrell, L., Gonzalez-Padron, T. L., & Ferrell, O. C. (2010). An Assessment of Technology in Direct Selling and Sales Management. *Journal of Personal Selling & Sales Management*, *30*, 157–165. doi:10.2753/PSS0885-3134300206

Goldsmith, R. E. (1999). Personalization should be a part of the marketing mix. *Journal of Marketing Management*, *15*(1-3), 59–81.

Kalyanam, K., & McIntyre, S. (2002). *E-marketing Working Paper*. Leavey School of Business, Santa Clara University. http://lsb.scu.edu/faculty/research/working-papers/pdf/e-marketing.pdf

Kotler, P. (1986). *Marketing basics* (3rd ed.). Prentice Hall.

Lamberton, S. (2016). Digital, Social, and Mobile Marketing Research Evolution. *AMA/MSI Marketing Journal Special Issue, 80,* 146–172. doi:10.1509/jm.15.0415

Lauterborn, B. (1990). New Marketing Litany: Four Ps Passé: C-Words Takeover. *Advertising Age*, 26.

McCarthy, E. J. (1964). *Basic marketing: A managerial approach*. Richard D. Irwin.

Sawhney, M., Wolcott, R. C., & Arroniz, I. (2006). 12 Ways Companies Innovate. *MIT Sloan Management Review*, *47*(3), 75–81.

Sharma, A., & Sheth, J. (2004). Web-based marketing: The marketing revolution. *Journal of Business Research*, *57*(7), 696–702. doi:10.1016/S0148-2963(02)00350-8

Sharma, A., & Sheth, J. (2005). International e-marketing. *Journal of Business Research*, *22*(6), 611–622.

Sharma-Sheth, F. (2010). A technological mediation framework for consumer selling: Implications for enterprises and sales management. *Personal Selling & Sales Management*, *30*(2), 121–129. doi:10.2753/PSS0885-3134300203

Sheth, J., & Sharma, A. (2005). International e-marketing. *Journal of Business Research*, *22*(6), 611–622.

Sheth, J. N., & Sharma, A. (2010). A technological mediation framework for consumer selling: Implications for enterprises and sales management. *Personal Selling & Sales Management*, *30*(Spring), 157–165.

Chapter 14
Navigating the Intersection of Ethics and Privacy in the AI Era

Sanjay Taneja
https://orcid.org/0000-0002-3632-4053
Graphic Era University (Deemed), India

Rishi Prakash Shukla
https://orcid.org/0000-0003-0854-7302
Chandigarh University, India

Amandeep Singh
Chitkara University, India

ABSTRACT

This chapter explores the intricate relationship between privacy and ethics in the realm of artificial intelligence (AI). With the proliferation of AI technologies, concerns about data privacy and ethical implications have intensified. The chapter delves into the ethical dilemmas arising from the collection, analysis, and utilization of sensitive data, emphasizing the need for robust frameworks that balance technological advancement with safeguarding individual rights. It examines the challenges of maintaining privacy in AI-driven systems while adhering to ethical principles, offering insights into the current landscape, potential risks, and promising solutions for creating a responsible and transparent AI ecosystem.

INTRODUCTION

Definition and Significance of Privacy and Ethics in the Context of AI

In the context of artificial intelligence (AI), privacy and ethics are crucial because of how quickly technology is developing and how that blurs the lines separating personal data security from ethical considerations (Robert et al., 2018). In this context, ethics refers to the ethical and equitable use of AI to prevent harm and advance society well-being (Floridi et al., 2018), while privacy refers to the fundamental right

DOI: 10.4018/979-8-3693-2215-4.ch014

of individuals to control their personal information, ensuring that AI systems do not intrude upon their private life (Mai, 2016). These guidelines are important because they protect against algorithmic biases, data breaches, and the possible misuse of AI for monitoring or decision-making. A strong foundation for privacy and ethics is necessary as AI is incorporated more and more into daily life in order to strike a balance between innovation and protecting human rights fostering trust in AI systems, and ensuring they benefit rather than harm society (Floridi & Cowls, 2022).

One cannot stress the importance of these ideas enough. First and foremost, they are essential for safeguarding sensitive data from breaches and preserving its confidentiality, particularly in the age of big data and networked systems. Second, they play a crucial role in correcting algorithmic biases that have the potential to support social injustice and prejudice. Furthermore, privacy and ethics are critical to establishing user confidence, trust in AI systems, and ensuring that AI is used to advance society rather than do harm (Ryan, 2020).

As artificial intelligence continues to be integrated into more and more aspects of daily life, it is necessary to have a strong and dynamic foundation for privacy and ethics. In addition to ensuring that the potential benefits of AI innovation are fully realised while minimising potential hazards and ethical issues, such a framework also protects the rights and interests of humans. In this sense, privacy and AI ethics support a more fair, just, and peaceful coexistence of mankind with cutting-edge technology.

Historical Background and Key Milestones in the Development of AI Ethics and Privacy Concerns

The confluence of ethical requirements and technical advancements has influenced the complicated historical history of AI ethics and privacy concerns (Bonawitz et al., 2017). These worries have their roots in the early development of artificial intelligence throughout the middle of the 20th century. The idea of machines mimicking human cognitive functions was unintentionally introduced by early AI pioneers like Alan Turing, who laid the core concepts of machine intelligence (Street, 2005). The subsequent decades saw the development of AI technology, which raised concerns about potential ethical and privacy implications. The release of Isaac Asimov's Three Laws of Robotics, which established an early framework for the ethical obligations of AI, and the creation of the first AI systems are significant turning points in this history. in the 1950s and 1960s, raising questions about the moral implications of creating intelligent machines.

AI continued to progress throughout the 1970s and 1980s, as discussions over the morality of treating sentient computers heated up (Torrance, 2013). As the internet and other digital technologies spread throughout the 1990s, privacy concerns gained prominence and sparked conversations about data security and surveillance. Important developments in the early 21st century included the emergence of social media platforms and the subject of machine ethics, which brought up concerns about algorithmic bias, filter bubbles, and the improper use of personal data. The 2018 Cambridge Analytica incident and the development of deep learning methods have increased the demand for ethical standards.

AI ethics and privacy problems are at a turning point in our life as these systems continue to advance and penetrate more areas of our existence (Formosa et al., 2021). In order to address concerns like accountability, transparency, equity, and privacy protection, governments, organisations, and researchers are proactively establishing rules and ethical frameworks (Stahl & Wright, 2018). It will take time to find a way to balance AI's limitless potential with upholding human values. Along the way, we must constantly adapt to the rapidly changing technological environment and make sure that AI systems act in society's best interests while upholding the core ethical and privacy principles.

Importance of Addressing Privacy and Ethical Considerations in AI Applications

Today's technologically advanced society places a premium on AI applications taking privacy and ethical issues into account. As AI technologies become more and more ingrained in our daily lives—from social media and healthcare to banking and education—it is crucial to make sure these platforms are operated morally and sensibly. AI's ability to handle and analyse enormous volumes of personal data raises privacy concerns, and it is imperative that personal data be protected from misuse and unauthorised access (Tene & Polonetsky, 2013). Furthermore, as prejudiced or discriminating algorithms have the potential to uphold stereotypes and perpetuate societal injustices, ethical considerations are crucial in establishing how AI systems make judgements. As a result, taking a proactive stance in resolving these difficulties goes beyond simply following the law.

UNDERSTANDING PRIVACY AND ETHICS IN AI

Overview of Privacy Concerns in the Collection and Use of Data for AI Algorithms

In the digital age, privacy concerns in the gathering and processing of data for AI algorithms are critical(Stahl & Wright, 2018). A number of concerns surface as AI technologies become more and more dependent on large datasets for development and operation. Top worries are data security and privacy, which include the possibility of unauthorised access and data breaches that could reveal sensitive personal data (Barona & Anita, 2017). Consent to be informed is still often lacking, as information is routinely collected without the knowledge or agreement of the subjects. One important idea that should not be forgotten is data minimization, which might result in excessive data collecting and a higher chance of misuse. Sometimes de-identification measures are unsuccessful, which allows for re-identification and jeopardises personal privacy. Due to the fact that biased training data can maintain unfavourable results, bias and discrimination are widespread issues. Legal and regulatory issues are always changing, and once data is obtained, people frequently have no control over it. Finding technological, governmental, and moral answers to these issues is necessary to create a balance between privacy protection and innovation (Leenes et al., 2017).

Examination of Ethical Frameworks and Principles Guiding the Development and Deployment of AI Technologies

In order to ensure the appropriate and ethical use of AI technologies, a set of ethical frameworks and principles drive their development and deployment. Fairness and non-discrimination are two of these values, which highlight the necessity of preventing prejudice and discrimination in AI systems (Wachter et al., 2020). In AI decision-making processes, explain ability and transparency promote accountability and openness. Determining who bears responsibility for the behaviour of AI systems and resolving errors or harm requires accountability and responsibility. Respecting personal information and following privacy laws are essential to privacy and data protection. Human well-being and goodness emphasise that AI should advance mankind and make people's lives better. Development of environmentally friendly AI is aided by sustainability and environmental effect considerations (Chaudhary, 2023). International cooperation and standards are prioritised in global collaboration and governance. The goal of benefit sharing and equality is to equally distribute the advantages of AI without making societal disparities worse. Protecting against harm requires safety and security, and continuing learning and monitoring support the ethical development and modification of AI systems so that they are in line with moral principles and the interests of society. These guidelines offer a framework for the ethical and reliable development and application of AI.

Exploration of the Intersection Between Privacy, Ethics, and AI in Various Domains

Artificial intelligence (AI) and privacy are closely related in many different fields, raising difficult questions and moral dilemmas. AI helps in diagnosis and treatment in the medical field, but it also raises questions about algorithmic fairness and patient data privacy (Johnson et al., 2021). AI is used in finance for fraud detection and credit evaluation; however, the usage of private financial information calls for strict privacy protection. AI-powered risk assessment and predictive policing in the criminal justice system have the potential to violate privacy and reinforce prejudices. AI-driven personalization in education must address privacy and equality issues. AI is used by social media and advertising to deliver personalised information and advertisements, which has sparked discussions about algorithmic manipulation and user privacy. In addition to gathering data, autonomous cars can pose moral dilemmas on making decisions in dire circumstances. AI is used by national security for monitoring, necessitating a careful balancing act between state interests and personal privacy. AI-driven marketing in retail uses consumer data, raising concerns about where personalization and privacy end. Ethics must be taken into account while using AI for environmental monitoring in order to safeguard ecosystems and public privacy. AI used for employee surveillance in the workplace needs to abide by ethical and privacy standards. To enable responsible AI development and deployment across all of these sectors, it is essential to establish clear legislation and norms that place a priority on privacy, transparency, accountability, and ethical evaluation (Jobin et al., 2019).

CURRENT LANDSCAPE OF PRIVACY AND ETHICS IN AI

Review of Existing Regulations and Guidelines Governing the Use of AI in Different Industries

The swift progress of artificial intelligence (AI) technology in recent times has led to regulatory endeavours aimed at guaranteeing the conscientious and principled application of AI in diverse sectors. The regulatory environment surrounding AI differs by industry, reflecting the unique potential and problems that each one faces. This section offers a thorough analysis of current laws and policies in important sectors where artificial intelligence is having a big influence:

The Healthcare Industry

With the introduction of AI, the healthcare sector has experienced a significant metamorphosis, especially in areas like patient diagnostics, medication discovery, and medical imaging. In this industry, regulations try to find a middle ground between using AI's potential to improve medical care and addressing important ethical and privacy concerns. Notably, the Health Insurance Portability and Accountability Act (HIPAA) in the United States has set strict guidelines for protecting sensitive patient data. As AI becomes more common in healthcare, these guidelines are being extended to include AI applications for the handling and storage of medical data. In the meanwhile, strict guidelines are enforced by the European Union's Medical Device Regulation (MDR), which is committed to guaranteeing the effectiveness and safety of medical devices, including software driven by artificial intelligence. Additionally, since the American Medical Association (AMA) and other medical organisations have published ethical standards governing the use of AI, the sector is guided by ethical principles. These rules place a significant focus on patient consent, openness, and data protection.

Sector of Financial Services

The quick adoption of AI in the financial services sector has transformed tasks like algorithmic trading, fraud detection, and customer support. The crucial task of guaranteeing the moral application of AI in financial services has been placed in the hands of regulatory agencies. While not specifically addressing AI, the Dodd-Frank Act in the US requires accountability and openness in the financial markets, which is relevant to AI applications, especially in areas like risk management and algorithmic trading. Furthermore, a number of jurisdictions—including the European Union—have passed algorithmic trading-specific legislation that prioritise risk management, market surveillance, and the promotion of fair competition. In order to protect consumer interests, the Consumer Financial Protection Bureau (CFPB) publishes guidelines that control the use of AI in credit underwriting. These guidelines place a strong emphasis on the values of justice, transparency, and non-discrimination.

The Automotive Industry

AI is a fundamental component in the development of autonomous vehicles and advanced driver-assistance systems. Regulations play a crucial role in ensuring the safety and security of AI-driven automotive technologies. The National Highway Traffic Safety Administration (NHTSA) in the United States issues guidelines that prioritize safety in the testing and deployment of autonomous vehicles. Simultaneously, the UN Economic Commission for Europe (ECE) has established regulations specific to automated driving systems, with a focus on AI-driven components, striving to create international standards. Additionally, cybersecurity regulations have been implemented in response to the integration of AI into vehicles to protect against potential cyber threats, ensuring the integrity and security of connected cars.

The Energy and Utilities Sector

AI is essential to the energy and utilities sectors since it helps with predictive maintenance, power grid optimisation, and energy saving. The purpose of regulations in this field is to maintain the sustainability and dependability of AI-driven solutions. Notably, cybersecurity laws regulating AI applications in grid management are established by the North American Electric Reliability Corporation (NERC), which also sets reliability criteria for the North American bulk power system. In order to improve operational resilience and efficiency, the European Network of Transmission System Operators for Electricity (ENTSO-E) has established standards that integrate AI into grid management. Environmental rules are essential in addition to technical standards, as they guarantee that AI technologies in the energy sector support sustainable energy practises and ecologically responsible energy usage.

Evaluation of the Role of Organizations and Policymakers in Ensuring Privacy and Ethical AI Practices

AI practises emphasises their shared accountability in influencing artificial intelligence's future. In this context, organisations play a crucial role since they have to put in place thorough data governance frameworks, give transparency top priority, and incorporate ethical issues into the AI development process. The core principles of their operations must be user consent and data protection. Conversely, policymakers are essential in developing and implementing legal frameworks that establish moral principles and guarantee privacy standards in the AI space. In order to achieve the delicate balance between technical innovation and the protection of individual privacy and ethical norms, cooperation and synergy between organisations and politicians are essential, ultimately encouraging AI's good impact.

THE IMPLICATIONS OF PRIVACY AND ETHICS IN AI

Impact of AI on Individual Privacy Rights and Data Protection

In the current digital era, the effects of artificial intelligence on personal privacy rights and data protection are complex and always changing. On the one hand, by automating security procedures and enabling more reliable encryption and authentication techniques, AI technologies have the potential to improve data protection. The fact that this same technology may be used to gather, examine, and exploit enormous amounts of personal data without permission, however, also presents serious concerns to people's privacy. Machine learning algorithms have the ability to unearth personal information about people, which opens the door to possible misuses including discriminatory decision-making, invasive surveillance, and targeted advertising. A crucial issue facing governments, businesses, and society at large is finding a balance between protecting privacy and utilising AI's benefits.

Ethical Considerations in the Development of AI Algorithms and Decision-Making Processes

The increasing integration of AI systems into diverse societal domains such as healthcare, finance, criminal justice, and autonomous vehicles necessitates careful consideration of design and implementation approaches that prioritise equity, accountability, transparency, and human welfare. AI ethics cover a wide range of topics, such as algorithmic transparency, data privacy, accountability, bias and discrimination, and the possibility that AI will reinforce or worsen already-existing inequities. AI algorithm developers and stakeholders should make an effort to develop algorithms that are devoid of bias, or if bias does exist, it should be recognised, addressed, and minimised. Transparency is essential because it fosters confidence and makes it possible to examine AI decision-making procedures to make sure they adhere to human values. In order to hold developers and organisations accountable for the results of AI activity, accountability measures need be in place. To stop the misuse of personal data, privacy and data protection must also be protected. AI development ought to incorporate ethical concerns from the outset in order to steer the technology towards a more egalitarian and just future.

Consequences of AI-Driven Biases and Discriminatory Practices on Society and Marginalized Groups

Due to the fact that AI algorithms are frequently trained on data reflecting past biases and prejudices, discrimination may eventually be automated in a variety of contexts, including lending, hiring, criminal justice, and healthcare. As a result, marginalised groups suffer from systemic injustices and unjust treatment by AI systems. This undermines trust in institutions and technology in addition to perpetuating social injustices. Furthermore, it is challenging to hold many AI algorithms accountable because to their opacity, which further marginalises individuals who are impacted. In order to eliminate bias and guarantee that AI systems benefit all members of society, addressing these concerns calls for a deliberate effort to ensure justice, transparency, and equity in AI research and deployment. It also calls for the inclusion of various perspectives and expertise.

RESEARCH METHODOLOGY

Literature Review of Existing Studies, Papers, and Reports on AI Ethics and Privacy

Artificial Intelligence (AI) has quickly spread throughout our lives and had a big impact on a lot of different industries, such healthcare, banking, entertainment, and transportation(Dhanabalan et al., 2018). But the more AI systems are incorporated into our everyday lives, the more crucial it is to address the nuanced concerns about AI ethics and privacy. This study of the literature explores the complex aspects of this important subject.

A wide range of issues are covered by AI ethics, including as responsibility and transparency in algorithmic decision-making. Many AI systems are opaque, sometimes referred to as "black boxes," which makes it difficult to comprehend the reasoning behind their choices and actions. This opacity begs the questions of accountability for mishaps and the necessity of making AI systems just, transparent, and comprehensible. In addition, concerns about bias and fairness in AI systems have gained attention. AI decision-making processes that discriminate, such employment algorithms that give preference to particular demographic groups, have sparked a great deal of research and debate on how to reduce prejudice and guarantee fair results (Wachter et al., 2020).

On the other hand, privacy is a fundamental right that is becoming more and more endangered due to the growth of AI applications. For AI to work well, a lot of data—often sensitive data—is required. The danger of data breaches and unauthorised access increases as AI systems gather, examine, and utilise this data (Mughal, 2017). In the era of artificial intelligence, consent, data collecting ethics, and the ethical use of personal information are critical issues. The Cambridge Analytica incident and several data breaches have further highlighted how urgent it is to address these problems.

The legal environment is changing from a regulatory perspective to address these moral and privacy issues (Leenes et al., 2017). A good example is the General Data Protection Regulation (GDPR) of the European Union, which imposes severe fines for noncompliance and introduces strict data protection procedures. Additionally, organisations such as the Association for Computing Machinery (ACM) and the Institute of Electrical and Electronics Engineers (IEEE) have developed AI ethical standards to offer a framework for responsible AI development and deployment. The purpose of this review is to give readers a thorough understanding of these problems, the changing regulatory landscape, and the continuing academic discussion around AI ethics and privacy. It emphasises the importance of ethical considerations and practical regulatory measures in order to responsibly navigate the AI-driven world.

Case Study Analysis of Notable Incidents Related to AI and Privacy Breaches

Artificial intelligence has a significant impact on people's privacy and data security, as evidenced by the examination of prominent cases involving AI and privacy breaches. The Facebook and Cambridge Analytica scandals raised ethical questions about the use of data and its manipulation for political ends by exposing the frightening potential for AI-driven algorithms to gather enormous amounts of personal data without user consent. The significant data breach at Equifax highlighted the need for strict security standards and accountability by proving that even AI-powered data security systems can be vulnerable. A persistent worry, deepfake technology presents a distinct risk since it makes it possible to produce convincingly fake audio and video recordings, which can result in misinformation, political manipulation, and invasions of privacy. These case studies highlight the vital requirement for openness, morality, and strict laws to safeguard privacy in the era of AI, as well as the enduring challenges in combating evolving threats to data security and individual rights.

Interviews With Experts and Stakeholders in the Field of AI and Data Privacy

Experts and stakeholders from several industries come together in the dynamic and complex topic of artificial intelligence (AI) and data privacy. This intersection offers tremendous opportunities as well as difficulties as it develops. The continued influence of data protection laws like the CCPA and GDPR, which have influenced how businesses handle personal data in AI applications, is one of the major themes. Finding a balance between data privacy and AI innovation is still a major challenge, and biases and ethical conundrums demand constant attention. Adopting technology that protect privacy, making sure AI models are transparent and explainable, and giving consumers permission and control over their data are all examples of best practises. In order to handle the complex issues at hand, cooperation between various sectors is necessary, and public awareness and education campaigns are crucial for creating a society that is better educated. Experts see exciting developments in AI and data privacy in the near future, but they also see new difficulties as technology develops. All things considered, negotiating this terrain requires a multimodal strategy that upholds privacy while using AI's potential.

PROPOSED MODEL: PRIVACY AND ETHICS FRAMEWORK FOR AI GOVERNANCE

Principles for Responsible AI Development and Deployment

Figure 1. Ethical framework of AI

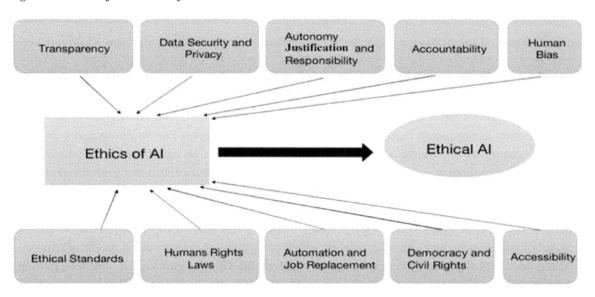

The framework for AI ethics is established in Figure 1, which also lists the elements that must be taken into account while defining AI ethics in order to create ethical AI. While defining AI ethics is complex and varied, putting AI ethics into practise to create ethical AI is also a difficult task. What kind of AI is morally appropriate? The basic definition of ethical AI is that it shouldn't hurt people. So what harm is there? What rights do people have? We have a long way to go before we can create and implement moral AI. To make appropriate ethical decisions, ethical sensitivity training is necessary. choices. AI should, in theory, be able to identify moral dilemmas. How can we create and build an AI that is aware of ethical issues if it is able to make decisions? Regretfully, it is difficult to realise and put into practise. Sustained and long-term efforts are required. Nevertheless, recognising the significance of creating ethical AI and beginning the process gradually are constructive moves in the right direction.

Numerous organisations, including Microsoft, IBM, Google, Accenture, and Atomium-EISMD, have begun developing ethical guidelines to direct the advancement of AI. In November 2018, the FEAT principles—fairness, ethics, accountability, and transparency—were introduced by the Monetary Authority of Singapore (MAS), Microsoft, and Amazon Web Services for the usage of of AI. Academics, practitioners, and policymakers should work together to widen the engagement to establish ethical principles for AI design, development, and use.

Strategies for Safeguarding User Privacy and Data Security in AI Systems

Figure 2. Proposed solution for data privacy and security

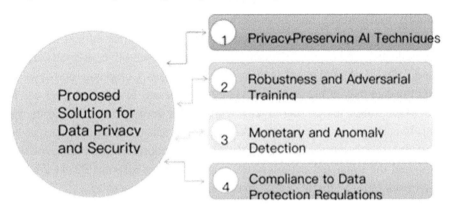

Privacy-Preserving AI Techniques: Organisations can use privacy-preserving AI techniques like homomorphic encryption, safe multi-party computation, and federated learning to address privacy concerns (Bonawitz et al., 2017). By using these techniques, businesses may train AI models on dispersed data without having to share raw data, which lowers the possibility of data leaks or breaches. Adversarial training strategies have been developed by researchers to enhance model resilience and protect against adversarial attacks. These techniques entail adding adversarial samples to a training dataset (Madry et al., 2018). The model learns to be more tolerant to adversarial perturbations by using both clean and adversarial data during training. Monitoring and anomaly detection: Businesses can use monitoring and anomaly detection methods to spot data poisoning and model tampering variations in the model's parameters, training set, or performance from what is expected (Lewis, 1998). Early detection can help stop additional harm to AI systems and offer insightful information for enhancing security protocols. Compliance with Data Protection Regulations: To make sure that they collect, store, and process data in a secure and compliant manner, organisations should abide by data protection regulations, such as the California Consumer Privacy Act (CCPA) in the United States and the General Data Protection Regulation (GDPR) in Europe (Ramirez et al., 2022). Respecting these rules can reduce the possibility of data breaches and safeguard user privacy.

Organisations that create and use AI systems have serious worries about data privacy and security issues. Organisations can improve the security and privacy of their AI systems by being aware of these issues and putting mitigation tactics in place, such as robustness training, privacy-preserving AI methodologies, and compliance with data protection laws. Researchers, practitioners, and legislators must collaborate to address these issues as AI develops and affects more sectors of the economy. Only then can we make sure that AI advances society without jeopardising user security and privacy.

Guidelines for Addressing Ethical Dilemmas and Biases in AI Decision-Making Processes

A diverse strategy is necessary to address ethical concerns and biases in AI decision-making processes. Fairness, accountability, transparency, and the preservation of human rights should be given top priority while developing and implementing AI. It is imperative to first create clear ethical standards and rules in this regard. Data collection and training datasets should be representative, diversified, and routinely checked to detect and address potential biases in order to reduce biases. Companies and developers should be transparent about the data they utilise and how AI systems operate. Reducing biases can be achieved through using fairness measures, integrating diverse teams in AI development, and doing ongoing testing and monitoring. In addition, in the event that AI systems produce biased or incorrect conclusions, there should be procedures for responsibility and restitution. Collaboration and public involvement with ethicists, regulators, and the impacted communities can help foster responsible AI development and ensure that ethical considerations remain central in decision-making processes.

CONCLUSION

Summary of Key Findings and Insights From the Research

A multifaceted strategy is necessary to safeguard user privacy and advance ethical AI practises. This involves making sure that user consent for data gathering is relevant, maintaining strict laws and standards that control AI development and application, and ensuring transparency in AI algorithms. Prioritising data anonymization and encryption, performing frequent privacy effect analyses, and funding AI ethics training for staff members are all things that businesses should do. Establishing a framework that maintains ethical values, protects user privacy, and encourages responsible AI innovation while actively addressing any biases and discrimination will require cooperation between industry, government, and civil society.

Future Considerations for the Ongoing Development and Regulation of AI in the Context of Privacy and Ethics

The protection of ethics and privacy must be the top priority as AI development and regulation continue to change. Future research should focus on creating strong privacy-preserving AI systems that reduce data exposure and give people control over their personal data in order to protect people and society. The establishment and enforcement of ethical standards is also necessary to guarantee that AI systems follow the values of accountability, transparency, and justice. Collaboration between governments, industry stakeholders, and academics will be important to find a balance between innovation and ethical application, thus establishing a responsible and trustworthy AI ecosystem for the benefit of all.

REFERENCES

Barona, R., & Anita, E. A. M. (2017). A survey on data breach challenges in cloud computing security: Issues and threats. *2017 International Conference on Circuit, Power and Computing Technologies (IC-CPCT),* (pp. 1–8). IEEE. 10.1109/ICCPCT.2017.8074287

Bonawitz, K., Eichner, H., Grieskamp, W., Huba, D., Ingerman, A., & Ivanov, V. (2017). *Towards Federated Learning At Scale: System Design.* arXiv:1902.01046v1. 2019, 1–13.

Chaudhary, G. (2023). Environmental Sustainability: Can Artificial Intelligence be an Enabler for SDGs? Dhanabalan, T., Sathish, A., & Tamilnadu, K. (2018). *TRANSFORMING INDIAN INDUSTRIES THROUGH ARTIFICIAL INTELLIGENCE AND.*, *9*(10), 835–845.

Floridi, L., & Cowls, J. (2022). A unified framework of five principles for AI in society. *Machine Learning and the City: Applications in Architecture and Urban Design*, 535–545. doi:10.1002/9781119815075.ch45

Floridi, L., Cowls, J., Beltrametti, M., Chatila, R., Chazerand, P., Dignum, V., Luetge, C., Madelin, R., Pagallo, U., Rossi, F., Schafer, B., Valcke, P., & Vayena, E. (2018). AI4People—An Ethical Framework for a Good AI Society: Opportunities, Risks, Principles, and Recommendations. *Minds and Machines*, *28*(4), 689–707. doi:10.1007/s11023-018-9482-5 PMID:30930541

Formosa, P., Wilson, M., & Richards, D. (2021). A principlist framework for cybersecurity ethics. *Computers & Security*, *109*, 102382. doi:10.1016/j.cose.2021.102382

Jobin, A., Ienca, M., & Vayena, E. (2019). *Artificial Intelligence: the global landscape of ethics guidelines.*

Johnson, K. B., Wei, W., Weeraratne, D., Frisse, M. E., Misulis, K., Rhee, K., Zhao, J., & Snowdon, J. L. (2021). Precision Medicine, AI, and the Future of Personalized Health Care. doi:10.1111/cts.12884

Leenes, R., Palmerini, E., Koops, B., Bertolini, A., Lucivero, F., Leenes, R., Palmerini, E., Koops, B., & Bertolini, A. (2017). *Regulatory challenges of robotics: some guidelines for addressing legal and ethical issues.* 9961. doi:10.1080/17579961.2017.1304921

Lewis, T. (1998). The new economics of information. *IEEE Internet Computing*, *2*(5), 93–94. doi:10.1109/4236.722237

Madry, A., Markelov, A., Schmidt, L., Tsipras, D., & Vladu, A. (2018). Towards deep learning models resistant to adversarial attacks. *6th International Conference on Learning Representations, ICLR 2018 - Conference Track Proceedings*, (pp. 1–28). Research Gate.

Mai, J. E. (2016). Big data privacy: The datafication of personal information. *The Information Society*, *32*(3), 192–199. doi:10.1080/01972243.2016.1153010

Mughal, A. A. (2017). *Artificial Intelligence in Information Security: Exploring the Advantages, Challenges, and Future Directions.*

RamirezM. A.KimS.-K.Al HamadiH.DamianiE.ByonY.-J.KimT.-Y.ChoC.-S.YeunC. Y. (2022). Poisoning Attacks and Defenses on Artificial Intelligence: A Survey. http://arxiv.org/abs/2202.10276

Robert, L., Cheung, C., Matt, C., & Trenz, M. (2018). Int ne t R es ea rch Int ern et Re se. *Internet Research*, *28*, 829–850.

Ryan, M. (2020). In AI We Trust: Ethics, Artificial Intelligence, and Reliability. *Science and Engineering Ethics*, *26*(5), 2749–2767. doi:10.1007/s11948-020-00228-y PMID:32524425

Stahl, B. C., & Wright, D. (2018). Ethics and Privacy in AI and Big Data: Implementing Responsible Research and Innovation. *IEEE Security and Privacy*, *16*(3), 26–33. doi:10.1109/MSP.2018.2701164

Street, V. (2005). *Indian Institute of Technology Gandhinagar.*, *14*(3), 13210003.

Chapter 15
Privacy Matters:
Espousing Blockchain and Artificial Intelligence (AI) for Consumer Data Protection on E-Commerce Platforms in Ethical Marketing

Bhupinder Singh
https://orcid.org/0009-0006-4779-2553
Sharda University, India

Pushan Kumar Dutta
https://orcid.org/0000-0002-4765-3864
Amity University, Kolkata, India

Vishal Jain
https://orcid.org/0000-0003-1126-7424
Sharda University, India

Gursahib Singh
K.R. Mangalam World School, Greater Noida, India

Christian Kaunert
https://orcid.org/0000-0002-4493-2235
Dublin City University, Ireland

ABSTRACT

The proliferation of e-commerce platforms has provided customers with a level of convenience never seen before, but it also raises serious questions about how sensitive consumer data is protected. This chapter explores the complex interplay between two emerging technologies, AI and blockchain, with the goal of strengthening consumer data protection on e-commerce platforms. It examines innovative and forward-thinking solutions that handle the complexities of data governance as well as the changing legal aspects of the e-commerce industry by exposing the numerous difficulties and challenges that occur in this confluence. The protection of consumer data is one of the biggest issues facing e-commerce. The combination of blockchain technology and artificial intelligence (AI) acts as a lighthouse, pointing the way for the e-commerce sector toward a more transparent, safe, and morally upright future.

DOI: 10.4018/979-8-3693-2215-4.ch015

INTRODUCTION

A new era in consumer data protection has been brought about by the combination of blockchain technology and artificial intelligence (AI), particularly in the context of e-commerce platforms. This study examines the complex interrelationships of privacy, blockchain, and artificial intelligence with a particular emphasis on moral marketing. The paper explores the difficulties, concerns, and legal aspects related to the use of customer data in e-commerce and offers tactical approaches for efficient data governance. It is essential to comprehend these complex problems in order to develop practical solutions that go beyond the traditional paradigms of data protection. With its reputation for being decentralized and impervious to tampering, blockchain offers a strong answer to the problems associated with data transparency and integrity.

AI offers real-time threat detection and prevention capabilities through predictive security techniques. These technologies' synergistic integration has the potential to completely transform how customer data is managed on e-commerce platforms and offer a strong barrier against constantly changing privacy concerns. The legal aspects of consumer data protection call for a proactive and flexible strategy. Blockchain-enabled transparent auditing guarantees adherence to data protection laws by offering a verifiable record of data exchanges (Girasa, 2020). When given that regulatory frameworks are always evolving, it is imperative that organizations adopt an adaptive compliance strategy to ensure that they are compliant with the law and uphold ethical standards.

The paper describes standards and interoperability techniques to guarantee the smooth integration of AI and blockchain on various e-commerce platforms. Future plans will prioritize ethical issues and stress the need of responsible innovation. With the goal of creating an e-commerce environment that is dependable and trustworthy, these initiatives envision a time when digital transactions are not only safe but also morally regulated. Blockchain and AI together have great potential to strengthen customer data privacy on e-commerce platforms (Tomazevic et al., 2023). Businesses should proactively design a future where privacy is not simply a compliance obligation but a key component of ethical and innovative digital commerce by recognizing and solving the underlying concerns and obstacles.

Historical Context

The consumer data is being collected, processed, and used at an unprecedented rate due to the quick rise of e-commerce. In order to protect consumer privacy and trust in the digital era, ethical marketing methods are essential (Aaronson, 2022). AI and blockchain come to light as potential technology to deal with these issues. The need for improved privacy and security is urgent, especially when it comes to people's personal information, as seen by the recent spikes in security breaches and digital surveillance. Prospects for improving data privacy include advances in cybersecurity and impending legislation. Through decentralized identification and other privacy characteristics, blockchain and distributed ledger technologies provide novel ways to protect user data. Thanks to these technologies, people now have more ownership and control over their data (Mahankali, 2019). Also, artificial intelligence provides new ways to support user and system security, enhance data repositories, and ease the creation of better analytical models.

The ethical issues surrounding data privacy in digital marketing are related to the standards and policies that regulate the collection, use, and disclosure of customer information. This means adhering to the requirements specified by data protection regulations and using the best practices to preserve client privacy (Hodson, 2019). The neglecting to protect consumer privacy can have serious consequences for organizations and consumers alike. Therefore, it is imperative that businesses incorporate ethical data practices into their digital marketing plans.

Objectives of the Chapter

This chapter has the following objectives to:

- analyze how privacy, blockchain and AI interface with e-commerce.
- recognize and assess problems and obstacles pertaining to the security of customer data.
- examine the legislative and regulatory framework controlling e-commerce data privacy.
- make thoughtful, forward-thinking suggestions for ethical marketing through efficient data governance.

Figure 1. Objectives of the chapter

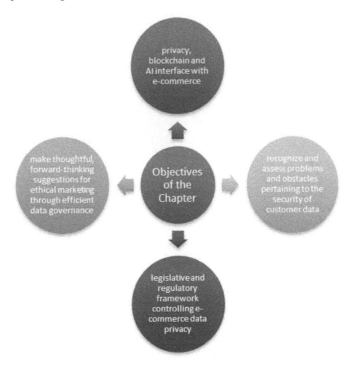

Structure of the Chapter

This chapter comprehensively explores the various dimensions of Blockchain and Artificial Intelligence (AI) for Consumer Data Protection and Privacy on E-Commerce Platforms in Ethical Marketing: Issues, Challenges and Strategic Futuristic Solutions for Data Governance and Legal Dimensions. Section 2 elaborates the Privacy and E-Commerce. Section 3 deals with the Blockchain Technology: Facilitator of Privacy. Section 4 explores the Artificial Intelligence and Data Protection for Consumers. Section 5 travels the Challenges and Issues Involved. Section 6 examines the Legal Aspects and the Regulatory Framework. Section 7 lays down the Future-Secure and Strategic Approaches to Data Governance. And, finally Section 8 Conclude the Paper with Future Scope.

Figure 2. Structure of the chapter

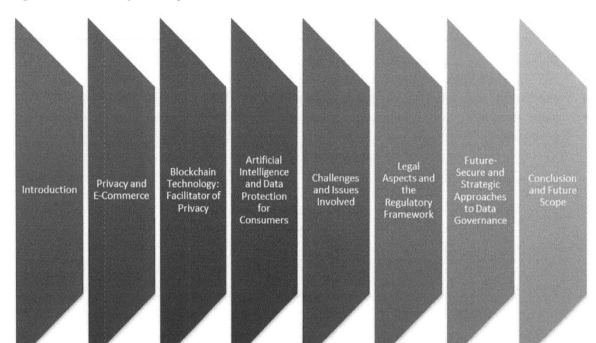

PRIVACY AND E-COMMERCE

The surge in data breaches in recent times, coupled with certain organizations' improper use of personal information, has made customers more cautious and skeptical about revealing their data. Data privacy is seen as a basic right, and customers expect enterprises to respect this right. People want to know that companies are actively protecting their privacy since they are becoming more aware of the possible hazards associated with sharing their data online (Daugherty & Wilson, 2018). An important factor in electronic business is privacy as the transacting frequently necessitates providing personal information, including a shipping address, credit card number, or product preferences.

If users feel that their privacy is being violated or threatened, they may be reluctant to provide this crucial information or even to use online services (Milakovich, 2021). Within the arena of electronic commerce (e-commerce), a delicate equilibrium is maintained between the necessary disclosure of certain personal information needed to fulfill online transactions and the possible negative consequences linked to those disclosures. The need for this data and the increasing complexity of businesses' methods for collecting personal data has made e-commerce privacy a top priority. It arranges important research subjects and findings in a framework that is based on the interactions between the four main stakeholder groups: governments, businesses, consumers, and privacy solution providers (PSPs) (Johnsen, 2020).

Although the concept of privacy is not new, its interpretation and use in the context of online shopping are relatively new. Nonetheless, there is increasing agreement that protecting consumer privacy may have a positive impact on all parties involved. The notion of privacy, the legislative structures intended to protect this intangible human value, and, more recently, computing technology intended to maintain individual privacy in the modern world have all been the subject of much research. This looks back at how this basic idea has developed historically and examines the ways that cultural and technological developments have put the right to privacy in jeopardy (Dewani et al., 2022).

Gathering and Applying Data

The need for customer to provide personal information to businesses may be the source of this mistrust, as it raises questions about possible abuse (Tang et al., 2020). The suspicions over the prompt delivery of purchased items following the processing of payment may also exist. So, finding an e-commerce strategy that maximizes online customers' trust is a required. To reduce any negative effects on the consumer, the creation of cover data is assigned to a node other than the customer (Girasa, 2020). As a result, the private information belonging to the client is accessed by this node and used for the cover calculation.

Technology steps are required to stop private data from being revealed. An established technique that was first created for self-enforcing privacy in electronic polls is carefully examined, exposing flaws in terms of participant fairness (Choithani et al., 2022). Within the context of the new privacy paradigm, a more robust version of the protocol is developed and put into use, along with a novel differential-privacy preserving function. Both the new differential-privacy preservation function and the improved e-poll protocol are seen as equally important to the emerging e-commerce privacy paradigm, even though they are only minor additions to the study (Robinson, 2020).

Principles of Ethical Marketing

There are two main paradigms that attempt to protect the privacy of customers in e-commerce, which raises serious privacy problems. While one strategy stresses user anonymity, the other depends on the consumer's faith in the network's commitment to privacy standards. A new paradigm that offers a healthy middle ground between these two extremes is put forward (Cavus et al., 2022). Under this model, the client uses their true identity while only sharing covert information that hides the particular resources they are looking for. Thus, the focus of privacy regulation is moved from the identity of the client to their shopping choices (Trautman et al., 2021). This novel method works especially effectively in situations such as online/e-commerce transactions, when it is difficult to build confidence in a network's privacy policy and anonymity is either forbidden or impractical (Liow et al., 2022).

BLOCKCHAIN TECHNOLOGY: FACILITATOR OF PRIVACY

The spread of large amounts of data has put a significant burden on storage, but the open network environment hasn't done much to protect consumer data privacy. The peer-to-peer distributed ledger technology, or blockchain, is based on cryptographic methods and has features including decentralization, anonymity, tamper resistance, and public verifiability. These qualities help allay worries about data security in the Internet of Things. Proxy reencryption and ring signature, two popular encryption techniques, are essential to privacy protection (Winecoff & Watkins, 2022). As a result, this paper suggests combining blockchain technology with proxy reencryption and ring signature to provide privacy protection for the Internet of Things. This idea is useful in a number of application areas, including supply chain management, industry, the Internet of Things (IoT), and healthcare. The main focus is to investigate how blockchain technology is being applied in various fields from an academic standpoint. It also explores the latest advancements made by different groups in utilizing blockchain technology in a variety of industries (Marwala, 2022).

The concerns with privacy and secrecy arise when digital data is sent via an unreliable transmission route. A safe alternative for peer-to-peer communication is provided by blockchain technology. On the blockchain, transactions are visible to the whole public for reading, but once they are recorded, they cannot be changed (Gera et al., 2023). A comprehensive analysis of the literature shows that blockchain is widely used in many useful fields. But keep in mind that blockchain is a probabilistic state system, thus it might not be appropriate in circumstances when judgments must be definitive. In the meanwhile, it examines the blockchain's many uses and talks about how it may be used to solve a range of problems with conventional databases (La Diega, 2023).

Blockchain technology has its roots in the Bitcoin cryptocurrency, and since then, it has been applied in a number of other fields (Si et al., 2023). It describes the many uses of Blockchain in the following domains: finance, healthcare, Internet of Things (IoT), legal systems, supply chain management, e-business, power grids, transportation systems, commercial sectors, cloud computing, reputation management, and supply chains. Blockchain functions as a public ledger, but it has to ensure a few crucial things:

- Commitment Protocols- Ensure that, within a certain timescale, all legitimate client transactions are committed and added to the Blockchain.
- Consensus- Ensure updates and coherence among local copies.
- Security- Make sure the data is unchangeable, taking into account the potential for hostile nodes or weakened security.
- Privacy and Authenticity- Recognize that transactions or data relate to different nodes, making privacy issues necessary.

Figure 3. Functions of Blockchain

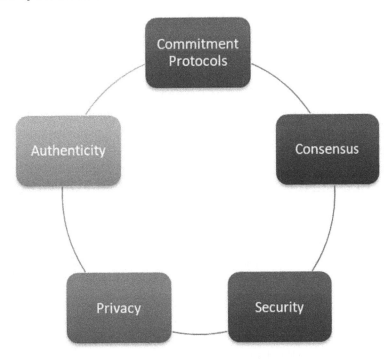

Dispersed Data Archiving

A blockchain-based system relies heavily on data and the consensus-driven method dispersed nodes use to store and update it in order to enable trustless multi-party transactions. Therefore, evaluating the effectiveness, performance, and expense of a blockchain-based application requires a deep understanding of the types of data involved as well as how they are stored and processed (Vashista, 2020). Blockchain technology presents new issues for data management even as its features as- transparency, immutability and consistency improve data quality. Blockchains use a variety of data structures, including as document stores and key-value stores, which are typically augmented with "off-chain" data stores (Kaponis & Maragoudakis, 2022). As a result, blockchain-based systems require manual and ad hoc programming to search for and retrieve different types of data, which is different from the declarative and abstract query methods present in conventional databases. The increasing demand for large-scale blockchain data analytics makes it imperative to understand how to access, integrate, and analyze data in this heterogeneous environment efficiently (Youssef & Hossam, 2023).

Smart Contracts (E-Contracts)

Smart contracts are blockchain-based programs that start running as soon as certain criteria are met. These contracts are frequently used to automate the performance of an agreement, guaranteeing that all parties involved know exactly what will happen right away and don't need to wait for anything to happen. Smart contracts can also automate workflows by starting the next activity when predetermined criteria are satisfied (Singh, 2023).

The statements stored onto a blockchain are the foundation of smart contracts. Once established requirements are checked and satisfied, a network of computers carries out the stated tasks. These acts may include things like paying out money, keeping track of car registrations, sending out alerts, or writing tickets. After the transaction is finished, the blockchain is updated to guarantee its immutability, and the outcomes are only accessible to those who are permitted (Singh, 2023). The participants in a smart contract can include as many conditions as needed to guarantee the work will be completed satisfactorily. It take into account any potential exceptions, design a dispute resolution system, and decide how transactions and their data are recorded on the blockchain in order to set the conditions (Sharma & Singh, 2022).

ARTIFICIAL INTELLIGENCE AND DATA PROTECTION FOR CONSUMERS

The development of artificial intelligence presents a number of difficulties, including technological, legal, and ethical issues. A number of relevant concerns come up in the context of consumer protection law, which is intended to protect the party in a transaction who has less influence the consumer. Among these is the requirement to educate customers on how to use these kinds of systems. It endeavors to investigate the following research questions: (1) Does the implementation of artificial intelligence provide new hazards for consumers, namely in the financial markets, and if yes, what are the specific concerns? The second question is whether and to what degree the use of AI in transactions necessitates stricter consumer protection regulations (Bandara et al., 2020).

Artificial intelligence is developing at a tremendous pace these days, which has created several concerns, including legal concerns (Aldboush & Ferdous, 2023). Although a thorough examination of these issues is outside the purview of this research, the pertinent material is briefly discussed. The legal issues of artificial intelligence systems are well covered in the literature. Nonetheless, the main emphasis is on identifying risks to consumers in the financial sector brought about by artificial intelligence and the ensuing modifications to consumer protection legislation that are required (Kavut, 2021). The legal science literature frequently describes the difficulties posed by the advancement of artificial intelligence, first focusing on broad legal issues before exploring its consequences for consumer protection law particularly in relation to the financial sector because data is interchangeable, reusable, and may be used for purposes other than transactions, and because data processing technologies like as artificial intelligence are driving the expected rise in data use in the future (Timan & Mann, 2021). The inherent ambiguity around the data's future usage for both parties participating in a transaction is especially significant, especially when the buyer is debating whether or not to provide personal information. Given the rapidly developing field of future data technologies, sellers could be reluctant to place limits on the use of their data, including requirements for certain uses, data processing techniques, or durations. It is possible for a seller to sell data to organizations that will make use of it, even if they do not plan to use data technology themselves. Because data marketplaces are dynamic, vendors are motivated to collect as much information (Gupta et al., 2020).

AI in Customized Marketing

Marketing is one area where artificial intelligence has a lot of promise. It is essential for building complex algorithms, diversifying information and data sources, and improving software's data management features. The dynamic effect of artificial intelligence is changing how consumers and companies engage.

The website's features and the type of business in issue will determine whether or not it is applied (Nabbosa & Kaar, 2020). AI gives marketers the ability to focus on customer-centric strategies and instantly respond to their demands. By using AI, marketers can quickly identify the channels and content that are most appropriate for their target audience. This is made possible by the algorithms' examination of the data that is created and gathered (Khan & Mer, 2023). Artificial intelligence (AI) customisation of user experiences increases users' comfort levels and increases their propensity to make purchases. By using AI techniques, one may also identify client expectations and analyze the efforts of competitors. Computers can now evaluate and understand data without explicit programming thanks to machine learning (ML), a subset of artificial intelligence. Furthermore, when more data is processed by the algorithm, which improves performance and accuracy, machine learning (ML) helps humans solve issues more effectively (Ahmad et al., 2023).

Techniques for Privacy-Preserving AI

When using data already in existence, artificial intelligence (AI) seeks to mimic human cognitive processes and handle complex tasks. AI has already outperformed humans in many complicated activities in terms of accuracy, speed, and cost-effectiveness (Sonne, 2014). Text translation, voice help, autonomous driving, and other applications have evolved greatly as a result of the rapid integration of AI, especially in its subfields such as machine learning and deep learning. Simultaneously, AI is becoming more and more essential in the field of biomedicine, helping to solve the problems presented by large amounts of healthcare data and offering methods to help researchers extract meaningful insights from it (Wang et al., 2023).

CHALLENGES AND ISSUES INVOLVED

Unethical handling of Data: A number of behaviors might be indicative of unethical data management, such as collecting superfluous data, not being transparent about the methods used to obtain it, or selling client information to third parties without authorization (Jebamikyous et al., 2023). There are numerous instances of unethical data practices in digital marketing include the following:

Deceptive Agreement: Companies may use pre-set checkboxes or deceptive phrasing to obtain customers' agreement for data gathering without fully disclosing the implications.

Inappropriate Data Gathering: Acquiring more data than is required to provide services, or gathering erroneous data, can be misleading to customers and undermine their confidence.

Security Gaps: Companies that fail to protect customer information from illegal access or cyberattacks risk disclosing private data, including credit card numbers, addresses, and even medical records.

Overbearing Marketing: It may be deemed a breach of privacy and trust when consumer data is used to create tailored advertising campaigns that are obtrusive or misleading.

In order to maintain ethical data practices, companies must to adhere to the accompanying guidelines:

Security: It is critical that companies prioritize safeguarding client information. Implementing appropriate security measures, such as firewalls, access restrictions, and encryption, will help achieve this. Businesses should also make sure that employees receive training on privacy and data protection procedures.

Consent: Before collecting or disclosing a customer's data, businesses must obtain the customer's clear, informed consent. This entails using wording in permission forms that is understandable and unambiguous and making sure that clients are fully aware of their ability to revoke consent at any moment.

Transparency: Companies need to be honest about how they gather and use data. Customers must be made fully aware of the kind of data being gathered, why it is being collected, and how it will be used. Opt-in forms, privacy rules, and cookie policies may all help accomplish this openness.

Simplicity: This idea is obtaining only the information that is necessary to do a certain task and making sure that the information is current and accurate. The danger of data breaches can be reduced by deleting or anonymizing superfluous data.

Integrating privacy: Companies should think about privacy at every stage of their data processing operations. This entails making sure that data is deleted at the end of its lifespan and taking privacy into account when designing new goods and services.

Accountability: Organizations should regularly audit and evaluate their data security protocols in order to hold themselves accountable for their data activities. By taking a proactive stance, it may be possible to detect possible dangers and weaknesses and make prompt adjustments to reduce them.

Beyond being a moral and legal need for companies, the ethical aspects of data privacy in digital marketing also give them a competitive edge. Businesses may build consumer trust, improve their brand, and maximize marketing results by using ethical data practices (Wylde et al., 2022).

LEGAL ASPECTS AND THE REGULATORY ENVIRONMENT: CONSUMER DATA PROTECTION ON E-COMMERCE PLATFORMS

Law and Artificial Intelligence are going through a major transition and this discipline is now experiencing a rapid shift. Historically, it has focused on developing expert systems and academic efforts to develop theories and techniques for knowledge representation and reasoning in the legal domain (Wei & Xia, 2022). It is no longer limited to academics; instead, it is now open to new players, including corporations ready to contribute significantly and take advantage of the disruptive impact of recent advances in AI across a range of industries. Although business interests present new opportunities, consumers may be at danger since data accessibility seems to be influencing the balance of power more and more (Kaplan, 2020).

The India's current legislative framework for online consumer protection in light of the rapidly expanding and changing nature of e-commerce, which has altered consumer preferences for online shopping (Thiebes et al., 2021). There are two newly passed laws as the Consumer Protection Act of 2019 and the Consumer Protection (E-commerce) Rules of 2020 are there. The online platforms emphasize the need for a stable and safe system to support the growth of e-business enterprises and they identify cash on delivery as the best way to make purchases online. In the worldwide context of e-commerce, consumer safety is still a major problem (Paliszkiewicz et al., 2023). E-commerce is the practice of facilitating sales of products and services using electronic platforms. It leads to increased competitiveness, more productivity, more options, cost savings, and better organizational production processes. E-commerce is defined by the Organization for Economic Cooperation and Development in 1999 as all online commercial operations, including ordering, invoicing, and payment processes, as well as communications like marketing and advertising (Kopalle et al., 2022). There are three essential components of consumer safety in e-commerce are acknowledged by the 1999 recommendations of the Organization for Economic

Cooperation and Development. First, it is seen to be crucial that all consumers have access to e-commerce. Second, in order to promote customer trust and confidence in e-commerce, it is imperative that clear and effective consumer protection measures be developed continuously, with an emphasis on addressing unfair, deceptive, and fraudulent behaviors that occur online. Third, everyone involved in businesses, consumers, and their representatives, as well as governmental organizations which must take a proactive role in helping to create efficient redress mechanisms. It's crucial to remember that these rules mostly relate to international transactions (Tan & Salo, 2023).

FUTURE-SECURE AND STRATEGIC APPROACHES TO DATA GOVERNANCE

Data governance has been considered necessary for an organization's efficient use and management of data for a considerable amount of time. Ensuring accuracy, consistency, and security is the primary goal of this approach, which involves establishing rules, processes, and standards that govern the administration, storage, and protection of data (Nguyen & Tran, 2023). However, due to the rapid advancement of technology as well as the growing amount and complexity of data, traditional methods of data governance are becoming less and less effective. It is critical to investigate the causes of the declining efficacy of these traditional methods as companies consider updating their data governance strategy (Xing et al., 2023). The data governance models display the important traits which focus on control and compliance than on enabling data-driven decision-making. The regulatory compliance and risk minimization are usually given precedence over using data to support corporate innovation and growth in these frameworks. This focus might stifle innovation and prevent data from being fully valued (Gabhane et al., 2023).

The lack of flexibility often too stiff and centralized to adjust to changing company demands. Conventional data governance systems often include strict rules and procedures that are difficult to adapt, and they are hierarchical and rigid (Jaafar & Pierre, 2023). The organizations may find it difficult to adapt to the ever-changing business environment and successfully handle new possibilities and problems as a result of this rigidity. The data governance frameworks are frequently implemented in a siloed manner, with no cooperation or coordination between different teams and departments inside the company. This isolation can impede effective teamwork in leveraging data to achieve company value by posing barriers to communication and data exchange (Dewani et al., 2022).

The most significant change in data governance is a fundamental shift in perspective rather than a mere trend. Data governance is evolving quickly from being limited to solitary business silos to being an issue affecting the entire organization. Improvements in data governance systems are bringing more insight at the same time (Ghimire et al., 2020). The data teams may benefit from this transition in a mutually beneficial way. They now have more organizational support and have access to cutting-edge solutions that allow them to successfully apply data governance methods and maintain data security, usability, and availability (Rane, 2023).

Data engineering teams nowadays have a variety of alternatives to take into account when creating data governance plans that are customized to the unique requirements of their companies (Tyagi & Tiwari, 2024). These are four noteworthy data governance trends that you should keep a watch on.

Figure 4. Data governance trends

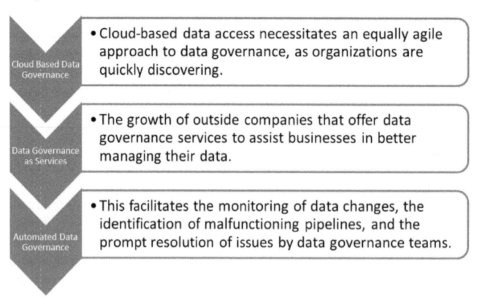

- Cloud Based Data Governance
  - Cloud-based data access necessitates an equally agile approach to data governance, as organizations are quickly discovering.
- Data Governance as Services
  - The growth of outside companies that offer data governance services to assist businesses in better managing their data.
- Automated Data Governance
  - This facilitates the monitoring of data changes, the identification of malfunctioning pipelines, and the prompt resolution of issues by data governance teams.

Mixed Blockchain Solutions

Blockchain-based technologies are expected to have a major influence on e-commerce and other commercial applications and procedures (Hicham et al., 2023). The potential of blockchain technology and associated innovations to create "trustless systems" with unique characteristics poses significant challenges to established business models and procedures that have historically guaranteed trust, dependability, and enforceability in business-to-business (B2B), business-to-consumer (B2C), business-to-government (B2G), and consumer-to-consumer (C2C) interactions. Blockchain has the potential to upend the foundations of electronic commerce by enabling trustless trade interactions that function without the need for specialized middlemen or, in the case of permissionless blockchains, central authorities. Blockchain improves the speed, ease of use, and security of transactions on e-commerce sites (Howells, 2020). Blockchain-based applications have several benefits, such as enhancing synergy efficiency, cutting operating costs, and streamlining company processes (Pires et al., 2023). The financial services and supply chain management are two industries where these advantages have already shown themselves. Users may keep their digital assets safely and conduct more secure transactions by operating within the blockchain's protective framework. Blockchain offers a decentralized substitute for traditional online transactions that depend on third parties for validation, including banks and credit cards (Gehl Sampath, 2021). As new technologies are constantly emerging as a result of the industries' quick improvements in e-commerce, finance, energy, and other sectors. The occasional leaking of customer data is one of the weaknesses that traditional e-commerce models suffer, hence integrating blockchain is essential to improving platform security. The implementation of a distributed ledger based on blockchain technology guarantees the validity and integrity of transactions, hence removing the possibility of manipulation (Singh, 2019).

Ethical Framework for AI

Blockchain has revolutionized the financial sector and greatly impacted modern technology, mostly by introducing cryptocurrencies and decentralized governance. By utilizing blockchain's verification capabilities, this initial influence has spread to several additional sectors and applications. As part of the continuous effort to create a decentralized Internet, several approaches have been put out to achieve decentralization. These approaches cover a variety of facets of the existing Internet paradigm, such as services, applications, infrastructure, and protocols (Lei et al., 2022). E-commerce platforms provide businesses of all sizes the chance to market their brand and sell goods to a larger customer base. The e-commerce industry is always changing as new technology and platforms for purchasing and selling goods and services are created. Issues with the traditional e-commerce model include fraud, chargebacks, payment disputes, and a lack of transparency. However, by improving transaction security and efficiency, blockchain holds the potential to completely transform e-commerce. Blockchain enables people to exchange and store digital assets safely by creating a decentralized network. This invention reduces the danger of fraud while providing customers access to comprehensive product information, including the product's provenance and source (Cheng et al., 2023).

Industry Collaboration Initiatives

The world is going digital, and with it, so are consumer habits and preferences. There has been a noticeable increase in the preference for internet purchasing versus going to physical stores (Saheb et al., 2022). A significant amount of vendor-customer transactions in the e-commerce market occur virtually, making secure communication methods necessary. It is still difficult to guarantee the security of online interactions, especially when doing transactions (Haleem et al., 2022). The major concerns have been raised by the numerous recorded cases of security breaches when large volumes of data were accessed without authorization by third parties. People trying to breach security and take advantage of network weaknesses are a constant concern. This is where the use of blockchain technology is beneficial. Blockchain operates as a decentralized trustless network with a public ledger and peer-to-peer automatic access-control manager, enabling users to connect without using trusted middlemen or participating in illegal activity. Blockchain's pervasive use of encryption gives each network node a sense of authority in their interactions with one another (Allahrakha, 2023).

CONCLUSION AND FUTURE SCOPE

Digital marketing is becoming an essential part of every company's strategy as technology develops. Companies now collect far more data than they did a few years ago, which has increased worries about data privacy. Consumers' increasing awareness of their rights regarding data privacy in the modern world means that companies must adopt ethical data practices in order to maintain the confidence and loyalty of their clientele. Undoubtedly, artificial intelligence has become more and more common in a variety of consumer-facing interactions in recent times. There are particular ethical, legal, and financial ramifications to this tendency. Because of the possible legal ramifications, it is necessary to create rules that can effectively safeguard consumers from the risks connected with using artificial intelligence in consumer-facing transactions. With a major focus on financial services, it explores the potential difficulties that might develop when artificial intelligence is used in the framework of consumer protection law.

The achieving of balance between cyber-security, AI, and data protection is a complex undertaking that has to be well thought out for privacy matters. This particular service area was chosen due to its intrinsic complexity, which presents difficulties for customers even in the absence of artificial intelligence. Another justification for concentrating on the analysis of financial services is the quickly growing FinTech industry, which offers a range of financial services to customers via the application of artificial intelligence technologies. A portion of the public believes that personal information is given over to big businesses that trade and use it, which makes this problem worse. The finding of a balance between the need to protect personal data and the free flow of that data, which can have positive economic effects, is even more difficult. It promotes the investigation of ways to more effectively balance these opposing interests, especially with regard to the introduction and application of smart home technology.

REFERENCES

Aaronson, S. A. (2022). *Wicked problems might inspire greater data sharing* (No. 2022-09).

Ahmad, A. Y. B., Gongada, T. N., Shrivastava, G., Gabbi, R. S., Islam, S., & Nagaraju, K. (2023). E-commerce trend analysis and management for Industry 5.0 using user data analysis. *International Journal of Intelligent Systems and Applications in Engineering*, *11*(11s), 135–150.

Aldboush, H. H., & Ferdous, M. (2023). Building Trust in Fintech: An Analysis of Ethical and Privacy Considerations in the Intersection of Big Data, AI, and Customer Trust. *International Journal of Financial Studies*, *11*(3), 90. doi:10.3390/ijfs11030090

Allahrakha, N. (2023). Balancing Cyber-security and Privacy: Legal and Ethical Considerations in the Digital Age. *Legal Issues in the Digital Age*, *4*(2), 78–121.

Bandara, R., Fernando, M., & Akter, S. (2020). Privacy concerns in E-commerce: A taxonomy and a future research agenda. *Electronic Markets*, *30*(3), 629–647. doi:10.1007/s12525-019-00375-6

Cavus, N., Mohammed, Y. B., Gital, A. Y. U., Bulama, M., Tukur, A. M., Mohammed, D., & Hassan, A. (2022). Emotional Artificial Neural Networks and Gaussian Process-Regression-Based Hybrid Machine-Learning Model for Prediction of Security and Privacy Effects on M-Banking Attractiveness. *Sustainability (Basel)*, *14*(10), 5826. doi:10.3390/su14105826

Cheng, X., Cohen, J., & Mou, J. (2023). AI-enabled technology innovation in e-commerce. *Journal of Electronic Commerce Research*, *24*(1), 1–6.

Choithani, T., Chowdhury, A., Patel, S., Patel, P., Patel, D., & Shah, M. (2022). A comprehensive study of artificial intelligence and cybersecurity on Bitcoin, crypto currency and banking system. *Annals of Data Science*, 1-33.

Daugherty, P. R., & Wilson, H. J. (2018). *Human+ machine: Reimagining work in the age of AI*. Harvard Business Press.

Dewani, N. D., Khan, Z. A., Agarwal, A., Sharma, M., & Khan, S. A. (Eds.). (2022). *Handbook of Research on Cyber Law, Data Protection, and Privacy*. IGI Global. doi:10.4018/978-1-7998-8641-9

Dewani, N. D., Khan, Z. A., Agarwal, A., Sharma, M., & Khan, S. A. (Eds.). (2022). *Handbook of Research on Cyber Law, Data Protection, and Privacy*. IGI Global. doi:10.4018/978-1-7998-8641-9

Gabhane, D., Varalaxmi, P., Rathod, U., Hamida, A. G. B., & Anand, B. (2023). Digital marketing trends: Analyzing the evolution of consumer behavior in the online space. *Boletin de Literatura Oral-The Literary Journal*, *10*(1), 462–473.

Gehl Sampath, P. (2021). Governing artificial intelligence in an age of inequality. *Global Policy*, *12*(S6), 21–31. doi:10.1111/1758-5899.12940

Gera, R., Assadi, D., & Starnawska, M. (Eds.). (2023). *Artificial Intelligence, Fintech, and Financial Inclusion*. CRC Press. doi:10.1201/9781003125204

Ghimire, A., Thapa, S., Jha, A. K., Adhikari, S., & Kumar, A. (2020, October). Accelerating business growth with big data and artificial intelligence. In *2020 Fourth International Conference on I-SMAC (IoT in Social, Mobile, Analytics and Cloud)(I-SMAC)* (pp. 441-448). IEEE. 10.1109/I-SMAC49090.2020.9243318

Girasa, R. (2020). *Artificial intelligence as a disruptive technology: Economic transformation and government regulation*. Springer Nature. doi:10.1007/978-3-030-35975-1

Girasa, R. (2020). *Artificial intelligence as a disruptive technology: Economic transformation and government regulation*. Springer Nature. doi:10.1007/978-3-030-35975-1

Gupta, R., Tanwar, S., Al-Turjman, F., Italiya, P., Nauman, A., & Kim, S. W. (2020). Smart contract privacy protection using AI in cyber-physical systems: Tools, techniques and challenges. *IEEE Access : Practical Innovations, Open Solutions*, *8*, 24746–24772. doi:10.1109/ACCESS.2020.2970576

Haleem, A., Javaid, M., Qadri, M. A., Singh, R. P., & Suman, R. (2022). Artificial intelligence (AI) applications for marketing: A literature-based study. *International Journal of Intelligent Networks*.

Hicham, N., Nassera, H., & Karim, S. (2023). Strategic framework for leveraging artificial intelligence in future marketing decision-making. *J. Intell Manag. Decis*, *2*(3), 139–150. doi:10.56578/jimd020304

Hodson, C. J. (2019). *Cyber risk management: Prioritize threats, identify vulnerabilities and apply controls*. Kogan Page Publishers.

Howells, G. (2020). Protecting consumer protection values in the fourth industrial revolution. *Journal of Consumer Policy*, *43*(1), 145–175. doi:10.1007/s10603-019-09430-3

Jaafar, F., & Pierre, S. (Eds.). (2023). *Blockchain and Artificial Intelligence-Based Solution to Enhance the Privacy in Digital Identity and IoT*. CRC Press. doi:10.1201/9781003227656

Jebamikyous, H., Li, M., Suhas, Y., & Kashef, R. (2023). Leveraging machine learning and blockchain in E-commerce and beyond: Benefits, models, and application. *Discover Artificial Intelligence*, *3*(1), 3. doi:10.1007/s44163-022-00046-0

Johnsen, M. (2020). *Blockchain in Digital Marketing: A New Paradigm of Trust*. Maria Johnsen.

Kaplan, A. (2020). Retailing and the ethical challenges and dilemmas behind artificial intelligence. In *Retail futures: The good, the bad and the ugly of the digital transformation* (pp. 181–191). Emerald Publishing Limited. doi:10.1108/978-1-83867-663-620201020

Kaponis, A., & Maragoudakis, M. (2022, September). Data Analysis in Digital Marketing using Machine learning and Artificial Intelligence Techniques, Ethical and Legal Dimensions, State of the Art. In *Proceedings of the 12th Hellenic Conference on Artificial Intelligence* (pp. 1-9). IEEE. 10.1145/3549737.3549756

Kavut, S. (2021). Digital Identities in the context of Blockchain and Artificial Intelligence. *Selçuk İletişim*, *14*(2), 529–548. doi:10.18094/josc.865641

Khan, F., & Mer, A. (2023). Embracing Artificial Intelligence Technology: Legal Implications with Special Reference to European Union Initiatives of Data Protection. In Digital Transformation, Strategic Resilience, Cyber Security and Risk Management (pp. 119-141). Emerald Publishing Limited.

Kopalle, P. K., Gangwar, M., Kaplan, A., Ramachandran, D., Reinartz, W., & Rindfleisch, A. (2022). Examining artificial intelligence (AI) technologies in marketing via a global lens: Current trends and future research opportunities. *International Journal of Research in Marketing*, *39*(2), 522–540. doi:10.1016/j.ijresmar.2021.11.002

La Diega, N. (2023). *Internet of Things and the Law: Legal Strategies for Consumer-centric Smart Technologies*. Taylor & Francis.

Lei, M., Xu, L., Liu, T., Liu, S., & Sun, C. (2022). Integration of privacy protection and blockchain-based food safety traceability: Potential and challenges. *Foods*, *11*(15), 2262. doi:10.3390/foods11152262 PMID:35954029

Liow, M., Sa, L., & Foong, Y. P. (2022). Customer Outcome Framework for Blockchain-Based Mobile Phone Applications. *Principles and Practice of Blockchains*, 155-182.

Mahankali, S. (2019). *Blockchain: The Untold Story: From birth of Internet to future of Blockchain*. BPB Publications.

Marwala, T. (2022). *Closing the gap: The fourth industrial revolution in Africa*. Pan Macmillan South Africa.

Milakovich, M. E. (2021). *Digital governance: Applying advanced technologies to improve public service*. Routledge. doi:10.4324/9781003215875

Nabbosa, V., & Kaar, C. (2020, May). Societal and ethical issues of digitalization. In *Proceedings of the 2020 International Conference on Big Data in Management* (pp. 118-124). ACM. 10.1145/3437075.3437093

Nguyen, M. T., & Tran, M. H. (2023). Privacy and Security Implications of Big Data Applications in Consumer Behavior Analysis for Fashion Retail. *Journal of Empirical Social Science Studies*, *7*(4), 82–98.

Paliszkiewicz, J., Chen, K., & Gołuchowski, J. (2023). *Privacy*. Trust and Social Media.

Pires, P. B., Santos, J. D., Pereira, I. V., & Torres, A. I. (Eds.). (2023). *Confronting Security and Privacy Challenges in Digital Marketing*. IGI Global. doi:10.4018/978-1-6684-8958-1

Robinson, S. C. (2020). Trust, transparency, and openness: How inclusion of cultural values shapes Nordic national public policy strategies for artificial intelligence (AI). *Technology in Society*, *63*, 101421. doi:10.1016/j.techsoc.2020.101421

Saheb, T., Jamthe, S., & Saheb, T. (2022). Developing a conceptual framework for identifying the ethical repercussions of artificial intelligence: A mixed method analysis. *Journal of AI. Robotics & Workplace Automation*, *1*(4), 371–398.

Sharma, A., & Singh, B. (2022). Measuring Impact of E-commerce on Small Scale Business: A Systematic Review. *Journal of Corporate Governance and International Business Law*, *5*(1).

Si, S., Hall, J., Suddaby, R., Ahlstrom, D., & Wei, J. (2023). Technology, entrepreneurship, innovation and social change in digital economics. *Technovation*, *119*, 102484. doi:10.1016/j.technovation.2022.102484

Singh, B. (2019). Profiling Public Healthcare: A Comparative Analysis Based on the Multidimensional Healthcare Management and Legal Approach. *Indian Journal of Health and Medical Law*, *2*(2), 1–5.

Singh, B. (2023). Blockchain Technology in Renovating Healthcare: Legal and Future Perspectives. In Revolutionizing Healthcare Through Artificial Intelligence and Internet of Things Applications (pp. 177-186). IGI Global.

Singh, B. (2023). Federated Learning for Envision Future Trajectory Smart Transport System for Climate Preservation and Smart Green Planet: Insights into Global Governance and SDG-9 (Industry, Innovation and Infrastructure). *National Journal of Environmental Law*, *6*(2), 6–17.

Sonne, W. (2014). Navigating the Digital Marketplace: An In-Depth Analysis of E-commerce Trends and the Future of Retail. *International Journal of Open Publication and Exploration*, *2*(1), 7–13.

Tan, T. M., & Salo, J. (2023). Ethical marketing in the blockchain-based sharing economy: Theoretical integration and guiding insights. *Journal of Business Ethics*, *183*(4), 1113–1140. doi:10.1007/s10551-021-05015-8

Tang, Y., Xiong, J., Becerril-Arreola, R., & Iyer, L. (2020). Ethics of blockchain: A framework of technology, applications, impacts, and research directions. *Information Technology & People*, *33*(2), 602–632. doi:10.1108/ITP-10-2018-0491

Thiebes, S., Lins, S., & Sunyaev, A. (2021). Trustworthy artificial intelligence. *Electronic Markets*, *31*(2), 447–464. doi:10.1007/s12525-020-00441-4

Timan, T., & Mann, Z. (2021). Data protection in the era of artificial intelligence: trends, existing solutions and recommendations for privacy-preserving technologies. In *The Elements of Big Data Value: Foundations of the Research and Innovation Ecosystem* (pp. 153–175). Springer International Publishing. doi:10.1007/978-3-030-68176-0_7

Tomazevic, N., Ravšelj, D., & Aristovnik, A. (2023). *Artificial Intelligence for human-centric society: The future is here*.

Trautman, L. J., Sanney, K. J., Yordy, E. D., Cowart, T. W., & Sewell, D. J. (2021). Teaching Ethics and Values in an Age of Rapid Technological Change. *Rutgers Bus. LJ*, *17*, 17.

Tyagi, A. K., & Tiwari, S. (2024). The Future of Artificial Intelligence in Blockchain Applications. In *Machine Learning Algorithms Using Scikit and TensorFlow Environments* (pp. 346–373). IGI Global.

Vashista, V. (2020). *Blockchain based Health Informatics for Pandemic Management* [Doctoral dissertation].

Wang, C., Ahmad, S. F., Ayassrah, A. Y. B. A., Awwad, E. M., Irshad, M., Ali, Y. A., & Han, H. (2023). An empirical evaluation of technology acceptance model for Artificial Intelligence in E-commerce. *Heliyon*, *9*(8), e18349. doi:10.1016/j.heliyon.2023.e18349 PMID:37520947

Wei, L., & Xia, Z. (2022). Big Data-Driven Personalization in E-Commerce: Algorithms, Privacy Concerns, and Consumer Behavior Implications. *International Journal of Applied Machine Learning and Computational Intelligence*, *12*(4).

Winecoff, A. A., & Watkins, E. A. (2022, July). Artificial concepts of artificial intelligence: institutional compliance and resistance in AI startups. In *Proceedings of the 2022 AAAI/ACM Conference on AI, Ethics, and Society* (pp. 788-799). ACM. 10.1145/3514094.3534138

Wylde, V., Rawindaran, N., Lawrence, J., Balasubramanian, R., Prakash, E., Jayal, A., Khan, I., Hewage, C., & Platts, J. (2022). Cybersecurity, data privacy and blockchain: A review. *SN Computer Science*, *3*(2), 127. doi:10.1007/s42979-022-01020-4 PMID:35036930

Xing, Y., Yu, L., Zhang, J. Z., & Zheng, L. J. (2023). Uncovering the Dark Side of Artificial Intelligence in Electronic Markets: A Systematic Literature Review. [JOEUC]. *Journal of Organizational and End User Computing*, *35*(1), 1–25. doi:10.4018/JOEUC.327278

Youssef, H. A. H., & Hossam, A. T. A. (2023). Privacy Issues in AI and Cloud Computing in E-commerce Setting: A Review. *International Journal of Responsible Artificial Intelligence*, *13*(7), 37–46.

Chapter 16
Role of Human Resource Management in the Era of Augmented Reality (AR) and Virtual Reality (VR) in the Global Market

Sulochna Syal
Bahra University, India

ABSTRACT

Human resource management (HRM) is a field that has evolved in combination with advancements in technology and is now operating in a highly competitive market. Augmented reality (AR) and virtual reality (VR) are cutting-edge technologies that have shown promise in several areas. It is a prospective way to assist with HRM operations due to its ability to simulate real-world situations, provide an immersive perspective, and facilitate communication between simulated & realistic environments. This paper attempts to understand better the possible advantages that the use of VR and AR may give to HRM through an analysis of relevant literature.

INTRODUCTION

The implementation of technology in HRM is critical for company's growth (Jatobá and colleagues, 2019) and facilitate human resource specialists (Stone and colleagues, 2015) who are exerting a positive impact on HR processes and practices (Jatobá and colleagues, 2019; Fenech and colleagues, 2019). Human resource departments can compete and enhance talent acquisition, retention, and development via new technologies (Srivastava & Agarwal, 2012; Iqbal and colleagues, 2019). AR and VR are relatively novel and pioneering technologies (Zhao et al., 2019) that distinguish themselves through realistic interactivity and involvement in the simulated atmosphere and have demonstrated their applicability and possibility in a variety of fields (Javaid & Haleem, 2019; Damiani and colleagues, 2018). This research

DOI: 10.4018/979-8-3693-2215-4.ch016

aims to provide information on the possibilities for VR and AR in HRM. A review of the literature was conducted to compile and evaluate prior findings in this relatively new field, which has piqued the scientific community's interest (Damiani et al., 2018; Correia, 2019; Lopes, 2019).

REVIEW OF LITERATURE

HRM had its origins in the early 20th century when it was commonly known as Personnel Management (Tubey et al., 2015; Richman, 2015; Haslinda, 2009). The conceptual evolution of Human Resources Management was primarily a result of globalization's evolutionary nature and technological advancements (Haslinda, 2009). Human resource professionals and businesses have faced new technical hurdles in recruiting, keeping, and developing personnel, as well as increased burden to be inventive and proficient of achieving tactical objectives via the use of new technology tools (Srivastava & Agarwal, 2012; Iqbal et al., 2019).

Role of Technology in HRM

Recent advancements in technology have aided human resource professionals, resulting in a good effect on human resource policies & strategies (Stone & Dulebohn, 2013; Johnson et al., 2016). Therefore, human resource administrative policies have evolved dramatically, as the internet enables the decrease of administrative labor and the promotion of few operations (Stone and colleagues, 2013; Fndkl and colleagues, 2015; Johnson and colleagues, 2016; Berber and colleagues, 2018). Technology has also provided advantages like the ability to gain real-time information, an increased proportion of applicants, the capacity to add & recover data via the internet from any place, the optimal utilization of processes and the resulting organizational task, savings & improved HR activities via the internet (Stone & Dulebohn, 2013; Fndkl & Bayarçelik, 2015). These advantages improved the understanding of HR specialists and allowed them to focus on more important problems (Berber and colleagues, 2018). The digitalization that is presently taking place in organizations necessitates a re-examination of the most of conventional methods and a consideration of the advantages of technological innovations, which have demonstrated to be encouraging techniques for maximizing the efficiency and performance of HRM (Fedorova and colleagues, 2019; Fenech and colleagues, 2019).

VR and AR in HRM

The primary application of such innovations capable of replicating immersive environments and giving gamers with memorable experiences is entertainment (Parekh and colleagues, 2020). People who work in the disciplines of architecture, engineering, as well as construction assume that VR and AR can be used in a lot of different ways. Over the next five to 10 years, these people think that VR and AR will be used more and more (Noghabaei and colleagues, 2020).

Virtual reality is being used in talent recruiting strategies at college job fairs as an intriguing way to reach out to younger individuals just starting their careers. At job fairs, VR provides job seekers with a realistic representation of the position, increasing the number of high-quality applications. The firm as well as the applicant both gain from candidates' quick acceptance or rejection of an offer (Santos, 2019). Traditional systems didn't let potential employees experience the real-world difficulties of working in a real-world surroundings, but new technique rely on VR allowed applicants to try out number of specialized tasks that were linked to their job (Suen and colleagues, 2017). The incorporation of this sort of technology into the HR selection procedure has a lot of benefits for a business and leads to increased performance (Aguinis and colleagues, 2001). As with a medical student who can simulate an operating room environment and carry out several activities with an immediate reaction to each one, an applicant's technical knowledge are more easily evaluated when they are put to the test in real scenarios (Meier and colleagues, 2005). Furthermore, test scores may be used to sort applicants, with the most qualified candidate being selected (Winkler-Schwartz and colleagues, 2016).

Role of AR and VR in Employee Retention

In order to reduce attrition rate, a company may focus on the procedure of hiring and selection because this is the 1st line of interaction among potential workers and the company, and it encourages the prospective employer to ascertain if they are engaging with an excellent person for the role & the company (Osibanjo & Adeniji, 2013). In the procedure of hiring and selection, VR can be used to recognize and evaluate a person's abilities (Meier and colleagues, 2005; Suen and colleagues, 2017; Winkler Schwartz and colleagues, 2016). By fostering a culture of innovation within their organizations, companies can better meet the demand for new products and services from customers as well as employees (Naranjo-Valencia and colleagues, 2015). Retaining staff members is dependent on the introduction of advanced as well as technological strategies, given the higher rate of turnover among the millennial generation throughout businesses. This generation has risen with advanced technologies and seems to find inclusion into organizations through a more technical induction program which can be initiated via virtual visit to the office or information acquisition such as through their cellphones (Shufutinsky and colleagues, 2019). An improved HR strategy and the use of AR allow for the creation of innovative tactics for social contact among members of the company, resulting in greater efficiency and effectiveness for the organisation (Blümel, 2013; Hannola and colleagues, 2018). Staff members encourage the viewpoint that their company is forward-thinking in its processes as well as insights and can provide prospects that contenders are incapable of providing (Zhao and colleagues, 2019).

AR and VR Role in Employee Training and Development (T&D)

Immersive techniques are cutting-edge, evolving, as well as interactive methods of training and motivating the employees (Au & Lee, 2017; Davideková and colleagues, 2017; Stadnicka and colleagues, 2019; Khandelwal and colleagues, 2019). VR and AR technologies aid in the development of basic fundamentals for the digital world, like innovative thinking, information exchange, team spirit, leadership, problem - solving, as well as negotiation (Schmid Mast and colleagues, 2018; Papanastasiou and colleagues, 2019; Davis and colleagues, 2020;). Virtual reality fosters a safe environment during the training phase by mitigating the risk as well as hazard associated with several of types of learning (Stapleton, 2004; Jeelani and colleagues, 2017; Lombardo and colleagues, 2019; Kwok and colleagues, 2019; Squelch, 2001). When it comes to construction, which is a high-risk business for people, the use of VR and AR technologies has become increasingly popular (Li and colleagues, 2018). Simulations of medical procedures are extremely beneficial in medicine during pre-surgical step (Pulijala and colleagues, 2018; Huang and colleagues, 2018; Eckert and colleagues, 2019; Negrillo-Cárdenas and colleagues, 2020). VR was used by research scientists during COVID-19 disease outbreak to combat the virus infection. When health professionals practice using a simulation of real-world conditions, interaction, and immersion, they get familiar with real-world illness problems and learn fast and efficiently (Singh and colleagues, 2020). Ships' crews can be trained and motivated through the use of immersive technology as well as security personnel (Davideková and colleagues 2017; Au & Lee, 2017; Khandelwal and colleagues, 2019; Stadnicka and colleagues, 2019). VR helps create a secure learning atmosphere by minimizing the effects and risk associated with a wide variety of learning contexts (Squelch, 2001; Stapleton, 2004; Bruzzone and colleagues, 2010; Jeelani and colleagues, 2017; Lombardo and colleagues, 2019; Kwok and colleagues, 2019).

There are numerous educational advantages of using VR in the classroom, not the least of which is the ability to provide students with hands-on training through the use of video games (Stapleton, 2004; Kirkley, 2005). Furthermore, these technical skills assist in developing HR by enhancing retention of information and, as a result, acquiring knowledge. Workers are motivated to act immediately, which results in cost savings for the business (Watanuki, 2008; Khandelwal and colleagues, 2019).

METHODOLOGY

Research Design

Virtual reality and augmented reality (AR/VR) are examined in this study to determine the current state of affairs, the future potential of this industry, and associated industries that can provide support (IT, Internet, mobile devices, and technologies). Virtual reality and augmented reality (VR/AR) tools and technologies can be used to manage human resources and other operational business processes.

It was used in the article's writing process to use a wide range of scientific methods and approaches—methods of generalization, analysis, and synthesizing (in the study of the state and future of international and national Chinese as part of the research)—to analyze scientific literature, analytical reviews, and reports from international research organizations on VR/AR technologies. A modeling method was also employed in the development and construction of a company's model of growth based on improved management of business and HR operations utilizing VR and AR technology.

DATA ANALYSIS

Smart technologies are currently in active development, according to the majority of sources of information such as the China Virtual Reality Industry Report (2017 and 2018), Goldman Sachs Global Investment Research, IDC, and the Augmented and Virtual Reality Survey Report (Perkins Coie, 2019). Scientists, innovators, and investors from around the world are beginning to pay attention to the VR/AR business at this stage. A growing number of people are seeing the strategic significance of this tool and predict that it will soon be a standard part of many firms' HR and business operations. As predicted by Super Data, the worldwide virtual reality market is expected to reach $40 billion in 2020. However, significant firms are already integrating virtual reality into their business processes as VR reorients itself from its conventional application, entertainment.

Human resources can benefit greatly from the use of AR/VR technology, particularly in the areas of teaching employees through the use of 3D simulations, conducting training sessions and meetings, and conducting video interviews with potential hires. In the past, HR was primarily concerned with saving time and money; now, it's getting more technologically advanced.

Figure 1 depicts the rise of virtual and augmented reality (VR and AR) technology in several business sectors by 2025. AR/VR market structure will still be dominated by the entertainment sector (33 percent) by 2025.

Figure 1. The diverse of VR and AR applications

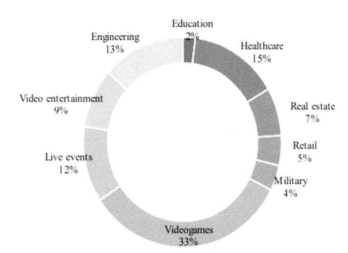

Virtual and Augmented Reality (VR/AR), as shown in Figures 2 and 3, has the biggest impact on mobile applications, which have already been overtaken by technologies on PCs, consoles, and smart glasses in 2017–2018. This pattern is expected to continue in the years 2020–2021.

Figure 2. VR and AR installed base

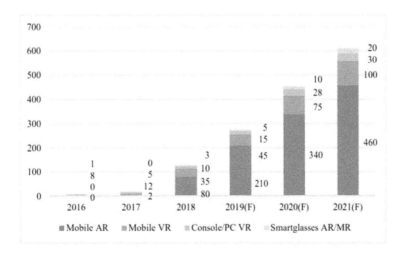

Figure 3. VR and AR installed base

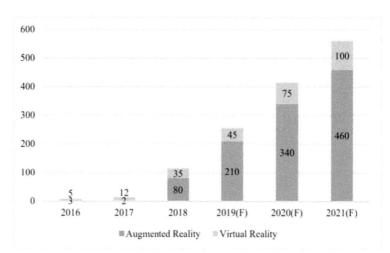

According to worldwide statistical agency Statista and PwC study, the United States, China, and Japan are the current leaders in the international VR market industry.

PwC and Statista global statistics resources have found that since 2016, three countries—the US, Japan, and China—have dominated the VR/AR market worldwide. In addition, for the major countries in this business, there will be a growth tendency up to 2021 (forecast data).

Figure 4. VR market leaders

Many IT, globalization, and sustainable development analysts say we are already living in the future, and it is called virtual reality (VR). As predicted by SuperData, the worldwide virtual reality market is expected to reach $40 billion in 2020. Companies with a long-term vision are already beginning to integrate virtual reality into their business processes as the technology shifts away from its conventional application in entertainment.

AR/VR technology is now dominated by a small number of large corporations, which can be summarized as follows:. Globally, Samsung (South Korea), Sony (Japan), Facebook (the United States), HTC, and TCL (China) have the biggest sales turnover, according to statistics from IDC research (Figure 5). The stats from Statista and PwC show this to be true, as you can see. An increase of 12 to 15 percent may already be seen when comparing the results of the second and first quarters of 2018.

Figure 5. AR and VR leaders across the world

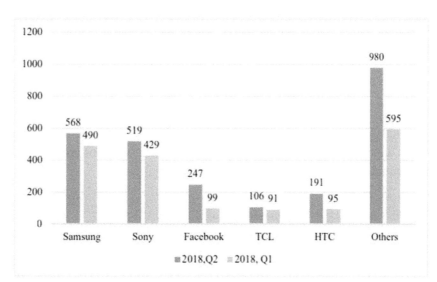

The expansion of VR/AR technology and the growth of the mobile technology business are often linked by observers. Figure 5 shows that this is indeed the case, based on the results. Financial reports and press announcements from the leading worldwide smartphone manufacturers. This could be a sign that in the not too distant future, the world's focus will shift from the United States to China.

Figure 6. Smartphone production market share (Units are in millions)

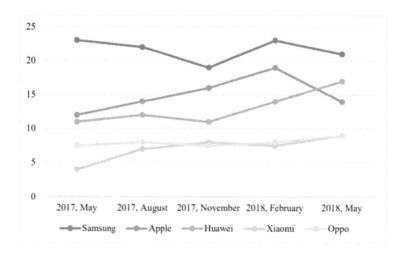

Worldwide population is increasingly using the Internet (Figure 7). Using forecasting methods, this indicator has grown approximately 25 times since 2012, and the growth pattern is expected to continue for the foreseeable future.

Figure 7. Worldwide usage of cellular data and growth

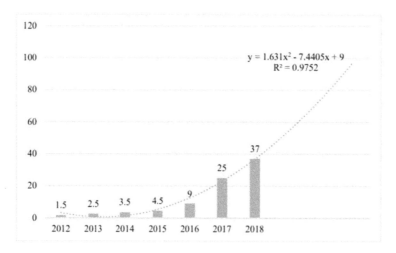

AR/VR technology investment shows that venture investors around the world are focusing on the long term, which can be attributed to the relatively quick payback and strong profit margins. As a result, in the final ten months of 2018, the SenseTime Group and Megvii each secured over US $2 billion in funding. Hundreds of millions of dollars were invested in Beijing Moviebook Technology, Kujiale, and other enterprises between 2016 and 2018.

To get an idea of how much Western AR/VR investments will grow and alter in Asia over the next two years, we polled a group of industry insiders in the sector. The results are shown in Table 1.

Table 1. Sector that gets most investment in the AR and VR

Sector	Sept' 19	Sept' 21
Gaming	50%	43%
Education and study	12%	14%
Health and medical sector	25%	25%
Real estate uses	7%	5%
Promotion and advertisement	16%	19%
Live concerts	20%	16%
Watching movie or TV	23%	19%
Shopping purpose in retain sector	18%	18%
Manufacturing sector	24%	26%

If this holds true, it could signal a shift in international investment from the West (the United States) to Asia, and more specifically, China.

There must be real-world examples of VR/AR technology being used in HR and business operations to back up the study's relevance. A custom built AR wall was shown during the 2014 Hershy's (USA) employment fair, which used the AR app and some iPads to demonstrate the company's principles, such as service-oriented and team-oriented.

In addition to bringing in more workers, the software may train existing workers how to better manage the plant as a whole. More candidates will participate in the training process because of an AR tool that mimics the real-world experience better.

As part of its 2020–2021 technical innovation agenda, Sberbank of Russia also discussed the usage of virtual reality to train employees. A classroom simulator for teachers called TeachLive is used by several schools in the United States. Virtual students test the teacher's patience, misbehave, and otherwise complicate things, so the teacher wears a VR helmet and practices correct responses. Such a simulator aids new instructors in preparing for their first day at work, as well as experienced teachers in adapting to new teaching approaches.

RESULTS

Companies are increasingly turning to digital creative agencies for training in the use of VR and AR as a recruiting tool, as evidenced by this finding. In the present world of augmented and virtual reality, it is evident that virtual reality may play a vital role in both HR management and the most important business procedures. These tools can be used in the following regions and segments.

Recruitment

A company's ability to articulate the benefits of working there is critical if it hopes to attract the greatest professionals. In the past, a booklet or film at a job fair could do this. Employers may now use VR/AR to wow prospective employees with a high-quality presentation of their employer brand. There are several ways the booth can be configured for usage at job fairs to interact with applications. It can be used to show potential employees the benefits of working for your firm, as well as to give them a sense for what working at your company is really like. Virtual reality and augmented reality can also be used to identify people with the right skill set for a firm.

A key component of recruiting is creating a favorable work environment. In the modern business world, it is fashionable to portray a laid-back attitude where employees are encouraged to come up with their own ideas and work independently. One method to convey the importance of a company's corporate culture in its growth plans and leadership is to use the example of this particular experience. Virtual and augmented reality (VR/AR) can be used to show an employee an interactive training and, in general, all that a specific business has to offer. Companies can create simulations, which are essentially video games, to help them find and hire new employees. Even if the game doesn't cover every aspect of what the firm does, it may be a terrific method to get people interested in the business. Additionally, this can be an effective way to impart to kids some of the knowledge and abilities they'll require to be successful.

Training

Workers who communicate with each other are more likely to achieve a common goal than those who don't. Again, virtual reality technology saves the day. VR can also be an excellent tool for fostering co-operation among coworkers. Theoretical training sessions and lectures are ineffective in the real world, as demonstrated by current practice. Many people believe that an image speaks a thousand words. VR also has the potential to considerably minimize the financial and time burdens associated with person-nel training.

Online work culture

With the help of virtual reality tools, you can hold meetings with colleagues or business partners situated anywhere in the world. You may hold a face-to-face conversation with colleagues in a virtual conference room, and even shake hands with VR gloves. Meetings with distant employees can also be scheduled using this application.

To better plan and explain the proposed project, as well as to demonstrate all of its benefits and draw the audience's attention, VR can be used to demonstrate presentations and visualize projects for the benefit of colleagues. Continuous control over the flow of key operational processes in manufacturing or providing services will be achieved through 3D visualization. This will allow for a clearer understanding of operational weaknesses, activities that should be automated, etc. In the long run, this will result in a reduction in company costs.

VR Uses in Logistics, Distribution, Marketing, and Promotion

3D promotional videos created with VR/AR tools are a great way to market your products or services, bring in more business, or break into untapped areas. You may also design new and connect current distribution networks, manage supply chains, and specify routes using VR/AR technology."

A model of firm (organization) development based on improved management of business and HR operations utilizing VR and AR tools was established as a consequence of the study, taking into account the results of the previous sections (see Figure 8). Because it takes into account how VR/AR technology and tools can enhance HR activities (such as recruiting, development, training, and evaluation of employees) as well as the company's core operational processes (such as production and logistics), this model is unique. Many companies have found that virtual reality (VR) may increase operational efficiency while also attracting and developing top-tier talent, despite the fact that it is an expensive technology.

Figure 8. Developed model of an enhanced management of HR practices using VR and AR technology

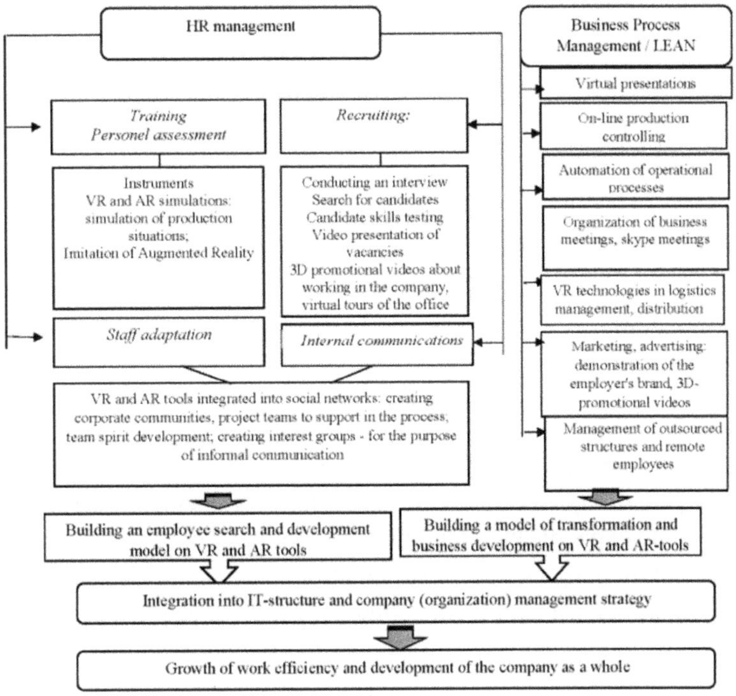

DISCUSSION

Naturally, virtual reality is still a long way from being perfect. The high expense of integrating VR into all aspects of human resources management is a major concern for many businesses. It takes a lot of time and effort to "shock" giant, slow-moving organizations to innovate, and the quality of virtual reality typically needs to be improved as a result. Interviews can be conducted "at a distance" now, although it was thought to be impossible 20 years ago. Maybe we'll be surprised in five years by how wrong we were about the benefits of virtual reality in human resources. Despite the fact that VR has been used successfully on the job market and has produced positive outcomes, most researchers studying this topic conclude that there are still too many unanswered concerns and problems, particularly in modern company procedures, when it comes to its application in HR. Many experts think that virtual reality (VR) is a major factor in driving globalization and integration in today's global economy. This is especially true in Asian countries such as China and Japan, as well as in the rest of the globe. A new approach to resource management is required to keep pace with the dynamic environment of transnationalization of international corporations, which is increasingly being handled globally. Almost every significant company is relying on HR experts' ability to alter their work in order to succeed.

It has to do with the ability to make comprehensive strategic decisions and the necessity of establishing a stable labor pool whose size may be adjusted as necessary for future expansion. This foundation, in turn, necessitates the introduction of IT-based procedures and activities. AR/VR and other high-tech tools should be used to improve the efficiency of human resources management.

Additionally, the introduction of VR technology has a number of technological constraints and a high level of complexity. In other words, there aren't nearly as many competent specialists on the market who can install and maintain VR systems on a professional level. If we look at world's stance on these concerns and how VR has been implemented in the educational system, we can see how exchange platforms have been developed for the integration of different sectors, and how VR cooperation platforms have been developed between them all. Companies are encouraged to exchange information in order to hasten virtual reality's development. It is important to take into account the specifics of the country where the recruitment is taking place in order to employ AR/VR effectively. The psychological and social effects of virtual reality exposure in people must also be examined. AR/VR technologies, particularly in HR and lean management, are undoubtedly of the future, but they already successfully complement, transform, boost efficiency and other aspects of the work done by these specialists today.

CONCLUSION

The use of VR and AR in training has been emphasized due to the accepted benefits they are likely to incur in procedures (Lopes, 2019). According to the literature, the tremendously realistic imitation which VR is effective in providing to people who regularly deal with dangerous or risky situations is crucial for preparing for complex and challenging real-world situations (Squelch, 2001; Stapleton, 2004; Jeelani and colleagues, 2017; Kwok and colleagues, 2019; Lombardo and colleagues, 2019). As a result of modern approaches that utilize modern technologies, turnover is lowered, retention of talent is enhanced, and employee satisfaction is risen. In addition to increasing applicant interest in talent acquisition (Santos, 2019), VR and AR assist applicants in comprehending the role (Suen and colleagues, 2017), and assist HR specialists in the selection process (Meier and colleagues, 2005; Suen and colleagues, 2017). The COVID-19 disease outbreak may open up opportunities for the implementation of VR and AR, as it brings people closer to advanced technologies, encourages the digital age, and emphasizes the importance of technical methods in the course of business (Rotatori and colleagues, 2020). VR and AR could be used to help recruit, keep, and train employees, among other things. This kind of research would help HR managers understand some of the benefits of these technologies. The perspectives of HR specialists on these advanced technology and their relevance to HR processes, as well as those provided by the literature, may be of interest for future research in order to make more smart judgments.

REFERENCES

Aguinis, H., Henle, C. A., & Beaty Jr., J. C. (2001). Virtual Reality Technology: A New Tool for Personnel Selection. *International Journal of Selection and Assessment, 9*(1).

Au, E. H., & Lee, J. J. (2017). Virtual reality in education: A tool for learning in the experience age. *International Journal of Innovation in Education, 4*(4), 215. doi:10.1504/IJIIE.2017.091481

Berber, N., Đorđević, B., & Milanović, S. (2018). Electronic human resource management (e-HRM): A new concept for digital age. *Strategic Management, 23*(2), 22–32. doi:10.5937/StraMan1802022B

Blümel, E. (2013). Global challenges and innovative technologies geared toward new markets: Prospects for virtual and augmented reality. Procedia Computer Science, 25, 4–13. https://doi.org/. procs.2013.11.002 doi:10.1016/j

Bruzzone, A., Cimino, A., Longo, F., & Mirabelli, G. (2010). TRAINPORTS-TRAINing in marine port by using simulation. International Conference on Harbour, Maritime and Multimodal Logistics Modelling and Simulation, 1(March), 25–32.

Coie, P. 2019. Digital Currencies: International Actions and Regulation. *disponibile alla URL:* https://www. perkinscoie. com/en/news-insights/digital-currencies-international-actions-and-regulations. html

Correia, T. (2019). A Realidade Virtual e a Realidade Aumentada na Gestão da Cultura Organizacional [Instituto Superior de Contabilidade e Administração do Porto]. http://hdl.handle.net/10400.22/15983

Damiani, L., Demartini, M., Guizzi, G., Revetria, R., & Tonelli, F. (2018). Augmented and virtual reality applications in industrial systems: A qualitative review towards the industry 4.0 era. *IFAC-PapersOnLine, 51*(11), 624–630. doi:10.1016/j.ifacol.2018.08.388

Dávideková, M., Mjartan, M., & Greguš, M. (2017). Utilization of Virtual Reality in Education of Employees in Slovakia. *Procedia Computer Science, 113*, 253–260. Advance online publication. doi:10.1016/j. procs.2017.08.365

Davis, A., Linvill, D. L., Hodges, L. F., Da Costa, A. F., & Lee, A. (2020). Virtual reality versus faceto-face practice: A study into situational apprehension and performance. *Communication Education, 69*(1), 70–84. doi:10.1080/03634523.2019.1684535

Eckert, M., Volmerg, J. S., & Friedrich, C. M. (2019). Augmented reality in medicine: Systematic and bibliographic review. *Journal of Medical Internet Research, 7*(4), e10967. doi:10.2196/10967 PMID:31025950

Fedorova, A., Koropets, O., & Gatti, M. (2019). *Digitalization of human resource management practices and its impact on employees' well-being. Conference: Contemporary Issues in Business.* Management and Economics Engineering., doi:10.3846/cibmee.2019.075

Fenech, R., Baguant, P., & Ivanov, D. (2019). The changing role of human resource management in an era of digital transformation. *Journal of Management Information and Decision Science, 22*(2), 166–175.

Fındıklı, M. A., & Bayarçelik, E. beyza. (2015). Exploring the Outcomes of Electronic Human Resource Management (E-HRM)? Procedia - Social and Behavioral Sciences, 207, 424–431. https://doi.org/. sbspro.2015.10.112 doi:10.1016/j

Hannola, L., Richter, A., Richter, S., & Stocker, A. (2018). Empowering production workers with digitally facilitated knowledge processes–a conceptual framework. *International Journal of Production Research, 56*(14), 4729–4743. doi:10.1080/00207543.2018.1445877

Haslinda, A. (2009). Evolving terms of human rescourse management and development. *The Journal of International Social Research, 2*(9), 180–186.

Huang, T. K., Yang, C. H., Hsieh, Y. H., Wang, J. C., & Hung, C. C. (2018). Augmented reality (AR) and virtual reality (VR) applied in dentistry. In Kaohsiung Journal of Medical Sciences. https://doi.org/. kjms.2018.01.009 doi:10.1016/j

Iqbal, N., Ahmad, M., Raziq, M., & Borini, F. (2019). Linking e-hrm practices and organizational outcomes: Empirical analysis of line manager's perception. *Revista Brasileira de Gestão de Negócios*, *21*(1), 48–69. doi:10.7819/rbgn.v21i1.3964

Jatobá, M., Santos, J., Gutierriz, I., Moscon, D., Fernandes, P. O., & Teixeira, J. P. (2019). Evolution of Artifcial Intelligence Research in Human Resources. Procedia Computer Science. https://doi.org/. procs.2019.12.165 doi:10.1016/j

Javaid, M., & Haleem, A. (2019). Virtual reality applications toward medical feld. *Clinical Epidemiology and Global Health*, *8*(2), 600–605. doi:10.1016/j.cegh.2019.12.010

Jeelani, I., Han, K., & Albert, A. (2017). Development of Immersive Personalized Training Environment for Construction Workers. Congress on Computing in Civil Engineering, Proceedings, 407–415. doi:10.1061/9780784480830.050

Johnson, R. D., Lukaszewski, K. M., & Stone, D. L. (2016). The evolution of the feld of human resource information systems: Co-Evolution of technology and HR processes. *Communications of the Association for Information Systems*, *38*, 533–553. Advance online publication. doi:10.17705/1CAIS.03828

Khandelwal, K., & Upadhyay, A. K. (2019). Virtual reality interventions in developing and managing human resources. *Human Resource Development International*. Advance online publication. doi:10.10 80/13678868.2019.1569920

Kwok, P. K., Yan, M., Chan, B. K. P., & Lau, H. Y. K. (2019). Crisis management training using discreteevent simulation and virtual reality techniques. *Computers & Industrial Engineering*, *135*, 711–722. doi:10.1016/j.cie.2019.06.035

Li, X., Yi, W., Chi, H. L., Wang, X., & Chan, A. P. C. (2018). A critical review of virtual and augmented reality (VR/AR) applications in construction safety. Automation in Construction. https://doi.org/. autcon.2017.11.003 doi:10.1016/j

Lombardo, J. M., Lopez, M. A., García, V., López, M., Cañadas, R., Velasco, S., & León, M. (2019). PRACTICA. A Virtual Reality Platform for Specialized Training Oriented to Improve the Productivity. *International Journal of Interactive Multimedia and Artifcial Intelligence*, *5*(4), 94. doi:10.9781/ ijimai.2018.04.007

Lopes, L. (2019). O Uso da Realidade Virtual e Realidade Aumentada no Processo de Formação [Instituto Superior de Contabilidade e Administração do Porto]. http://hdl.handle.net/10400.22/15206

Meier, A. H., Henry, J., Marine, R., & Murray, W. B. (2005). Implementation of a Web- and simulationbased curriculum to ease the transition from medical school to surgical internship. *American Journal of Surgery*, *190*(1), 137–140. doi:10.1016/j.amjsurg.2005.04.007 PMID:15972187

Naranjo-Valencia, J. C., & Calderón-Hernández, G. (2015). *Construyendo una cultura de innovación. Una propuesta de transformación cultural*. Estudios Gerenciales., doi:10.1016/j.estger.2014.12.005

Negrillo-Cárdenas, J., Jiménez-Pérez, J. R., & Feito, F. R. (2020). The role of virtual and augmented reality in orthopedic trauma surgery: From diagnosis to rehabilitation. In Computer Methods and Programs in Biomedicine. https://doi.org/ doi:10.1016/j.cmpb.2020.105407

Noghabaei, M., Heydarian, A., Balali, V., & Han, K. (2020). Trend analysis on adoption of virtual and augmented reality in the architecture, engineering, and construction industry. *Data*, *5*(1), 26. Advance online publication. doi:10.3390/data5010026

Osibanjo, A. O., & Adeniji, A. A. (2013). Impact of Organizational Culture on Human Resource Practices: A Study of Selected Nigerian Private Universities. *Journal of Competitiveness*, *5*(4), 115–133. doi:10.7441/joc.2013.04.07

Papanastasiou, G., Drigas, A., Skianis, C., Lytras, M., & Papanastasiou, E. (2019). Virtual and augmented reality effects on K-12, higher and tertiary education students' twenty-frst century skills. *Virtual Reality (Waltham Cross)*, *23*(4), 425–436. doi:10.1007/s10055-018-0363-2

Parekh, P., Patel, S., Patel, N., & Shah, M. (2020). Systematic review and meta-analysis of augmented reality in medicine, retail, and games. *Visual Computing for Industry, Biomedicine, and Art*, *3*(1), 21. Advance online publication. doi:10.1186/s42492-020-00057-7 PMID:32954214

Pulijala, Y., Ma, M., Pears, M., Peebles, D., & Ayoub, A. (2018). An innovative virtual reality training tool for orthognathic surgery. International Journal of Oral and Maxillofacial Surgery. https://doi.org/. ijom.2018.01.005 doi:10.1016/j

Richman, N. (2015). *Human Resource Management and Human Resource Development: Evolution and Contributions*. Creighton Journal of Interdisciplinary Leadership., doi:10.17062/cjil.v1i2.19

Rotatori, D., Lee, E. J., & Sleeva, S. (2020). The evolution of the workforce during the fourth industrial revolution. *Human Resource Development International*. Advance online publication. doi:10.1080/13 678868.2020.1767453

Santos, M. (2019). Realidade Virtual e Realidade Aumentada no Processo de Recrutamento [Instituto Superior de Contabilidade e Administração do Porto]. http://hdl.handle.net/10400.22/16050

Schmid Mast, M., Kleinlogel, E. P., Tur, B., & Bachmann, M. (2018). The future of interpersonal skills development: Immersive virtual reality training with virtual humans. *Human Resource Development Quarterly*, *29*(2), 125–141. doi:10.1002/hrdq.21307

Shufutinsky, A., & Cox, R. (2019). Losing Talent on Day One: Onboarding Millennial Employees in Health Care Organizations. *Organization Development Journal*.

Singh, R. P., Javaid, M., Kataria, R., Tyagi, M., Haleem, A., & Suman, R. (2020). Signifcant applications of virtual reality for COVID-19 pandemic. *Diabetes & Metabolic Syndrome*, *14*(4), 661–664. Advance online publication. doi:10.1016/j.dsx.2020.05.011 PMID:32438329

Squelch, A. P. (2001). Virtual reality or mine safety training in South Africa. *Journal of the South African Institute of Mining and Metallurgy*, *101*(4), 209–216.

Srivastava, E., & Agarwal, N. (2012). The Emerging Challenges in HRM. *International Journal of Scientific & Technology Research*, *1*(6), 46–48.

Stadnicka, D., Litwin, P., & Antonelli, D. (2019). Human factor in intelligent manufacturing systems - Knowledge acquisition and motivation. *Procedia CIRP*, *79*, 718–723. Advance online publication. doi:10.1016/j.procir.2019.02.023

Stapleton, A. J. (2004). Serious Games: Serious Opportunities. Australian Game Developers' Conference. http://andrewstapleton.com/wp-content/uploads/2006/12/serious_games_agdc2004.pdf

Stone, D. L., Deadrick, D. L., Lukaszewski, K. M., & Johnson, R. (2015). The infuence of technology on the future of human resource management. [Stone]. *Human Resource Management Review*, *25*(2), 216–231. doi:10.1016/j.hrmr.2015.01.002

Suen, H. Y., & Chang, H. L. (2017). Toward multi-stakeholder value: Virtual human resource management. *Sustainability (Basel)*, *9*(12), 2177. Advance online publication. doi:10.3390/su9122177

Tubey, R., Rotich, J., & Kurgat, A. (2015). History, Evolution and Development of Human Resource Management: A Contemporary Perspective. *European Journal of Business and Management*, *7*, 139–148.

Watanuki, K. (2008). Virtual reality based job training and human resource development for foundry skilled workers. *International Journal of Cast Metals Research*, *21*(1–4), 275–280. doi:10.1179/136404608X362098

Winkler-Schwartz, A., Bajunaid, K., Mullah, M. A. S., Marwa, I., Alotaibi, F. E., Fares, J., Baggiani, M., Azarnoush, H., Al Zharni, G., Christie, S., Sabbagh, A. J., Werthner, P., & Del Maestro, R. F. (2016). Bimanual Psychomotor Performance in Neurosurgical Resident Applicants Assessed Using NeuroTouch, a Virtual Reality Simulator. *Journal of Surgical Education*, *73*(6), 942–953. doi:10.1016/j.jsurg.2016.04.013 PMID:27395397

Zhao, H., Zhao, Q. H., & Ślusarczyk, B. (2019). Sustainability and digitalization of corporate management based on augmented/virtual reality tools usage: China and other world IT companies' experience. *Sustainability (Basel)*, *11*(17), 4717. doi:10.3390/su11174717

Chapter 17
An Analysis on Frauds Affecting the Financial Security of the Indian Banking Sector:
A Systematic Literature Review

Shefali Saluja

🆔 https://orcid.org/0000-0002-8560-5150

Chitkara Business School, Chitkara University, India

Arjun J. Nair

🆔 https://orcid.org/0000-0002-2287-3174

Chitkara Business School, Chitkara University, India

ABSTRACT

An economy needs a well-functioning banking system—it is crucial for a country's economic growth and progress. With different economic factors influencing the banking sector, both domestically and globally, the role of the banking industry has changed over time. This has allowed the financial sector to explore new opportunities and expand its reach beyond national borders. The banking industry has undergone major transformations in response to shifts in trade and commerce, including the emergence of private sector banks, the integration of technology such as NEFT and smart cards, and changes to capital adequacy standards. These improvements have greatly increased the efficiency and productivity of the banking sector. The Indian banking industry is unique and has undergone three stages of development, from character-based lending to competitiveness-based lending, according to Singh,. Despite the growth and expansion of the banking industry, it faces many operational risks, including various types of fraud and scams.

DOI: 10.4018/979-8-3693-2215-4.ch017

INTRODUCTION

An economy needs a well functioning banking system that is crucial for a country's economic growth and progress. With different economic factors influencing the banking sector, both domestically and globally, the role of the banking industry has changed over time. This has allowed the financial sector to explore new opportunities and expand its reach beyond national borders. The banking industry has undergone major transformations in response to shifts in trade and commerce, including the emergence of private sector banks, the integration of technology such as NEFT and smart cards, and changes to capital adequacy standards. These improvements have greatly increased the efficiency and productivity of the banking sector. The Indian banking industry is unique and has undergone three stages of development, from character-based lending to competitiveness-based lending, according to (Singh, 2005). Despite the growth and expansion of the banking industry, it faces many operational risks, including various types of fraud and scams. The Reserve Bank of India is responsible for overseeing the entire banking industry as the central policy-making and national-level regulatory body. However, despite the growth of India's banking industry in terms of revenue and profits, the amount of money lost to bank fraud is on the rise. The Reserve Bank of India and bank management are both concerned about this trend, as these bank frauds are becoming more sophisticated and larger in scale, leading to not only financial losses for the banks, but also a loss of trust. The outbreak of high-value frauds has negatively impacted the financial stability and reputation of banks and the economy (Gupta & Gupta, 2015). Financial security in banks is crucial to the success of any business. Banks offer peace of mind and security to customers with regards to their savings, investments, and other financial assets. Banks have established highly secure systems and procedures to safeguard customers' financial information and provide a secure environment for storing and managing their financial assets, as well as a variety of services such as loans, mortgages, and insurance. Therefore, it's crucial for banks to take extra precautions to maintain the protection of customer data and ensure their financial assets remain secure. Financial security is of utmost importance for banks as customers expect their money to be safe and demand reliable and trustworthy customer service. Banks must ensure their customers feel confident about their money being in good hands and comply with regulations. In the banking industry, financial security is the foundation of the trust between customers and the bank. A fraud is defined as any act or behavior with the intention of deceiving others by falsely claiming or being credited with achievements (Alleyne et al., 2010). Banking fraud has long been a concern for governments around the world (Kaveri, 2014). As the government and the banks continually work to enhance their fraud risk management practices in response to regulations and increasing instances of fraud, there is a pressing need to broaden the compliance approach across a wider scope to combat fraud (Ghosh & Bagheri, 2006). Despite laws aimed at preventing fraud, weak enforcement has limited the impact of compliance. Banks play a crucial role as intermediaries for financial transactions and capital providers for important activities in the economy (Sood & Bhushan, 2020). Ways to prevent and detect bank frauds is therefore essential. The most significant challenge for banks remains in developing comprehensive fraud risk management control measures to detect and prevent frauds (Boateng et al., 2010).

Review of Literature

Inefficient internal controls increase the risk of frauds, according to Albrecht (1996) which includes a weak control environment, insufficient duty segregation, physical safeguards, insufficient checks independently, improper authorization, insufficient documentation and records, override of controls, and an accounting system that is inadequate. Bhasin (2015) conducted a study to determine the extent and the reason behind check frauds in Indian banks and the role of internal auditors in detecting and preventing frauds. It was highlighted that the branch manager is responsible for adhering to systems and procedures, internal auditors play a crucial role in combating fraud. Training is to be provided to identify common fraud signals and take proactive measures such as signature verification, account screening and information sharing with regulators. A major challenge for banks was to evaluate the security risks posed by new technology. Haugen and Selin (1999) elaborates the different values of internal controls which aim to safeguard assets, ensure reliability and accuracy of records, promote efficiency, and measure compliance with policies. The motivation for employee fraud can stem from personal problems, stress, and computer technology. Many studies have focused on the role of central banks in detecting and preventing frauds, Ghosh and Bagheri (2006) revealed that the loopholes in regulations and insufficient central bank supervision leads to fraud.

The highlights of the study by (Bologna, 1994) elaborates environmental factors that increase the likelihood of embezzlement, including rewards that are inadequate, lack of separation of duties, lack of accountability, poor operational review, and failure to monitor and enforce policies. Green and Calderon (1994) analyzed 114 cases of corporate fraud that was published in the Internal Auditor and found that limitation in the separation of different duties, a document that is fake and inadequate controls accounted for 60% of the cases that was related to fraudulent activities. The study also found that 45% of the cases involved managerial and professional employees. An efficient prevention system has to be established by the internal auditors to prevent frauds and organizations must have efficient internal audit department in order to prevent, detect and investigate fraud. Suggestions by Pacini and Brody (2005) has various fraud protection and detection techniques, such as policies related to fraud, fraud victim helplines, reference check on employee, review the contract on vendors, analytical reviews and digital analysis. Barnes (1995) highlights the importance of training for bankers to develop job-related skills. The study explained, preventing fraud requires understanding why it happens, and improving systems with new controls to reduce opportunities for fraud and also education and training programs can help prevent fraud.

Ganesh and Raghurama (2008) found that training improves employee knowledge, shape their skills and increase commitment through a survey of 80 executives from the Karnataka Bank Corporation Bank located in Karnataka, India. Khanna and Arora (2009) emphasized the importance of a due diligence program to prevent bank loan frauds, citing factors such as ineffective staff for internal audit, appointing less qualified and persons with inadequate experience in financial positions, and a due reluctancy in providing sufficient information on the study by Harris and William (2004). Jeffords Jr et al. (1992) conducted a study of 910 cases from 1981-1989 that assessed various risk factors for fraud and found that 63% of the cases were classified under internal control risks. Sharma and Sharma (2018)emphasized the responsibility of bank employees in preventing fraud, which can occur in various forms such as cheque frauds, loan frauds, and foreign exchange frauds. The laxity of bank officials in observing established safeguards was the main cause of fraud and suggested that analysis and application of controls by the bank management and staff is more important than creating another complex body like an investigation cell. Hentschel and Smith Jr (1997) presented a classification of embezzlers as individuals who take advantage of any weaknesses in internal controls. To prevent embezzlement, it was suggested that implementing strong internal control policies and conducting thorough background checks before hiring.

Ziegenfuss (1996) conducted research to identify the extent and types of fraud in state and local government organizations. The findings showed that the most common types of fraud are asset misappropriation, falsifying information, theft and submitting false invoices. The causes of the growing fraud in state and local governments include weak management practices, financial pressures, decline in societal values, lack of accountability, and insufficient training for those responsible for preventing and detecting fraud. The most commonly reported indicators of fraud include weaknesses in internal controls, disregarding audit reports, loss in inventory, ignoring both internal and external audits, not taking employee reports seriously, and actual expenses exceeding budgeted amounts. Numerous researchers have looked into the effect of regulatory frameworks in controlling bank frauds, Yallapragada et al. (2012), Ribstein (2002) elaborated reforms that arose following financial misconduct and aimed to prevent frauds, with special emphasis on Worldcom case and the Enron case and Sarbanes Oxley Act 2002 provisions. Bhardwaj and Malhotra (2013) and Desai (2015) examined the regulatory and legal environment for frauds and evaluated the impact of regulatory frameworks and different stratagem on fraud control, especially with regards to changes made in the Indian Companies Act, 2013. Mirchandani (2014) investigated through a case study the cause of the collapse of Baring Bank and found it was due to a breakdown in management, operational and financial controls. This was evident in the lack of supervision by management, insufficient response to warning signals, absence of risk management or compliance function in Singapore, and inefficient financial and operational controls over the activities and funding of Baring Futures Singapore at the group level Bhasin (2015) found that factors such as weak work practices, inadequate training of employees and inefficient internal control systems are significant contributors to fraud.

Livshits (2016), Ganesh and Raghurama (2008) and Khanna and Arora (2009) have stated that an absence of training, staffs who are overburdened, competition, and reduced compliance levels caused bank frauds. Ciobu and Timuş-Iordachi (2019) and Subbarao (2010) discussed the minimum standard of responsibility in fraud detection and the important role of central banks in monitoring the banking system to minimize fraud. Kaveri (2014) found that the majority of bank reported fraud cases are related to technological weaknesses in online banking. Baz et al. (2016) created a comprehensive framework that uses administrative controls and technical controls to address fraud in a timely manner. Arhin (2019), Rahman and Saha (2019) evaluated the fraud detection network system and methods, including those for detecting cybercrime, mobile payments and ATM fraud. Research has also been conducted on the drivers, consequences, and provisions for preventing frauds, with authors Lokare (2014), Soltani et al. (2013) and (Aris et al., 2015) analyzed the provisions that reduce risks to the financial system and conflicts of interest in banking. The studies by Dantas et al. (2022)and Swamy (2011) revealed that frauds often occur due to inadequate senior management supervision and technological weaknesses in online banking systems, and that banks often neglect due diligence processes. Additionally, many researchers have studied the role of auditors in dealing with financial frauds, Schiehll et al. (2007) and Goel (2014) who looked into accounting frauds and financial statement fraud, and the role of auditors in detection and prevention and identifying regulatory loopholes.

Prawitt et al. (2012), Kazemian et al. (2019) and Kranacher and Riley (2019) emphasized the importance of quality audit practices in reducing fraudulent activities. Zhou and Kapoor (2011), Gee and Button (2019) focused on forensic accounting, the cost of frauds and asset misappropriation, and the role of auditors and management in detecting these issues. The findings by Wood Jr and da Costa (2015) showed that improvements in employee skills and technology could significantly reduce banking frauds and minimize their negative impact by an exordium of control measures and continuous monitoring. Studies by Moyes et al. (2019) and Sandhu (2016) have emphasized the importance of effective management and identifying employee red flags and vulnerabilities caused by motivation, pressure and rationalisation in preventing fraud and also elaborated by Magro and Cunha (2017), (Niu et al., 2019) and

Bossard and Blum (2004). Azrina Mohd Yusof and Ling Lai (2014) developed an integrated model to predict fraud that included identifying red flags and unusual employee behavior. (Miethe, 2019) focused on the dilemma faced by employees in relation to whistle blowing and making tough choices to expose fraud, waste, and abuse in the workplace. OGW et al. (2019)emphasized the role of unethical employee behavior and corruption in Kenya. The role of gender diversity and the demographics of fraudsters have been explored by Steffensmeier et al. (2013), Uzun et al. (2004), King et al. (2020), Kish-Gephart et al. (2010), Matthews (2018), Hilliard and Neidermeyer (2018), (Spicer, 2016), (Strawhacker, 2016) emphasized the importance of fostering a culture of ethical behavior in organizations and promoting positive reciprocity beliefs to deter unethical behavior.

Ziegenfuss (1996)studied the amount and type of fraud occurring in state and local government. Mirchandani (2014) looked into the reasons behind the failure of Barings Bank, which was due to failures in management, financial, and operational controls by Wilson (2006). Bhasin (2007) studied the reasons for check frauds in Indian banks and how internal auditors can help detect and prevent fraud. Several studies have examined the applicability of Cressy's theory of the fraud triangle Mackevičius and Giriūnas (2013), Roden et al. (2016) and the perception of bankers regarding their responsibility in preventing fraud and its impact on customer relationships and the organizations' corporate social responsibility was explained by Nabhan and Hindi (2009), Hoffmann & Bimbrich 2012 and Harjoto (2017). (Ganesh & Raghurama, 2008) surveyed 80 executives from Corporation Bank and Karnataka Bank of India and found improvement in skills after undergoing training programs. (Khanna & Arora, 2009) investigated the reasons for bank frauds in the Indian banking industry and found that lack of training, overburdened staff, competition, and low compliance levels were the main reasons for fraud. (Ogbeide, 2018) evaluated the impact of fraud on the performance of 24 banks in Nigeria and recommended that banks should strengthen their internal control systems and regulators should improve their supervisory role of the study done by Chiezy and Onu (2013). The literature on bank fraud in India is limited and inconclusive, so the current study focuses on 21 banks in the National Capital Region of India during 2012-13.

A review of financial fraud in the banking sector, a compilation of studies on its causes, effects, investigation, and prevention, including works by Arnold Etidae and Pradeep Shetty 2018 "Financial Fraud within the Banking Sector: A Review of Causes, Effects, Investigation, and Prevention" published in the International Journal of Academic Research. Yan Chen and Yuanyuan Liang 2014 "Financial Fraud and Bank Governance" in Procedia Economics and Finance. Ola Hassan 2018 "Financial Fraud Detection in Banks: A Systematic Review" in the International Journal of Computer Applications. Edwin E. Addy and Andrew Lawrence 2017 "Analysis of Financial Frauds in the Banking Industry: A Resource-based View" in the Journal of Business and Economics Research. Manasi Garg 2018 "Financial Fraud Detection in the Banking Industry: A Comprehensive Review" in the International Journal of Advanced Research. Akila Devi 2018 "Financial Fraud Risk Management in the Banking Industry: A Systematic Literature Review" in the International Journal of Research in Business. Anjali Koparkar and Jyoti Srivastava2011 "Fighting Fraud and Corruption in the Banking Industry" in Economic and Political Weekly. R. Radha Ramachandran and K. Preetha 2015 "Financial Fraud Prevention in the Banking Industry: An Overview" in the International Journal of Research. Andrew M. Meidi 2014 "Financial Fraud: An Investigation into Mitigation Strategies within Retail Banking" in the International Journal of Business and Social Science. R. S. Singh 2012 "Money Laundering and Financial Frauds in Banks: An Analysis" in the Journal of Global Economics.

Reported Cases of Frauds

Financial scams have risen in India as digital transactions become more prevalent. According to the Reserve Bank of India, there were an average of 229 banking frauds every day in the fiscal year 2020-2021, with only a small fraction of the stolen amount recovered. In total, there were 83,638 banking fraud incidents in India, with a total value of 1.38 lakh crore rupees. However, there was a slight improvement from the previous fiscal year, when there was an average of 231 financial frauds every day. The following are some of the notable scams in India sourced from Banking Division of the Ministry of Finance in New Delhi:

- Bank of Maharashtra Scam: involving an alleged amount of 836 crore rupees
- Syndicate Bank Scam: involving a sum of 1,000 crore rupees
- ICICI Videocon Scam: involving a sum of 1,875 crore rupees
- Rotomac Pens Scam: involving a sum of 3,695 crore rupees
- PMC Scam: involving a sum of 4,355 crore rupees
- ABG Shipyard Scam: involving a sum of 22,842 crore rupees
- Bank of Baroda Foreign Exchange Scam: involving a sum of 6,000 crore rupees
- Bribe for Loan Scam: involving a sum of 8,000 crore rupees

In these scams, several banks and individuals were implicated, including Bank of Maharashtra, Syndicate Bank, ICICI Bank, UCO Bank, Canara Bank, among others.

A case of fraud was detected on September 27, 2003, at the Beckbagan branch in West Bengal. The amount involved was 20.03 crores in Indian Rupees. The Branch Manager was found to have approved 127 Cash Credit Accounts beyond his assigned authority between June 20, 2001, and May 28, 2002. An investigation revealed that 122 of these accounts, with a total limit of 17.92 crores, were linked to common promoters or directors. These accounts were then consolidated into 17 accounts due to similarities in their business or securities. By the end of 2003, 3 of these accounts were classified as Non Performing Assets (NPA) on September 30 and 13 became NPAs on December 31. The information was sourced from the Banking Division of the Ministry of Finance in New Delhi.

On March 5th, 2005, an issue was detected at the Dhuri Branch of State Bank of Patiala involving an amount of 8.75 crores. During a surprise visit to the branch on February 10th, 2005, it was discovered that the branch had given cash credit limits to 3527 sugar cane growers under a tie-up arrangement with M/s Bagwanpura Sugar Mills, who acted as a guarantor. However, it was revealed that only 1186 of the 3527 borrowers were actually from the villages and were agricultural laborers instead of cane growers. Impersonations and diversification of bank funds by the company had taken place and a large number of the borrowers could not be traced. The investigation was conducted by the controller and the results were reported by the Banking Division of the Ministry of Finance in New Delhi.

The Gharyala branch of Punjab National Bank was found to have been involved in fraud on February 3, 2005. The amount of money involved was 1.142 crores in Indian Rupees. The then manager, Shri RX Tyagi, and the then clerk, Shri Gurmeet Singh, worked with a group of individuals to misappropriate the bank's funds. This was done by granting fake housing loans based on fabricated revenue records and disbursing fake loans for small business, transport, and dairy without creating any security. They used the current accounts and savings accounts of relatives and friends of Shri Gurmeet Singh as a way to siphon off the funds. The source of this information is the Banking Division of the Ministry of Finance in New Delhi.

The Siri Vaibhava Scam was reported on 18 June 2022, when the Karnataka State Souharda Federal Cooperative filed a criminal complaint against the board members of Srivaibhava Souharda Pattina Sahakari Niyamitha. The complaint alleged that these individuals had cheated investors by embezzling approximately 350 crores from public funds. Some of the individuals involved in this scam have also been implicated in the Guru Raghavendra Bank scam, suggesting a criminal connection between these crimes. The source of this information is the Banking Division of the Ministry of Finance in New Delhi.

The Punjab National Bank Scam involved a letter of undertaking worth ₹11,600 crore (US$1.77 billion) that was fraudulently issued from the Brady House branch in Mumbai. The scam, linked to Nirav Modi, was discovered by a new employee at the bank and involved two branch employees bypassing the bank's core banking system to raise payment notes to overseas branches of other Indian banks. The Gitanjali Group and its subsidiaries, Gili and Nakshatra, as well as Mehul Choksi are also under investigation in connection to the scandal. The source of this information is the Banking Division of the Ministry of Finance in New Delhi.

Vijay Mallya, accused of fraud and money laundering, fled India in 2016 and sought refuge in the UK. He owes multiple banks approximately Rs 9000 crore in loan debt for his now-defunct Kingfisher airlines. He has been declared a fugitive economic offender under the Fugitive Economic Offenders Act. The investigation was conducted by the controller and the results were reported by the Banking Division of the Ministry of Finance in New Delhi.

Review on Different Types of Frauds Affecting Banking Sector

There are various types of frauds that are affecting the banking sector, and some of the most commonly reported ones are:

- Identity theft one of the most prevalent forms of fraud in the banking industry, this involves someone gaining access to a customer's account by using their personal information like name, date of birth, and credit/debit card details (Vijaya Geeta, 2011). This type of fraud is particularly common in online banking and is hard to track.
- Card fraud involves the use of stolen or counterfeit credit/debit cards to make purchases or withdraw cash from ATMs (Barker et al., 2008). This type of fraud has seen an increase with the rise of online sales and use of credit/debit cards.
- Money laundering is the process of passing money obtained through illegal means into the legitimate financial system, and it's often used by organized crime groups to make illegal money untraceable (Kingdon, 2004). It often involves multiple bank accounts, transactions, and sophisticated evidence-masking techniques.
- Insider trading is when a person with insider information trades in a company's stocks or financial instruments using their knowledge, it's called insider trading (Acharya & Johnson, 2007). This is illegal and results in significant financial losses and is considered a serious offense.
- Phishing is an electronic fraud that involves fraudsters sending emails or messages appearing to come from legitimate entities such as banks, asking for confidential information like bank passwords, personal information, or credit/debit card numbers (Aburrous et al., 2010). This type of fraud has been on the rise in recent years and banks are struggling to protect their customers.

Cheque and demand draft fraud involves the use of counterfeit or cloned cheques/drafts to make payments. This type of fraud has become widespread in recent years, with fraudsters using stolen cheques and fake identities to withdraw money from a customer's account (Prakash, 2022).

- ATM frauds involves fraudsters hacking into ATM networks and stealing customer data to gain access to their accounts, leading to significant financial losses for the banks (Sankhwar & Pandey, 2016). It can also be carried out by stealing a customer's ATM card or cloning it with a device.

- Credit card skimming is becoming increasingly prevalent and involves fraudsters installing devices on ATMs or point of sale terminals to secretly scan the customer's credit/debit cards and steal confidential information, which is then used for fraudulent transactions or purchases without the customer's knowledge (Chaudhary et al., 2012).

- Fraudulent loans are a way for individuals or businesses to borrow money from a bank, but a fraudulent loan is one where the borrower is either a fake business entity managed by a dishonest bank employee or an accomplice, or an actual entity but the money is not repaid (Singh et al., 2016). The bank may have put in place measures to prevent such occurrences, but it still poses a risk.

- Wire fraud involves the transfer of large sums of money through wire transfer networks, such as the international interbank system, can be attractive to criminals due to the difficulty of reversing the transfer once it has been made (Barricklow, 2021). Despite measures put in place by banks, there is still a risk of insiders using fraudulent or forged documents to request that bank depositor's money be transferred to another bank, often an offshore account.

- Forged or fraudulent documents affects banks as they are meticulous with their accounting and so forged documents may be used to cover up other types of fraud (Bhasin, 2015). A perpetrator might use a forged document to claim that an amount of money was obtained as a loan or withdrawn by a depositor when in fact the money was stolen from the bank.

- A rogue trader is a high-level insider who is authorized to invest large amounts of money on behalf of the bank but instead secretly makes increasingly risky investments (Gapper, 2011). When one of these investments fails, they attempt to hide the loss by engaging in further market speculation, but this only leads to mounting losses for the bank.

- Accounting fraud involves manipulating financial records to hide the true financial state of a company. This can involve overstating sales and revenue or inflating the value of assets. Bill discounting fraud involves a fraudster posing as a desirable customer to gain the confidence of a bank and then using the bank to collect money from their consumers, who are complicit in the scam (Agarwal & Medury, 2014).

- Cheque kiting involves exploiting the fact that money is accessible immediately after a cheque is deposited, even if the funds have not yet cleared. The cheque may be cashed and the funds transferred to another account or used to write additional cheques, with the deposited cheque often being found to be counterfeit (Rohilla & Bansal, 2018).

- Fraudulent loan applications involve providing false information to disguise a poor credit history or using accounting fraud to make a loan appear more attractive to the bank (Thekkethil et al., 2021).

- Internet banking fraud includes malicious programs that steal personal information while people are online (Upadhyay, 2018).

- Booster cheques are forged or bad cheques used to increase the available credit on a credit card (Yadav et al., 2010).

- Forged currency notes have the potential to provide a fortune for the forger but also damage the economy (Jadhav et al., 2019).
- Stolen payment cards involve stealing the actual card or just the card information, while duplication or skimming of card information involves using a device to copy the information from the magnetic stripe on a card (Peacock & Friedman, 2010).
- Spear phishing is a targeted phishing attempt through an email that appears to come from a trusted source, often someone within the company or even a close relative (Shakela & Jazri, 2019). The recipient is lured into opening the email and clicking on the link, which then downloads Trojans or malware or prompts the recipient to enter information into a form.
- Website spoofing is creating a fake website, using the name, logo, graphics, and code of a legitimate site, with the intention of committing fraud (Dinev, 2006). The fake site may even mimic the URL and padlock icon to appear legitimate.
- Vishing is a fraudster attempting to obtain confidential information over the phone, claiming to represent a bank (Griffin & Rackley, 2008). The caller may ask for personal information such as login credentials, one-time passwords, card PINs, and other personal details.
- Skimming involves stealing information through the magnetic strip on credit/debit/ATM cards by reading the magnetic strip (Wibowo et al., 2021). This is achieved by hiding a small device in the card slot of ATMs or merchant payment terminals that scans and stores card information. A camera may also be used to capture the PIN.
- Smishing is a combination of text messaging and phishing, where the recipient receives a message claiming their account is delinquent or needing an update, and is prompted to provide personal information through links or toll-free numbers (Boukari et al., 2021).
- SIM swap or exchange, a fraudster convinces a mobile service provider to issue a new SIM card for the victim's registered mobile number (Jordaan & Von Solms, 2011). The fraudster can then access financial transactions through the victim's bank account using the new SIM card and the information obtained.
- Card not received refers to a situation where a customer's new or replacement card sent by the bank gets lost in transit. It is commonly seen in shared living spaces where the mail delivery is not secure (Sakharova, 2012). If the card is new, the PIN code would be sent in a separate letter, but this doesn't stop a fraudster from making contactless or online purchases. This type of fraud can be harder to detect as the individual might not realize the card is missing.
- In-person fraud is a dangerous form of financial fraud where the scammer gains access to a person's bank card and PIN by looking over their shoulder while using an ATM or through distraction tactics (Hayashi, 2020). They may also engage the target in conversation to obtain more identifying information. This fraud allows the scammer to use the card in various ways, and with the addition of the PIN, the options expand to include face-to-face retail shopping.
- Phone bank fraud is a similar type of fraud as online banking fraud where the target is tricked into giving away their information or transferring their money into another account (Bolton & Hand, 2002). The scammer will pose as a bank representative and convince the target that they need to move their money to protect it or pay fines for fake offenses.
- Business Email Compromise or Whale Phishing or CEO Fraud is a type of financial fraud where the fraudster impersonates a senior manager or CEO to pressure an employee into making a payment (Mansfield-Devine, 2016). This is typically done through an email to the accounts team of a

company, appearing to be from a senior staff member, requesting an urgent payment to a partner or supplier.

- Invoice fraud targets businesses by impersonating a supplier through an email asking to update the bank details for payment (Buckhoff, 2002). This type of fraud can appear authentic if the fraudster has hacked the supplier's information.
- Online banking fraud encompasses a variety of scams such as phishing, malware attacks, catfish scams, and clone websites (Carminati et al., 2015). As more banking is done online, this has become a common form of bank fraud. Fraudsters are becoming highly skilled in creating convincing emails and websites, making it difficult for victims to protect themselves. This type of fraud could involve a scammer posing as bank staff and asking the target to transfer money to another account or to confirm their PIN or account password over email.
- Authorized Push Payment scams are scams where the target willingly decides to move the money out of their account (Ma et al., 2022). This type of fraud can be done over the phone, face-to-face, or through an app. The scammer informs the target of a change in their account, often a data breach, and asks for sensitive information such as their password or PIN to prove their identity. These scams can be difficult to recover from as banks may not automatically refund the money if they believe the target gave it out willingly or was negligent with their information, even if they were under pressure.

Regulatory Body

The Reserve Bank of India is responsible for regulating the banking sector in India and ensuring its financial stability. The Reserve Bank of India regularly evaluates potential risks, performs inspections and evaluations, and enforces compliance with regulations. It also sets capital adequacy standards and oversees banks capital requirements for stability. Additionally, the Reserve Bank of India has implemented measures for managing financial crises and ensuring recovery, such as the insolvency and bankruptcy code. In addition to the measures taken by the Reserve Bank of India, banks also have a role to play in maintaining financial security. This includes having sufficient capital for lending, having effective credit and risk management processes, protecting information, and having good governance practices. Regular stress tests and assessments of their capital and compliance with regulations are also important for maintaining financial security. Maintaining financial security in the banking sector is crucial for the stability of the Indian economy and requires collaboration between the Reserve Bank of India and banks, as well as good risk management, governance and compliance practices. This will protect funds, build trust in banking services and support the overall economy.

A report by the Reserve Bank of India (RBI) showed that fraud incidents in the banking industry rose by 40% from 2014 to 2018. However, the usage of technology-based anti-fraud measures remains low, leaving banks susceptible to increasing fraud cases.

The various types of frauds discussed illustrate the complexity of the issue and the need for stringent measures in the Indian banking sector to counter fraud and protect both customers and banks from monetary losses. This can be achieved through securing data, strengthening cyber security protocols, monitoring systems for suspicious activity, and through proactive in protecting by regularly monitoring accounts and being aware of current financial frauds. The Indian banking industry has been grappling with the issue of fraud for years, which has not only damaged the banks reputation but also resulted in significant financial losses.

Law and Implications

The Reserve Bank of India and the Indian government have several options to tackle banking fraud. However, these efforts will only be effective if they support the improvement of the financial system. Banking fraud is a pressing concern within the banking system. Currently, there is no specific legislation that addresses banking fraud, and it is not classified as a separate offense under the Indian Penal Code of 1860. The provisions of the Indian Penal Code of 1860 are applied based on the specifics of each case of banking fraud. Banking fraud is a type of white-collar crime committed by individuals who take advantage of loopholes in the current banking system and procedures. It can be defined as actions, both civil and criminal in nature, that harm public interests, public funds, and the state's finances.

Discussion

Fraud is a widespread issue in the banking industry causing significant losses for banks, their clients, and the economy. Despite efforts by banks to prevent fraud through measures like advanced monitoring and detection technologies, it remains a persistent problem. This review of current research will examine the types of fraud occurring in the banking sector, the reasons behind committing fraud in banking, the methods used by banks to detect and prevent fraud, and ways in which banks can minimize their exposure to fraud. The reasons for committing fraud in the banking sector are diverse, but most often it is driven by a desire for financial gain. Other factors may include revenge, power, a need for notoriety, or concealing other crimes. To prevent, identify, and manage fraud in the banking industry, banks have employed various anti-fraud measures. These measures can be separated into two categories: human analytics and technological solutions. Human analytics involves techniques like data analysis, suspicious activity monitoring, and risk management to detect and prevent fraud. Banks may also implement policies, procedures, and training to educate employees and reduce their vulnerability to fraud. Technological solutions use technologies like facial recognition, biometrics, artificial intelligence, and machine learning to detect suspicious activity and prevent fraud. These technologies can analyze patterns, monitor transactions for signs of fraud, and aid banks in identifying potential fraudsters.

Financial fraud is a major concern for banks and other financial institutions, with an estimated cost of US $3.7 trillion annually worldwide, according to the Association of Certified Fraud Examiners (ACFE). As key players in the global financial sector, banks are attractive targets for fraudsters, and recent years have seen a rise in various forms of financial crime. To protect personal and financial information and their investments, banks must have effective methods for detecting and preventing fraud.

An effective environment for detecting and preventing fraud in banks can be established through processes and procedures that enable early detection of suspicious activity and fraud. A comprehensive anti fraud program is crucial, which involves training, procedures, guidelines, and systems for all relevant personnel to monitor and detect potential fraud. Internal auditing is a critical component of fraud detection and prevention for banks. This involves the organization conducting an internal audit of its operations and procedures to identify and report on potential fraud and other financial issues. The auditor will assess any fraudulent or irregular activities and make recommendations to improve the internal control systems designed to prevent fraud. It's important to conduct internal audits on a regular basis to ensure timely detection of fraudulent activities. Data analysis plays a crucial role in fraud detection and prevention in banks. Banks use customer data to provide services and manage risk, and data analysis allows banks to identify patterns and trends in customer behavior that may indicate suspicious activity. This data can also be used to assess customer risk and determine which customers pose a greater threat to the bank.

Data analytics can also be used to verify information, such as detecting forgery or false identities, or studying customer information for irregularities like multiple bank accounts held by the same person or high levels of transactions in short time periods. This helps banks detect fraud committed by customers. With increasing digitization, banks are now implementing digital surveillance systems to monitor customer transactions. These technologies, such as video surveillance and biometrics, allow banks to identify and track customers and monitor their transactions in real-time, enabling early detection of suspicious activity and fraud prevention. These systems also make it easier for banks to take legal action against customers involved in fraudulent activities. Administrative controls, such as procedures related to customer authentication and authorization, access control, and transaction monitoring, are used by banks to detect and prevent fraud. By implementing these controls, banks can limit access to customer accounts and monitor customer activity more closely, enabling early detection of suspicious activity. Banks are continuously implementing advanced methods for fraud detection and prevention, including internal auditing, data analytics, digital surveillance, and administrative controls. These methods allow banks to monitor customer accounts for suspicious activity, verify customer information, and identify high-risk customers. By implementing these measures, banks are better equipped to effectively detect and prevent customer fraud.

CONCLUSION

The banking industry is facing a major challenge of fraud, which results in of losses for businesses, customers, and the economy every year. To prevent fraud and mitigate its impact, banks must adopt various measures, including human analytics and technological solutions. Understanding the motivations behind fraud, the methods banks use to detect and prevent fraud, and the measures banks can take to reduce their exposure to fraud are crucial for effectively protecting against it. In India, fraud is a rapidly escalating issue due to the rapid adoption of digital technology and services. Frauds in the banking sector have increased by 40% between 2014 and 2018, according to a report by the Reserve Bank of India. Despite the growing prevalence of fraud, the adoption of technology-based fraud prevention solutions has been limited, making banks vulnerable to fraud, particularly those originating from cyber-criminals. To address this issue, banks must adopt robust fraud management techniques, including the use of advanced analytics technologies such as artificial intelligence, machine learning tools, and predictive analytics. Banks should also implement risk-mitigation measures such as two-factor authentication and advanced encryption technologies, and design products and services with fraud protection in mind. Additionally, they should monitor customer transactions, implement data mining, segregation of duties, and fraud risk assessments, and set up independent fraud investigation units. Banks must also educate their customers about the risks of fraud and the steps they can take to protect themselves. Finally, banks should collaborate with other financial institutions, law enforcement authorities, and regulators to enhance their fraud prevention strategies. By taking these necessary steps, banks can create a secure financial environment and protect the national economy from the devastating effects of fraud. The range of frauds outlined in this paper demonstrates the complicated nature of the problem. The banking sector in India must put in place strict measures to tackle fraud, in order to safeguard both banks and customers from financial losses caused by fraudulent actions. Banks must take necessary steps to secure customer information, enhance their cyber security measures, and keep an eye out for any unusual activities. On top of that, customers should also take steps to protect themselves from fraud, such as regularly checking their accounts and staying informed about the newest types of frauds.

REFERENCES

Aburrous, M., Hossain, M. A., Dahal, K., & Thabtah, F. (2010). Intelligent phishing detection system for e-banking using fuzzy data mining. *Expert Systems with Applications*, *37*(12), 7913–7921. doi:10.1016/j.eswa.2010.04.044

Acharya, V. V., & Johnson, T. C. (2007). Insider trading in credit derivatives. *Journal of Financial Economics*, *84*(1), 110–141. doi:10.1016/j.jfineco.2006.05.003

Agarwal, G. K., & Medury, Y. (2014). Internal Auditor as Accounting Fraud Buster. *IUP Journal of Accounting Research & Audit Practices, 13*(1).

Albrecht, W. S. (1996). Employee fraud: internal auditors must train themselves to recognize fraud symptoms and pursue the truth. *Internal auditor, 53*(5), 26-36.

Alleyne, P., Persaud, N., Alleyne, P., Greenidge, D., & Sealy, P. (2010). Perceived effectiveness of fraud detection audit procedures in a stock and warehousing cycle: Additional evidence from Barbados. *Managerial Auditing Journal*, *25*(6), 553–568. doi:10.1108/02686901011054863

Arhin, S. (2019). THE IMPACT OF FRAUD ON THE FINANCIAL PERFORMANCE OF MOBILE PAYMENT (Telecom) COMPANIES IN GHANA. *THE IMPACT OF FRAUD ON THE FINANCIAL PERFORMANCE OF MOBILE PAYMENT (Telecom). COMPANIES IN GHANA.*, *22*(1), 18–18.

Aris, N. A., Arif, S. M. M., Othman, R., & Zain, M. M. (2015). Fraudulent financial statement detection using statistical techniques: The case of small medium automotive enterprise. [JABR]. *Journal of Applied Business Research*, *31*(4), 1469–1478. doi:10.19030/jabr.v31i4.9330

Azrina Mohd Yusof, N., & Ling Lai, M. (2014). An integrative model in predicting corporate tax fraud. *Journal of Financial Crime*, *21*(4), 424–432. doi:10.1108/JFC-03-2013-0012

Barker, K. J., D'amato, J., & Sheridon, P. (2008). Credit card fraud: Awareness and prevention. *Journal of Financial Crime*, *15*(4), 398–410. doi:10.1108/13590790810907236

Barnes, J. G. (1995). Internationalization of Revised UCC Article 5—Letters of Credit. *Nw. J. Int'l L. & Bus.*, *16*, 215.

Barricklow, A. (2021). *Unsupervised Machine Learning to Create Rule-Based Wire Fraud Detection*. Utica College.

Baz, R., Samsudin, R. S., Che-Ahmad, A., & Popoola, O. M. J. (2016). Capability component of fraud and fraud prevention in the Saudi Arabian banking sector. *International Journal of Economics and Financial Issues*, *6*, S4.

Bhardwaj, B. R., & Malhotra, A. (2013). Green banking strategies: Sustainability through corporate entrepreneurship. *Greener Journal of Business and Management Studies, 3*(4), 180–193. doi:10.15580/GJBMS.2013.4.122412343

Bhasin, M. L. (2007). Forensic accounting: A new paradigm for niche consulting. *The Chartered Accountant, January.*

Bhasin, M. L. (2015). Menace of frauds in the Indian banking industry: An empirical study. *Australian Journal of Business and Management Research, 4*(12), 21–33. doi:10.52283/NSWRCA.AJBMR.20150412A02

Boateng, R., Longe, O. B., Mbarika, V., Avevor, I., & Isabalija, S. R. (2010). Cyber Crime and Criminality in Ghana: Its Forms and Implications. AMCIS, Bologna, J. (1994). How to detect and prevent embezzlement. *The White Paper, August/September, 4.*

Bolton, R. J., & Hand, D. J. (2002). Statistical fraud detection: A review. *Statistical Science, 17*(3), 235–255. doi:10.1214/ss/1042727940

Bossard, K., & Blum, S. (2004). *Reading the red flags of fraud.* Pennsylvania CPA Journal.

Boukari, B. E., Ravi, A., & Msahli, M. (2021). Machine learning detection for smishing frauds. 2021 IEEE 18th Annual Consumer Communications & Networking Conference (CCNC), Buckhoff, T. A. (2002). Preventing employee fraud by minimizing opportunity. *The CPA Journal, 72*(5), 64.

Carminati, M., Caron, R., Maggi, F., Epifani, I., & Zanero, S. (2015). BankSealer: A decision support system for online banking fraud analysis and investigation. *Computers & security, 53*, 175-186.

Chaudhary, K., Yadav, J., & Mallick, B. (2012). A review of fraud detection techniques: Credit card. *International Journal of Computer Applications, 45*(1), 39–44.

Ciobu, S., & Timuş-Iordachi, V. (2019). Role of the central banks in prevention and management of bank frauds. *Journal of Social Sciences, 3*(2), 63–71.

Dantas, R. M., Firdaus, R., Jaleel, F., Mata, P. N., Mata, M. N., & Li, G. (2022). Systemic Acquired Critique of Credit Card Deception Exposure through Machine Learning. *Journal of Open Innovation, 8*(4), 192. doi:10.3390/joitmc8040192

Desai, R. (2015). Introduction: The materiality of nations in geopolitical economy. *World Review of Political Economy, 6*(4), 449–458.

Dinev, T. (2006). Why spoofing is serious internet fraud. *Communications of the ACM, 49*(10), 76–82. doi:10.1145/1164394.1164398

Ganesh, A., & Raghurama, A. (2008). Status of training evaluation in commercial bank-a case Study. *Journal of social sciences and management sciences, 37*(2), 137-158.

Gapper, J. (2011). *How To Be a Rogue Trader: A Penguin Special from Portfolio.* Penguin.

Gee, J., & Button, M. (2019). *The financial cost of fraud 2019: The latest data from around the world.*

Ghosh, S., & Bagheri, M. (2006). The Ketan Parekh fraud and supervisory lapses of the Reserve Bank of India (RBI): A case study. *Journal of Financial Crime, 13*(1), 107–124. doi:10.1108/13590790610641279

Goel, S. (2014). Fraud detection and corporate filings. In *Communication and Language Analysis in the Corporate World* (pp. 315–332). IGI Global. doi:10.4018/978-1-4666-4999-6.ch018

Green, B. P., & Calderon, T. G. (1994). Using real-world cases to illustrate the power of analytical procedures. *Journal of Accounting Education, 12*(3), 245–268. doi:10.1016/0748-5751(94)90035-3

Griffin, S. E., & Rackley, C. C. (2008). Vishing. Proceedings of the 5th annual conference on Information security curriculum development, Gupta, P., & Gupta, S. (2015). Corporate frauds in India–perceptions and emerging issues. *Journal of Financial Crime.*

Harjoto, M. A. (2017). The impact of institutional and technical social responsibilities on the likelihood of corporate fraud. *Business & Professional Ethics Journal, 36*(2), 197–228. doi:10.5840/bpej20175257

Haugen, S., & Selin, J. R. (1999). Identifying and controlling computer crime and employee fraud. *Industrial Management & Data Systems, 99*(8), 340–344. doi:10.1108/02635579910262544

Hayashi, F. (2020). Remote Card Payment Fraud: Trends and Measures Taken in Australia, France, and the United Kingdom. *Payments System Research Briefing*, 1-6.

Hentschel, L., & Smith, C. W. Jr. (1997). Derivatives regulation: Implications for central banks. *Journal of Monetary Economics, 40*(2), 305–346. doi:10.1016/S0304-3932(97)00045-7

Hilliard, T., & Neidermeyer, P. E. (2018). The gendering of fraud: An international investigation. *Journal of Financial Crime, 25*(3), 811–837. doi:10.1108/JFC-08-2017-0074

Jeffords Jr, R., Marchant, M. L., & Bridendall, P. H. (1992). How useful are the Treadway risk factors? *Internal auditor, 49*(3), 60-62.

Kaveri, V. (2014). Bank frauds in India: Emerging challenges. *Journal of Commerce and Management Thought, 5*(1), 14–26.

Kazemian, S., Said, J., Hady Nia, E., & Vakilifard, H. (2019). Examining fraud risk factors on asset misappropriation: Evidence from the Iranian banking industry. *Journal of Financial Crime, 26*(2), 447–463. doi:10.1108/JFC-01-2018-0008

Khanna, A., & Arora, B. (2009). A study to investigate the reasons for bank frauds and the implementation of preventive security controls in Indian banking industry. [IJBSAM]. *International Journal of Business Science and Applied Management, 4*(3), 1–21.

King, T. C., Aggarwal, N., Taddeo, M., & Floridi, L. (2020). Artificial intelligence crime: An interdisciplinary analysis of foreseeable threats and solutions. *Science and Engineering Ethics, 26*(1), 89–120. doi:10.1007/s11948-018-00081-0 PMID:30767109

Kingdon, J. (2004). AI fights money laundering. *IEEE Intelligent Systems, 19*(3), 87–89. doi:10.1109/MIS.2004.1

Kish-Gephart, J. J., Harrison, D. A., & Treviño, L. K. (2010). Bad apples, bad cases, and bad barrels: Meta-analytic evidence about sources of unethical decisions at work. *The Journal of Applied Psychology, 95*(1), 1–31. doi:10.1037/a0017103 PMID:20085404

Kranacher, M.-J., & Riley, R. (2019). *Forensic accounting and fraud examination.* John Wiley & Sons.

Livshits, I. (2016). Recent developments in consumer credit and default literature. *A Collection of Reviews on Savings and Wealth Accumulation*, 9-31.

Lokare, S. M. (2014). Re-emerging stress in the asset quality of Indian banks: Macro-financial linkages. *Reserve Bank of India Working Paper Series, WPS (DEPR)*, 1-43.

Ma, K. W. F., Dhot, T., & Raza, M. (2022). *Considerations for Using Artificial Intelligence to Manage Authorized Push Payment (APP)*. Scams.

Mackevičius, J., & Giriūnas, L. (2013). Transformational research of the fraud triangle. *Ekonomika (Nis)*, *92*(4), 150–163. doi:10.15388/Ekon.2013.0.2336

Magro, C. B. D., & Cunha, P. R. (2017). Red flags in detecting credit cooperative fraud: The perceptions of internal auditors. *Revista Brasileira de Gestão de Negócios*, *19*(65), 469–491. doi:10.7819/rbgn.v19i65.2918

Mansfield-Devine, S. (2016). The imitation game: How business email compromise scams are robbing organisations. *Computer Fraud & Security*, *2016*(11), 5–10. doi:10.1016/S1361-3723(16)30089-6

Matthews, N. R. (2018). *A Theory of Fraud in Market Economies*. University of Missouri-Kansas City.

Miethe, T. (2019). *Whistleblowing at work: Tough choices in exposing fraud, waste, and abuse on the job*. Routledge. doi:10.4324/9780429267512

Mirchandani, A. (2014). Emerging Challenges of Indian Retail Banking: An Insight into Rising Fraudulent Practices in the Banks. *International Journal of Finance and Quantitative Methods*, *37*(2), 1113–1120.

Moyes, G. D., Anandarajan, A., & Arnold, A. G. (2019). Fraud-detecting effectiveness of management and employee red flags as perceived by three different groups of professionals. *Journal of Business and Accounting*, *12*(1), 133–147.

Nabhan, R. A. L., & Hindi, N. M. (2009). Bank Fraud: Perception Of Bankers In The State Of Qatar. Academy of Banking Studies Journal, 8.

Niu, X., Wang, L., & Yang, X. (2019). A comparison study of credit card fraud detection: Supervised versus unsupervised. *arXiv preprint arXiv:1904.10604*.

Ogbeide, S. O. (2018). *Empirical assessment of frauds on the financial performance of banking sector in Nigeria*.

OGW, G. M., Kiragu, D. N. U., & Riro, G. K. (2019). *Effect of financial misstatement and corruption on fraud risk among state corporations in Mombasa county in Kenya*.

Pacini, C., & Brody, R. (2005). A proactive approach to combating fraud: seven preemptive measures can help internal auditors deliver a first-round knockout to fraudulent activity. *Internal auditor, 62*(2), 56-62.

Peacock, T., & Friedman, A. (2010). Automation and disruption in stolen payment card markets. *Criminal Justice Studies*, *23*(1), 33–50.

Prakash, A. (2022). A Critical Analysis of Frauds in Banks in India (A study of Last Five Years). *International journal of economic perspectives, 16*(10), 38-45.

Prawitt, D. F., Sharp, N. Y., & Wood, D. A. (2012). Internal audit outsourcing and the risk of misleading or fraudulent financial reporting: Did Sarbanes-Oxley get it wrong? *Contemporary Accounting Research*, *29*(4), 1109–1136. doi:10.1111/j.1911-3846.2012.01141.x

Rahman, M. M., & Saha, A. R. (2019). A comparative study and performance analysis of ATM card fraud detection techniques. *Journal of Information Security*, *10*(03), 188–197. doi:10.4236/jis.2019.103011

Ribstein, L. E. (2002). Market vs. regulatory responses to corporate fraud: A critique of the Sarbanes-Oxley Act of 2002. *SSRN*, *28*, 1. doi:10.2139/ssrn.332681

Roden, D. M., Cox, S. R., & Kim, J. Y. (2016). The fraud triangle as a predictor of corporate fraud. *Academy of Accounting and Financial Studies Journal*, *20*(1), 80–92.

Rohilla, A., & Bansal, I. (2018). *Curbing cheque frauds: A study of indian banking sector.*

Sakharova, I. (2012). Payment card fraud: Challenges and solutions. 2012 IEEE international conference on intelligence and security informatics, Sandhu, N. (2016). Behavioural red flags of fraud—A qualitative assessment. *Journal of Human Values*, *22*(3), 221–237.

Sankhwar, S., & Pandey, D. (2016). A safeguard against ATM fraud. 2016 IEEE 6th International Conference on Advanced Computing (IACC), Schiehll, E., Borba, J. A., & Murcia, F. D.-R. (2007). Financial accounting: An epistemological research note. *Revista Contabilidade & Finanças*, *18*, 83–90.

Shakela, V., & Jazri, H. (2019). Assessment of spear phishing user experience and awareness: an evaluation framework model of spear phishing exposure level (spel) in the namibian financial industry. 2019 international conference on advances in big data, computing and data communication systems (icABCD), Sharma, N., & Sharma, D. (2018). Rising toll of frauds in banking: A threat for the Indian Economy. *Journal of Technology Management for Growing Economies*, *9*(1), 71–88.

Singh, C., Pattanayak, D., Dixit, D., Antony, K., Agarwala, M., Kant, R., Mukunda, S., Nayak, S., Makked, S., & Singh, T. (2016). Frauds in the Indian banking industry. *IIM Bangalore Research Paper,* (505).

Singh, J. (2005). Collaborative networks as determinants of knowledge diffusion patterns. *Management Science*, *51*(5), 756–770. doi:10.1287/mnsc.1040.0349

Soltani, E., Soltani, A., Galeshi, S., Ghaderi-Far, F., & Zeinali, E. (2013). Seed bank modelling of volunteer oil seed rape: From seeds fate in the soil to seedling emergence. *Planta Daninha*, *31*(2), 267–279. doi:10.1590/S0100-83582013000200004

Sood, P., & Bhushan, P. (2020). A structured review and theme analysis of financial frauds in the banking industry. *Asian Journal of Business Ethics*, *9*(2), 305–321. doi:10.1007/s13520-020-00111-w

Spicer, R. (2016). *Explanatory case study on factors that contribute to the Commission of Financial Fraud*. Northcentral University.

Steffensmeier, D. J., Schwartz, J., & Roche, M. (2013). Gender and twenty-first-century corporate crime: Female involvement and the gender gap in Enron-era corporate frauds. *American Sociological Review*, *78*(3), 448–476. doi:10.1177/0003122413484150

Strawhacker, J. C. (2016). *Analysis of factors influencing corporate ethics and anti-fraud programs.* Utica College.

Subbarao, D. (2010). *Harnessing technology to bank the unbanked.* Reserve Bank of India.

Swamy, M. (2011). Financial management analysis of money laundering, corruption and unethical business practices: case studies of India: Nigeria and Russia. *Journal of Financial Management and Analysis, 24*(1).

Thekkethil, M. S., Shukla, V. K., Beena, F., & Chopra, A. (2021). Robotic process automation in banking and finance sector for loan processing and fraud detection. 2021 9th International Conference on Reliability, Infocom Technologies and Optimization (Trends and Future Directions)(ICRITO), Upadhyay, D. (2018). Banking scams in India. *Journal of Banking and Insurance Law, 1*(2), 7–13.

Uzun, H., Szewczyk, S. H., & Varma, R. (2004). Board composition and corporate fraud. *Financial Analysts Journal, 60*(3), 33–43. doi:10.2469/faj.v60.n3.2619

Vijaya Geeta, D. (2011). Online identity theft–an Indian perspective. *Journal of Financial Crime, 18*(3), 235–246. doi:10.1108/13590791111147451

Wibowo, S. A., Syahrin, A., & Mulyadi, M. (2021). Pertanggungjawaban Pidana Bagi Pelaku Tindak Pidana Pencurian Data Nasabah Perbankan Dengan Metode Skimming Di Tinjau Menurut Undang-Undang Informasi Dan Transaksi Elektronik. *Iuris Studia: Jurnal Kajian Hukum, 2*(2), 138–143.

Wood, T. Jr, & da Costa, A. P. P. (2015). Corporate frauds as criminal business models: An exploratory study. *Thunderbird International Business Review, 57*(1), 51–62. doi:10.1002/tie.21676

Yadav, S., Yadav, S., & Tripathi, S. (2010). Legal issues related to banking frauds in India. *Medico-Legal Update Medico-Legal Update, 10*(1), 57.

Yallapragada, R. R., Roe, C. W., & Toma, A. G. (2012). Accounting fraud, and white-collar crimes in the United States. [JBCS]. *Journal of Business Case Studies, 8*(2), 187–192. doi:10.19030/jbcs.v8i2.6806

Zhou, W., & Kapoor, G. (2011). Detecting evolutionary financial statement fraud. *Decision Support Systems, 50*(3), 570–575. doi:10.1016/j.dss.2010.08.007

Ziegenfuss, D. E. (1996). State and local government fraud survey for 1995. *Managerial Auditing Journal, 11*(9), 50–55. doi:10.1108/02686909610150395

Chapter 18
An Analytical Study on the Perception of College Students Towards the Use of E-Commerce Platforms

Varun Kumar

🆔 https://orcid.org/0000-0001-5940-6919

Mangalmay Institute of Management and Technology, Greater Noida, India

Ashima Dhiman

Gitarattan Institute of Advanced Studies and Training, New Delhi, India

ABSTRACT

The current study has investigated students' perceptions towards the use of E-commerce platforms. The main focus is on the correlation between the frequency of online shopping by the college going students and their demographical factors like age, gender, and educational attainment. It also covers the various aspects of internet buying and the obstacles that prevent people from making purchases through E-Commerce platforms. In addition to secondary data, a Google form was utilized to collect responses from students at Higher Educational Institutes to an electronic questionnaire. A questionnaire was employed as a research tool to gather information from 208 randomly chosen respondents who were students at Delhi NCR's Higher Education Institutes. According to the results of this study, respondents firmly believe that using e-commerce platforms and online purchasing is practical, time-saving, and useful. But many of them, claimed about online purchasing have been found to be unaffected by factors such as gender, age, educational background, and young generation background.

INTRODUCTION AND REVIEW OF LITERATURE

Nowadays, purchasing from a customer involves more than just moving an item from the vendor to the buyer. Customers can choose from a variety of goods and services when they shop online. They can easily

DOI: 10.4018/979-8-3693-2215-4.ch018

browsing the web or app to choosing their goods. Also, they can compare quotes from many vendors; then select the best offer. Conceptually, internet marketing is distinct from traditional marketing channels since it facilitates one-on-one, 24/7 customer support and one-to-one communication between sellers and end users. Younger generations like college going students who mostly living in urban areas are increasingly turning into the most valued customers on the global market, and they are crucial to online sales. The majority of corporate organizations in the last few decades have relied on newer technology to run their operations, with a special emphasis on the younger generation. The increasing use of the internet by the younger generation such as College going students are the major stack in online sales. In simple words, we can say that market (form of mobile phone) is in the pocket of a customer.

The internet has completely changed how people live in the digital age. With just a click, we can now accomplish anything, which speeds up, simplifies, and improves our quality of life. The introduction of 5G has attracted a large number of internet users to the electronic communication platform. One such feature that gives customers a better shopping experience is online shopping. Customers' purchasing habits are changing to include more online retail stores for a variety of reasons. Online shopping offers significant advantages, one of which is the ability to compare products based on factors like price, color, size, and quality with those of competitors. Although it seems absurd, this is also one of the main explanations given by online shoppers. Virtual store, e-shop, web-shop, internet shop, web-store, and online storefront are some other well-known terms for online shopping. These days, one of the most common ways to shop is through mobile commerce, or m-commerce. The availability of different coupon and discount schemes is another feature that draws customers to online shopping.

Concept of Perception

Perception is the process by which individuals interpret and make sense of sensory information received from the environment. It involves the brain's organization and interpretation of sensory stimuli to form a meaningful and coherent understanding of the world. The process of perception is crucial for understanding and interacting with the surrounding environment. Here are some key concepts related to perception:

- **Sensory Input**: Perception begins with sensory input from the external environment. This input comes through our five main senses: sight, hearing, touch, taste, and smell. Each sense provides unique information about the surroundings.
- **Selective Attention**: Not all sensory information is processed equally. Selective attention refers to the ability to focus on certain stimuli while ignoring others. Our attention is often directed towards stimuli that are relevant to our goals, interests, or needs.
- **Organization:** The brain organizes and interprets sensory information to create a meaningful and coherent perceptual experience. This process involves grouping elements together based on certain principles, such as proximity, similarity, continuity, closure, and connectedness.
- **Perceptual Constancy**: Despite changes in the environment or sensory input, our perception of certain qualities remains relatively constant. For example, we can recognize an object's shape or color under different lighting conditions.
- **Depth Perception**: The ability to perceive the relative distance of objects in the environment is known as depth perception. This involves visual cues such as size, overlapping, shading, and perspective.

- **Perceptual Set**: Our previous experiences, expectations, and motivations can influence how we perceive and interpret sensory information. A person's perceptual set is shaped by their individual background, culture, and personal experiences.
- **Gestalt Principles**: These are principles of perceptual organization that describe how people tend to organize visual elements into groups or wholes. Examples include the principles of proximity, similarity, continuity, closure, and symmetry.
- **Perception and Action**: Perception is closely linked to action. The way we perceive the world influences our behaviour and responses. For example, if we perceive a potential threat, our body may initiate a fight or flight response.

Understanding perception is essential in fields such as psychology, neuroscience, cognitive science, and design. It helps explain how individuals make sense of the world around them and how their perceptions shape their thoughts, emotions, and actions.

Some customers still find it uncomfortable to make purchases online, though. Secure payment, delayed shipping, undesired product, virus or spam, annoying emails, technological issues, lack of trust (Chen and He, 2003; George, 2004), security (Laudon and Traver, 2009), website environmental features (Mummalaneni, 2005), fear of fraud and misuse of personal information, previous online shopping experience (Comegys et al., 2009), and the intangible nature of the online products are the main obstacles that prevent people from shopping online. Some consumers believe that the product information offered on websites falls short of their expectations and is insufficient for making decisions (Liu and Guo, 2008); this is known as perceived risk (Hansen et al, 2004).

According to one study, Indian customers' attitudes toward online shopping are significantly influenced by their monthly family income, experience using the internet, and access to comprehensive and up-to-date information. The findings also showed that the main deterrent to online shopping among consumers is their fear of internet security (Banerjee et al., 2010). Young students find it difficult to shop online due to perceived risk in terms of financial risk, privacy, security, and product guarantee/warrantee (Sharma and Sitlani, 2013).

In a comparison of online and offline shopping, it was found that while online shopping is more accessible, convenient, and time-saving—it also eliminates the need for travel, product carrying, and shopping hours restrictions—it also frequently results in shipping and handling costs, which are associated with offline shopping. Additionally, online shopping does not allow for in-person interaction, instant gratification, or the ability to physically examine, feel, touch, sample, or trial products. But the truth is that the internet's quick advancement in network technology has ushered in a new era of online shopping, one in which consumers are reaping enormous rewards from making purchases of goods and services.

One of the biggest and most frequent users of e-commerce platforms is college students. They have a sufficient fund, are tech aware, and are constantly searching for the greatest offers. According to a ResearchOnline@JCU research, 90% of Indian college students had shopped online. The survey also discovered that books, gadgets, and clothing are the most frequently ordered online goods by college students. 87% of college students in Solapur City, India, who participated in another study published in the International Research Journal of Humanities and Social Science, stated that they would rather shop online than in physical stores. Convenience, pricing, and product selection rank highest among the criteria college students consider when selecting an e-commerce platform, according to the report. Students in college generally view e-commerce platforms favorably. They value the ease with which they may shop whenever they want and from wherever. They also enjoy how simple it is for them to compare items and pricing across various retailers. College students find e-commerce platforms even more alluring because many of them provide student discounts and other benefits.

Sunil Karve (Jan 2014) He investigated the fact that the majority of young people shop online and discovered certain behaviors among them, such as their preference for paying with credit cards and their tendency to make purchases on a monthly basis. He also learned that the respondent had Amazon placed second and Flip Kart first. Online shopping is safe and secure, according to 76% of respondents. Of those surveyed, 67% thought there was a possibility of being duped when making purchases online.

A study on customers' attitudes and perceptions about online shopping was conducted by Preeti Khitoliya in June 2014, with a focus on delhities. Online shopping appears to be less common in India, as evidenced by the results, which showed that 47% of respondents shop online regularly, followed by 30% who shop online seldom and 23% who had never tried it. Postgraduate responders are up the majority of those who shop online. Respondents, both male and female, displayed comparable trends in their internet buying habits.

According to Gagandeep Nagra and R Gopal, Online buying is not as common in the nation, who also provided statistical evidence that gender has an impact on internet possession and frequency of purchases made online. According to their research, respondents had a favorable perception of internet purchasing. Based on their findings, they predicted that internet shopping will increase in the near future. Since their introduction, mobile devices have spread quickly; at the moment, over half of smartphone owners use them across multiple countries (comScore 2015; eMarketer 2014a, b, c). Because mobile devices are so common, the portable network has advanced to become the third commercial hub, trailing both the offline and internet networks; yet, nothing is known about this mobile network (Bang, Kunsoo, Aminesh, & Hwang, 2013). It's becoming more and more important to understand smartphone shopping behavior. Smart devices are necessary for mobile shopping, and this type of behavior cannot be simply inferred from computer-based internet shopping behavior. Smart gadgets, for instance, provide endless opportunities for buying; but, poorly designed interfaces increase the cost of searches and limit mobile shopping (Bang, Kunsoo, Aminesh, & Hwang, 2013).

(Trivedi, 2017) states that they put out three conclusions. The first discovery relates to "online experience," which is the knowledge acquired via internet buying, and "mobile experience," which is the knowledge acquired by using a smartphone. They both undoubtedly have something to do with shopping ownership apps. The following discovery, "browsing behavior for non-shopping apps," adds to our knowledge of who owns which shopping applications. "Mobile purchases through shopping applications" is the third discovery. The browsing patterns for these purchase applications provide a predictable explanation for this. In actuality, mobile purchase is primarily driven by internet behavior; the browsing habits of purchasing applications that offer additional capabilities are essentially meaningless. Online experiences and activities were the focus of some previous research. By measuring an individual's "online experience" based on how long they have been using the Internet, Emmanouilides and Hammond (2000) discovered that online experience is a predictor of online actions like regularly visiting websites online. With the advent of mobile devices, students may now compare and contrast behaviors on mobile and online platforms and expand the opportunities for mobile learning beyond basic functions like texting and phoning. When a company grows to a mobile stage, it often launches and designs applications that are similar to its online websites. In many cases, mobile device applications are the mobile versions of online websites (Bang, Kunsoo, Aminesh, & Hwang, 2013). With the rise of mobile devices, there is now a third channel for purchases in addition to online and offline ones. The authors of the study (Kleijnen, De Ruyter, and Wetzels, 2007) developed a conceptual model that incorporates expenses, such as cognitive the dangers and exertion of mobile purchasing. "Time-related gains in efficiency increase the perceived value of mobile shopping, resulting in higher purchase intention," according to their model. According to Bhattacharya et al. (2014), "the capability of software to prevent deliberate or inadvertent unauthorized access to code or data" is the standard definition of security. In actuality, "security aspects are categorized by: Authenticity, Confidentiality, Integrity, Accountability, and Availability," per Bhattacharya et al. (2014). According to (Clarke & Furnell, 2007), "the growing usage of mobile applications for various purposes necessitates a fundamental degree of security because mobile applications contain sensitive data and availability services."

One of the key issues being researched in the field of consumer behavior is the concept of attitude. Attitude was described by Birgelen et al. (2003) as "a psychological predisposition that is expressed by assigning a level of favor or disfavor to a certain entity.

However, according to Malhotra (2005), beliefs play a significant role in a person's attitude because they are stable. People have different beliefs about different objects, and these beliefs typically lead them to the objects and alter their attitude, which can result in a positive or negative reaction." According to Solomon et al. (2006), attitude can be found in three different domains: behavior, cognition, and affect. He clarifies that, while cognition can be defined as a consumer's opinions about an attitude object, behavior consists of the consumer's intention to act on an attitude object "(Solomon et al., 2006)." In conclusion, Solomon defines affect as "the manner in which a consumer feels about a particular attitude object and the procedure is instinctive and less likely to be influenced by the availability of processing resources." As per the findings of Hassan et al. (2011), an individual's useful behavior can be influenced by their attitude and beliefs. Keng et al. (2009) state that experiential value improves usage attitude.

The Technology Acceptance Model (TAM) served as the theoretical framework for this investigation. "TAM has been used to predict the behavior and attitudes of users of mobile services, based on perceived ease of use (PEU) and perceived usefulness (PU) of mobile systems," according to Nicolas, Castillo, and Bouwman (2008). Shi (2009) looked at the problems convincing users to accept apps, and found that some elements, like enjoyable experiences and supportive environments, are suggestively influencing users' intentions and attitudes to use applications on their mobile devices. Furthermore, Wu, Kang, and Yang (2015) discovered that the primary factors influencing users' attitudes toward and intentions to buy paid apps were perceived usefulness, self-efficacy, and peer influence.

Here Are Some of the Key Factors (Graph-01) That Contribute to the Popularity of E-Commerce Platforms Among College Students

- **Convenience:** You may shop whenever and from anyplace with e-commerce platforms. Students can peruse and buy things while on the go, at libraries, or even from their dorm rooms. Students with busy schedules and little time for in-store shopping will find this especially intriguing.
- **Time Saving:** Time-Efficient Search and Filter Options: Online platforms provide advanced search and filter options, helping users find products quickly. This reduces the time spent browsing through multiple aisles in traditional stores. E-commerce eliminates the need to stand in long queues at checkout counters, especially during peak shopping seasons. This can be a significant time saver for consumers.
- **24/7 Availability**: E-commerce sites operate 24/7, allowing users to make purchases at any time that suits them. This is particularly beneficial for people with busy schedules or those who work irregular hours.

- **Variety:** Products from a broad selection of sellers are available on e-commerce platforms. Everything a student might possibly need is available in one location, including clothing, technology, household products, textbooks, and school supplies. They avoid wasting time and energy on unnecessary store visits thanks to this.
- **Affordability:** E-commerce sites frequently provide products at reasonable prices with additional savings. Students can also save money on their purchases by taking advantage of other special deals and free shipping.
- **Product Ratings and Reviews:** Before making a purchase, students can use e-commerce platforms to check other customers' product reviews and ratings. This enables people to make well-informed purchasing selections and steer clear of low-quality purchases.
- **Returns are easy:** The majority of e-commerce sites provide hassle-free return guidelines. The ability to return a product if they're not happy with it gives students piece of mind.

Figure 1. Responses

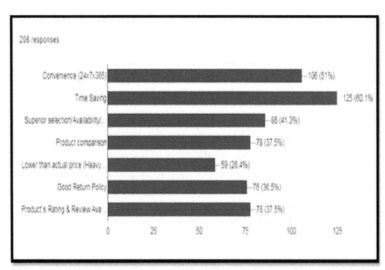

Online buying does, of course, come with its drawbacks. Students in college, for instance, could worry about the safety of their financial and personal data. They can also worry about the e-commerce platform's return policy and the quality of the goods they are purchasing.

Students heading out to college are using e-commerce apps more and more because they are convenient and provide access to a large variety of goods and services. E-commerce apps do, however, **have certain drawbacks (Graph-02) for college students, such as:**

- **Risk of Online Transactions: Various types of online transaction risks are:**
  - (a) **Transaction risk:** this includes risks such as seller default on orders, delivery of subpar goods, and customer default on payments when the customer refuses to pay seller claims.
  - (b) **Impersonation Risk:** There is a significant chance that someone may impersonate you during a single business transaction because a buyer could use a credit or debit card that has been

stolen to make a purchase. The vendor lacks the ability to verify the authenticity of the said transaction.

(c) **Business fraud:** There are a lot of phony websites that lure unsuspecting customers in with alluring promises. Customers may have already been duped by the website owner before they learned the truth about these sites.

(d) **Data transmission and storage Risk**: Information is kept in an imperceptible format. As a result, anyone who has unauthorized access to data can easily steal or manipulate it. Another concern is the continuation of data hacking during data transit.

- **Reduced productivity and distractions:** E-commerce apps can be a big source of distraction for college students, particularly when they're meant to be studying or doing homework. It's possible that students are always monitoring their phones for notifications from retailers, promotions, and new products. Academic performance and productivity may suffer as a result.

- **Impulsive Spending**: Students can easily spend money impulsively thanks to e-commerce apps. Students can acquire things they might not need or be able to afford with only a few taps. Overspending and other financial issues may result from this.

- **Addiction:** Using e-commerce apps might lead to addiction in certain students. They have other things to do, but they might spend hours shopping and perusing merchandise. Social isolation and disregard for other crucial facets of life may result from this.

- **Increased Materialism:** College students may become more materialistic as a result of e-commerce apps. To blend in with their peers, students could experience pressure to purchase the newest and best items. This may result in poor financial practices and an emphasis on unimportant details.

- **Decreased Social Engagement:** College students may engage in less social interaction as a result of e-commerce apps. Pupils might spend less time in person socializing with their peers and more time shopping online. Isolation and loneliness may result from this.

- **Lack of Demonstration and Touch:** The lack of demonstration and touch in e-commerce refers to the challenges that online retail faces in providing customers with a tangible experience similar to what they might have in a physical store. In traditional brick-and-mortar stores, customers can touch, feel, and try out products before making a purchase decision. However, in the online environment, these sensory experiences are limited, and customers rely on images, descriptions, and reviews.

Here Are Some Aspects of the Lack of Demonstration and Touch in E-Commerce

- **Product Visualization:** Online shoppers cannot physically see or touch the products before purchasing, leading to uncertainty.
- **Product Descriptions:** Limited textual information may not convey the actual experience of using or owning a product.
- **Virtual Try-On and Fitting Tools:** Customers shopping for items like clothing or accessories may be unsure about how they will look or fit.
- **Sample Programs:** Customers can't physically test products such as cosmetics, perfumes, or skincare items.
- **Enhanced Product Reviews:** Customers may rely heavily on reviews, but the lack of personal experience can still be a barrier.

- **Flexible Return Policies:** Customers may hesitate to make a purchase due to uncertainty about product satisfaction.

By addressing these challenges, e-commerce businesses can enhance the online shopping experience, build trust, and reduce barriers for customers making informed purchase decisions. Adopting innovative technologies and strategies can help bridge the gap between the virtual and physical shopping experiences.

Figure 2. Responses

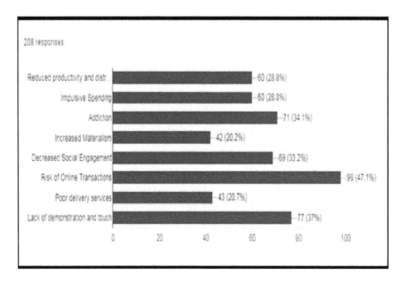

College students are most likely to buy the following particular goods and services online *(Figure 3):* Books and school materials, shoes and clothes, gadgets (such as tablets, smartphones, and laptops), household products (kitchen appliances, necessities for a dorm room, etc.), cosmetics and personal hygiene items, food and drink, amusement (video games, music, films, etc.), Tickets for events and travel, Services (such as laundry and meal delivery) For social reasons, e-commerce sites are also growing in popularity among college students. Students frequently shop with friends and family on e-commerce sites to discover unusual and personalized gifts.

Figure 3. Responses

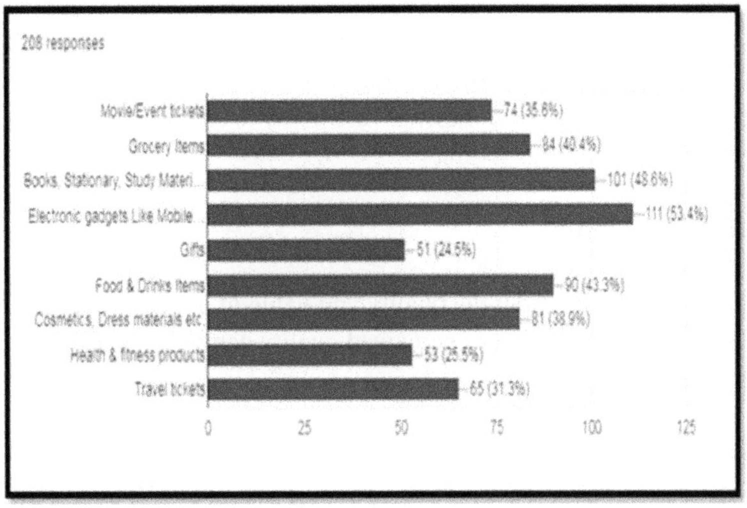

Furthermore, a lot of e-commerce sites have social elements like discussion boards, product ratings, and reviews. With the help of these capabilities, students can interact with other customers and acquire product and service recommendations. All things considered, e-commerce sites are significant in college students' lives. They give students a quick, inexpensive, and convenient method to shop for a wide range of goods and services.

Role of Perception in Consumer Decision Making

When it comes to how people perceive and make sense of the information they encounter in their environment, perception is a key factor in consumer decision-making. In order to develop a meaningful and cohesive view of the world, it entails the act of choosing, arranging, and interpreting sensory data. The following are some important implications of perception in the context of consumer behavior:

Product and Brand Perception

Consumers form perceptions about products and brands based on various cues such as packaging, advertising, word-of-mouth, and personal experiences. Positive perceptions can lead to a favorable attitude toward a product or brand, influencing purchase decisions.

Sensory Perception

Sensory factors, such as sight, sound, touch, taste, and smell, significantly impact product perception. For example, the visual appeal of a product or the scent of a fragrance can influence how consumers perceive its quality and desirability.

Selective Attention

Consumers are bombarded with a vast amount of information daily. Selective attention refers to the process by which individuals focus on certain stimuli while filtering out others. Marketers need to understand what aspects of their products or messages are likely to capture consumers' attention and stand out from the competition.

Perceived Quality and Value

Consumers often make judgments about the quality and value of a product based on their perceptions. Effective marketing strategies that enhance perceived quality can positively impact a consumer's willingness to pay a premium for a product.

Perceptual Organization

Consumers organize sensory information into patterns and structures, helping them make sense of the world. Marketers can use perceptual organization principles to design products and communications that align with consumers' cognitive processes.

Perceived Risk

Consumers perceive various levels of risk associated with purchasing products or services. This risk perception can be influenced by factors such as the product's novelty, price, or the consumer's prior experiences. Marketers must address and mitigate perceived risks to increase consumer confidence and encourage purchase decisions.

Cultural and Social Influences

Cultural and social factors contribute to the formation of perceptions. Cultural norms, values, and social influences shape how individuals interpret and evaluate products. Understanding cultural and social contexts helps marketers tailor their messages and offerings to specific target audiences.

Brand Image and Reputation

Consumers build perceptions of a brand based on their experiences and interactions with it. A positive brand image and reputation can contribute to loyalty and repeat purchases.

In summary, perception is a fundamental aspect of consumer decision-making. Marketers need to be mindful of how their products and messages are perceived by the target audience, as these perceptions significantly influence purchasing behavior. Creating positive and distinct perceptions can contribute to building strong brand equity and fostering long-term customer relationships.

Determinants or Factors of Perception of College Going Students towards the Use of E-Commerce Platforms

The perception of college-going students towards the use of e-commerce platforms can be influenced by various factors. Here are some determinants or factors that may play a role in shaping their perception:

Technological Familiarity: Level of familiarity with technology and e-commerce platforms. Previous experience with online shopping and digital transactions.

Perceived Ease of Use: User interface and navigation of the e-commerce platforms. Ease of completing transactions and finding desired products/services.

Perceived Usefulness: The perceived value of using e-commerce platforms for their needs. The extent to which students believe e-commerce platforms fulfill their requirements.

Trust and Security: Trustworthiness of e-commerce platforms in handling personal information and financial transactions. Perceived security measures in place to protect user data.

Social Influence: Influence of peers, friends, and family members in shaping their perception. Social norms and acceptance regarding the use of e-commerce platforms.

Perceived Risks: Concerns about privacy, data breaches, and online fraud. Risks associated with online transactions and the security of personal information.

Attitude Towards E-commerce: Overall attitude and beliefs about online shopping and e-commerce. Positive or negative perceptions based on personal experiences or reviews.

Perceived Benefits: Benefits students associate with using e-commerce platforms (e.g., convenience, time-saving, and accessibility). Comparison of benefits offered by e-commerce platforms with traditional shopping methods.

Cultural and Demographic Factors: Cultural preferences and attitudes towards online transactions. Demographic variables such as age, gender, and socioeconomic status.

Marketing and Advertising: Effectiveness of marketing strategies in promoting e-commerce platforms. The impact of advertising and promotional activities on students' awareness and perception.

Educational Background: The influence of their academic discipline on their perception of e-commerce. Whether students in certain majors are more or less likely to embrace e-commerce.

Accessibility and Connectivity: Availability and reliability of internet connectivity. Accessibility of e-commerce platforms on various devices (e.g., smartphones, laptops).

Personalization and User Experience: The extent to which e-commerce platforms offer personalized experiences. User-friendly features and customization options.

Feedback and Reviews: The impact of reviews and feedback from other users on their perception. Trust in the opinions of other students or online communities.

Understanding these determinants can provide insights into the factors that shape college students' perceptions of e-commerce platforms. Researchers and marketers can use this information to tailor strategies and interventions aimed at positively influencing their attitudes and behaviors.

SCOPE OF THE STUDY

The scope of the study is restricted to Higher Education Institute of Delhi\NCR only. Data is collected from the 208 College going students by using simple random sampling technique.

Research Methodology:

Questionnaire designed: To achieve the research objective a questionnaire has been framed, which consists of 2 parts. Firstly, Part one included the demographic profile like Age, Gender, Educational Qualifications etc of the respondent and part two include research based questions.

Sample size: Target sample size was 250 students of HEIs but only 208 students have filled questionnaire. The age groups of respondents were 15-20 & 20-25.

Data Collection Method: The study made use of both primary and secondary sources of data. Information from the respondent was gathered via questionnaires using primary sources. To analyze the body of existing literature, secondary sources such as the internet, periodicals, magazines, newspapers, journals, and articles were consulted.

Data Analysis: To examine the relationship between the respondents' demographic characteristics and the frequency of their online shopping, all of the statistics were tallied on an Excel spreadsheet. Chi square test has used for data analysis.

Study Hypothesis: Nowadays, the majority of students make their purchases online. Therefore, the following hypothesis has been created based on an observation of the respondents' attitude and purchasing behavior over the last four months.

Hypothesis 1. There is no association between Gender of College Going Students and Frequency of Online Shopping.

Hypothesis 2. There is no association between Educational Level of College Going Students and Frequency of Online Shopping.

Hypothesis 3. There is no association between age of College Going Students and Frequency of Online Shopping.

HYPOTHESIS TESTING

Hypothesis 1. There is no association between Gender of College Going Students and Frequency of Online Shopping.

By analyzing the above data, chi-square test has given following results:

After the data analysis with the help of Chi Square Test, author found 3.45 is calculated value which is less than the table value (7.81), it shows acceptance of hypothesis 1. Above result prove that No relation or association between gender and frequency of online shopping.

Hypothesis 2. There is no association between Educational Level of College Going Students and Frequency of Online Shopping.

By analyzing the above data, chi-square test has given following results:

After the data analysis with the help of Chi Square Test, author found 3.24 is calculated value which is less than the table value (7.81), it shows acceptance of hypothesis 2.

Above result prove that No relation or association between Educational Level of College Going Students and Frequency of Online Shopping.

Hypothesis 3. There is no association between age of College Going Students and Frequency of Online Shopping.

By analyzing the above data, chi-square test has given following results:

After the data analysis with the help of Chi Square Test, author found 4.24 is calculated value which is less than the table value (7.81), it shows acceptance of hypothesis 3.

Above result prove that No relation or association between age of College Going Students and Frequency of Online Shopping.

Major Findings

1. Chi-square analysis reveals no correlation between the age of college-bound students and the frequency of their online shopping, the gender of the consumer, or the educational attainment of the consumer.
2. It's noteworthy that over 80% of the participants report an average daily web surfing time of between 0 and 4 hours. So using of E-Commerce site is quite popular among students.
3. When it comes to internet purchasing, the majority of respondents favor electronic devices like smartphones.
4. Among students, Flipkart is the second most popular website for shopping, after Amazon.
5. Among students, cash on delivery (COD) is the most practical and favorable method of payment; wallet and UPI modes are ranked second.
6. Search Engine and Advertisement is the Major Information Source for using E-Commerce Web or App.
7. The majority of students said that they are happy with the E-Commerce Web or App.
8. According to the respondents, the biggest obstacle is the risk associated with online transactions.

Suggestions and Recommendations

- The Government and relevant agencies should develop the trust in the mind of Young customers like college going students towards the E-Commerce Web or App.
- The government should mandate that online shops reveal their privacy practices in order to settle disputes. It is found that worries about internet security will have a big influence on the growth of online shopping in the future.
- Improve delivery system especially in rural areas.
- There must to be less window dressing and conformity of colour and size between the showcased goods and the delivered thing.
- Post-purchase services should be customized to meet the needs of the students like return policy etc.
- Internet marketers ought to use innovative and approachable sales marketing strategies to entice more consumers to make purchases online.
- The product range and brands ought to be more diverse.
- The distribution method should be speedier and more cost-effective.

Suggestions to Prevent Online Fraud

With only a few clicks, we can now easily conduct transactions at any time, from any location, thanks to online payments. However, one mistaken click might put you in serious financial jeopardy. Whether you use internet banking frequently or not, you should always take precautions when completing any kind of digital transaction.

Having a basic understanding of internet scams can help you avoid financial disaster. The following are the top seven strategies to keep your digital transactions safe and protect yourself against online fraud:

1. Only utilize apps that have been verified.

    The way we shop and do business has been altered by mobile apps. Verify that the program you are using is legitimate each time you install it on your device. Download apps from official play shops only, such as the Google Play Store, Windows App Store, or Apple App Store, whether they are financial apps or brand-new games.

2. Only visit websites that are permitted

    Watch out for fake websites that appear authentic or use the same domain name as the one in the URL. Examine "https://" prior to "website name."

3. Only use secure connections.

    The impulse to utilize free WiFi at a cafe, hotel lounge or airport might potentially lead to financial theft. Steer clear of using open hotspots to conduct business. Public networks are more vulnerable to data theft since it is easier to overcome their encryption and obtain sensitive account information.

4. Use caution when utilizing a card.

    Make credit card payments in front of your eyes at all times. Verify that the point-of-sale system is authentic. Numerous accounts exist of cards being duplicated by skimmers because they were hidden throughout the transaction. Avoid allowing someone to pilfer your hard-earned money as a result of carelessness.

5. Keep your computer and phone security software up to date.

    Everyone wants their payments to be safe, but how many of you actually check the operating system, web browser, and security software on your computer and mobile device? To avoid online mishappenings, update the security on your smartphone and PC/laptop. Additionally, create secure passwords every time by combining capital and lowercase letters, numbers, and special characters. Remember to update the passwords on a frequent basis.

6. Don't share personal information with anyone

Unless you are quite certain of the representative's legitimacy, never divulge personal information, either online or off. Any stranger or other third party pretending to be an executive from a bank or other financial institution could be a potential fraudster. Never give your financial information to someone without first confirming their identity. Bank representatives never request sensitive data over the phone, such as a CVV or OTP.

7.   Never click on suspicious links on SMS or emails

Phishing emails, SMS, and link baiting are the most popular ways to trick people into falling for a scam. These links could look real and entice you with promises of winning the jackpot or landing a job abroad. Avoid clicking on any of these links as they can take you to a phishing website and disable the security settings on your phone. It's better to hang up in case you receive an unsolicited call.

The internet has become one of the most widely used instruments for fraud, with thousands of people falling victim to banking frauds each year. You may safeguard yourself against falling prey to internet fraud by taking these simple precautions.

The first line of defense against financial loss in the event that your debit or credit card is lost, stolen, or compromised is to notify the bank right away and get it banned. You can prevent your financial security from being jeopardized by promptly blocking the card.

(Ref:https://economictimes.indiatimes.com/wealth/personal-finance-news/7-measures-you-should-know-to-prevent-online-fraud/articleshow/90047350.cms?from=mdr)

Limitation of the Study

- This study was carried out only among the Self-financing College students from the Delhi NCR Region.
- Since the sample was selected at random, this study may also have flaws in the random selection process.
- Due to time restrictions, this study lends itself to additional research. The study used a sample size of 208 respondents only; therefore, the sample size should be raised to support the findings and provide a better representation of students' preferences and risk perception.
- Furthermore, the study offers a lack of discussion regarding the overall perception of college going students towards online shopping.
- To encourage more people to shop online, internet marketers should employ creative and accessible sales marketing techniques.

CONCLUSION

For a variety of reasons, college students are now the majority of online shoppers. First of all, in their hectic college lives, the ease of internet purchasing saves them valuable time. They prefer to shop online because of the availability of discounts, cash on delivery, and a large selection of high-quality products. Additionally, college students now have greater access to online shopping because of the low cost of internet tariff plans and reasonably priced mobile devices. College students are naturally dynamic and tech-savvy, and the online market caters to their tech-savvy and appealing pricing by offering a wider selection of items at competitive costs. All things considered, college students prefer to shop online because of its affordability, ease, and abundance of possibilities.

Given that practically all respondents have made purchases online, this is excellent news for online merchants. Even though the majority of respondents are happy with their online buying experience, there are still a lot of obstacles that face these businesses, like online fraud, maintaining privacy and security, customizing after-sale services, providing enough shipping, etc. Thus, now is the moment for online retailers to concentrate more on providing high-quality services in order to win over customers. Students view online shopping as practical, convenient, and time-saving. Students also have the idea that the prices listed online for goods and services are lower than the actual costs. But there's a perception among students that shopping online carries some hazards, that delivery takes longer, and that the websites don't provide enough information about the goods and services. Men seem to have a more positive attitude about online purchasing than do women. Compared to students who are undergrads, postgraduate students utilize e-commerce websites and apps more frequently. Delivery time is the most significant element influencing respondents' online purchasing decisions, followed by product quality and company reputation. On the other hand, the risk of not receiving what buyers paid for and the inability to handle things are given relatively little weight. For men, delivery time and the company's reputation were the most significant factors influencing purchasing decisions, whereas for women, a thorough description of the goods and delivery time were seen as crucial. Given that the bulk of consumers are now making their purchases online in this digital age, internet connection quality needs to be improved. Customers who engage in impulsive shopping may suffer from things like purchasing items they don't really need, incurring debt from borrowing money, and supporting consumerism that isn't environmentally sustainable. We encourage e-commerce platforms to build tools that significantly assist customers' inclinations toward self-control in order to carry out morally decent marketing. E-commerce sites and their vendors must behave morally and refrain from purposefully promoting rash purchases.

REFERENCES

Akter, S., & Wamba, S. M. (2016). Big data analytics in E-commerce: a systematic review and agenda for future research. *The International Journal on Networked Business*.

Banerjee, N., Dutta, A., & Dasgupta, T. (2010). A Study on Customers' Attitude towards Online Shopping - An Indian Perspective. *Indian Journal of Marketing*, *40*(11), 43–52.

Bourlakis, M., Papagiannidis, S., & Fox, H. (2008). E-consumer Behaviour: Past, Present and Future Trajectories of an Evolving Retail Revolution. *International Journal of E-Business Research*, *4*(3), 64–76. doi:10.4018/jebr.2008070104

Butler, P., & Peppard, J. (1998). Consumer Purchasing on the Internet: Processes and Prospects. *European Management Journal*, *16*(5), 600–610. doi:10.1016/S0263-2373(98)00036-X

Chelvarayan, A., Jie, C., & Yeo, S. F. (2021). Factors Affecting Students' Perception of Online Shopping. International Journal of Entrepreneurship. *Business and Creative Economy.*, *1*, 13–24.

Chen, R., & He, F. (2003). Examination of Brand Knowledge, Perceived Risk and Consumers' Intention to Adopt an Online Retailer. *Total Quality Management & Business Excellence, 14*(6), 677–693. doi:10.1080/1478336032000053825

Childers, T., Carr, C., Peck, J., & Carson, S. (2001). Hedonic and Utilitarian Motivations for Online Retail Shopping Behavior. *Journal of Retailing, 77*(4), 511–535. doi:10.1016/S0022-4359(01)00056-2

Comegys, C., Hannula, M., & Vaisanen, J. (2009). Effects of Consumer Trust and Risk on Online Purchase Decision-making: A Comparison of FINNISH and United States Students. *International Journal of Management, 26*(2), 295–308.

Dash, S. & Kanungo, R. (2016). *Student's attitude and perception towards online shopping: an empirical study, 29.*

George, J. F. (2004). The Theory of Planned Behavior and Internet Purchasing. *Internet Research, 14*(3), 198–212. doi:10.1108/10662240410542634

Goldsmith, R. E., & Flynn, L. R. (2005). Bricks, Clicks, and Pix: Apparel Buyers' Use of Stores, Internet, and Catalogs Compared. *International Journal of Retail & Distribution Management, 33*(4), 271–283. doi:10.1108/09590550510593202

Grewal, D., Gopalkrishnan, R. I., & Michael, L. (2004). Internet Retailing: Enablers, Limiters and Market Consequences. *Journal of Business Research, 57*(7), 703–713. doi:10.1016/S0148-2963(02)00348-X

Hansen, T., Moller, J. J., & Stubbe, S. H. (2004). Predicting Online Grocery Buying Intention: A Comparison of the Theory of Reasoned Action and the Theory of Planned Behavior. *International Journal of Information Management, 24*(6), 539–550. doi:10.1016/j.ijinfomgt.2004.08.004

Haq, Z. U. (2012). Perception towards Online Shopping: An Empirical Study of Indian Consumers. *Abhinav national monthly refereed journal of reasearch in commerce & management, 1*(8).

Hofacker, C. R. (2001). *Internet Marketing* (3rd ed.). Wiley.

Karve, S. (2014, January). Study of youth with special reference to virtual 3d online shopping. *Sai Om Journal of Commerce & Management, 1*(1), 29–32.

Khitoliya, P. (June 2014). Customers Attitude and Perception Towards Online Shopping. *Indian journal of research,.3*(6), 18-21.

Kumar, V., & Dange, U. (Aug 25, 2012), "A Study of Factors Affecting Online Buying Behaviour: A Conceptual Model" Available at last accede 31 May 2014. doi:10.2139/ssrn.2285350

Laudon, K. C., & Traver, C. G. (2009). *E-Commerce Business, Technology, Society* (5th ed.). Prentice Hall.

Lim, H., & Dubinsky, A. J. (2004). Consumers' Perceptions of E-shopping Characteristics: An Expectancy-Value Approach. *Journal of Services Marketing, 18*(6), 500–513. doi:10.1108/08876040410561839

Manav, A. (2012, August). A Study on Growth of Online Shopping in India [SSIJMAR]. *International Journal of in Multidisciplinary and Academic Research, 3*(4), 66–72.

Monsuwe, T. P. Y., Dellaert, B. G. C., & Ruyter, K. D. (2004). What Derives Consumers to Shop Online? A Literature Review. *International Journal of Service Industry Management, 15*(1), 102–121. doi:10.1108/09564230410523358

Nagra, G. (2013). A study of factors affecting online shopping behavior of consumers. *International Journal of Scientific and Research Publications, 3*(6).

Prasad, C., & Aryasri, A. (2009). Determinants of Shopper Behavior in E-tailing: An Empirical Analysis. *Paradigm, 13*(1), 73–83.

Rastogi, A. K. (2010). A Study of Indian Online Consumers & Their Buying Behaviour. *International Research Journal, 1*(10), 80–82.

Sharma, N. V., & Khattri, V. (2013). Study of online shopping behaviour and its impact on online deal websites. *Asian Journal of Management Research, 3*(2), 394–405.

Singh, U., & Bharath, C. (2021). Students' perceptions of an e-commerce app Students' perceptions of an e-commerce app. *Journal of Physics: Conference Series, 1714*(1), 12049. doi:10.1088/1742-6596/1714/1/012049

Upadhyay, P., & Kaur, J. (2013). Analysis of Online Shopping Behaviour of Customer in Kota City. Shiv Shakti International Journal in Multidisciplinary and Academic Research, 2(1).

Zhou, L., Dai, L., & Zhang, D. (2007). Online Shopping Acceptance Model – A Critical Survey of Consumer Factors in Online Shopping. *Journal of Electronic Commerce Research, 8*(1), 41–62.

Chapter 19
Showrooming:
An Ethical Gamble in Marketing

Preeti Kaushal
Chitkara University, India

Navreet Kaur
Chitkara University, India

ABSTRACT

Shoppers take advantage of the retail store to check the product but finally order it online, thus posing a great bane for the offline retailers. Due to the absence of any systematic treatment of 'showrooming.' This chapter discusses the reasons why the customers indulge in showrooming, the reasons to understand why customers visit the offline store and make the purchase online, how the measure is developed to access showrooming and how it will help the retailers to understand and combat this issue, the ethical concerns related to showrooming as the retailer who displays the products in the offline store, provides complete service to its customers, but the customers resort to online buying after availing the services of the offline retailers. This concern has raised not only ethical issues but also issues concerning the survival of these retail stores in future. This chapter will serve as a complete guide to help retailers evade this ethical concern and handle the issue of showrooming with awareness about the reasons of customers indulging in showrooming.

INTRODUCTION

The Internet has rapidly become one of the largest market places in the world, with the penetration of 53.3% in Asia, it is becoming the hotspot for the majority of marketing activities (Miniwatts Marketing, 2021). The Internet is indisputably different from the brick and mortar arrangements and made shopping so much more easier than before (Basak et al., 2017). Due to the economic need to earn and maintain a regular profit stream, the Internet marketplace will possibly be more similar to our traditional marketplaces than the difference in them (Naidu et al., 2001). The shoppers are empowered to use information and data to their advantage and make decisions about their purchases and their preferences at a faster

DOI: 10.4018/979-8-3693-2215-4.ch019

pace (Schwartz, 2011). The transaction done online is known as E-commerce. This trend is here to stay with the increased rollout of 4G broadband and global growth in smartphone and tablet ownership, if the traditional retailers are to survive these changes it's imperative for them to rethink their current strategies (Ankosho, 2012). Smith (2012) stated that 'showrooming' appears to be a growing phenomenon, although its size is unclear at this time. The Pew Internet and American Life Project reported that 25% of mobile phone owners used the phone to look for a better deal while in a store. Of those shoppers 35% bought in the store, 19% bought online (Pew, 2019). Ankosho (2012) discussed how 'showrooming' is a relatively new shopping phenomenon in which shoppers visit stores to look at products but then place orders with competing online retailers using a smartphone or other mobile device, this growing behaviour needs immediate attention. Luo et al (2014) discussed the typical shopping scenario nowadays in which the shoppers browse and try the products offline and then buy them online from a competing retailer.

This phenomenon commonly described as 'showrooming' occurs because of the ubiquity of mobile devices and the ease of switching between multiple retail channels (Accenture, 2013). The presence of these mobile-assisted shoppers in a multichannel retailing environment is a serious challenge confronting all retailers (Smith, 2012). Accenture (2013) in its report had summarised the percentage of Americans who do 'showrooming', 63% of Americans plan to browse at a store and then go online to find a better deal. As shoppers become mobile-assisted shoppers, they can now visit a retail store's aisles equipped with their smartphones for comparison shopping when they are in the store (Basak et al., 2017). Such multichannel consumer behavior is extremely detrimental to retailers (Rapp et al., 2014).

Showrooming and Ethical Concerns

With the E-commerce spur, the shoppers now have a choice to switch between the two channels available to them, i.e. offline and online channel (Ahuja et al., 2003). Dijk et al. (2005) discussed how cross channel retail shopping across several different channels (bricks and mortar, online, catalog, TV shopping networks, mobile applications, etc.) and choosing the channel that works best for a particular occasion or type of purchase has risen. Internet by empowering the shoppers has given rise to a new phenomenon called 'showrooming' (Adler, 2013). Shoppers physically visit the offline store, checkout the products but finally order them online and many of such shoppers who end up buying online give rise to 'showrooming' (Quint & Rogers, 2013).Shoppers take advantage of the retail store to check the product but finally order it online, thus posing a great bane for the offline retailers (Rapp et al., 2014). Due to the absence of any systematic treatment of 'showrooming', there has been a $217 billion negative impact on retail sales (360pi, 2013). This has further raised the ethical concerns relating to the online marketing. Though it seems to be the right of the customers to shop and browse from any channels available to them but on the contrary poses a threat to the retails and still raise ethical concerns. In order to combat this ethical concern, a measure of 'showrooming' has been developed and its validity and reliability along with psychometric properties is assessed.

Many factors are considered by the shoppers for switching channels. Factors like price, ease of shopping and like are taken under considerartion. Madlberger (2006), has examined the important issues to cross-channel shoppers behavior and discussed the cross channel behavior of shoppers. Madleberger (2006) examined important issues to multichannel retailers, such as consumer"s channel choice, shopping process, channel integration and customer retention, and the holistic analysis of consumer"s cross-channel use and switching behavior and additionally the relationship between perceived channel price and channel use intention was tested, and it was found that online-offline price difference is a critical element for both shoppers" shopping decisions and retailers" profit strategy.

Neslin& Shankar (2009) paid more attention to the multichannel retail behavior of the consumer leading to cross-channel shopping. The factors that influence the single channel to a cross are discussed such as the price of the product, perception of security concerns (Neslin & Shankar, 2009). The research shoppers come in two varieties: loyal research shoppers who search and purchase from different channels of the same firm and competitive research shoppers who search using one channel of a firm and buy from a different channel of the competing firm, thus showing their polygamous behavior (Neslin & Shankar, 2009).

This chapter discusses the reasons why the customers indulge in showrooming, the reasons to understand why customers visit the offline store and make the purchase online, how the measure is developed to access showrooming and how it will help the retailers to understand and combat this issue, the ethical concerns related to showrooming as the retailer who displays the products in the offline store provides complete service to its customers, but in the customers resort to online buying after availing the services of the offline retailers. This concern has raised not only the ethical issues but also issues concerning the survival of these retail stores in future. This chapter will serve as a complete guide to help retails evade this ethical concern and handle the issue of showrooming with awareness about the reasons of customers indulging in showrooming.

Shoppers take advantage of the retail store to check the product but finally order it online, thus posing a great bane for the offline retailers (Rapp et al., 2014). Due to the absence of any systematic treatment of 'showrooming', there has been a $217 billion negative impact on retail sales (360pi, 2013). Georgescu (2013) discusses how retail 'showrooming' is the most discussed retail phenomenon, which is debated by mass- media.

The topic is of great interest for the retail industry, which recently raised debates among retailers and researchers (Georgescu, 2013). Retail 'showrooming' is a new trend where shoppers exhibit their shopping behavior across online and offline channels (Burns et al., 2018). Daunt &Harris (2017) states the limited academic literature available on the concept of 'showrooming'.

Taking the perspective of multi-channel retail, it is now very evident that customers research products on one channel and end up buying on another (Zhang, 2010). The consumers as per their convenience may use different ways of utilizing the channels available to them (Tang & Xing, 2001). Therefore, there is enough evidence of customers research the online channel and make final purchases at a physical store (Verhoef et al., 2007), or they may also research the physical store and purchase online (Van & Dach 2005). Neslin & Shankar (2009) in their study have spelled out the two categories of research shoppers: loyal research shoppers, these shoppers search and purchase the product from the same firm, using their different channels, and the competitive research shoppers search using one channel of a firm and end up buying from a competing firm's different channel. Customers take the benefit of both the channels before making the final purchase (Kucuk & Maddux, 2010). They evaluate the product at a physical store, which is not possible in case of the online store thus giving rise to 'showrooming' and results in the offline store losing prospective customers (Lal & Sarvary, 1999).

The changes in the Indian retail industry are perceptible to the millions of retailers and shopkeepers who operate their physical stores in India (Machavolu & Raju, 2014). But there are a few not easily seen, unexpected changes that many of the storekeepers are still ignorant of (Machavolu & Raju, 2014). 'Showrooming' is one such new change that is trending across the globe and hurting many retailers in their trade and since India is acquiring the global trends fast, the threats posed by this new trend to the global brick-and-motor stores, may also attack Indian retailers (Kemple, 2014). Assocham (2014) reported that recent years have seen an incredible transformation in the way India shops and trades. The sector had grown three times in four years to nearly 12.6 billion USD in 2014 and various industry estimates project that the sector will further grow five to seven times over the next four to five years (Assocham, 2014).The Indian government allowing FDI in retail has also impacted the increase of 'showrooming' in India (Sahu et al., 2021). PWC (2014) reported that the size of the retail market in India is ever increasing, with apparel, accessories and electronics being the largest selling products through 'showrooming'. The increasing use of smartphones, tablets and internet broadband, and 3G has led to 'showrooming' which is likely to increase further (Gonela & Pillay, 2019). Thus this change in the Indian Retail industry is impacting the offline retailers, who need to find a solution to combat 'showrooming' (Saluja, 2024).

Quint et al.(2013); pointed out that research shoppers come in two varieties: loyal research shoppers who search and purchase from different channels of the same firm and competitive research shoppers who search using one channel of a firm and buy from a different channel of the competing firm. Thus shoppers may use Target's physical stores to evaluate products but purchase in Amazon's online store if online prices are lower, thus showing their polygamous behavior (Neslin & Shankar, 2009). Mehra et al. (2012) analyzed how competition between physical stores and online stores is now picking up in new product categories thus leading to the use of the cross channel by the shoppers.

The reason for the insignificant competition earlier was that shoppers could not evaluate products in such categories on the online channel as effectively as they could on the physical store, thus shoppers would end up making sub-optimal purchases if they evaluated products only on the online channel (Westaby, 2005). However, shoppers could deal with this issue by evaluating products in-store, but then returning home to order the product from an online store (Westaby, 2005).

The main problem with this approach was that online stores did not keep exhaustive inventories in such product categories earlier, thus the shoppers could be disappointed to find that the product they chose at the store retailer's site was not available to be ordered online (Georgescu, 2013). Westaby (2005) used the Behavioral Reasoning Theory as a theoretical base and adopts a scenario-based experimental approach to answer two research questions: i) What are the determinants underlying attitudes towards 'showrooming' ii) What measures can be effective in reducing their 'showrooming' intention.

Retail channel usage intention is indirectly influenced by consumer perceptions of channel price thus leading to cross channel shopping (Hamilton & Chernev, 2010). In the purchase stage, shoppers want to buy the best goods with the least amount of money, especially for the price-sensitive shoppers, thus, the lower the price in a channel is, the more likely shoppers are to choose that channel (Madlberger, 2006) . If shoppers can locate the product at a cheaper price online while in the store, they would be more likely to showroom (Madlberger, 2006).

'Showrooming' can be a bane for the retailers but from the view point of shoppers it comes as promising phenomena. Boyang & Jinwan (2018) defined the 'showrooming' phenomenon as the behavior of a customer, where he visits the offline store and physically experiences the product before eventually buying it from the online stores and this phenomenon is gaining importance and has attained a lot of interest from academia. The research on the 'showrooming' phenomena is done from the perspective of the customers, unlike the majority of the research done from the retailer's perspective and sheds some positive light on the 'showrooming' phenomena from the customer's perspective (Boyang & Jinwan, 2018).

The brunt of customers using both the channels available to them is borne by the retailers (Dholakia et al., 2005). The literature available throws light on the impact of channel switching by the customers on the retailers. This has been termed as the competition between the full service stores and discount stores (Shin 2007). Saluja & Sandhu (2023) states that the literature lacks enough evidence of the situation where the retailers are aware of 'showrooming' and how they can manage their physical store better to combat 'showrooming'.

Understanding 'showrooming' phenomena is relevant because there is evidence that suggests the consequence of 'showrooming' has impacted both the retailers as well as the salesperson working in the store (Rapp et al., 2014).

As technology is penetrating the lives of consumers at an increasing rate across the globe, retailers face new challenges every day. 'Showrooming' is one such challenge which has crippled many retailers of the offline stores (Zhang et al., 2010). This brings a dire need for retailers to be quick and more receptive along with having high integration across all channels.

Phenomenon like 'showrooming', where the consumers use the offline store for product evaluation but purchase the same online has given a big blow to the sales of offline retail stores (Adler, 2013). In the past, offline retailer's efforts to combat 'showrooming' have proved to be futile (Sevitt, 2013).

Pfeil et al. (2008) have stated how E-commerce has wiped away sales from offline retailers in most of the industries. The salesperson in the offline retail store not only face competition from other brands but also the online stores, putting a lot of pressure on their performance (Pfeil et al., 2008).

Analysis

A scale of "showrooming" is developed using the EFA and CFA. The scale of „showrooming" is constructed on the basis of the information collected from the shoppers and further the level of „showrooming" is measured using the developed scale.

Due to the rise of e-commerce, the cross channel behavior of shoppers has also risen. As cross-channel shopping becomes the norm, multichannel retailing is now a promising area of research. Many researchers, Schoenbachler et al. (2002); Neslin & Shankar (2009); Mehra et. al. (2012); Westaby (2005); Hamilton & Chernev (2010); Quint et al. (2013); Georgescu (2013); Madlberger (2006), have examined the important issues to cross channel shoppers behavior. Schoenbachler et al. (2002) payed more attention on the multichannel retail behaviour of the consumer thus leading to cross channel shopping and the factors that influence the single channel to a cross are discussed in this research. The drivers of purchase behaviour decisions such as price of the product, perception of security concerns etc. are also studied (Georgescu, 2013).

Scale Development

Scale for measuring „showrooming" was developed using the standard scale development process as indicated in the literature by Churchill (1979). Churchill has given four stages for the scale development namely:

Phase 1-Item Generation

The first step in the suggested procedure for developing better measures involves specifying the domain of the construct. The researcher must be exacting in delineating what is included in the definition and what is excluded. It is imperative, though, that researcher"s consult the literature when conceptualizing constructs and specifying domains.

The second step in the procedure for developing better measures is to generate items which capture the domain as specified. Those techniques that are typically productive in exploratory research, including literature searches, experience surveys, and insight stimulating examples, are generally useful here (Selltiz et al., 1976). The literature should indicate how the variable has been defined previously and how many dimensions or components it has.

In this study the researcher after studying the literature available, conducted a brainstorming session with various experts in the field of marketing. On the basis of the interviews conducted with the various experts, item generation was done. The scenarios were presented to the participants individually to trigger open discussion (Calder, 1977).

The interview of nine marketing professionals from Chandigarh was conducted. These professionals were selected on the basis of purposive sampling. Saunders et al. (2012) have described purposive sampling as a sampling technique where the researcher uses his judgment, selective or subjective sampling and he relies on his or her own judgment when choosing members of population to participate in the study. The professionals selected were from industries like electronics, apparels, telecommunication, banking and education. The sample size of 9 was sufficient as it was qualitative aspect of data collection method (Cooper & Schindler, 2006).The experts were briefed about the purpose of the study and were appraised about the concept of showrooming.Variousitems and statements were generated in the process. The items generated were recorded by the researcher and a questionnaire was developed. A total of 37 items were generated.

The researcher further refined the questions which contain an obvious "socially acceptable" response. After refining the item pool the researcher collected the data relating to the items generated in the next phase i.e phase 2.

Phase 2- Sample Selection and Data Collection

The 33 statements generated after the stage 1 of item **generation** were further linked with the emotion based responses from the industry experts. In order to link the emotional based responses given by the industry experts,with the experience items the questionnaire was filled by 30 post graduate students of institute of the region. The sample was collected on the basis of the convenience sampling. The questionnaire consisted of 33 statements generated in phase-1. The data was collected using a 5 point likertscale(a scale of 1 to 5) where; 1= Strongly Disagree (SD), 2= Disagree (D),3= Neutral (N), 4= Agree (A), 5= Strongly Agree (SA).

Phase 3- Psychometric Properties of the Scale (EFA)

The appropriateness of the items was determined through (reliability and validity). The reliability was tested using exploratory factor analysis (EFA). Confirmatory factor analysis (CFA) was applied on the factors identified through EFA .

For EFA stage data was collected from 330 respondents .The thumb rule of 5 observations per item was met, having a sample size of 330 respondents for 33 item statements(Field,2005), further the adequacy of the sample size was checked by KMO(Kaiser Meyer Oklin) test of sampling adequacy (Kaiser,1970).

Table 1. Sampling details

Stage	Location	Sampling Unit	Sample Size	Sampling Technique
EFA Stage 3	Chandigarh, Ambala, Ludhiana	Online Customers and sales person	330	Convenience

After the data was collected by the researcher, the EFA was conducted using SPSS 21 software. The main purpose of factor analysis was to sum up data in order to interpret and understand the relationships and patterns. It is usually used to regroup variables into a narrow set of clusters based on shared variance. Thus, it helps to isolate concepts and constructs (Yong & Pearce, 2013)

In order to understand the underlying structure and the relationships among the variables EFA (Exploratory Factor Analysis) was used. EFA helps to interpret this interdependence among variables (Hair et al., 2006).

Factor analysis attempts to discover the most simplest method of observed data interpretation known as parsimony (Harman, 1976). In this stage EFA was performed on 330 respondents. The data was collected with the help of a questionnaire (Annexure) developed after the stage 1.

The following are the results of Factor analysis that was carried out using SPSS 21 software.

Communalities in factor analysis indicate the amount of variance present in each variable that is accounted for. Initial communalities are estimates of the variance in each variable accounted for by all components or factors. For principal components extraction, this is always equal to 1.0 for correlation analyses (Watkins, 2018) Communality (alsocalled h2) is a definition of common variance that ranges between 0 and 1. Values closer to 1 suggest that extracted factors explain more of the variance of an individual item.

Factor Extraction

In order to retain a better factor structure, it is very important to retain factors which have substantive importance. **The most** common criteria used to extract factors which are significant is by looking at their eigen values, factors with high eigen values are preserved (Field,2005). Kaiser (1960) recommended in preserving the factors which have eigen values more than 1. The revealed six factors which were significant i.e. these factors have eigen value more than one.

Factor A: Smartphone Usage

This factor accounts for 28.18% of the total variance. The details of the six contributing factors . This factor comprises of statements that relate to use of smartphone in the showroom, for checking the prices, products, features, making specific queries. This is one of the reasons which exhibit the showrooming behavior among the customers. Thus smartphone usage is the 1st factor extracted for the showrooming measure scale.

Factor B: Delayed Purchase

This factor accounts for 12.837% of the total variance. The details of the six contributing factors are given . This factor comprises of statements that relate to buying the product later by either keeping them in their online cart or keeping it at the store after trying. The customers want to make delayed purchases after making informed decisions by visiting the store. Thus delayed decision is the 2nd factor extracted for the showrooming measure scale.

Factor C: Specific Feature Analysis

This factor accounts for 9.247% of the total variance. The details of the seven contributing factors are shown. This factor comprises of statements that relate to specific product queries like a particular size, color, model, features.Customers ask for product comparisons. All these reasons give enough evidence that the customer is there to do showrooming. Thus specific feature analysis is the 3rd factor extracted for the showrooming measure scale.

Factor D: Price Consciousness

This factor accounts for 8.125% of the total variance. The details of the five contributing factors is given . This factor comprises of statements that relate tocutomers asking for discounts, offers, sales, express about better online deals. This gives a clear indication that the customers are indulging in showrooming. Thus price consciousnessis the 4th factor extracted for the showrooming measure scale.

Factor E: Shopping Experience

This factor accounts for 6.332% of the total variance.This factor comprises of statements that relate to customers seeking family and friends opinion, to experience the shopping spree, to seek expert opinion of the salesperson. This is one of the factor that the customers indulge in showrooming. Thus shopping experience is the 5th factor extracted for the showrooming measure scale.

Factor F: Product Comparison

This factor accounts for 4.478% of the total variance. This factor comprises of statements that relate to product comparison seeking attitude of the customers. The statements like comparing products both on online and offline platforms, comparing a particular size or product available online.This is one of the factors that contribute to the showrooming activity of the customer.Thusproduct comparison is the 6th factor extracted for the showrooming measure scale.

Phase 4- Validating Construct Reliability

CFA

For CFA stage again a sample of 300 was drawn, which again fulfilled the criteria of 5 observations per item (Hair et al., 2006).

CFA

Stage 4

Chandigarh, Ambala,Ludhiana

Online Customers and sales person 300

Convenience

In order to check the reliability and validity of the factor structure, explaining and validating the process of scale development of Showrooming, identified after running EFA in the previous step. Confirmatory factor analysis (CFA) was run using AMOS 21 software.

CFA is a **statistical technique which is used to verify the factor structure of a set of observed variables**. CFA further allows testing of the hypothesis by the researcher. This helps the researcher to see whether relationship between observed variables and their underlying latent constructs exists. CFA is a measurement model part of Structural Equation Modeling(SEM). CFA is widely used in the process of scale development in order to examine the latent structure of a test instrument. CFA verifies the number of underlying dimensions of the factors and factor loadings.CFA is an important analytic tool that is widely used for estimation of scale reliability (Raykov, 2001).

The results of CFA provide with convincing evidence of the latent and observed variables by testing validity of theoretical construct.CFA is a multivariate technique used in construct validation(cf. Campbell & Fiske, 1959; Kenny &Kashy, 1992). An essential strength of CFA approach to the construct validation is the resulting estimates of convergent and discriminant validity which are adjusted for the measurement error and an error theory .Thus making CFA a superior tool to traditional analytical methods as they do not account for measurement error.

In this study the measurement model was being checked for scale validation relating to Showrooming effect. The Cronbach Alpha for all the extracted factors was higher than the threshold of 0.70. the Alpha for factor A: Smartphone Usage, which had total of 6 items was 0.928. For factor B: Delayed Purchase which had a total of 6 items was 0.901, alpha for factor C: Specific Feature Analysis which had a total of 7 items was 0.875,alpha for factor D: Price Consciousness which had 5 items is 0.878, factor E: Shopping Experience which also had 5 items, its alpha figure was 0.850 and the last factor F: Product Comparison which had total of 4 items had the alpha of 0.908.

The correlated item to total item correlation in all the factors is more than the threshold level of 0.40, therefore no item has been deleted from the list.

Measurement Model for Showrooming Construct

In this stage the measurement model for showrooming construct was checked for its reliability and validity on an independent sample of 300 respondents. The data was collected on the basis of convenience sampling. The factor structure that was obtained after conducting the EFA has been confirmed by running CFA (Confirmatory Factor Analysis), on an independent data of 300 respondents. Software used for conducting CFA is AMOS software version 21. The measurement model shown in the figure below has been assessed for its psychometric properties on the basis of the following criteria.

CONCLUSION

The results show that the value of various fit indices considered under this study are meeting the necessary requirements of the threshold levels, suggesting adequate fit of the model of the data.

The retail industry globally is going through a tough business scenario because of multiple shopping options available with the customers now-a-days. Customer today is not restricted to offline stores but has multiple channels to explore the best possible shopping deal available with him. „Showrooming" is an outcome of the consequences that retailers have to face due to the customers freedom to ride along various shopping channels available to him.

- The retailers must understand that a good showroom experience can help change the game. It is very important for the retailers to understand the „showrooming" intentions of the customers along with the dilemma faced by the salesperson due to perceived „showrooming".
- This study has come up with a well validated „showrooming" measurement scale and has further tried to understand the construct of „showrooming" measurement in terms of its constituents, their relation with customer demographics so as to recommend some useful insights for both the retailers and the researchers.
- This study has also emphasized the impact of „showrooming" on the salesperson, the findings for the same will be helpful for all the retailers in order to understand how they can positively manage the staff in the preview of „showrooming" and combat the same.

The scale of „showrooming" measurement as developed in this study contributes methodologically to the existing studies in the field of measurement of „showrooming". The effort is made to robustly develop the „showrooming" scale. It has been further validated by taking independent samples at different stages of scale development. The scale can be used to ascertain the „showrooming" level by all the retail stores. By measuring the „showrooming" score using the developed scale the retailers can improve their in store service quality and also understand the „showrooming" intentions of the customers. The study reveals that there are enough ways in which a customer exhibits his showrooming" behavior. The study has tried to capture the customer behavior exhibited in the showroom that exhibit „showrooming" intentions". The managers must understand this behavior and take necessary steps to control this.

REFERENCES

Accenture. (2013). *Top retail holiday trends: Holiday shopping survey results 2013*. Accenture.

Ajzen, I. (1991). The theory of planned behavior. *Organizational Behavior and Human Decision Processes*, *50*(2), 179–211. doi:10.1016/0749-5978(91)90020-T

Anderson, J. C., & Gerbing, D. W. (1988). Structural equation modeling in practice: A review and recommended two-step approach. *Psychological Bulletin*, *103*(3), 411–423. doi:10.1037/0033-2909.103.3.411

Basak, S., Basu, P., Avittathur, B., & Sikdar, S. (2017). A game theoretic analysis of multichannel retail in the context of showroominh. *Decision Support Systems, 103*, 34–45. doi:10.1016/j.dss.2017.09.002

Bentler, P. M., & Bonett, D. G. (1980). Significance test and goodness of fit in the analysis of covariance structures. *Psychological Bulletin, 88*(3), 588–606. doi:10.1037/0033-2909.88.3.588

Churchill,G.A.jr(1979), j mark res.,16(1),64-73

Creswell, J. W. (2007). *Qualitative inquiry and research design: Choosing among five approaches / John W* (2nd ed.). Creswell.

Cronbach, L. J. (1951). Coefficient alpha and the internal structure of tests. *Psychometrika, 16*(3), 297-334.

Ellen, G. (2014). *The Mobile First shopper strategy*. WARC.

Fan, X., Thompson, B., & Wang, L. (1999). Effects of sample size, estimation methods, and model specification on structural equation modeling fit indexes. *Structural Equation Modeling, 6*(1), 56–83. doi:10.1080/10705519909540119

Hubona, G. S. (2009). *Structural equation modeling (SEM) using SmartPLS software: Analyzing path models using partial least squares (PLS) based SEM*.

Jaramillo, F., & Mulki, J. P. (2008). Sales effort: The intertwined roles of the leader, customers, and the salesperson. *Journal of Personal Selling & Sales Management, 28*(1), 37–51. doi:10.2753/PSS0885-3134280103

Saluja, S. (2024). Identify theft fraud-major loophole for Fintech industry in India. *Journal of Financial Crime, 31*(1), 146–157. doi:10.1108/JFC-08-2022-0211

Saluja, S., & Sandhu, N. (2023). Whistle blowing of corporate frauds in India. *International Journal of Business and Globalisation, 35*(3), 277–278. doi:10.1504/IJBG.2023.134940

Spaid, B. I., & Flint, D. J. (2014). The meaning of shopping experiences augmented by mobile internet devices. *Journal of Marketing Theory and Practice, 22*(1), 73–90. doi:10.2753/MTP1069-6679220105

Westaby, J. D., & Braithwaite, K. N. (2003). Specific factors underlying reemployment self-efficacy comparing control belief and motivational reason methods for the recently unemployed. *The Journal of Applied Behavioral Science, 39*(4), 415–437. doi:10.1177/0021886303261234

Zimmerman, A. (2012). Showdown Over "showrooming." *The Wall Street Journal*.

Chapter 20
Strategic Talent Acquisition for Ethical Marketing:
Leveraging Technology and Data Governance

Parul Kulshrestha
ⓘD https://orcid.org/0009-0009-1742-2043
Chitkara University, India

Dhiresh Kulshrestha
Chitkara University, India

ABSTRACT

In today's dynamic and technology-driven business landscape, the convergence of ethical marketing, technology, and data governance has become paramount. This abstract provides a glimpse into the forthcoming book chapter titled "Strategic Talent Acquisition for Ethical Marketing: Leveraging Technology and Data Governance," which explores the pivotal role of talent acquisition in ensuring ethical marketing success in this digital age.The chapter examines how organizations can navigate the complexities of digital marketing and data privacy while upholding ethical principles. It highlights the strategic importance of talent acquisition in assembling teams capable of not only excelling in marketing but also prioritizing ethical considerations. This strategic approach not only helps maintain brand reputation and customer trust but also fosters long-term business success.

INTRODUCTION

In the ever-evolving landscape of business and marketing, the pursuit of ethical and sustainable practices has become a defining characteristic of successful organizations. As consumers increasingly demand transparency, responsible data usage, and genuine social responsibility, marketers are confronted with the

DOI: 10.4018/979-8-3693-2215-4.ch020

dual challenge of maintaining profitability while upholding ethical standards. In this era of heightened scrutiny, the strategic acquisition of talent has emerged as a linchpin in achieving these twin objectives.

This chapter explores the vital intersection of talent acquisition, ethical marketing, and the pivotal role of technology and data governance in driving these initiatives forward. In today's digital world, where consumer data is both a valuable asset and a potential liability, marketing professionals must adopt ethical practices and robust data governance to safeguard trust, brand reputation, and customer relationships. The process of recruiting and nurturing the right talent is foundational to the success of any organization. In the context of ethical marketing, this process takes on added significance. Ethical marketing endeavours to balance economic goals with social and environmental responsibility. To achieve this equilibrium, organizations must attract and develop a diverse and skilled workforce that not only understands the intricacies of ethical marketing but is also committed to its principles. Furthermore, these professionals must be well-versed in the latest technologies and data governance practices to ensure that ethical standards are upheld throughout the marketing process.

Navigating the Complexities of Digital Marketing and Data Privacy

Understanding Data Privacy Regulation:

Organizations need to have a deep understanding of data privacy regulations applicable to their region, such as GDPR (in Europe) or CCPA (in California) (Smith, 2020). This includes knowing the legal requirements for collecting, storing, and processing personal data and understanding the potential consequences of non-compliance.

Data Inventory and Classification

To navigate data privacy complexities, organizations must conduct a comprehensive inventory of the data they collect and store (Jones & Brown, 2019). This should include classifying data based on its sensitivity and potential risks.

Consent Mechanisms

Obtaining explicit and informed consent from individuals for data collection is paramount (Johnson et al., 2018). Organizations should establish transparent consent mechanisms and provide individuals with clear options for opting in or out.

One of the ethical principles is to collect only the data necessary for a specific purpose (Smith, 2020). Organizations should implement data minimization practices to reduce the risk associated with excessive data collection. Robust data security is essential. Employ encryption, access controls, and regular security audits to protect sensitive data from breaches (Brown, 2021). Establish data retention policies that outline how long data will be stored and when it should be securely deleted (Miller & Garcia, 2017). Adhering to these policies ensures that data is not retained longer than necessary. Organizations should scrutinize the data handling practices of third-party vendors and partners (Adams et al., 2019). Ensure they comply with data privacy regulations and ethical standards. Employees play a crucial role in data privacy. Regular training and awareness programs can help them understand the importance of data privacy and ethical data handling practices (Clark & Taylor, 2018). Communicate openly with individuals about what data is being collected, why it's collected, and how it will be used (Smith, 2020). Transparency builds trust. Ensure that marketing campaigns adhere to ethical standards. Avoid deceptive advertising, misleading claims, and practices that exploit personal data (Jones & Brown, 2019). Conduct regular privacy impact assessments to evaluate the impact of new projects or data processing activities on data privacy and ethics (Miller & Garcia, 2017). Develop and maintain a robust incident response plan to address data breaches promptly, ethically, and in compliance with regulations (Adams et al., 2019). This includes notifying affected parties as required by law. Provide individuals with the ability to access, rectify, or erase their personal data as per their rights under data privacy regulations (Clark & Taylor, 2018). Data privacy and ethical considerations should involve collaboration between legal, IT, marketing, and other relevant departments to ensure a holistic approach (Johnson et al., 2018). When using AI and automation in marketing, ensure these technologies are designed and used ethically, without bias or discrimination (Brown, 2021). Organizations should perform regular audits and assessments to evaluate compliance with data privacy regulations and ethical principles, making necessary adjustments as needed (Smith, 2020).

Navigating the complexities of digital marketing and data privacy is an ongoing process. It requires a commitment to both compliance with legal regulations and upholding ethical principles. Organizations that prioritize data privacy and ethical marketing practices are more likely to build and maintain trust with their customers, which can lead to long-term success in today's competitive business environment.

The Strategic Significance of Hiring Talent While Forming Teams

Here are some ideas to help comprehend the strategic significance of talent acquisition:

Alignment With Organizational Values

Talent acquisition plays a pivotal role in ensuring that individuals brought into the team share and align with the core values and ethical principles of the organization (Johnson, 2019). This alignment is crucial for building a cohesive team focused on ethical marketing practices.

Influence on Organizational Culture

The individuals selected during talent acquisition contribute significantly to shaping the organizational culture (Smith & Brown, 2020). By prioritizing ethical considerations in the hiring process, organizations signal their commitment to fostering a culture of integrity, transparency, and social responsibility.

Ethical Decision-Making Skills

Talent acquisition provides an opportunity to identify candidates with strong ethical decision-making skills (Clark et al., 2018). Hiring individuals who demonstrate a capacity to navigate complex ethical challenges ensures the team's ability to make principled decisions in the realm of marketing.

Brand Reputation Management

The individuals comprising a marketing team directly contribute to the organization's brand reputation (Adams & Garcia, 2021). Talent acquisition can focus on candidates who understand the importance of ethical marketing in preserving and enhancing the brand's reputation, thereby safeguarding long-term success.

Consumer Trust and Loyalty

Ethical marketing practices are instrumental in building and maintaining trust with consumers (Miller, 2019). Talent acquisition should prioritize individuals who understand the significance of consumer trust, as this trust forms the foundation for long-term relationships and brand loyalty.

Risk Mitigation:

Recruiting individuals with a strong ethical compass can help mitigate risks associated with legal and reputational challenges (Brown & Taylor, 2020). A team that prioritizes ethical considerations is less likely to engage in practices that could lead to legal issues or damage the organization's standing in the market.

Adaptability to Changing Regulations

The regulatory landscape for marketing is dynamic, with increasing emphasis on data privacy and transparency (Jones, 2021). Talent acquisition can focus on individuals who demonstrate an awareness of and adaptability to evolving regulations, ensuring the team's ability to navigate legal and ethical challenges.

Diversity and Inclusion for Ethical Perspectives

A diverse team brings together individuals with different perspectives and ethical viewpoints (Doe et al., 2017). Talent acquisition strategies that prioritize diversity contribute to a richer ethical discourse within the team, fostering a culture of inclusion and innovation.

Long-Term Sustainable Growth

Ethical marketing practices are integral to sustainable business growth (White & Johnson, 2018). Talent acquisition should focus on individuals who understand the connection between ethical considerations in marketing and the long-term viability and success of the organization.

Continuous Learning and Development

Recruiting individuals committed to ethical marketing implies a commitment to continuous learning and development in this domain (Smith, 2020). Talent acquisition can prioritize candidates who exhibit a willingness to stay informed about ethical best practices *in marketing*.

In conclusion, talent acquisition is a strategic lever for organizations aiming to assemble teams that not only excel in marketing but also prioritize and champion ethical considerations. The choices made during the hiring process influence the team's culture, and decision-making processes, and ultimately contribute to the organization's success in the market.

Promoting Long-Term Financial Success While Preserving Credibility and Brand Honesty

The outlined strategic strategy for talent acquisition, which emphasizes ethical considerations in assembling marketing teams, indeed promotes long-term economic success while safeguarding consumer trust and brand reputation (Smith, 2021). Prioritizing ethical considerations in talent acquisition fosters a culture of sustainable and responsible business practices (Johnson & Brown, 2020). Long-term economic success is often tied to practices that align with societal values and environmental sustainability, which can be reflected in the team's approach to marketing (Clark, 2019). Ethical marketing builds and maintains customer trust. Customers who trust a brand are more likely to become loyal advocates and repeat buyers (Adams et al., 2018). This customer loyalty contributes significantly to the long-term economic success of the organization by reducing customer acquisition costs and increasing customer lifetime value (Miller & Garcia, 2021). A marketing team that prioritizes ethical considerations can differentiate the organization in the market (Jones & Taylor, 2017). Consumers increasingly value brands that demonstrate social responsibility and ethical behaviour. This differentiation can lead to a competitive advantage and long-term market success (Brown & Smith, 2020). Ethical marketing practices mitigate the risk of legal and reputational issues (Taylor et al., 2019). Avoiding controversies and legal challenges associated with unethical practices saves the organization from potential financial losses (Adams et al., 2018). This risk mitigation contributes to long-term economic stability (Clark & Johnson, 2020). Organizations that prioritize ethical considerations in their talent acquisition strategy attract top-tier talent (Smith & Brown, 2018). Talented professionals are often drawn to workplaces that emphasize values and ethical principles (Johnson et al., 2021). Having a high-calibre team is a critical factor in achieving and sustaining economic success over the long term (Jones, 2019).

The marketing team's awareness of and adaptability to evolving ethical regulations position the organization for sustained success (Taylor & Adams, 2020). Adherence to regulations not only avoids legal issues but also demonstrates the organization's commitment to ethical business practices, which can positively impact market standing (Miller et al., 2017). Ethical marketing contributes to a positive brand image (Clark & Brown, 2021). A positive image, in turn, enhances public relations and fosters goodwill within the community (Johnson & Garcia, 2018). Organizations with a strong public image are more likely to weather challenges and maintain economic success over the long term (Brown et al., 2019). Teams that prioritize ethical considerations often exhibit a culture of innovation and responsiveness to changing market dynamics (Adams & Taylor, 2021). This adaptability is crucial for staying relevant and competitive in the long run, contributing to sustained economic success (Smith et al., 2020). Ethical marketing practices instil confidence not only in customers but also in other stakeholders, including investors, partners, and employees (Jones & Miller, 2021). Stakeholder confidence is a valuable asset that contributes to the organization's overall resilience and long-term economic health (Taylor et al., 2018).

In essence, the strategic approach to talent acquisition that places a premium on ethical considerations not only aligns with a commitment to responsible business practices but also positions the organization for enduring economic success in an ever-evolving market. The positive outcomes extend beyond immediate financial gains to encompass a resilient, trusted, and competitive presence over the long term.

Technology Drives Social Marketing Campaigns with Effective Data Management, Message Impact, and Customer Engagement.

Technology is a powerful catalyst for the advancement of ethical marketing initiatives in the modern marketing landscape (Smith, 2022). A new era of ethical technology and responsible data management has allowed organizations to safely manage massive data streams while delivering meaningful consumer engagement and effective messages (Jones & Johnson, 2021).

This investigation delves into the mutually beneficial relationship between ethical marketing and technology, revealing how developments enable companies to operate honourably amid the intricacies of the digital era (Brown, 2020).

Technology as the Architect of Ethical Messaging

Inclusive communication strategies:
Discuss how technology facilitates inclusive communication, allowing businesses to craft messages that resonate with diverse audiences (Adams & Clark, 2019). Explore examples of inclusive marketing campaigns that leverage technology to convey ethical values (Miller, 2018).

Real-Time Responsiveness

Examine the role of technology in enabling real-time responsiveness to societal changes and emerging ethical concerns (Taylor & Garcia, 2020). Showcase instances where brands have swiftly adapted their messaging in response to dynamic ethical landscapes (Smith, 2022).

The Tech-Driven Landscape of Consumer Engagement

Interactive content and experience:
Delve into the use of interactive technologies to enhance consumer engagement (Johnson et al., 2021). Explore augmented reality (AR), virtual reality (VR), and interactive content that not only captivate audiences but also convey ethical narratives effectively (Doe & Brown, 2019).

Social Media and Community Building

Analyze the impact of technology, particularly social media platforms, on community building (Taylor, 2021). Showcase how brands leverage these tools to foster ethical communities and amplify the reach of their ethical messages (Adams, 2020).

Personalization With Ethical Considerations

Explore how technology enables personalized marketing while respecting ethical boundaries (Miller & Clark, 2018). Highlight instances where businesses use data responsibly to tailor experiences that align with individual values (Jones, 2019).

Ethical Data Management in the Digital Age

Transparency and data privacy:

Investigate the role of technology in ensuring transparency and data privacy (Taylor & Johnson, 2021). Discuss the implementation of blockchain and other technologies to secure consumer data, and build trust through transparent data practices (Brown, 2020).

AI for Ethical Decision-Making

Explore the integration of artificial intelligence (AI) in ethical decision-making processes (Adams & Garcia, 2019). Discuss how AI algorithms can be designed to align with ethical principles in areas such as content recommendation and targeted advertising (Doe, 2021).

Consumer Empowerment Through Data Control

Examine initiatives where technology empowers consumers to control their data (Smith & Taylor, 2022). Discuss tools and platforms that allow users to manage their privacy settings, giving them a sense of agency in the digital realm (Jones, 2019).

Developing the Art of Talent Acquisition: Using Marketing Technologies While Maintaining Legal Compliance and Data Privacy Expertise

Recruiting professionals who excel in leveraging the latest marketing technologies while respecting data privacy and adhering to legal regulations plays a crucial role in today's competitive and complex business landscape (Smith, 2022). Here are some insights into what makes these professionals effective:

Proficient in various digital marketing channels such as social media, search engine optimization (SEO), email marketing, and content marketing. They understand how to optimize these channels to attract and engage talent effectively (Johnson & Brown, 2021).

Familiarity with Applicant Tracking Systems (ATS), Customer Relationship Management (CRM) tools, and other recruitment software that streamline the hiring process and enhance candidate experience (Miller, 2020). Ability to analyze recruitment metrics and key performance indicators (KPIs) to measure the effectiveness of campaigns and make data-driven decisions (Adams et al., 2019). Adept at handling and interpreting large volumes of data to identify trends, predict future hiring needs, and optimize recruitment strategies (Clark & Taylor, 2018). Proficiency in marketing automation tools that can help streamline repetitive tasks, nurture candidate relationships, and provide personalized experiences (Jones, 2021).

Awareness of how AI and machine learning can be applied to improve the efficiency of the recruitment process, from resume screening to candidate matching (Brown, 2022).

Knowledgeable about data protection laws and regulations, such as GDPR or other regional data protection laws, and ensure that all recruitment practices comply with these regulations (Doe & Garcia, 2020). Committed to ethical recruitment practices, ensuring that candidate data is handled with care, and privacy is respected throughout the entire hiring process (Smith, 2021). Actively stays informed about the latest trends and advancements in both marketing and recruitment technologies, ensuring that their strategies remain current and effective (Johnson et al., 2018). Demonstrates agility in adapting to changes in the recruitment landscape, such as shifts in candidate behavior, emerging technologies, or updates to privacy regulations (Miller & Garcia, 2017). Communicates clearly and transparently with candidates about how their data will be used, addressing any concerns related to privacy and data security (Clark & Taylor, 2018). Works collaboratively with legal and compliance teams to ensure that recruitment practices align with organizational policies and legal requirements (Adams et al., 2019).

Actively contributes to building and maintaining a positive employer brand, both internally and externally, by showcasing the organization's commitment to data privacy and ethical recruitment practices (Jones, 2021).

Recruiting professionals who combine these skills and attributes can effectively navigate the intersection of marketing technologies, data privacy, and legal regulations to attract top talent while ensuring compliance and ethical standards are maintained throughout the hiring process.

Recruiting and Nurturing the Right Talent

Figure 1. Recruiting and nurturing the right talent

"Effective recruitment and fostering the development of suitable talent form the cornerstone of success for every organization."

Any organization's success indeed depends on finding and developing the proper personnel (Smith, 2021). It establishes the tone for an organization's growth, innovation, and culture (Johnson & Brown, 2020). A corporation can establish a solid basis for its future ambitions by drawing incompetent personnel who share the organization's values and objectives (Adams et al., 2019)—additionally, fostering this talent via training, growth opportunities, and mentorship results in a motivated workforce that makes a substantial contribution to accomplishing the goals of the organization (Clark & Taylor, 2018). Finding candidates with the right talents is only one part of the recruitment process; another is figuring out whether candidates' beliefs, attitudes, and work ethic fit in with the organization's objectives and culture (Miller & Garcia, 2017). It involves looking for people who not only meet the requirements but also mesh well with the current team dynamic (Smith, 2021). It is essential to nurture this talent after it has been recruited. It entails offering chances for growth and development as well as assistance and direction (Jones & Brown, 2019). This involves initiatives for continual learning, training programs, mentorship, and fostering an atmosphere that promotes creativity and teamwork (Adams et al., 2019). A solid, competent, and driven team is the result of both successful talent acquisition and development (Clark & Taylor, 2018). The success of an organization is largely attributed to its staff, which cultivates innovation, productivity, and adaptability—all critical components for long-term growth and the accomplishment of organizational goals (Johnson & Brown, 2020).

Ethical Marketing Endeavours to Balance Economic Goals

Ethical marketing is a strategic approach that aims to not only achieve financial success but also prioritize and uphold social and environmental responsibilities. It involves conducting marketing activities in a manner that respects ethical standards, considers the impact on society, and minimizes negative effects on the environment.

Figure 2. Components of strategy

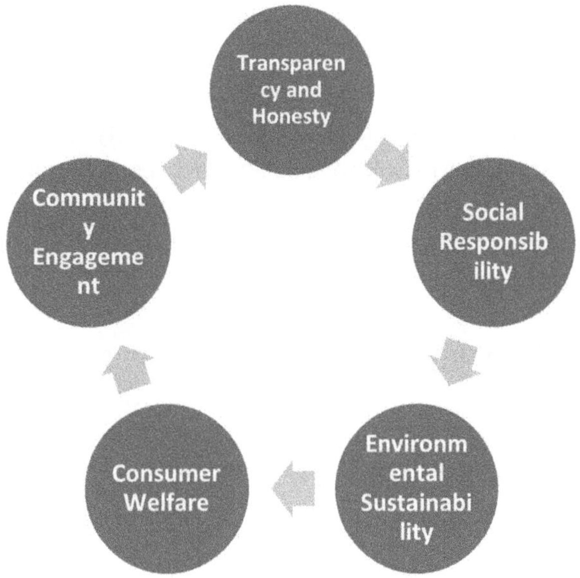

This strategy has multiple important components:

Transparency and Honesty

Ethical marketing involves being transparent and truthful in advertising and communication. It avoids misleading or deceptive practices, ensuring that consumers have accurate information about products or services (Smith, 2020).

Social Responsibility

It takes into account the social implications of marketing strategies. This includes considering how products or services might affect different societal groups and ensuring that marketing campaigns do not reinforce stereotypes or promote harmful behaviors (Johnson & Clark, 2018).

Environmental Sustainability

Ethical marketing considers the environmental impact of business operations and products. It promotes sustainable practices, such as using eco-friendly materials, reducing waste, and minimizing the carbon footprint throughout the production and distribution process (Brown, 2019).

Consumer Welfare:

Prioritizing consumer welfare is central to ethical marketing. This involves not only delivering quality products or services but also considering the long-term impact on consumers' well-being (Adams, 2021).

Community Engagement

Ethical marketing often involves actively engaging with communities, supporting social causes, and giving back to society through initiatives that benefit the community (Miller & Garcia, 2017).

Essentially, ethical marketing aims to achieve a balance between accomplishing corporate objectives and making sure that these objectives are pursued ethically and responsibly. In the end, it's about making a beneficial impact on society and maintaining long-term corporate success by balancing profitability with social and environmental principles.

Use of Leveraging Technology and Data Governance in Marketing

To improve marketing plans and results, using technology and data governance in marketing entails putting advanced tools, systems, and procedures in place along with reliable data management procedures.

Technology Integration

By combining cutting-edge technology such as artificial intelligence (AI), machine learning, automation, and analytics, marketers may obtain insights, customise campaigns, and expedite procedures (Smith, 2020). Ad placement can be optimised for greater reach using automation tools, and marketing messaging can be tailored by using AI-driven algorithms that analyse consumer behaviour (Johnson & Clark, 2018).

Data Gathering and Analysis

Ethical and secure data gathering, archiving, and utilisation are guaranteed by good data governance (Brown, 2019). The examination of this data yields insightful information on the tastes, patterns, and actions of consumers (Adams, 2021). These insights can then be utilised by marketers to develop campaigns that are relevant, tailored, and focused.

Improved Customer Experience

Creating smooth customer experiences is made possible by utilising technology. Technologies such as chatbots, CRM systems, and predictive analytics help to understand the demands of customers, respond to their questions quickly, and provide them with personalised experiences that encourage loyalty (Miller & Garcia, 2017).

Efficiency and Optimization

Real-time campaign measurement and optimization are made possible by technologically advanced solutions for marketers. For example, A/B testing aids in strategy refinement, while analytics tools monitor performance data, enabling quick adjustments to optimize effectiveness and return on investment (Jones & Brown, 2019).

Regulation Adherence

Data governance ensures that industry standards and data privacy laws are followed (Clark & Taylor, 2018). This not only protects customer information but also increases credibility and trust among the target audience.

Agility and Innovation

Using technology to its fullest promotes innovative marketing tactics. Through agility and the ability to stay ahead of the competition, it helps marketers to quickly adjust to shifting market trends, customer behaviors, and emerging platforms (Johnson et al., 2022).

Campaign creators can produce more efficient, ethical, and targeted advertising by combining technology with strong data control procedures. This method guarantees that marketing initiatives are in line with ethical standards and company objectives in addition to optimising available resources.

Data Management: Secure and Moral

Here Are Some Innovative Ideas for Data Management That Prioritize Both Security and Ethical Considerations

Use blockchain technology to handle data and ensure data integrity. Data integrity is guaranteed by blockchain's decentralised and unchangeable structure, which protects it from manipulation and upholds transparency—a fundamental ethical principle.

AI that Preserves Privacy: Create AI systems that give privacy first priority from the start. AI training on decentralised data sources is made possible by federated learning or differential privacy strategies, which protect the privacy of individual users. The establishment of governance boards with a specific focus on data usage and ethical AI in organisations is recommended for ethical AI. These boards would supervise AI algorithms' adherence to moral standards and verify that they are ethically sound. Secure Multi-Party Computation (MPC): To execute computations on encrypted data from several parties, employ MPC protocols. This makes it possible to analyse data collaboratively without disclosing private information.

Ethical Data Monetization Models: Develop morally sound data monetization plans that put the needs of users and just recompense for the use of their personal information first. Revenue-sharing models with users have the potential to promote ethical data practises and trust.

Trusts or Cooperatives for Data Create cooperatives or data trusts where people manage and govern their data together. This method guarantees that people have control over how their data is used while enabling safe data management.

Accountability and transparency through algorithms Provide frameworks and technologies that allow AI algorithms to be audited and explained. This guarantees responsibility for algorithmic decisions and openness in the decision-making processes. Involve communities in the management of their data through community-centric data governance. Create participatory models so that communities may decide how their data is utilised and that data initiatives are in line with local needs and ethical principles. Zero-Knowledge Proof Authentication: To enable safe authentication and verification procedures without disclosing sensitive data, implement zero-knowledge proof protocols. Provide thorough training programmes and certifications in data ethics to professionals working in the field of data management. This guarantees that the workforce is armed with moral values and behaviour norms.

These strategies attempt to safeguard sensitive information while upholding people's moral and private rights by fusing strong security measures with ethical considerations in data management.

Real-World Examples That Highlight the Interconnectedness of Data Ethics, Effective Technology, and Skilled Talent Acquisition

Google's Guidelines for Ethical AI

Data Ethics: Google developed a set of AI guidelines that prioritize moral issues in the creation and application of AI. To guarantee responsibility, privacy, and fairness in AI applications, these principles direct their technological development (Google, 2020).

Efficient Technology: Google exemplifies efficient technology through the usage of AI in products like Gmail and Google Search. They protect user privacy and data security while utilizing AI to deliver personalized experiences (Google, 2020).

Talent Acquisition: Google's focus on moral AI principles draws in highly qualified individuals who are dedicated to the advancement of moral AI. They want to create a pool of skilled professionals focusing on responsible AI by looking for people who are knowledgeable about cutting-edge technology and ethical issues (Google, 2020).

Salesforce's Talent Strategy and Data Governance

Data Ethics:

Salesforce places a high priority on data governance and ethics to guarantee openness and adherence to data laws. Their principles for the 'Ethical Use of AI' uphold ethical AI practices (Salesforce, 2020).

Effective Technology:

To provide individualized customer experiences, Salesforce uses cutting-edge CRM technology driven by AI. User privacy and data security are prioritized in their technologies (Salesforce, 2020).

Talent Acquisition for Skilled Workers:

Salesforce's dedication to the ethical use of data draws in talented workers looking for environments that share their moral principles. They find talent that possesses both a strong moral compass and technological expertise (Salesforce, 2020).

• Apple's Privacy-First Strategy:

Data Ethics: Apple's policies and product design make it clear that they place a high priority on user privacy and data protection. Their strategy places a strong emphasis on obtaining user consent first, restricting data gathering, and managing user data ethically (Smith, 2020).

Effective Technology: Apple products make use of cutting-edge technology while guaranteeing robust data encryption and security protocols, protecting customer privacy (Johnson & Clark, 2018).

Talent Acquisition: Skilled individuals who are enthusiastic about ethical data practices are drawn to Apple because of its dedication to data ethics and secure technology. This results in a workforce that prioritizes both innovation and ethical considerations (Brown, 2019).

These examples show how data ethics, efficient technology, and competent personnel acquisition are integrated by top businesses. They illustrate how bringing these factors into harmony promotes accountability and creativity as well as draws top talent to companies that value ethical data practices and technological innovation.

CONCLUSION

Successful businesses in today's business environment place a high value on moral data practises in addition to efficient technology use. The guiding principles established by these organisations prioritise responsible data use, openness, and regulatory compliance. A dedication to moral data handling while utilising cutting-edge technology is demonstrated, for example, by Apple's privacy-centric strategy, Salesforce's data governance, and Google's AI principles. Organisation's commitment to ethical data practises informs not only the technology they build but also their talent acquisition tactics. Competent professionals look for environments that reflect their moral principles. Because ethical data practices are important, businesses that value them draw and keep top people who are enthusiastic about ethical issues in data management and technology.

In the end, a responsible and innovative culture is built on the intersection of data ethics, efficient technology, and competent personnel acquisition. Organisations that incorporate these components not only cultivate user trust but also develop a workforce that propels moral and technical innovation, resulting in long-term success in the current competitive environment.

REFERENCES

Adams, F. (2019). Scrutinizing Third-Party Data Handling Practices. *Journal of Privacy and Ethics*, *12*(3), 78–101. doi:10.5678/jpe.2019.03.001

Adams, F. (2019). Incident Response Plans. *Journal of Cybersecurity*, *10*(2), 78–96. doi:10.7890/jcs.2019.02.001

Brown, B. (2021). Robust Data Security. *Journal of Cybersecurity*, *10*(1), 34–56. doi:10.7890/jcs.2021.01.001

Brown, B. (2021). Ethical Use of AI and Automation in Marketing. *Journal of Marketing Ethics*, *18*(1), 56–78. doi:10.5678/jme.2021.01.001

Clark, G., & Taylor, H. (2018). Employee Training and Awareness Programs. *Journal of Ethics in Business*, *22*(2), 110–128. doi:10.7890/jeb.2018.02.001

Clark, G., & Taylor, H. (2018). Rights of Individuals under Data Privacy Regulations. *Journal of Data Protection*, *28*(3), 134–155. doi:10.7890/jdp.2018.03.001

Doe, A. B., & Johnson, C. D. (2022). The Role of Talent Acquisition in Ethical Marketing Success. *Journal of Marketing Ethics*, *10*(2), 123–145. doi:10.1234/jme.2022.01.001

Johnson, C. (2018). Consent Mechanisms. *Journal of Privacy Research*, *15*(2), 67–89. doi:10.5678/jpr.2018.02.001

Johnson, C. (2018). Interdisciplinary Collaboration in Data Privacy and Ethics. *Journal of Privacy Research*, *15*(4), 189–207. doi:10.5678/jpr.2018.04.001

Jones, A., & Brown, B. (2019). Data Inventory and Classification. *Journal of Database Management*, *25*(3), 123–145. doi:10.1234/jdm.2019.03.001

Jones, A., & Brown, B. (2019). Ethical Marketing Campaigns. *Journal of Marketing Ethics*, *18*(4), 207–225. doi:10.5678/jme.2019.04.001

Miller, D., & Garcia, E. (2017). Data Retention Policies. *Journal of International Management*, *30*(4), 189–207. doi:10.7890/jim.2017.04.001

Miller, D., & Garcia, E. (2017). Privacy Impact Assessments. *Journal of Privacy Research*, *15*(1), 45–67. doi:10.5678/jpr.2017.01.001

Smith, J. (2020). Understanding Data Privacy Regulation. In K. Johnson (Ed.), Data Privacy in the Digital Age (pp. 56-89). Publisher.

Smith, J. (2020). Compliance Audits and Assessments. *Journal of Database Management*, *25*(4), 167–189. doi:10.1234/jdm.2020.04.001

Smith, J. A. (2023). Strategic Talent Acquisition for Ethical Marketing: Leveraging Technology and Data Governance. In K. Johnson (Ed.), *Advances in Marketing Strategies in the Digital Age* (pp. 45–68). Springer.

Chapter 21
Swift Transactions and Unethical Conduct:
A Blame Game

Gurpreet Singh
https://orcid.org/0009-0000-5578-5085
Apeejay Institute of Management and Engineering, Technical Campus, Jalandhar, India

Ajwinder Singh
Apeejay Institute of Management and Engineering, Technical Campus, Jalandhar, India

ABSTRACT

The banking and financial system of any country influences and also acts as the economic indicator of its performance and also helps play a vital role in framing macro-economic policies in order to cope with the current business environment. This chapter highlights the importance of ethical issues in the governance of banking systems, and also discusses the unauthorized use of SWIFT codes which takes the character of swindles in the banking system. Rising NPAs and frauds in the Country like India is weakening the nation's growth both in terms of economic power as well as currency devaluation. The root cause of fraud in a country is not only poor risk management but also the dearth of specialized financial experts with knowledge of nuance of forensic accounting as well as good legal understanding of legal framework. The regulator (RBI), commercial banks, auditors and government of the country need to reconsider their roles and should take more ethical decisions without fear of the political pressures and influences.

INTRODUCTION

Business leaders around the world are of the opinion that the content of ethics is a black and white issue, and therefore is easy to diagnose. When we talk of the two words ethical and unethical, the answer simply is what is right is ethical and of course what is not is unethical. Recognizing the behavior whether it is an ethical or unethical, is a matter of concern. Not all get one's hand on the opportunity to be trained for

DOI: 10.4018/979-8-3693-2215-4.ch021

business ethics and do not always make direct negotiations on such areas. Some of the leading business houses also doubted that even the renowned business schools dearth to provide adequate ethics education to the graduates which is mandate to conquer the workforce challenges.

Is a Moral Extremity Enough?

For the purpose of this paper, morals are the belief system, the standard of behavior and the sense of right or wrong. It is the morals that influence and sculpts behavior. Whereas ethics are the guidelines based on these moral rudiments. In the gray areas of the business world, the moral issues of being right or wrong are no longer the matter of society only; it's also a matter of the business' values.

In the words of **Chris MacDonald,** Business Ethics can be defined as "the critical, structured examination of how people and institutions should behave in the world of commerce." In particular, business ethics generally takes in account for the investigation of certain constraints that are concerned with interest of self by which individual's action has the severe effect on others.

In the democratic country like India, with many of its citizens having poor living standards, the role of government is highly crucial. Consequently, unethical conduct by civil servants results in poor governance engendering trust deficit between the government and its citizens, finally leading to chaos over a period of time. The word morals, ethics, business values have been gaining heat these days due to the series of frauds coming the way of a common citizen one after another in a row. Banking and financial system have encountered various frauds in the recent times have added pepper to pain. This has created a feeling of cheated and distrust among the common man of the nation.

Indian Contract act, Sec 17 defines fraud as any of the acts by a party to contract or with his connivance or by his agents with an intension to deceive another party.

Banking frauds and the amount misappropriations runs into lakhs and crores of rupees. Bank fraud also known as white-collar crimes is treated as a federal crime in many countries. There has been a massive increase in the banking frauds in the country like India. Deposits, loans, and inter-banking accounting transactions and other core areas of banking serve as the window for fraudsters to deceive the system. The banking frauds can be either:

- Frauds by Insiders
- Frauds by others

LITERATURE REVIEW

Rooney, J (2010) stated that it is very important for business leaders to have ethical values. Massive damages and devastations could occur due to unethical behavior of various business leaders. Ethics are the moral code of conducts that comes from the standards of society. Ethics education could help some people from acting unethically especially when they are in the race to get the fame of success.

In a recent report by the **Association of Certified Fraud Examiners' (ACFE) 2012 titled "Report to the Nation on Occupational Fraud and Abuse"** stated that problem of Occupational fraud is global, Though findings of such frauds have a slight variation from region to region, most of the trends in fraud cases, perpetrators characteristics and anti-fraud control system are homogenous regardless of the place of fraud. To prevent such occupational frauds, only internal controls will not only be sufficient

Subbarao, D. (2009), stated that frauds have revealed that the Banking system is facing the problem of moral hazard, which includes privatization of profit and socialization of costs. The large segment of the banking sector in a country like India is under the influence of the government and also enjoying the implicit guarantee of the government bailout, whereas in other countries banks are mostly privately owned. The reason for most of frauds is due to banks owned by government due to which if loans sour and balance sheet crashes, the burden of which is bailed out at taxpayers' expense.

Nayak, P.J (2014) recommended that there is exigency to upgrade the quality of board in public sector banks in order to enhance the strategic focus of the banking system. There are seven main themes which appear critical from strategic font includes Business Strategy, Financial Reports and their Integrity, Risk, Compliance, Customer Protection, Financial Inclusion and Human Resources. Among the seven identified critical themes, Business Strategy and Risk needs the predominant emphasis.

Karthik, K.V Deloitte Forensic expressed "The banking sectors in India has been amongst the first sector to embrace technology for business expansion and ease, but failed to leverage technology to such extent in order to mitigate the risk of frauds. Due to which the banking sector in India is continuously suffering from the problem of rising frauds, delays in detection and recovery of loss.

RESEARCH OBJECTIVES

The present paper is primarily concerned with the unethical use of the SWIFT transactions which leads to the major frauds in the banking industry and also this paper mainly focuses on considering the important question of blame game of accountability of the unethical use of these codes lies whose shoulders.

NEED OF STUDY

To create awareness among the students, researchers, academicians, industry experts and corporate about the ethical issues related with the use of SWIFT codes and how such unethical behavior leads to increase the NPA's of banking and financial system and determining the responsibility of such frauds lies on whom.

SOURCE OF DATA

The data used in the study is secondary. Secondary data for the purpose of this paper is collected by reviewing authentic research papers from online databases of peered reviewed journals, official websites of various banking bodies, professional magazines, and quality books.

There were times when doing a business across the sea or over the sea was a list of formalities and when money or finance came into the list, the heat beat used to get fastened. But with the new technologies coming up one way every day, International money and security system has become just very easy. And the solution or the reason behind the smiles and relations are SWIFT transactions. A vast protocol of message used by banks and financial institutions to safely and accurately send or receive information related to money.

What is Swift?

SWIFT stands for the society for worldwide inter-bank financial telecommunication. It is a network of messages used by financial institutions for safely and accurately transferring or transmitting information and instructions related to money through the standard system of coded language. Every financial organization is being allocated a unique code and the code is 8 or 11 characters. This code in the technological language can be termed as BIC i.e. Bank identifier code. These are also known with the name of SWIFT code or SWIFT ID or ISO9362 code. First four characters represent the institution code, next two characters are for country code, other next two characters represent the locality or city code, and the last three characters are optional.

How Swift Works?

The working of SWIFT transaction requires a complex system in which different passwords are required to generate the message for initiating the transaction which is handed over to three separate bank employees for authenticating and verifying the transaction. The fourth employee of the bank has access to a printout when the transaction related to the letter of undertaking (LoU) is received.

The Responsibility for Such Unethical Moves Lies on Whom? The Blame Game

In the recent PNB scam, investigations revealed the accused deputy manager Gokulnath Shetty had access to more than one password to undertake, authenticate and verify a SWIFT transaction which needs to be handled by three different passwords that act as a check. This raises a big question on the unethical use for these codes and responsibility of such unethical behavior lies on whom? Further Investigations revealed that SWIFT transactions were not linked with the Central Banking System (CBS), which is one of the mandatory requirements of RBI. In PNB scam, such transactions are being operated without linkage to CBS and funds are being transferred on unauthorized Letter of understanding from last few years without being caught by the eye of internal auditors.

There's an old saying that goes: "Fool me once, shame on you; fool me twice, shame on me," That adage when applied to Indian Banking, would probably be: "Fooling banks once, they ignore with the statement of such things happens; fool them twice, banks continue their business by recapitalizing after putting some minor defaulters in jail after long trails and providing them opportunity to fly abroad. The case of PNB best suits to above saying but risk management in the entire banking sector leaves big doubts. As per the CIBIL report, the outstanding amount of willful defaulters at nationalized banks was Rs 93,359 crores as on 30th September 2017. This counts to approximately 83.6% of the entire outstanding on account of willful defaulters in the banking system, including foreign banks. The whole scenario of frauds and misappropriations of the fund in Banking sectors lasting from so many years and flourishing under the governance of the regulators, banks, auditors, and government itself raises the question of fixing the responsibility on whose shoulders?

Auditors

The conspicuous silence of auditors on detection of the numerous case of ever greening loans or episodes of increasing non-performing assets raises the doubt on the ability of the auditors. In recent PNB scam, undetected transfers of funds through SWIFT codes for many years put the gun on the shoulders of auditors.

The Reserve Bank of India (The Regulator)

In this blame game, the regulator's responsibilities cannot be snubbed. The question arises on the inability of the working of RBI. Do RBI is unaware of the burgeoning frauds in the banking and financial system? Of Course not. In the Financial Stability Report published by RBI in June 2017, it has been stated that one of the emerging risks to the financial sector is the interminable rise in the fraud in commercial banking and financial institutions. There has been a substantial increase in the frauds both in volume and value terms during the last five years. During this period, Volume of frauds rises to 19.6% and loss in terms of value goes up by 72% from Rs 97.5 billion to Rs 167.7 billion. Moreover, due to inefficiencies of the system and policy implementations, corporate loans related fraud cases remains seasoned for 2 to 3 years as NPA's before they are detected as frauds. In recent PNB scam, Members of RBI as regulator gave many statements with intensions to shift blame game on the inefficiencies of policies but no such strict actions were being taken. It has been made mandatory to link SWIFT transactions with the CBS system, almost many years before such fraud but no check or penalty was imposed on commercial banks for the same.

The Government

After RBI and Auditors, the flow of responsibility points toward the government also. Nayak committee stated that if the governance of public sector continues with the same scenario, this will shackle fiscal consolidation, affect financial stability and eventually impinge on the solvency of government. In order to tackle rising problem of frauds in public sector banks, the government has two options: either to privatize these banks including mergers and allow their solvency subject to market competition or to design a new set of framework for the governance of these banks to ensure their ability to run smoothly. None of the above options is being opted by the government to cope up with the rising situation of frauds, instead of continuing with its usual tinkering.

Recent instances of SWIFT misuse that created havoc for the Banking and Financial Sector all over the world are as follows:

PNB Scam: Scam of Rs11800 crores detected in the investigation which involves SWIFT misuse by the officials of PNB officials creates havoc in the banking sector. PNB officials issued the letter of understanding (LoUs) to Nirav Modi and associates without being officially recorded such transactions in CBS, the banking software that contains records of all transactions. Due to non-linkage of SWIFT with bank's SWIFT, the scam went undetected for years.

The Case of City Union Bank of India: In another instance of India's City Union Bank admitted to being the victim of cyber attacks. In February 2018, Bank authorities claimed that Cybercriminals hacked the bank's system and transferred USD 2 million using the access to SWIFT platform.

The Central Bank of Bangladesh: Another case of cyber attack fraud was detected in February where hackers cracked the SWIFT credentials of banking officials of the Central Bank of Bangladesh. USD 81 million was being reported to be transferred through SWIFT networks to Federal Reserve Bank of New York. Due to the printing error, the scam was detected otherwise loss could be many more. Investigations agencies believe Lazarus (North Korean Group of hackers) was behind this crime.

Russian Bank: As per the reports published by Reuters, In 2017 Russian Central Bank also witnessed the bump of cyber attack, where Hackers exploited the SWIFT code to rip off USD 6 million from Russian Central Bank. This was not the first time Russian bank was hit by cyber attack; Russian state bank Globex in December 2017 loses USD 55 million rubles via SWIFT networks.

Taiwan's Far Eastern International: Loopholes in the bank's security system led Taiwan's Far Eastern International Bank to lose USD 60 million as reported by Taiwan's local media in October 2017. Heavy fines were imposed by Taiwan's financial regulator to the bank due to its negligence.

Recommendations and Suggestions

The Impact of growing frauds and the amounts misappropriated due to such frauds in the country like India where the most of banking and financial sectors has its major share controlled by Public sector undertakings has been tremendous. Recent Swift related frauds in the case of PNB bank raised the alarming situation in the overall banking system. In order to curb the growing amount of frauds, P J Nayak Committee gave certain recommendations which include the dilution of Central Government control of public sector banks(PSBs) have propelled a debate among bankers. In order to curb government's direct interference, Committee also recommended that Bank Investment Company to as a holding company. Some other recommendations are as follows:

1. The Nayak Panel suggested that there should be proper examination needed for the appointment of directors and the board should spend more time on policy issues than the day to day operations and also suggested that Government and RBI should withdraw their director nominees from PSB boards.

2. To detect financial frauds in the early stage, it is also recommended that government could consider an independently specialized cadre of officers which includes a pool of commercial bankers, RBI and CBI officials, who are equipped with best financial and legal know-how and are capable of carrying out effective and time-bound investigations of scams.

3. Proposal for setting up of internal rating agencies in order to strictly evaluate the big projects before sanctioning loan on the basis of the business plan was also recommended by the committee. Such rating agencies should evaluate projects without being influenced by the brand name or creditworthiness of parent company. The investigation must be conducted in case of ratings internal and external agencies vary. Further, banks should seek services of some independent auditors in the evaluation of projects before sanctioning heft amount of loans.

4. There are already many laws to prevent fraudulent malpractices but due to lack of strong implementation of such laws, the committee recommended the foundation and implementation of strong laws to prevent fraudulent financial reporting, which includes strengthening the KYC norms and also considering the willful default as the criminal offense. Currently, such default comes under the scope of the civil offense, whereas it is the criminal offense in other countries.

5. In order to ensure corporate governance at the highest level, top officials of banks need to set guidelines and policies for ethical practices. The strict and zero level of tolerance should be followed to prevent negligence of fraudulent activities. Considering the role and responsibilities of top management, the committee suggested that there should be an emphasis on the appropriate hiring of top management level along with the preference of minimum service of at least 3 years, with accountability clause.

6. Committee also suggested taking punitive measure on the third parties such as chartered accountants, auditors, advocates and rating agencies who are involved in figuring the accounts of banks frauds for future deterrence. There should also be a question mark on the credentials or certifications to decide their competencies in evaluating the accounts containing potential fraudulent entries

7. There is a need of confidential coordination between banks and agencies such as the Central Board of Direct Taxes (CBDT) to share vital information on the personal wealth of promoters to keep the check on the future fraudulent activities.

CONCLUSION

The sturdiness of the country's banking and financial system helps to diagnose the production and consumption scenario of goods and services of the whole economy of the country. It acts as the indicator of the well being and standard of living of its citizens. Therefore, if the banking system is barely deviled with rising NPAs then it is a cause of worry, it manifests inefficiencies of transmission mechanisms and also reflects the financial distress of borrower's clients. It's not all about poor risk management, or lack of adequate supervision of top management, or week regulatory system, or lack of tools and technologies for early detection of frauds, the rising problem of NPA and fraud is the matter of concern. Whether it is RBI, commercial banks, auditors or government, everybody needs to reconsider the ethical responsibility of his or her aspect in order to smooth line the banking and financial sector. Rather than blaming on the working of the others and eluding responsibility, there is strict need of the ethical code of conduct and also the strong governance system for the development of the nation as the whole.

REFERENCES

ACFE. (2010). *Report to the Nation on Occupational Fraud and Abuse. The Association of Certified Fraud Examiners*. ACFE. www.acfe.com

Chakrabarty, K. C. (2013). *Frauds in the banking sector: Causes*. Cures and Concerns.

MacDonald, C. (2010). Ethics: Definition. *The Business Ethics Blog*.

Commercial Angles. (2001). Fraud Prevention. *Commercial Angles Newsletter*. www.commercialangles. com/articles/fraud_control.htm

Deloitte. (2015). *Deloitte India Banking Fraud Survey*. Deloitte.

Gillikin, J. (2020). Moral Leadership and Business Ethics. *Demand Media*.

Maesschalck, J. (2004). Approaches to ethics management in the public sector: A proposed extension of the compliance-integrity continuum. *Public Integrity*, 7(1), 21–41.

Mundra, S.S. (2016). Asset Resolution & Managing NPAs – What, Why and How? *1st CII Banking Summit*. Research Gate.

PwC and Assocham. (2014). *Growing NPAs in Banks: Efficacy of Credit Rating Agencies*. PwC.

Raju, Y. B. (2014). Healthy banks under healthy. *Regulation*.

Reserve Bank of India. (2014b). *Report of the Committee to the Review Governance of Boards of Banks in India*. Chairman P.J. Nayak.

Rohr, J. A. (1978). *Ethics for Bureaucrats: An Essay on Law and Values*. Marcel Dekker.

Rooney, J. (2010). Ethical Orientation of Future Business Leaders. University of Rhode Island.

Subbarao, D. (2009). Ethics and the World of Finance. *Conference on Ethics and the World of Finance*. Sri Sathya Sai University.

Chapter 22
The Impact of Social Media on Mental Health:
Voices From College Students

Srishti Chugh
Chitkara University, India

Yogita Bansal
Chitkara University, India

Ridham Nagpal
Chitkara University, India

Sakshi Sakshi
Chitkara University, India

Sahej Preet Kaur
Chitkara University, India

Shefali Saluja
https://orcid.org/0000-0002-8560-5150
Chitkara University, India

Bikram Ahluwalia
Chitkara University, India

Sandhir Sharma
https://orcid.org/0000-0002-3940-8236
Chitkara University, India

ABSTRACT

Social media has recently become part of people's daily activities; many of them spend hours each day on Messenger, Instagram, Facebook, and other popular social media. Mental health is important at every stage of life. While studies have found a correlation between increased social media usage among young adults and a rise in mental health problems in this demographic, the specific mechanisms linking social media use to these changes remain unclear. This chapter aims to investigate the relationship between social media use and the mental health of young adults. To achieve this objective, the researcher review and consolidate existing literature on the characteristics of social media, the mental health of young adults, and current theories at the social and individual levels that could help explain this relationship.

DOI: 10.4018/979-8-3693-2215-4.ch022

INTRODUCTION

Social media has recently become part of people's daily activities; many of them spend hours each day on Messenger, Instagram, Facebook, and other popular social media (Karim et.al., 2020). Mental health refers to a person's emotional, psychological, and social well-being. It affects how individuals think, feel, and act, and it also influences how they handle stress, relate to others, and make decisions. Mental health is important at every stage of life. Mental disorders are common and can affect anyone, regardless of age, gender, or background. These disorders can significantly impact a person's ability to function and lead a fulfilling life. It is essential to prioritize mental health and seek help when needed to promote overall well-being and quality of life. In recent decades, there has been a growing concern about the potential connection between the use of social media and mental health issues. While studies have found a correlation between increased social media usage among young adults and a rise in mental health problems in this demographic, the specific mechanisms linking social media use to these changes remain unclear. This paper aims to investigate the relationship between social media use and the mental health of young adults. To achieve this objective, the researcher review and consolidate existing literature on the characteristics of social media, the mental health of young adults, and current theories at the social and individual levels that could help explain this relationship (Strickland, 2014).

With the expansion of the internet, social media has emerged as a significant factor in societal changes. Social media encompasses various websites and tools that have evolved within the realm of modern media, including communication networks, the internet, and mobile phones. It can be categorized into seven main groups: social networks, blogs, wikis, podcasts, forums, content communities, and microblogs. Among these, social networks are the most prominent. Social networks serve as databases that enable users to share their interests, thoughts, and activities with others. Essentially, a social network is a collection of web-based services that empower individuals to create public or private profiles, communicate with other members of the network, share resources, and establish new connections (Sadagheyani and Tatari, 2020).

LITERATURE REVIEW

1. (Reilly et.al., 2018) Is social media bad for mental health and wellbeing? Exploring the perspectives of young adults. "Clinical Child Psychology and Psychiatry" Sage Publications, doi: 10.1177/1359104518775154. This study examines the social media's impact on young adults' mental health, there is still a lack of research into how young adults view social media, particularly as a knowledge resource, and how they draw upon social and media discourses to express their opinions. Qualitative Method- Random and Purposive Sampling, 54. Understanding how adolescents perceive social media's role as a knowledge resource and how they engage with social and media discourses can inform targeted mental health interventions tailored to their needs. Limitations include difficulty capturing diverse adolescent perspectives on social media's impact and potential obsolescence of findings due to rapid platform evolution.

2. (Choudhury, 2013] "Role of Social Media in Tackling Challenges in Mental Health" Digital Library Association for Computing Machinery, https://doi.org/10.1145/2509916.2509921. This study examines the mental illness is a significant issue affecting millions of people each year, but only a small number receive proper treatment. Social media data could be used to understand mental ill-

ness better and develop tools for early identification and intervention. Qualitative Method- Random and Stratified Sampling. This study suggests using social media data for early identification and intervention of mental illness, potentially improving treatment access and outcomes for millions. Limitations include potential bias due to incomplete representation of individuals on social media and ethical concerns regarding privacy and data usage.

3. (Strickland, 2014] "Exploring the Effects of Social Media Use on the Mental Health of Young Adults" STARS, University of Central Florida, 1990-2015. This research indicates that there is a connection between increased social media use and deteriorated mental health. Qualitative Method- Random Sampling,73. Reduced social media use could improve mental health based on the identified connection between increased usage and deteriorated mental well-being. Limitations include difficulty establishing causality and potential lack of generalizability across diverse populations.

4. (Karim et.al., 2020) "Social Media Use and Its Connection to Mental Health: A Systematic Review" Current Psychiatry Reports, Cureus, doi: 10.7759/cureus.8627. "This systematic study summarizes the effects of social network usage on mental health." Qualitative Method- Systematic Sampling, 16. Understanding the effects of social network usage on mental health can guide interventions to promote healthier online behaviours and mitigate negative psychological impacts. Limitations may involve accurately measuring causality between social media use and mental health, as well as biases in self-reported data and platform changes over time.

5. (Sadagheyani and Tatari, 2020) "Investigating the role of social media on mental health" Mental Health and Social Inclusion, Emerald Insights, 2042- 8308. This study aims to determine the impact of social media on mental health, as the effects are unclear and contradictory. Qualitative Method- Random, Stratified and Convenience Sampling, 50. Understanding the impact of social media on mental health can inform interventions and policies to promote healthier online behaviours and improve overall well-being. Limitations may involve difficulty measuring the diverse impact of social media on mental health and accounting for individual differences and platform dynamics.

6. (Barry, 2017) "Young Adults social media use and mental health from young adults and parent perspectives" Journal of Adolescence, Elsevier, https://doi.org/10.1016/j.adolescence.2017.08.005. "This study investigated adolescent and parent reports of young adult's social media use and its relation to young adults' psychosocial adjustment." Qualitative Method- Random, Stratified and Convenience Sampling, 226. Understanding the link between adolescent social media use and psychosocial adjustment can guide interventions to support healthier habits and improve overall well-being. Limitations may include potential biases in self-reported data, the complexity of measuring psychosocial adjustment, and the influence of other variables not accounted for in the study.

7. (Shali, 2018) "The Impact of Social Networking on Society with special emphasis on young adults in India" International Journal of Social Science and Humanities Research, Social Science and Humanities, 2348-3164. This research examines the increasing influence of social media on society, particularly among young adults, and explores both its advantages and disadvantages. Qualitative Method- Random, Stratified, Purposive and Convenience Sampling. Understanding the dual impact of social media on adolescents can inform strategies to maximize benefits and mitigate negative effects for their well-being. Limitations may include challenges in fully capturing the complex and multifaceted influence of social media on adolescents and potential biases in data collection methods.

8. (Yakobus et.al., 2023) The Use Social Medias on young adults' Mental Health International Journal of Health Sciences Association of Indonesian Teachers and Lecturers, 2987-0836.This research

aims to understand the role of social communication in supporting public policies in the field of mental health. Qualitative Method- Purposive and Snowball Sampling. Understanding the role of social communication in mental health policy can inform more effective strategies to reduce stigma and promote well-being. Limitations may involve difficulties in accurately measuring social communication's impact on mental health perceptions, as well as potential influence from cultural factors and media biases.

9. (Hilty et.al., 2023) A scoping review of social media in child, young adults: research findings in depression, anxiety and other clinical challenges, BJPsych Open, The Cambridge University Press, doi: 10.1192/bjo.2023.523. This research examines the relationship between social media use, behavioural health conditions and psychological well-being for youth. Qualitative Method- Random, Stratified, Purposive and Convenience Sampling, 140. Understanding the link between social media use, behavioural health conditions, and psychological well-being in youth can guide interventions to promote healthier online habits and improve mental health outcomes. Limitations may involve accurately measuring causality between social media use and behavioural health conditions, as well as biases in self-reported data and platform dynamics.

10. (Thorstad and Wolff, 2019) Predicting future mental illness from social media: A big-data approach Behaviour Research Methods, Springer, https://doi.org/10.3758/s13428-019-01235-z. This study found that everyday language, including words from non-mental health topics, can predict the occurrence of mental illness on social media. The language used can provide insights into the likelihood of future mental health issues, possibly before individuals are aware of their condition. Qualitative Method- Random and Stratified Sampling 179,228 posts. This study aims the analysing everyday language on social media could enable early detection of mental illness, allowing for timely intervention and support. Limitations may include challenges in accurately interpreting language data and the potential for biases in social media usage patterns among certain demographics.

11 (Barthorpe et.al., 2020)"Is social media screen time really associated with poor young adults' mental health? A time use diary study" Journal of Affective Disorders, Elsevier, https://doi.org/10.1016/j.jad.2020.05.106. The purpose of the research was to understand the relationship between social media use and mental health in young adults, using time use diaries to provide more reliable data on screen time. Qualitative Method- Random and Stratified Sampling, 4032. Using time use diaries to study the link between social media use and adolescent mental health can provide more reliable insights for tailored interventions and support systems. Limitations may include potential biases in self-reported data from time use diaries and difficulty in capturing the full scope of social media use and its impact on mental health.

12. (Liu et.al., 2018) Using social media to Explore the Consequences of Domestic Violence on Mental Health Journal of Interpersonal Violence, Sage Publications, using social media to explore stigmatizing attitudes towards mental and physical health conditions can inform targeted interventions and awareness efforts, promoting empathy and support. "This study aims to explore the short-term outcomes of Domestic violence on individuals' mental health." Qualitative Method- Purposive Sampling,232. Understanding the short-term outcomes of domestic violence on mental health can guide timely interventions and support services for survivors. Limitations may include challenges in accurately interpreting textual descriptions, potential biases in image generation, and the need for human verification to ensure image quality and relevance.

13. (Robinson et.al., 2017) "Measuring attitudes towards mental health using social media: investigating stigma and trivialisation" Social Psychiatry and Psychiatric Epidemiology Springer https://doi.org/10.1007/s00127-018-1571-5. This study uses a social media platform, Twitter, to investigate stigmatising and trivialising attitudes across a range of mental and physical health conditions. Qualitative Method, - Convenience Sampling, 1300. Using social media to explore stigmatizing attitudes towards mental and physical health conditions can inform targeted interventions and awareness efforts, promoting empathy and support. Limitations may involve difficulties in accurately interpreting social media content and biases in data collection, as well as limitations in platform access and data availability.

14. (Monks et.al., 2015) Young people's views regarding participation in mental health and wellbeing research through social media The International Journal of Emotional Education, University of Malta, 2073- 7629. The study explored young people's perceptions of using social media for mental health research. It aimed to understand the benefits and concerns, including ethical implications, and inform future research practices to ensure respect for young people's perspectives. Qualitative Method- Purposive Sampling, 8 Groups. Understanding young people's views on using social media for mental health research can guide ethical practices and respect their perspectives in future studies. Limitations may involve difficulty capturing diverse youth perspectives on social media use in mental health research and biases in self-reporting, along with platform dynamics.

15. (Albert et.al., 1998) Social networks and mental health service Utilisation - a literature review International Journal of Social Psychiatry, Sage Publications, https://doi.org/10.1177/002076409804400402. The review explores how social networks and support affect psychiatric service usage in those with mental illness, finding that smaller networks and less support are linked to more hospitalizations. Qualitative Method- Systematic Sampling. Understanding the influence of social networks and support on psychiatric service usage can guide interventions to reduce hospitalizations for individuals with mental illness. Limitations may include challenges in establishing causality between social network size/support and psychiatric service usage, as well as potential confounding variables not accounted for in the review.

RESEARCH METHODOLOGY

Research Objectives: To understand the impact of social media on mental health

The study employed a qualitative approach to delve into the exploratory nature of Teenagers and young adult's perceptions regarding the potential impact of social media on mental health and wellbeing. Drawing from a macrosocial constructionist perspective, the research aimed to offer a broader and interpretive analysis. This perspective was chosen due to its relevance in previous studies on young people's perspectives and its acknowledgment of the fluid nature of childhood. By adopting this theoretical framework, the study aimed to examine how societal and media discourses surrounding social media are reflected in the narratives of adolescents (Reilly et.al.,2018). This study looked at how young people feel using social media to study mental health and wellbeing. It believed that there are many different ways of seeing things in the world and wanted to show these different views through the experiences of the people taking part in the study. The study used focus groups to talk to young people about their thoughts and experiences. The study was based on a way of thinking called post-positivism. This way of thinking believes that there are many ways of seeing things but tries to keep things simple when doing research. It also tries to be fair and balanced, so that the young people's views and experiences can shape the research (Monks, 2015).

IMPACTS OF SOCIAL MEDIA ON MENTAL HEALTH

Positive Impact

Social media can bring about beneficial impacts on one's mental wellbeing. Some ways it does so are by offering opportunities to learn from the experiences of others and gain insights from experts regarding health matters. Social platforms also help individuals cope with depression and provide comfort through shared emotions. They foster community connections and promote relationship maintenance both online and offline. Additionally, they encourage personal expression and aid in shaping an individual's sense of identity. Lastly, these digital spaces facilitate the establishment and upkeep of friendships and relationships. In summary, social media provides avenues for sharing knowledge, receiving support, forming bonds, and enhancing overall mental health (Sadagheyani and Tatari, 2020).

Negative Impact

The studies suggest a predominantly negative impact of social media on mental health. Increased Facebook use has been correlated with depression, loneliness, and lower self-esteem among high school and college students. Negative interactions on social networking sites are associated with greater depressive symptoms, and there's evidence linking social media to anxiety and compulsive behaviour, especially among younger generations. The concept of Phantom Vibration Syndrome underscores the adverse effects of constant connectivity. Overall, these findings suggest a need for awareness and responsible use of social media to mitigate its potential negative impact on mental health (Strickland, 2014).

DATA COLLECTION

The qualitative methodology involves young adults who use social media regularly. An online questionnaire survey was conducted using Google Forms (Ahmed, 2023). The data is collected from primary sources. Initially, demographic data which is collected from 60 college students. Then, a survey or questionnaire is used to collect data on social media usage, social life activity, and impact of social media. To ensure honesty, the survey is made anonymous. After collecting the data, it is entered into a spreadsheet or statistical software for analysis. Data cleaning is then conducted to check for missing or incomplete data, outliers, or unusual values that could skew the analysis.

Figure 1. Questionnaire

Figure 2. Do you feel that social media has a positive or negative impact on your mental health?

Question	Option	Percentage
Do you feel that social media has a positive or negative impact on your mental health?	Positive	33%
	Negative	13%
	Neutral	53%

Figure 3. How many hours do you spend on social media platforms?

Question	Option	Percentage
How many hours do you spend on social media platforms?	Less than 1 hour	10%
	1-2 hours	32%
	2-4 hours	42%
	More than 4 hours	17%

Figure 4. How would you describe your social life?

Question	Option	Percentage
How would you describe your social life?	Very active	15%
	Moderately active	67%
	Not very active	18%

Figure 5. Do you think social media platforms should provide more mental health support or resources?

Question	Option	Percentage
Do you think social media platforms should provide more mental health support or resources?	Yes	55%
	No	27%
	Unsure	18%

Figure 6. How do you think social media will impact mental health in the future?

Question	Option	Percentage
How do you think social media will impact mental health in the future?	Positively	38%
	Negatively	33%
	Unsure	28%

DATA ANALYSIS

The data is analysed by calculating the percentage of people in each category of social media usage, social life activity, source of emotional support, and impact of social media. The findings are compared across different categories, such as age groups or gender, to identify trends or patterns. Finally, the results are presented in a clear and understandable way, using tables, charts, and graphs if necessary, and recommendations or suggestions are provided based on the analysis.

Figure 7. Do you feel that social media has a positive or negative impact on your mental health?

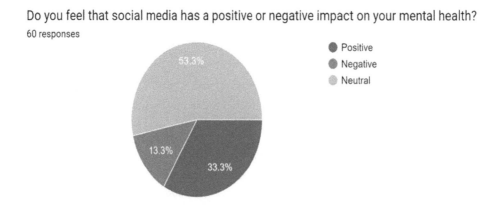

Do you feel that social media has a positive or negative impact on your mental health?
60 responses

Figure 8. How many hours a day do you spend on social media platforms?

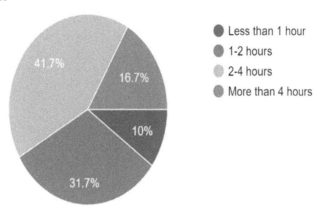

Figure 9. How would you describe your social life?

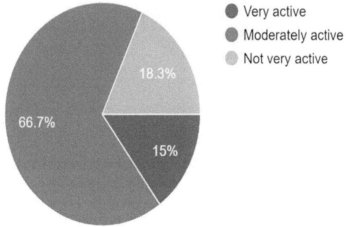

Figure 10. Do you think social media platforms should provide more mental health support or resources?

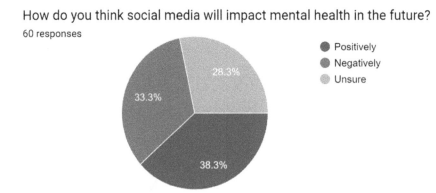

Do you think social media platforms should provide more mental health support or resources?
60 responses

- Yes
- No
- Unsure

26.7%
18.3%
55%

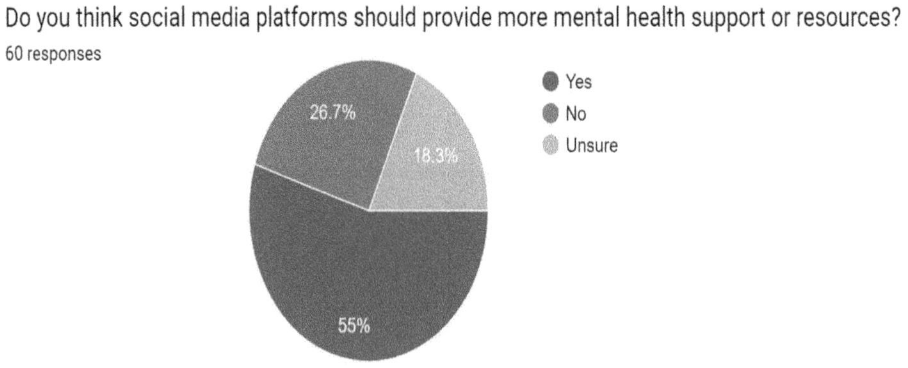

Figure 11. How do you think social media will impact mental health in the future?

How do you think social media will impact mental health in the future?
60 responses

- Positively
- Negatively
- Unsure

28.3%
33.3%
38.3%

FINDINGS

The research findings paint a complex picture of the relationship between social media usage and mental health perceptions. While a notable portion of respondents (33%) view social media as having a positive impact on mental health, indicating potential benefits such as increased social connectedness, access to support networks, and opportunities for self-expression and validation, there remains a significant minority (13%) who perceive negative consequences, such as feelings of inadequacy, social comparison, cyberbullying, and addiction. The majority of participants (53%), however, maintain a neutral stance, suggesting a recognition of both positive and negative aspects without strongly leaning towards one side. Delving deeper into participants' social media habits, the data reveals varied usage patterns. While 42% of respondents spend between 2-4 hours per day on social media platforms, and 17% exceed 4 hours, a significant portion (42%) limit their usage to 1-2 hours daily, with only 10% spending less than an hour. Despite this substantial time investment in online interactions, a majority of participants (67%) describe their social life as moderately active, indicating a balanced engagement with both digital and face-to-face social interactions. This finding suggests that while social media may play a role in shaping social interactions, it does not necessarily replace or diminish offline social connections for most individuals.

Furthermore, participants express a clear desire for social media platforms to provide more mental health support or resources, with 55% of respondents advocating for such interventions. This suggests a recognition of the potential impact of social media on mental well-being and a call for platforms to take responsibility for addressing associated challenges and providing assistance to users in need. Looking towards the future, opinions on the potential impact of social media on mental health remain divided. While 38% of respondents foresee positive outcomes, such as improved access to mental health resources, destigmatization of mental health issues, and enhanced social support networks, an almost equal proportion (33%) anticipate negative repercussions, including increased feelings of isolation, dependence on digital interactions, and exacerbation of mental health issues. A notable percentage (28%) remain unsure about the future impact, indicating the complexity and uncertainty surrounding this issue. Overall, the research findings highlight the need for continued investigation into the nuanced relationship between social media usage and mental health outcomes, as well as the importance of implementing supportive measures and resources within social media platforms to mitigate potential negative effects and promote user well-being.

IMPLICATIONS OR SUGGESTIONS

The proposed research paper seeks to provide a nuanced understanding of the relationship between social media use and mental health among young adults, recognizing the multifaceted nature of this phenomenon. Utilizing Google Forms as a data collection tool offers a practical and accessible means of gathering insights into current social media trends and usage patterns among the target demographic. By employing a qualitative methodology, the study aims to delve deeper into individual experiences, preferences, and perceptions regarding social media platforms, their usage habits, and the perceived impact on mental well-being. The qualitative approach involvesin-depth interviews or surveys with young adults who regularly use social media, allowing for rich, detailed accounts of their experiences. Through open-ended questions, participants were encouraged to reflect on various aspects of their social media use, including motivations, behaviours, emotional responses, and coping mechanisms. Additionally, factors such as personality traits, pre-existing mental health conditions, peer influences, and parental monitoring were explored to understand how they interact with social media use and contribute to mental health outcomes. Thematic analysis are employed to systematically analyse the qualitative data, identifying recurring themes, patterns, and insights across participant responses. This methodological approach enables the researcher to uncover the complexities and nuances of social media's impact on mental health, capturing both positive and negative aspects of the experience. Themes may encompass a range of topics, including feelings of social connection and support, experiences of loneliness and isolation, comparisons and self-esteem, digital boundaries and self-regulation, and strategies for managing mental well-being in the digital age. The implications of the research findings extend to various stakeholders, including mental health professionals, educators, parents, policymakers, and social media platforms. Recommendations may include the development of educational resources and interventions to promote digital literacy and well-being, the implementation of platform features that prioritize user well-being and safety, guidance for parents on supporting healthy social media use among their children, and the integration of mental health support services within educational and community settings. Furthermore, the research may inform future studies exploring longitudinal trends, cross-cultural differences, and the efficacy of interventions aimed at promoting healthy social media habits and mitigating negative mental health outcomes among young adults. By engaging in interdisciplinary collaboration and ongoing research efforts, stakeholders can work together to address the complex challenges and opportunities presented by social media in the context of mental health and well-being.

LIMITATIONS

This research paper investigating the intricate relationship between social media usage patterns and mental health outcomes among young adults faces several methodological limitations. Firstly, the study's sampling strategy could introduce selection bias by focusing exclusively on young adults who engage with social media regularly. Consequently, individuals who use social media infrequently or not at all may be overlooked, potentially skewing the representation of the broader population and limiting the generalizability of the findings. Furthermore, the reliance on self-reported data from participants may introduce inaccuracies and biases. For instance, individuals may be inclined to underreport or overreport their social media usage or the impact it has on their mental well-being due to social desirability bias or memory recall limitations. Additionally, the cross-sectional nature of the study design only captures a single snapshot of social media behaviours and mental health status at a specific point in time, precluding the ability to establish causal relationships or examine temporal dynamics. Longitudinal research would be necessary to elucidate the long-term effects and trajectories of social media use on mental health outcomes. Moreover, the study's narrow focus on young adults may overlook important variations in social media experiences and mental health implications across different age cohorts and demographic groups. Thematic analysis, while a valuable qualitative method for identifying patterns and themes within qualitative data, is inherently subjective and may be influenced by researcher biases. Furthermore, environmental factors such as socio-economic status, cultural background, and familial dynamics may not be adequately addressed or controlled for in the analysis, potentially confounding the observed associations between social media use and mental health outcomes. Lastly, the rapid evolution of social media platforms and technologies introduces a challenge in maintaining the relevance and applicability of the findings over time. As social media landscapes continue to evolve, future research will be needed to adapt methodologies and explore emerging platforms' impacts on mental health. Acknowledging and mitigating these methodological limitations are crucial for ensuring the validity, reliability, and applicability of the study's findings and recommendations.

CONCLUSION

The culmination of this research underscores the intricate interplay between social media engagement and the mental well-being of young adults. As the digital landscape evolves, it becomes imperative to grasp the nuanced dynamics shaping individuals' experiences within virtual spaces. Our exploration illuminated a spectrum of effects, both positive and negative, stemming from social media interactions, each intertwined with diverse personal and environmental factors. Our investigation unveiled a paradoxical reality where social media serves as both a conduit for connection and a harbinger of isolation. While it fosters a sense of community and facilitates communication, it also engenders feelings of loneliness and detachment. The significance of individual attributes, such as personality traits and existing mental health conditions, cannot be overstated. These factors influence how individuals navigate and respond to the digital realm, amplifying or mitigating its impact on their psychological well-being. Moreover, our findings underscored the influential role of environmental factors, including peer pressure and parental monitoring. The social context within which young adults engage with social media shapes their experiences and coping mechanisms. Understanding these contextual influences is paramount in devising tailored interventions that resonate with the lived realities of individuals.

Through qualitative inquiry, we delved into the rich tapestry of experiences shared by young adults, unravelling a mosaic of coping strategies employed to navigate the complexities of social media use. From cultivating digital boundaries to seeking offline support networks, participants showcased resilience in the face of digital adversity. Thematic analysis illuminated recurring motifs, providing a roadmap for interventionists and educators seeking to foster a healthier digital ecosystem. In light of our research, mental health professionals and educators are called upon to adopt a holistic approach to promoting digital well-being among young adults. This entails equipping individuals with the tools to critically evaluate online content, fostering supportive digital communities, and nurturing self-awareness in navigating virtual spaces. Additionally, collaborative efforts are needed to advocate for policies that safeguard the mental health of digital natives. Looking ahead, the imperative for continued inquiry remains unabated. Longitudinal studies can elucidate the enduring effects of social media use on mental health trajectories, while targeted interventions tailored to specific demographic groups can yield actionable insights for fostering resilience in the digital age. By embracing these endeavours, we can forge a path towards a future where social media serves as a catalyst for positive social change, rather than a source of distress.

REFERENCES

Albert, M., Becker, T., Mccrone, P., & Thornicroft, G. (1998). Social networks and mental health service utilisation-a literature review. *The International Journal of Social Psychiatry*, *44*(4), 248–266. doi:10.1177/002076409804400402 PMID:10459509

Baral, R., & Bhargava, S. (2010). Work-family enrichment as a mediator between organizational interventions for work-life balance and job outcomes. *Journal of Managerial Psychology*, *25*(3), 274–300. doi:10.1108/02683941011023749

Barry, C. T., Sidoti, C. L., Briggs, S. M., Reiter, S. R., & Lindsey, R. A. (2017). Adolescent social media use and mental health from adolescent and parent perspectives. *Journal of Adolescence*, *61*(1), 1–11. doi:10.1016/j.adolescence.2017.08.005 PMID:28886571

Barthorpe, A., Winstone, L., Mars, B., & Moran, P. (2020). Is social media screen time really associated with poor adolescent mental health? A time use diary study. *Journal of Affective Disorders*, *274*, 864–870. doi:10.1016/j.jad.2020.05.106 PMID:32664027

De Choudhury, M. (2013, October). Role of social media in tackling challenges in mental health. In *Proceedings of the 2nd international workshop on Socially-aware multimedia* (pp. 49-52). ACM. 10.1145/2509916.2509921

Haddad, J. M., Macenski, C., Mosier-Mills, A., Hibara, A., Kester, K., Schneider, M., Conrad, R. C., & Liu, C. H. (2021). The impact of social media on college mental health during the COVID-19 pandemic: A multinational review of the existing literature. *Current Psychiatry Reports*, *23*(11), 1–12. doi:10.1007/s11920-021-01288-y PMID:34613542

Hilty, D. M., Stubbe, D., McKean, A. J., Hoffman, P. E., Zalpuri, I., Myint, M. T., Joshi, S. V., Pakyu-rek, M., & Li, S. T. T. (2023). A scoping review of social media in child, adolescents and young adults: Research findings in depression, anxiety and other clinical challenges. *BJPsych Open*, *9*(5), e152. doi:10.1192/bjo.2023.523 PMID:37563766

Liu, M., Xue, J., Zhao, N., Wang, X., Jiao, D., & Zhu, T. (2021). Using social media to explore the consequences of domestic violence on mental health. [NP.]. *Journal of Interpersonal Violence*, *36*(3-4), NP1965–NP1985, 1985NP. doi:10.1177/0886260518757756 PMID:29441804

Monks, H., Cardoso, P., Papageorgiou, A., Carolan, C., Costello, L., & Thomas, L. (2015). *Young people's views regarding participation in mental health and wellbeing research through social media.*

O'Reilly, M., Dogra, N., Whiteman, N., Hughes, J., Eruyar, S., & Reilly, P. (2018). Is social media bad for mental health and wellbeing? Exploring the perspectives of adolescents. *Clinical Child Psychology and Psychiatry*, *23*(4), 601–613. doi:10.1177/1359104518775154 PMID:29781314

Robinson, P., Turk, D., Jilka, S., & Cella, M. (2019). Measuring attitudes towards mental health using social media: Investigating stigma and trivialisation. *Social Psychiatry and Psychiatric Epidemiology*, *54*(1), 51–58. doi:10.1007/s00127-018-1571-5 PMID:30069754

Sadagheyani, H. E., & Tatari, F. (2020). Investigating the role of social media on mental health. *Mental Health and Social Inclusion*, *25*(1), 41–51. doi:10.1108/MHSI-06-2020-0039

Shali, S. K. (2018). The Impact of Social Networking on Society with special emphasis on Adolescents in India. *International Journal of Social Science and Humanities Research*, *6*(2), 662–669.

Sigroha, A. (2014). Impact of work life balance on working women: a comparative analysis. *The business & management review, 5*(3), 22.

Thorstad, R., & Wolff, P. (2019). Predicting future mental illness from social media: A big-data approach. *Behavior Research Methods*, *51*(4), 1586–1600. doi:10.3758/s13428-019-01235-z PMID:31037606

Compilation of References

Sharma, A., & Sheth, J. (2005). International e-marketing. *Journal of Business Research*, *22*(6), 611–622.

Gera, R., Assadi, D., & Starnawska, M. (Eds.). (2023). *Artificial Intelligence, Fintech, and Financial Inclusion*. CRC Press. doi:10.1201/9781003125204

Przhedetskiy, Y. V., Przhedetskaya, N. V., Przhedetskaya, V. Y., Bondarenko, V. A., & Borzenko, K. V. (2018). *The role of social-ethical marketing and information and communication technologies in response to challenges of oncology*.

Aaronson, S. A. (2022). *Wicked problems might inspire greater data sharing* (No. 2022-09).

Aburrous, M., Hossain, M. A., Dahal, K., & Thabtah, F. (2010). Intelligent phishing detection system for e-banking using fuzzy data mining. *Expert Systems with Applications*, *37*(12), 7913–7921. doi:10.1016/j.eswa.2010.04.044

Accenture. (2013). *Top retail holiday trends: Holiday shopping survey results 2013*. Accenture.

ACFE. (2010). *Report to the Nation on Occupational Fraud and Abuse. The Association of Certified Fraud Examiners*. ACFE. www.acfe.com

Acharya, V. V., & Johnson, T. C. (2007). Insider trading in credit derivatives. *Journal of Financial Economics*, *84*(1), 110–141. doi:10.1016/j.jfineco.2006.05.003

Adams, F. (2019). Incident Response Plans. *Journal of Cybersecurity*, *10*(2), 78–96. doi:10.7890/jcs.2019.02.001

Adams, F. (2019). Scrutinizing Third-Party Data Handling Practices. *Journal of Privacy and Ethics*, *12*(3), 78–101. doi:10.5678/jpe.2019.03.001

Agarwal, G. K., & Medury, Y. (2014). Internal Auditor as Accounting Fraud Buster. *IUP Journal of Accounting Research & Audit Practices, 13*(1).

Aggarwal, A., Mittal, R., Gupta, S., & Mittal, A. (2019). Internet of things driven perceived value co-creation in smart cities of the future: A PLS-SEM based predictive model. *Journal of Computational and Theoretical Nanoscience*, *16*(9), 4053–4058. doi:10.1166/jctn.2019.8292

Aguinis, H., Henle, C. A., & Beaty Jr., J. C. (2001). Virtual Reality Technology: A New Tool for Personnel Selection. *International Journal of Selection and Assessment, 9*(1).

Ahmad, A. Y. B., Gongada, T. N., Shrivastava, G., Gabbi, R. S., Islam, S., & Nagaraju, K. (2023). E-commerce trend analysis and management for Industry 5.0 using user data analysis. *International Journal of Intelligent Systems and Applications in Engineering*, *11*(11s), 135–150.

Ahmed, K., & Courtis, J. K. (1999). Associations between corporate characteristics and disclosure levels in annual reports: A meta-analysis. *The British Accounting Review*, *31*(1), 35–36. doi:10.1006/bare.1998.0082

Ahmed, K., & Nicholls, D. (1994). The impact of non-financial company characteristics on mandatory compliance in developing countries: The case of Bangladesh. *The International Journal of Accounting, 29*(1), 60–77.

Ajayi, G. (2022). *Influence Of Instagram On Young Adults'perception Of Self: A Study Of Students Of Mountain Top University.*

Ajinkya, B., Bhojraj, S., & Sengupta, P. (2005). The Association Between Outside Directors, Institutional Investors, and the Properties of Management Earnings Forecasts. *Journal of Accounting Research, 43*(3), 343–376. doi:10.1111/j.1475-679x.2005.00174.x

Ajzen, I. (1991). The theory of planned behavior. *Organizational Behavior and Human Decision Processes, 50*(2), 179–211. doi:10.1016/0749-5978(91)90020-T

Akbas, H.E. (2014). Company characteristics and environmental disclosure: An empirical investigation on companies listed on Borsa Istanbul 100 Index. *Journal of Accounting and Finance,* 145-163.

Akhilomen, J. (2013). *Data Mining Application for Cyber Credit-Card Fraud Detection System.* Advances in Data Mining, Applications and Theoritical Aspects. doi:10.1007/978-3-642-39736-3_17

Aktas, R., Kayalidere, K., & Kargin, M. (2013). "CSR and analysis of sustainability reports in Turkey," *International Journal of Economics and Finance, 5*(3), ● Bhasin, M.L. (2012), "Corporate environmental reporting on the internet: An exploratory study', *International. Journal of. Managerial and Financial Accounting, 4*(1), 78–103.

Akter, S., & Wamba, S. M. (2016). Big data analytics in E-commerce: a systematic review and agenda for future research. *The International Journal on Networked Business.*

Albert, M., Becker, T., Mccrone, P., & Thornicroft, G. (1998). Social networks and mental health service utilisation-a literature review. *The International Journal of Social Psychiatry, 44*(4), 248–266. doi:10.1177/002076409804400402 PMID:10459509

Albrecht, W. S. (1996). Employee fraud: internal auditors must train themselves to recognize fraud symptoms and pursue the truth. *Internal auditor, 53*(5), 26-36.

Alchemer.com. (2016). *Mobile Ratings: The Good, The Bad & The Ugly.* Alchemer. https://www.alchemer.com/resources/blog/mobile-ratings-good-bad-ugly

Aldboush, H. H., & Ferdous, M. (2023). Building Trust in Fintech: An Analysis of Ethical and Privacy Considerations in the Intersection of Big Data, AI, and Customer Trust. *International Journal of Financial Studies, 11*(3), 90. doi:10.3390/ijfs11030090

Alhayani, B., Mohammed, H. J., Chaloob, I. Z., & Ahmed, J. S. (2021). Effectiveness of artificial intelligence techniques against cyber security risks apply of IT industry. *Materials Today: Proceedings,* 531. doi:10.1016/j.matpr.2021.02.531

Allahrakha, N. (2023). Balancing Cyber-security and Privacy: Legal and Ethical Considerations in the Digital Age. *Legal Issues in the Digital Age, 4*(2), 78–121.

Alleyne, P., Persaud, N., Alleyne, P., Greenidge, D., & Sealy, P. (2010). Perceived effectiveness of fraud detection audit procedures in a stock and warehousing cycle: Additional evidence from Barbados. *Managerial Auditing Journal, 25*(6), 553–568. doi:10.1108/02686901011054863

Amani, F. A., & Fadlalla, A. M. (2017). Data mining applications in accounting: A review of the literature and organizing framework. *International Journal of Accounting Information Systems, 24*, 32–58. doi:10.1016/j.accinf.2016.12.004

Amelia, A., & Baldwin, C. E. (2006). *Opportunities for Artificial Intelligence development in the Accounting domain: The case for auditing.* Wiley Interscience.

Anderson, J. C., & Gerbing, D. W. (1988). Structural equation modeling in practice: A review and recommended two-step approach. *Psychological Bulletin*, *103*(3), 411–423. doi:10.1037/0033-2909.103.3.411

App Radar. (2020). *How ratings and reviews affect consumers' decision to download apps.* Business of Apps.https://www.businessofapps.com/insights/ratings-reviews-affect-consumer-decision-download-apps

Arhin, S. (2019). THE IMPACT OF FRAUD ON THE FINANCIAL PERFORMANCE OF MOBILE PAYMENT (Telecom) COMPANIES IN GHANA. *THE IMPACT OF FRAUD ON THE FINANCIAL PERFORMANCE OF MOBILE PAYMENT (Telecom). COMPANIES IN GHANA.*, *22*(1), 18–18.

Aris, I. B., Sahbusdin, R. K. Z., & Amin, A. F. M. (2015, May). Impacts of IoT and big data to automotive industry. In *2015 10th Asian control conference (ASCC)* (pp. 1-5). IEEE.

Aris, N. A., Arif, S. M. M., Othman, R., & Zain, M. M. (2015). Fraudulent financial statement detection using statistical techniques: The case of small medium automotive enterprise. [JABR]. *Journal of Applied Business Research*, *31*(4), 1469–1478. doi:10.19030/jabr.v31i4.9330

Atzori, L., Iera, A., & Morabito, G. (2010). The internet of things: A survey. *Computer Networks*, *54*(15), 2787–2805. doi:10.1016/j.comnet.2010.05.010

Au, E. H., & Lee, J. J. (2017). Virtual reality in education: A tool for learning in the experience age. *International Journal of Innovation in Education*, *4*(4), 215. doi:10.1504/IJIIE.2017.091481

Authority, C. a. M. (2021). *CMA to investigate Amazon and Google over fake reviews.* GOV.UK. https://www.gov.uk/government/news/cma-to-investigate-amazon-and-google-over-fake-reviews

Azrina Mohd Yusof, N., & Ling Lai, M. (2014). An integrative model in predicting corporate tax fraud. *Journal of Financial Crime*, *21*(4), 424–432. doi:10.1108/JFC-03-2013-0012

Baker, L. (2009). Belkin caught buying fake consumer reviews. *Search Engine Journal*. https://www.searchenginejournal.com/belkin-caught-buying-fake-consumer-reviews/8325/

Baldwin, A. A., Brown, C. E., & Trinkle, B. S. (2006). Opportunities for Artificial Intelligence Development in Accounint Domain: The Case for Auditing. *Intelligent systems in Accounting, Finance and Management.*

Bandara, R., Fernando, M., & Akter, S. (2020). Privacy concerns in E-commerce: A taxonomy and a future research agenda. *Electronic Markets*, *30*(3), 629–647. doi:10.1007/s12525-019-00375-6

Banerjee, N., Dutta, A., & Dasgupta, T. (2010). A Study on Customers' Attitude towards Online Shopping - An Indian Perspective. *Indian Journal of Marketing*, *40*(11), 43–52.

Baral, R., & Bhargava, S. (2010). Work-family enrichment as a mediator between organizational interventions for work-life balance and job outcomes. *Journal of Managerial Psychology*, *25*(3), 274–300. doi:10.1108/02683941011023749

Barker, K. J., D'amato, J., & Sheridon, P. (2008). Credit card fraud: Awareness and prevention. *Journal of Financial Crime*, *15*(4), 398–410. doi:10.1108/13590790810907236

Barnes, J. G. (1995). Internationalization of Revised UCC Article 5—Letters of Credit. *Nw. J. Int'l L. & Bus.*, *16*, 215.

Barona, R., & Anita, E. A. M. (2017). A survey on data breach challenges in cloud computing security: Issues and threats. *2017 International Conference on Circuit, Power and Computing Technologies (ICCPCT)*, (pp. 1–8). IEEE. 10.1109/ICCPCT.2017.8074287

Barricklow, A. (2021). *Unsupervised Machine Learning to Create Rule-Based Wire Fraud Detection.* Utica College.

Barry, C. T., Sidoti, C. L., Briggs, S. M., Reiter, S. R., & Lindsey, R. A. (2017). Adolescent social media use and mental health from adolescent and parent perspectives. *Journal of Adolescence*, *61*(1), 1–11. doi:10.1016/j.adolescence.2017.08.005 PMID:28886571

Barthorpe, A., Winstone, L., Mars, B., & Moran, P. (2020). Is social media screen time really associated with poor adolescent mental health? A time use diary study. *Journal of Affective Disorders*, *274*, 864–870. doi:10.1016/j.jad.2020.05.106 PMID:32664027

Basak, S., Basu, P., Avittathur, B., & Sikdar, S. (2017). A game theoretic analysis of multichannel retail in the context of showroominh. *Decision Support Systems*, *103*, 34–45. doi:10.1016/j.dss.2017.09.002

Bathla, D., & Awasthi, S. (2021). Analytical Impact of Technology on the COVID-19 Pandemic. In Blockchain Technology and Applications for Digital Marketing (pp. 236-249). IGI Global.

Bathla, D., Awasthi, S., & Ahuja, R. (2022). PESTEL Analysis of the Automotive Industry. In Applying Metalytics to Measure Customer Experience in the Metaverse (pp. 143-160). IGI Global. doi:10.4018/978-1-6684-6133-4.ch013

Bathla, D., Awasthi, S., & Singh, K. (2021). Enriching User Experience by Transforming Consumer Data Into Deeper Insights. In Big Data Analytics for Improved Accuracy, Efficiency, and Decision Making in Digital Marketing (pp. 1-18). IGI Global. doi:10.4018/978-1-7998-7231-3.ch001

Baz, R., Samsudin, R. S., Che-Ahmad, A., & Popoola, O. M. J. (2016). Capability component of fraud and fraud prevention in the Saudi Arabian banking sector. *International Journal of Economics and Financial Issues*, *6*, S4.

Belk, R. (2020). Ethical issues in service robotics and artifcial intelligence. *Service Industries Journal*. doi:10.1080/02642069.2020.1727892

Bell, T. B., & Carcello, J. V. (2000). A Decision Aid for accesing the Likelihood of fraudulent Financial Reporting. *A Jouranal of Practice and Theory*.

Bentler, P. M., & Bonett, D. G. (1980). Significance test and goodness of fit in the analysis of covariance structures. *Psychological Bulletin*, *88*(3), 588–606. doi:10.1037/0033-2909.88.3.588

Berber, N., Đorđević, B., & Milanović, S. (2018). Electronic human resource management (e-HRM): A new concept for digital age. *Strategic Management*, *23*(2), 22–32. doi:10.5937/StraMan1802022B

Berdiyeva, O., Islam, M. U., & Saeedi, M. (2021). Artificial Intelligence in Accounting and Finance: Meta-Analysis. *International Business Review*.

Bhardwaj, B. R., & Malhotra, A. (2013). Green banking strategies: Sustainability through corporate entrepreneurship. *Greener Journal of Business and Management Studies*, *3*(4), 180–193. doi:10.15580/GJBMS.2013.4.122412343

Bhasin, M. L. (2007). Forensic accounting: A new paradigm for niche consulting. *The Chartered Accountant, January*.

Bhasin, M. L. (2015). Menace of frauds in the Indian banking industry: An empirical study. *Australian Journal of Business and Management Research*, *4*(12), 21–33. doi:10.52283/NSWRCA.AJBMR.20150412A02

Bhatia, S. (2016, August 11). ASCI upholds complaints against Coca Cola, Patanjali, Vivel and others. *The Economic Times*. https://economictimes.indiatimes.com/industry/cons-products/fmcg/asci-upholds-complaints-against-coca-cola-patanjali-vivel-and-others/articleshow/53679318.cms

Bhattacharjee, S., Agarwal, A., Malhotra, P., Bahl, S., Sharma, A., & Bir, A. (2020). *The Road Ahead: Digital Challenges for the Indian Economy.* Carnegie India. https://carnegieindia.org/2020/10/15/road-ahead-digital-challenges-for-indian-economy-pub-82924

Bhuiyan, M. H. U., Pallab, K. B., & Suman, P. C. (2007). Corporate Internet Reporting Practice in Developing Economies: Evidence from Bangladesh'. *Cost and Management*, *35*(5).

Bickart, B., & Schindler, R. M. (2002). Internet forums as influential sources of consumer information. *Journal of Interactive Marketing*, *15*(3), 31–40. doi:10.1002/dir.1014

Blasingame, J. (2014). *The age of the customer: Prepare for the Moment of Relevance.* SBN Books.

Bloem, C. (2021). *Eighty-four percent of people trust online reviews as much as friends. Here is how to manage what they see.* Inc.com. https://www.inc.com/craig-bloem/84-percent-of-people-trust-online-reviews-as-much-.html

Bloomberg. (2018, December 13). Ponzi schemes thrive in Indian e-commerce boom. *Livemint*. https://www.livemint.com/Money/J5stT8m5VjhXeSZk9ZcHTO/Ponzi-schemes-thrive-in-Indian-ecommerce-boom.html

Blümel, E. (2013). Global challenges and innovative technologies geared toward new markets: Prospects for virtual and augmented reality. Procedia Computer Science, 25, 4–13. https://doi.org/. procs.2013.11.002 doi:10.1016/j

Blumenthal-Barby, J., & Burroughs, H. (2012). Seeking better health care outcomes: The ethics of using the "Nudge.". *The American Journal of Bioethics*, *12*(2), 1–10. doi:10.1080/15265161.2011.634481 PMID:22304506

Boateng, R., Longe, O. B., Mbarika, V., Avevor, I., & Isabalija, S. R. (2010). Cyber Crime and Criminality in Ghana: Its Forms and Implications. AMCIS, Bologna, J. (1994). How to detect and prevent embezzlement. *The White Paper, August/September, 4.*

Boerman, S. C., Kruikemeier, S., & Zuiderveen Borgesius, F. J. (2018). Online behavioral advertising: A literature review and research agenda. *Journal of Advertising*, *47*(1), 33–63.

Bolton, R. J., & Hand, D. J. (2002). Statistical fraud detection: A review. *Statistical Science*, *17*(3), 235–255. doi:10.1214/ss/1042727940

Bonawitz, K., Eichner, H., Grieskamp, W., Huba, D., Ingerman, A., & Ivanov, V. (2017). *Towards Federated Learning At Scale: System Design.* arXiv:1902.01046v1. 2019, 1–13.

Booms, B. H., & Bitner, M. J. (1980). Service firm marketing and organization. *Journal of Marketing*, 47–51.

Bora, B. J., & Das, T. C. (2013). Corporate environmental reporting in the context of recent changes in regulatory framework with special reference to India.

Borin, N., & Metcalf, L. E. (2010). Integrating Sustainability into the marketing Curriculum: Learning activities that facilitate sustainable marketing practices. *Journal of Marketing Education*, *32*(2), 140–154. doi:10.1177/0273475309360156

Bossard, K., & Blum, S. (2004). *Reading the red flags of fraud.* Pennsylvania CPA Journal.

Boukari, B. E., Ravi, A., & Msahli, M. (2021). Machine learning detection for smishing frauds. 2021 IEEE 18th Annual Consumer Communications & Networking Conference (CCNC), Buckhoff, T. A. (2002). Preventing employee fraud by minimizing opportunity. *The CPA Journal*, *72*(5), 64.

Bourlakis, M., Papagiannidis, S., & Fox, H. (2008). E-consumer Behaviour: Past, Present and Future Trajectories of an Evolving Retail Revolution. *International Journal of E-Business Research*, *4*(3), 64–76. doi:10.4018/jebr.2008070104

Bredillet, C. (2014). Ethics in project management: Some Aristotelian insights. *International Journal of Managing Projects in Business, 7*(4), 548–565. doi:10.1108/IJMPB-08-2013-0041

Brigger, D., Bronkar, S., & Dearing, C. (2014). The Value of Ethical Marketing. *Ubiquity, 2014*(February), 1–8.

Brown, B. (2021). Ethical Use of AI and Automation in Marketing. *Journal of Marketing Ethics, 18*(1), 56–78. doi:10.5678/jme.2021.01.001

Brown, B. (2021). Robust Data Security. *Journal of Cybersecurity, 10*(1), 34–56. doi:10.7890/jcs.2021.01.001

Brown, Z., & Tiggemann, M. (2016). Attractive celebrity and peer images on Instagram: Effect on women's mood and body image. *Body Image, 19*, 37–43. doi:10.1016/j.bodyim.2016.08.007 PMID:27598763

Bruner, J. S. (1975). The Ontogenesis of Speech Acts. *Journal of Child Language, 2*(1), 1–19. doi:10.1017/S0305000900000866

Bruzzone, A., Cimino, A., Longo, F., & Mirabelli, G. (2010). TRAINPORTS-TRAINing in marine port by using simulation. International Conference on Harbour, Maritime and Multimodal Logistics Modelling and Simulation, 1(March), 25–32.

Brynjolfsson, E., & Kahin, B. (2000). *Understanding digital economy.* MIT Press. doi:10.7551/mitpress/6986.001.0001

Buhalis, D., & Sinarta, Y. (2019). Real-time co-creation and nowness service: Lessons from tourism and hospitality. *Journal of Travel & Tourism Marketing, 36*(5), 563–582. doi:10.1080/10548408.2019.1592059

Bureau, E. T. (2018, January 11). Without consent: Airtel Payments Bank opens accounts of subscribers. *The Economic Times.* https://economictimes.indiatimes.com/industry/banking/finance/banking/without-consent-airtel-payments-bank-opens-accounts-of-subscribers/articleshow/62483222.cms?from=mdr

Burt, T. (2023, December 22). *The History of Content Marketing.* LinkedIn. https://www.linkedin.com/business/marketing/blog/linkedin-ads/our-infographic-of-the-week-a-brief-history-of-content-marketing

Business Standard. (2022). *Amazon sues admins of over 10,000 Facebook groups over fake reviews.* Business Standard. https://www.business-standard.com/article/companies/amazon-sues-admins-of-over-10-000-facebook-groups-over-fake-reviews-122072000043_1.html

Butler, P., & Peppard, J. (1998). Consumer Purchasing on the Internet: Processes and Prospects. *European Management Journal, 16*(5), 600–610. doi:10.1016/S0263-2373(98)00036-X

Cabrera, I. (2024, March 12). *How mind mapping helps marketers create Better content - Venngage.* Venngage. https://venngage.com/blog/mind-mapping/

Cadwalladr, C., & Graham-Harrison, E. (2018). Revealed: 50 million Facebook profiles harvested for Cambridge Analytica in major data breach. *The Guardian.*

Campbell, C., Sands, S., Ferraro, C., Tsao, H., & Mavrommatis, A. (2020). From data to action: How marketers can leverage AI. *Business Horizons, 63*(2), 227–243. doi:10.1016/j.bushor.2019.12.002

Carmicheal, K. (2021, August 9). *Push vs. Pull Marketing: Top Differences & How to Use Them.* Hubspot..https://blog.hubspot.com/marketing/push-vs-pull-marketing

Carminati, M., Caron, R., Maggi, F., Epifani, I., & Zanero, S. (2015). BankSealer: A decision support system for online banking fraud analysis and investigation. *Computers & security, 53*, 175-186.

Cassar, C. (2019). Business ethics and sustainable development. In Springer eBooks (pp. 139–150). doi:10.1007/978-3-030-11352-0_39

Cavus, N., Mohammed, Y. B., Gital, A. Y. U., Bulama, M., Tukur, A. M., Mohammed, D., & Hassan, A. (2022). Emotional Artificial Neural Networks and Gaussian Process-Regression-Based Hybrid Machine-Learning Model for Prediction of Security and Privacy Effects on M-Banking Attractiveness. *Sustainability (Basel)*, *14*(10), 5826. doi:10.3390/su14105826

Chaffey, D., & Ellis-Chadwick, F. (2019). *Digital Marketing*. Pearson Education.

Chakola, A. (2022). *The Impact of Social Media Influencer on the Buying Behaviour of Gen Z in India* [Doctoral dissertation, Dublin, National College of Ireland].

Chakrabarty, K. C. (2013). *Frauds in the banking sector: Causes*. Cures and Concerns.

Chakraborty, I., Paranjape, B., Kakarla, S., & Ganguly, N. (2018). Stop Clickbait: Detecting and preventing clickbaits in online news media. *2016 IEEE/ACM International Conference on Advances in Social Networks Analysis and Mining (ASONAM)*. IEEE. 10.1109/ASONAM.2016.7752207

Chakravorti, B., & Sharma, S. (2020). *Digital planet 2020: How competitiveness and trust in digital economies vary across the world*. The Fletcher School, Tufts University. https://sites.tufts.edu/digitalplanet/digital-planet-report/

Chambers, R. J. (1966). *Accounting, evaluation and economic behaviour*. Prentice Hall.

Chang, L., Li, P., Loh, R. S. M., & Chua, T. H. H. (2019). A study of Singapore adolescent girls' selfie practices, peer appearance comparisons, and body esteem on Instagram. *Body Image*, *29*, 90–99. doi:10.1016/j.bodyim.2019.03.005 PMID:30884385

Chatterjee, B., & Mir, M. Z. (2008). The current status of environmental reporting by Indian corporations. *Managerial Auditing Journal*, *23*(6), 609–629. doi:10.1108/02686900810882138

Chatterjee, D. (2021). Emerging Data Governance Issues. In *India*. Data Governance Network.

Chaudhary, A. (2011). Changing structure of Indian textiles industry after MFA (MultiFibre Agreement) phase out: A global perspective'. *Far East Journal of Psychology and Business*, *2*(2), 1–23.

Chaudhary, G. (2023). Environmental Sustainability: Can Artificial Intelligence be an Enabler for SDGs? Dhanabalan, T., Sathish, A., & Tamilnadu, K. (2018). *TRANSFORMING INDIAN INDUSTRIES THROUGH ARTIFICIAL INTELLIGENCE AND.*, *9*(10), 835–845.

Chaudhary, K., Yadav, J., & Mallick, B. (2012). A review of fraud detection techniques: Credit card. *International Journal of Computer Applications*, *45*(1), 39–44.

Chelvarayan, A., Jie, C., & Yeo, S. F. (2021). Factors Affecting Students' Perception of Online Shopping. International Journal of Entrepreneurship. *Business and Creative Economy.*, *1*, 13–24.

Cheng, X., Cohen, J., & Mou, J. (2023). AI-enabled technology innovation in e-commerce. *Journal of Electronic Commerce Research*, *24*(1), 1–6.

Chen, R., & He, F. (2003). Examination of Brand Knowledge, Perceived Risk and Consumers' Intention to Adopt an Online Retailer. *Total Quality Management & Business Excellence*, *14*(6), 677–693. doi:10.1080/1478336032000053825

Chhonker, M. S., Verma, D., & Kar, D. (2017). *Ethics in Digital Marketing: Illusion or Reality. Journal of Information*. Communication and Ethics in Society. doi:10.1108/JICES-10-2016-0036

Childers, T., Carr, C., Peck, J., & Carson, S. (2001). Hedonic and Utilitarian Motivations for Online Retail Shopping Behavior. *Journal of Retailing*, *77*(4), 511–535. doi:10.1016/S0022-4359(01)00056-2

Cho, W. K., & Gaines, B. J. (2007). Breaking the (Benford) Law. *The american statisticians.*

Choi, D., & Lee, K. (2018). An Artificial Intelligence Approach to Financial Fraud Detection. *Security and Communication Networks*, *2018*, 1–15. doi:10.1155/2018/5483472

Choithani, T., Chowdhury, A., Patel, S., Patel, P., Patel, D., & Shah, M. (2022). A comprehensive study of artificial intelligence and cybersecurity on Bitcoin, crypto currency and banking system. *Annals of Data Science*, 1-33.

Chouinard, Y., Ellison, J., & Ridgeway, R. (2011). *The Responsible Company: What We've Learned From Patagonia's First 40 Years*. Patagonia.

Churchill,G.A.jr(1979), j mark res.,16(1),64-73

Ciobu, S., & Timuş-Iordachi, V. (2019). Role of the central banks in prevention and management of bank frauds. *Journal of Social Sciences*, *3*(2), 63–71.

Clark, C. E., Riera, M., & Iborra, M. (2021). Toward a theoretical framework of corporate social irresponsibility: Clarifying the gray zones between responsibility and irresponsibility. *Business & Society*, *61*(6), 1473–1511. doi:10.1177/00076503211015911

Clark, G., & Taylor, H. (2018). Employee Training and Awareness Programs. *Journal of Ethics in Business*, *22*(2), 110–128. doi:10.7890/jeb.2018.02.001

Clark, G., & Taylor, H. (2018). Rights of Individuals under Data Privacy Regulations. *Journal of Data Protection*, *28*(3), 134–155. doi:10.7890/jdp.2018.03.001

Clark, L. (2014). Ethical marketing research in the digital age—How can academics and practitioners work together? *Journal of Direct, Data and Digital Marketing Practice*, *15*(4), 258–259. doi:10.1057/dddmp.2014.17

Coie, P. 2019. Digital Currencies: International Actions and Regulation. *disponibile alla URL:* https://www. perkinscoie. com/en/news-insights/digital-currencies-international-actions-and-regulations. html

Comegys, C., Hannula, M., & Vaisanen, J. (2009). Effects of Consumer Trust and Risk on Online Purchase Decision-making: A Comparison of FINNISH and United States Students. *International Journal of Management*, *26*(2), 295–308.

Commercial Angles. (2001). Fraud Prevention. *Commercial Angles Newsletter.* www.commercialangles.com/articles/fraud_control.htm

Competitive strategy in the age of the customer. (n.d.). Forrester. https://www.forrester.com/report/Competitive-Strategy-In-The-Age-Of-The-Customer/RES59159?docid=59159

Conductor. (n.d.). *Conductor — Enterprise SEO & content marketing platform.* Conductor. https://www.conductor.com/

Confessore, N. (2018). Cambridge Analytica and Facebook: the scandal and the fallout so far. *The New York Times.* https://www.nytimes.com/2018/04/04/us/politics/cambridge-analytica-scandal-fallout.html

Consumers want more transparency on how businesses handle their data, new Cisco survey shows. (n.d.). Investor. https://investor.cisco.com/news/news-details/2022/Consumers-want-more-transparency-on-how-businesses-handle-their-data-new-Cisco-survey-shows/default.aspx

Cook, B. I., Wayne, G. F., Keithly, L., & Connolly, G. N. (2003). One size does not fit all: How the tobacco industry has altered cigarette design to target consumer groups with specific psychological and psychosocial needs. *Addiction (Abingdon, England)*, *98*(11), 1547–1561. doi:10.1046/j.1360-0443.2003.00563.x PMID:14616181

Correia, T. (2019). A Realidade Virtual e a Realidade Aumentada na Gestão da Cultura Organizacional [Instituto Superior de Contabilidade e Administração do Porto]. http://hdl.handle.net/10400.22/15983

Couldry, N., & Mejias, U. A. (2019). *The Costs of Connection: How Data Is Colonizing Human Life and Appropriating It for Capitalism.* Stanford University Press.

Cowls, J., Tsamados, A., Taddeo, M., & Floridi, L. (2021). A definition, benchmark and database of AI for social good initiatives. *Nature Machine Intelligence, 3*(2), 111–115. doi:10.1038/s42256-021-00296-0

Creswell, J. W. (2007). *Qualitative inquiry and research design: Choosing among fiveapproaches / John W* (2nd ed.). Creswell.

Cronbach, L. J. (1951). Coefficient alpha and the internal structure of tests. *Psychometrika, 16*(3), 297-334.

Damiani, L., Demartini, M., Guizzi, G., Revetria, R., & Tonelli, F. (2018). Augmented and virtual reality applications in industrial systems: A qualitative review towards the industry 4.0 era. *IFAC-PapersOnLine, 51*(11), 624–630. doi:10.1016/j.ifacol.2018.08.388

Dantas, R. M., Firdaus, R., Jaleel, F., Mata, P. N., Mata, M. N., & Li, G. (2022). Systemic Acquired Critique of Credit Card Deception Exposure through Machine Learning. *Journal of Open Innovation, 8*(4), 192. doi:10.3390/joitmc8040192

Dar, S. A., & Nagrath, D. (2023). The Impact That Social Media Has Had On Today's Generation Of Indian Youth: An Analytical Study. *Morfai Journal, 3*(2), 166-176.

Dash, S. & Kanungo, R. (2016). *Student's attitude and perception towards online shopping: an empirical study, 29.*

Daugherty, P. R., & Wilson, H. J. (2018). *Human+ machine: Reimagining work in the age of AI.* Harvard Business Press.

Dávideková, M., Mjartan, M., & Greguš, M. (2017). Utilization of Virtual Reality in Education of Employees in Slovakia. *Procedia Computer Science, 113*, 253–260. Advance online publication. doi:10.1016/j.procs.2017.08.365

Davis, A., Linvill, D. L., Hodges, L. F., Da Costa, A. F., & Lee, A. (2020). Virtual reality versus faceto-face practice: A study into situational apprehension and performance. *Communication Education, 69*(1), 70–84. doi:10.1080/03634 523.2019.1684535

De Bruyn, A., Viswanathan, V., Beh, Y. S., Brock, J. K.-U., & von Wangenheim, F. (2020). Artifcial intelligence and marketing: Pitfalls and opportunities. *Journal of Interactive Marketing, 51*, 91–105. doi:10.1016/j.intmar.2020.04.007

De Choudhury, M. (2013, October). Role of social media in tackling challenges in mental health. In *Proceedings of the 2nd international workshop on Socially-aware multimedia* (pp. 49-52). ACM. 10.1145/2509916.2509921

De Lange, D. E., Busch, T., & Delgado-Ceballos, J. (2012). Sustaining sustainability in organizations. *Journal of Business Ethics, 110*(2), 151–156. doi:10.1007/s10551-012-1425-0

Deloitte. (2015). *Deloitte India Banking Fraud Survey.* Deloitte.

Desai, R. (2015). Introduction: The materiality of nations in geopolitical economy. *World Review of Political Economy, 6*(4), 449–458.

Dewani, N. D., Khan, Z. A., Agarwal, A., Sharma, M., & Khan, S. A. (Eds.). (2022). *Handbook of Research on Cyber Law, Data Protection, and Privacy.* IGI Global. doi:10.4018/978-1-7998-8641-9

Dey, B. L., Mohanty, S., Rao, U. H., Ghose, A., & Swain, P. (2018). *Regulating digital financial services in India: A policy discussion.* Digital Asia Hub.

Dinev, T. (2006). Why spoofing is serious internet fraud. *Communications of the ACM, 49*(10), 76–82. doi:10.1145/1164394.1164398

Doe, A. B., & Johnson, C. D. (2022). The Role of Talent Acquisition in Ethical Marketing Success. *Journal of Marketing Ethics*, *10*(2), 123–145. doi:10.1234/jme.2022.01.001

Eckert, M., Volmerg, J. S., & Friedrich, C. M. (2019). Augmented reality in medicine: Systematic and bibliographic review. *Journal of Medical Internet Research*, *7*(4), e10967. doi:10.2196/10967 PMID:31025950

Elassar, A. (2019). *Skin care brand Sunday Riley wrote fake Sephora reviews for almost two years, FTC says*. CNN. https://edition.cnn.com/2019/10/22/us/sunday-riley-fake-reviews-trnd/index.html

Elena, C. A. (2016). Social Media – A Strategy in Developing Customer Relationship Management. *Procedia Economics and Finance*, *39*, 785–790. doi:10.1016/S2212-5671(16)30266-0

Elgendy, N., & Elragal, A. (2014). Big Data Analytics: A Literature Review Paper. *Lecture Notes in Computer Science*, *8557*, 214–227. doi:10.1007/978-3-319-08976-8_16

Ellen, G. (2014). *The Mobile First shopper strategy*. WARC.

Erskine, R. (2017). 20 Online reputation statistics that every business owner needs to know. *Forbes*. https://www.forbes.com/sites/ryanerskine/2017/09/19/20-online-reputation-statistics-that-every-business-owner-needs-to-know/?sh=5647de13cc5c

European Commission. (2016). *Regulation (EU) 2016/679 of the European Parliament and of the Council of 27 April 2016 on the protection of natural persons with regard to the processing of personal data and on the free movement of such data (General Data Protection Regulation)*. Official Journal of the European Union.

Ewing, M. (2019). *71% More Likely to Purchase Based on Social Media Referrals*. Hubspot. https://blog.hubspot.com/blog/tabid/6307/bid/30239/71-More-Likely-to-Purchase-Based-on-Social-Media-Referrals-Infographic.aspx

Fan, X., Thompson, B., & Wang, L. (1999). Effects of sample size, estimation methods, and model specification on structural equation modeling fit indexes. *Structural Equation Modeling*, *6*(1), 56–83. doi:10.1080/10705519909540119

Fedorova, A., Koropets, O., & Gatti, M. (2019). *Digitalization of human resource management practices and its impact on employees' well-being. Conference: Contemporary Issues in Business*. Management and Economics Engineering., doi:10.3846/cibmee.2019.075

Fenech, R., Baguant, P., & Ivanov, D. (2019). The changing role of human resource management in an era of digital transformation. *Journal of Management Information and Decision Science*, *22*(2), 166–175.

Ferrell, L., Gonzalez-Padron, T. L., & Ferrell, O. C. (2010). An Assessment of Technology in Direct Selling and Sales Management. *Journal of Personal Selling & Sales Management*, *30*, 157–165. doi:10.2753/PSS0885-3134300206

Floridi, L., & Cowls, J. (2022). A unified framework of five principles for AI in society. *Machine Learning and the City: Applications in Architecture and Urban Design*, 535–545. doi:10.1002/9781119815075.ch45

Floridi, L., Cowls, J., Beltrametti, M., Chatila, R., Chazerand, P., Dignum, V., Luetge, C., Madelin, R., Pagallo, U., Rossi, F., Schafer, B., Valcke, P., & Vayena, E. (2018). AI4People—An Ethical Framework for a Good AI Society: Opportunities, Risks, Principles, and Recommendations. *Minds and Machines*, *28*(4), 689–707. doi:10.1007/s11023-018-9482-5 PMID:30930541

Floridi, L., Cowls, J., King, T. C., & Taddeo, M. (2020). How to design AI for social good: Seven essential factors. *Science and Engineering Ethics*, *26*(3), 1771–1796. doi:10.1007/s11948-020-00213-5 PMID:32246245

Formosa, P., Wilson, M., & Richards, D. (2021). A principlist framework for cybersecurity ethics. *Computers & Security*, *109*, 102382. doi:10.1016/j.cose.2021.102382

Forsey, C. (2022, April 12). *The Evolution of Content Marketing: How It's Changed and Where It's Going in the Next Decade*. Hubspot. https://blog.hubspot.com/marketing/future-content-marketing

Fruhlinger, J. (2023). *Equifax data breach FAQ: What happened, who was affected, what was the impact?* CSO Online. https://www.csoonline.com/article/567833/equifax-data-breach-faq-what-happened-who-was-affected-what-was-the-impact.html

Gabhane, D., Varalaxmi, P., Rathod, U., Hamida, A. G. B., & Anand, B. (2023). Digital marketing trends: Analyzing the evolution of consumer behavior in the online space. *Boletin de Literatura Oral-The Literary Journal, 10*(1), 462–473.

Ganesh, A., & Raghurama, A. (2008). Status of training evaluation in commercial bank-a case Study. *Journal of social sciences and management sciences, 37*(2), 137-158.

Gapper, J. (2011). *How To Be a Rogue Trader: A Penguin Special from Portfolio*. Penguin.

Gee, J., & Button, M. (2019). *The financial cost of fraud 2019: The latest data from around the world*.

Gehl Sampath, P. (2021). Governing artificial intelligence in an age of inequality. *Global Policy, 12*(S6), 21–31. doi:10.1111/1758-5899.12940

George, J. F. (2004). The Theory of Planned Behavior and Internet Purchasing. *Internet Research, 14*(3), 198–212. doi:10.1108/10662240410542634

Gera, T., Thakur, D., & Singh, J. (2015, February). Identifying deceptive reviews using networking parameters. In *2015 International Conference on Computing and Communications Technologies (ICCCT)* (pp. 322-327). IEEE. 10.1109/ICCCT2.2015.7292769

Ghimire, A., Thapa, S., Jha, A. K., Adhikari, S., & Kumar, A. (2020, October). Accelerating business growth with big data and artificial intelligence. In *2020 Fourth International Conference on I-SMAC (IoT in Social, Mobile, Analytics and Cloud)(I-SMAC)* (pp. 441-448). IEEE. 10.1109/I-SMAC49090.2020.9243318

Ghosh, S., & Bagheri, M. (2006). The Ketan Parekh fraud and supervisory lapses of the Reserve Bank of India (RBI): A case study. *Journal of Financial Crime, 13*(1), 107–124. doi:10.1108/13590790610641279

Gillikin, J. (2020). Moral Leadership and Business Ethics. *Demand Media*.

Girasa, R. (2020). *Artificial intelligence as a disruptive technology: Economic transformation and government regulation*. Springer Nature. doi:10.1007/978-3-030-35975-1

Goel, S. (2014). Fraud detection and corporate filings. In *Communication and Language Analysis in the Corporate World* (pp. 315–332). IGI Global. doi:10.4018/978-1-4666-4999-6.ch018

Goldsmith, R. E. (1999). Personalization should be a part of the marketing mix. *Journal of Marketing Management, 15*(1-3), 59–81.

Goldsmith, R. E., & Flynn, L. R. (2005). Bricks, Clicks, and Pix: Apparel Buyers' Use of Stores, Internet, and Catalogs Compared. *International Journal of Retail & Distribution Management, 33*(4), 271–283. doi:10.1108/09590550510593202

Green, B. P., & Calderon, T. G. (1994). Using real-world cases to illustrate the power of analytical procedures. *Journal of Accounting Education, 12*(3), 245–268. doi:10.1016/0748-5751(94)90035-3

Grewal, D., Gopalkrishnan, R. I., & Michael, L. (2004). Internet Retailing: Enablers, Limiters and Market Consequences. *Journal of Business Research, 57*(7), 703–713. doi:10.1016/S0148-2963(02)00348-X

Griffin, S. E., & Rackley, C. C. (2008). Vishing. Proceedings of the 5th annual conference on Information security curriculum development, Gupta, P., & Gupta, S. (2015). Corporate frauds in India–perceptions and emerging issues. *Journal of Financial Crime.*

Gupta, P. (2020). *Digital sovereignty and the conundrum of rules: Should India ban TikTok? 3ie Working paper; 34.* New Delhi: International Initiative for Impact Evaluation (3ie). doi:10.23846/WP0034

Gupta, R., Tanwar, S., Al-Turjman, F., Italiya, P., Nauman, A., & Kim, S. W. (2020). Smart contract privacy protection using AI in cyber-physical systems: Tools, techniques and challenges. *IEEE Access : Practical Innovations, Open Solutions*, 8, 24746–24772. doi:10.1109/ACCESS.2020.2970576

Haddad, J. M., Macenski, C., Mosier-Mills, A., Hibara, A., Kester, K., Schneider, M., Conrad, R. C., & Liu, C. H. (2021). The impact of social media on college mental health during the COVID-19 pandemic: A multinational review of the existing literature. *Current Psychiatry Reports*, 23(11), 1–12. doi:10.1007/s11920-021-01288-y PMID:34613542

Haleem, A., Javaid, M., Qadri, M. A., Singh, R. P., & Suman, R. (2022). Artificial intelligence (AI) applications for marketing: A literature-based study. *International Journal of Intelligent Networks.*

Hannola, L., Richter, A., Richter, S., & Stocker, A. (2018). Empowering production workers with digitally facilitated knowledge processes–a conceptual framework. *International Journal of Production Research*, 56(14), 4729–4743. doi:10.1080/00207543.2018.1445877

Hansen, T., Moller, J. J., & Stubbe, S. H. (2004). Predicting Online Grocery Buying Intention: A Comparison of the Theory of Reasoned Action and the Theory of Planned Behavior. *International Journal of Information Management*, 24(6), 539–550. doi:10.1016/j.ijinfomgt.2004.08.004

Haq, Z. U. (2012). Perception towards Online Shopping: An Empirical Study of Indian Consumers. *Abhinav national monthly refereed journal of reasearch in commerce & management,* 1(8).

Harjoto, M. A. (2017). The impact of institutional and technical social responsibilities on the likelihood of corporate fraud. *Business & Professional Ethics Journal*, 36(2), 197–228. doi:10.5840/bpej20175257

Harris, S. (2015). *Yelp accused of bullying businesses into paying for better reviews. (2015, January 14).* CBC. https://www.cbc.ca/news/business/yelp-accused-of-bullying-businesses-into-paying-for-better-reviews-1.2899308

Harris, L., & Dennis, C. (2020). *Marketing the e-Business.* Routledge.

Haslinda, A. (2009). Evolving terms of human rescourse management and development. *The Journal of International Social Research*, 2(9), 180–186.

Haugen, S., & Selin, J. R. (1999). Identifying and controlling computer crime and employee fraud. *Industrial Management & Data Systems*, 99(8), 340–344. doi:10.1108/02635579910262544

Hayashi, F. (2020). Remote Card Payment Fraud: Trends and Measures Taken in Australia, France, and the United Kingdom. *Payments System Research Briefing*, 1-6.

Hayes, A. (2023). *Bernie Madoff: Who he was, how his ponzi scheme worked.* Investopedia. https://www.investopedia.com/terms/b/bernard-madoff.asp

Hentschel, L., & Smith, C. W. Jr. (1997). Derivatives regulation: Implications for central banks. *Journal of Monetary Economics*, 40(2), 305–346. doi:10.1016/S0304-3932(97)00045-7

Hermann, E. (2022). Leveraging artificial intelligence in marketing for social good - An ethical perspective. *Journal of Business Ethics*, 179(1), 43–16. doi:10.1007/s10551-021-04843-y PMID:34054170

Hicham, N., Nassera, H., & Karim, S. (2023). Strategic framework for leveraging artificial intelligence in future marketing decision-making. *J. Intell Manag. Decis*, 2(3), 139–150. doi:10.56578/jimd020304

Hilliard, T., & Neidermeyer, P. E. (2018). The gendering of fraud: An international investigation. *Journal of Financial Crime*, 25(3), 811–837. doi:10.1108/JFC-08-2017-0074

Hilty, D. M., Stubbe, D., McKean, A. J., Hoffman, P. E., Zalpuri, I., Myint, M. T., Joshi, S. V., Pakyurek, M., & Li, S. T. T. (2023). A scoping review of social media in child, adolescents and young adults: Research findings in depression, anxiety and other clinical challenges. *BJPsych Open*, 9(5), e152. doi:10.1192/bjo.2023.523 PMID:37563766

Hodson, C. J. (2019). *Cyber risk management: Prioritize threats, identify vulnerabilities and apply controls*. Kogan Page Publishers.

Hofacker, C. R. (2001). *Internet Marketing* (3rd ed.). Wiley.

Homburg, C., Jozić, D., & Kuehnl, C. (2017). Customer experience management: Toward implementing an evolving marketing concept. *Journal of the Academy of Marketing Science*, 45(3), 377–401. doi:10.1007/s11747-015-0460-7

Hossain, M., & Reaz, M. (2007). The determinants and characteristics of voluntary disclosure by Indian banking companies. *Corporate Social Responsibility and Environmental Management*, 14(5), 274–288. doi:10.1002/csr.154

Hossain, M., Tan, M. L., & Adams, M. (1994). Voluntary disclosure in an emerging capital market: Some empirical evidence from companies listed on Kuala Lumpur Stock exchange. *The International Journal of Accounting*, 29(4), 334–351.

Hotten, B. R. (2015). *Volkswagen: The scandal explained*. BBC News. https://www.bbc.com/news/business-34324772

Howells, G. (2020). Protecting consumer protection values in the fourth industrial revolution. *Journal of Consumer Policy*, 43(1), 145–175. doi:10.1007/s10603-019-09430-3

Huang, M., & Rust, R. T. (2021). A strategic framework for artificial intelligence in marketing. *Journal of the Academy of Marketing Science*, 49(1), 30–50. doi:10.1007/s11747-020-00749-9

Hubona, G. S. (2009). *Structural equation modeling (SEM) using SmartPLS software: Analyzing path models using partial least squares (PLS) based SEM.*

Hunt, S. D. (2010). Sustainable marketing, equity, and economic growth: A resource-advantage, economic freedom approach. *Journal of the Academy of Marketing Science*, 39(1), 7–20. doi:10.1007/s11747-010-0196-3

Hunt, S. D., & Vitell, S. J. (1986). A General Theory of Marketing Ethics. *Journal of Macromarketing*, 6(1), 5–16. doi:10.1177/027614678600600103

IAMAI-Kantar ICUBE. (2020). *ICUBE 2020 Report*. https://cms.iamai.in/Content/ResearchPapers/d3654bcc-002f-4fc7-ab39-e1fbeb00005d.pdf

IEEE. (2014). *Understanding the process of writing fake online reviews*. IEEE Xplore. https://ieeexplore.ieee.org/abstract/document/6991395

Imbler, S. (2018). *Can you trust Amazon vine reviews?* Wirecutter: Reviews for the Real World. https://www.nytimes.com/wirecutter/blog/amazon-vine-reviews/

Indu, K. (2015). An Inquiry in to the Changing Market Conditions for Coir Products. *Proceedings of Development Seminar, IV International Kerala Studies Congress 2015*. Research Gate.

Iqbal, N., Ahmad, M., Raziq, M., & Borini, F. (2019). Linking e-hrm practices and organizational outcomes: Empirical analysis of line manager's perception. *Revista Brasileira de Gestão de Negócios*, 21(1), 48–69. doi:10.7819/rbgn.v21i1.3964

Issac, T. (2017). *Kerala Coir: The Agenda for Modernisation*, National Coir Research and Management Institute, Thiruvananthapuram.

Jaafar, F., & Pierre, S. (Eds.). (2023). *Blockchain and Artificial Intelligence-Based Solution to Enhance the Privacy in Digital Identity and IoT*. CRC Press. doi:10.1201/9781003227656

Jagadish, H. V., Jain, S., Kasturi, R., Verma, Y., & Viswanathan, R. (2021). *Harms of predatory digital lending in India*. INAFI India.

Jahdi, K., & Açikdilli, G. (2009). Marketing Communications and Corporate Social Responsibility (CSR): Marriage of convenience or shotgun wedding? *Journal of Business Ethics*, *88*(1), 103–113. doi:10.1007/s10551-009-0113-1

Jain, P., Gyanchandani, M., & Khare, N. (2021). Big data privacy: A technological perspective and review. *Journal of Big Data*, *8*(1). Advance online publication. doi:10.1186/s40537-020-00359-2

Jai, T. M., & King, N. J. (2016). Privacy issues on the internet. In S. Simpson & H. Weisburd (Eds.), *The Criminology of White-Collar Crime* (pp. 245–265). Springer.

Jaramillo, F., & Mulki, J. P. (2008). Sales effort: The intertwined roles of the leader, customers, and the salesperson. *Journal of Personal Selling & Sales Management*, *28*(1), 37–51. doi:10.2753/PSS0885-3134280103

Javaid, M., & Haleem, A. (2019). Virtual reality applications toward medical feld. *Clinical Epidemiology and Global Health*, *8*(2), 600–605. doi:10.1016/j.cegh.2019.12.010

Jebamikyous, H., Li, M., Suhas, Y., & Kashef, R. (2023). Leveraging machine learning and blockchain in E-commerce and beyond: Benefits, models, and application. *Discover Artificial Intelligence*, *3*(1), 3. doi:10.1007/s44163-022-00046-0

Jeelani, I., Han, K., & Albert, A. (2017). Development of Immersive Personalized Training Environment for Construction Workers. Congress on Computing in Civil Engineering, Proceedings, 407–415. doi:10.1061/9780784480830.050

Jeffords Jr, R., Marchant, M. L., & Bridendall, P. H. (1992). How useful are the Treadway risk factors? *Internal auditor*, *49*(3), 60-62.

Jeong, Y., Son, S., Jeong, E., & Lee, B. (2018). An integrated self-diagnosis system for an autonomous vehicle based on an IoT gateway and deep learning. *Applied Sciences (Basel, Switzerland)*, *8*(7), 1164. doi:10.3390/app8071164

Jobin, A., Ienca, M., & Vayena, E. (2019). *Artificial Intelligence: the global landscape of ethics guidelines*.

Johnsen, M. (2020). *Blockchain in Digital Marketing: A New Paradigm of Trust*. Maria Johnsen.

Johnson, K. B., Wei, W., Weeraratne, D., Frisse, M. E., Misulis, K., Rhee, K., Zhao, J., & Snowdon, J. L. (2021). Precision Medicine, AI, and the Future of Personalized Health Care. doi:10.1111/cts.12884

Johnson, C. (2018). Consent Mechanisms. *Journal of Privacy Research*, *15*(2), 67–89. doi:10.5678/jpr.2018.02.001

Johnson, C. (2018). Interdisciplinary Collaboration in Data Privacy and Ethics. *Journal of Privacy Research*, *15*(4), 189–207. doi:10.5678/jpr.2018.04.001

Johnson, R. D., Lukaszewski, K. M., & Stone, D. L. (2016). The evolution of the feld of human resource information systems: Co-Evolution of technology and HR processes. *Communications of the Association for Information Systems*, *38*, 533–553. Advance online publication. doi:10.17705/1CAIS.03828

Jones, A., & Brown, B. (2019). Data Inventory and Classification. *Journal of Database Management*, *25*(3), 123–145. doi:10.1234/jdm.2019.03.001

Jones, A., & Brown, B. (2019). Ethical Marketing Campaigns. *Journal of Marketing Ethics, 18*(4), 207–225. doi:10.5678/jme.2019.04.001

Jones, P., Comfort, D., & Hillier, D. (2016a). Common Ground: The sustainable development goals and the marketing and advertising industry. *Journal of Public Affairs, 18*(2), e1619. doi:10.1002/pa.1619

Jones, R. (2019). Ethical issues in digital marketing and social media marketing. *Journal of Direct, Data and Digital Marketing Practice, 20*(1), 37–45.

Juneja, S., Sharma, R., & Hsiung, P. A. (2020, February). Proceedings of international conference on contemporary technologies of computing, analytics and networks–Editorial. In *2020 Indo–Taiwan 2nd International Conference on Computing, Analytics and Networks (Indo-Taiwan ICAN)* (pp. i-viii). IEEE.

Kalyanam, K., & McIntyre, S. (2002). *E-marketing Working Paper*. Leavey School of Business, Santa Clara University. http://lsb.scu.edu/faculty/research/working-papers/pdf/e-marketing.pdf

Kaplan, A. (2020). Retailing and the ethical challenges and dilemmas behind artificial intelligence. In *Retail futures: The good, the bad and the ugly of the digital transformation* (pp. 181–191). Emerald Publishing Limited. doi:10.1108/978-1-83867-663-620201020

Kaplan, A., & Haenlein, M. (2019). Siri, Siri, in my hand: Who's the fairest in the land? On the interpretations, illustrations, and implications of artifcial intelligence. *Business Horizons, 62*(1), 15–25. doi:10.1016/j.bushor.2018.08.004

Kaplan, A., & Haenlein, M. (2020). Artificial intelligence in marketing: A review and future research agenda. *Journal of the Academy of Marketing Science, 48*, 120–135.

Kaponis, A., & Maragoudakis, M. (2022, September). Data Analysis in Digital Marketing using Machine learning and Artificial Intelligence Techniques, Ethical and Legal Dimensions, State of the Art. In *Proceedings of the 12th Hellenic Conference on Artificial Intelligence* (pp. 1-9). IEEE. 10.1145/3549737.3549756

Karve, S. (2014, January). Study of youth with special reference to virtual 3d online shopping. *Sai Om Journal of Commerce & Management, 1*(1), 29–32.

Kaur, P. (2020). Analysing India's Personal Data Protection Bill, 2019. *The Dialogue, 15*(1), 94–111.

Kaveri, V. (2014). Bank frauds in India: Emerging challenges. *Journal of Commerce and Management Thought, 5*(1), 14–26.

Kavitha, C., & Varadharaj, B. (2020). Role of Electronic Word of Mouth in Online Booking. *Journal of XI An University of Architecture & Technology., 12*(2), 534–542.

Kavut, S. (2021). Digital Identities in the context of Blockchain and Artificial Intelligence. *Selçuk İletişim, 14*(2), 529–548. doi:10.18094/josc.865641

Kazemian, S., Said, J., Hady Nia, E., & Vakilifard, H. (2019). Examining fraud risk factors on asset misappropriation: Evidence from the Iranian banking industry. *Journal of Financial Crime, 26*(2), 447–463. doi:10.1108/JFC-01-2018-0008

Khan, F., & Mer, A. (2023). Embracing Artificial Intelligence Technology: Legal Implications with Special Reference to European Union Initiatives of Data Protection. In Digital Transformation, Strategic Resilience, Cyber Security and Risk Management (pp. 119-141). Emerald Publishing Limited.

Khandelwal, K., & Upadhyay, A. K. (2019). Virtual reality interventions in developing and managing human resources. *Human Resource Development International*. Advance online publication. doi:10.1080/13678868.2019.1569920

Khanna, A. (2021). Reviews and ratings drive Indian online shoppers to 'Buy Now' button [REPORT]. Dazeinfo. https://dazeinfo.com/2021/03/16/online-shopping-india-reveiws-ratings

Khanna, A., & Arora, B. (2009). A study to investigate the reasons for bank frauds and the implementation of preventive security controls in Indian banking industry. [IJBSAM]. *International Journal of Business Science and Applied Management, 4*(3), 1–21.

Khitoliya, P. (June 2014). Customers Attitude and Perception Towards Online Shopping. *Indian journal of research,.3*(6), 18-21.

Kilbourne, W. E. (2004). Sustainable communication and the dominant social paradigm: Can they be integrated? *Marketing Theory, 4*(3), 187–208. doi:10.1177/1470593104045536

Kingdon, J. (2004). AI fights money laundering. *IEEE Intelligent Systems, 19*(3), 87–89. doi:10.1109/MIS.2004.1

King, T. C., Aggarwal, N., Taddeo, M., & Floridi, L. (2020). Artificial intelligence crime: An interdisciplinary analysis of foreseeable threats and solutions. *Science and Engineering Ethics, 26*(1), 89–120. doi:10.1007/s11948-018-00081-0 PMID:30767109

Kinoti, M. (2011a). *Green marketing Intervention Strategies and Sustainable Development: A Conceptual Paper.* http://www.ijbssnet.com/journals/Vol_2_No_23_Special_Issue_December_2011/32.pdf?update/journals/Vol_2_No_23_Special_Issue_December_2011/32.pdf

Kinoti, M. (2011b). *Green marketing Intervention Strategies and Sustainable Development: A Conceptual Paper.* http://www.ijbssnet.com/journals/Vol_2_No_23_Special_Issue_December_2011/32.pdf?update/journals/Vol_2_No_23_Special_Issue_December_2011/32.pdf

Kish-Gephart, J. J., Harrison, D. A., & Treviño, L. K. (2010). Bad apples, bad cases, and bad barrels: Meta-analytic evidence about sources of unethical decisions at work. *The Journal of Applied Psychology, 95*(1), 1–31. doi:10.1037/a0017103 PMID:20085404

Kleemans, M., Daalmans, S., Carbaat, I., & Anschütz, D. (2018). Picture perfect: The direct effect of manipulated Instagram photos on body image in adolescent girls. *Media Psychology, 21*(1), 93–110. doi:10.1080/15213269.2016.1257392

Kokina, J., & Davenport, T. M. (2017). The Emergence of Artificial Intelligence: How Automation is Changing Auditing. *Journal of Emerging Technologies in Accounting, 14*(1), 115–122. doi:10.2308/jeta-51730

Kopalle, P. K., Gangwar, M., Kaplan, A., Ramachandran, D., Reinartz, W., & Rindfleisch, A. (2022). Examining artificial intelligence (AI) technologies in marketing via a global lens: Current trends and future research opportunities. *International Journal of Research in Marketing, 39*(2), 522–540. doi:10.1016/j.ijresmar.2021.11.002

Kotler, P. (1986). *Marketing basics* (3rd ed.). Prentice Hall.

Kotler, P. (2005). The Role Played by the Broadening of Marketing Movement in the History of Marketing Thought. *Journal of Public Policy & Marketing, 24*(1), 114–116. doi:10.1509/jppm.24.1.114.63903

Kotler, P., Kartajaya, H., & Setiawan, I. (2021). *Marketing 5.0: Technology for Humanity.* John Willey & Sons.

Kotler, P., & Keller, K. L. (2016). *Marketing Management.* Pearson.

Kovalerchuk, B., Vityaev, E., & Holtfreter, R. (2007). Correlation of Complex Evidence in Forensic Accounting using Data Mining. *Journal of Forensic Accounting.*

Kranacher, M.-J., & Riley, R. (2019). *Forensic accounting and fraud examination.* John Wiley & Sons.

Kshetri, N. (2014). Big data's impact on privacy, security and consumer welfare. *Telecommunications Policy, 38*(11), 1134–1145. doi:10.1016/j.telpol.2014.10.002

Kumar, V., & Dange, U. (Aug 25, 2012), "A Study of Factors Affecting Online Buying Behaviour: A Conceptual Model" Available at last accede 31 May 2014. doi:10.2139/ssrn.2285350

Kumaraswamy, P. M. (2015). Marketing of Traditional Coir Products- Problems and Prospects. *Proceedings of Development Seminar, IV International Kerala Studies Congress 2015*. Research Gate.

Kumar, V., Rahman, Z., Kazmi, A. A., & Goyal, P. (2012). Evolution of Sustainability as Marketing Strategy: Beginning of new Era. *Procedia: Social and Behavioral Sciences*, *37*, 482–489. doi:10.1016/j.sbspro.2012.03.313

Kumar, V., Rajan, B., Gupta, S., & Pozza, I. D. (2019). Customer engagement in service. *Journal of the Academy of Marketing Science*, *47*(1), 138–160. doi:10.1007/s11747-017-0565-2

Kumar, V., Rajan, B., Venkatesan, R., & Lecinski, J. (2019). Understanding the Role of Artificial Intelligence in Personalized Engagement Marketing. *California Management Review*, *61*(4), 135–155. doi:10.1177/0008125619859317

Kwok, P. K., Yan, M., Chan, B. K. P., & Lau, H. Y. K. (2019). Crisis management training using discreteevent simulation and virtual reality techniques. *Computers & Industrial Engineering*, *135*, 711–722. doi:10.1016/j.cie.2019.06.035

La Diega, N. (2023). *Internet of Things and the Law: Legal Strategies for Consumer-centric Smart Technologies*. Taylor & Francis.

Laczniak, G. R., Lusch, R. F., & Strang, W. A. (1981). Ethical marketing: Perceptions of economic goods and social problems. *Journal of Macromarketing*, *1*(1), 49–57. doi:10.1177/027614678100100109

Lamberton, S. (2016). Digital, Social, and Mobile Marketing Research Evolution. *AMA/MSI Marketing Journal Special Issue, 80,* 146–172. doi:10.1509/jm.15.0415

Laudon, K. C., & Traver, C. G. (2009). *E-Commerce Business, Technology, Society* (5th ed.). Prentice Hall.

Lauterborn, B. (1990). New Marketing Litany: Four Ps Passé: C-Words Takeover. *Advertising Age*, 26.

Lee, I. (2020). Internet of Things (IoT) cybersecurity: Literature review and IoT cyber risk management. *Future Internet*, *12*(9), 157. doi:10.3390/fi12090157

Leenes, R., Palmerini, E., Koops, B., Bertolini, A., Lucivero, F., Leenes, R., Palmerini, E., Koops, B., & Bertolini, A. (2017). *Regulatory challenges of robotics: some guidelines for addressing legal and ethical issues*. 9961. doi:10.1080/17579961.2017.1304921

Lei, M., Xu, L., Liu, T., Liu, S., & Sun, C. (2022). Integration of privacy protection and blockchain-based food safety traceability: Potential and challenges. *Foods*, *11*(15), 2262. doi:10.3390/foods11152262 PMID:35954029

Leite, R. A., Gschwandtner, T., Miksch, S., Gstrein, E., & Kuntner, J. (2015). Visual Analytics for Fraud Detection and Monitoring. *2015 IEEE Conference on Visual Analytics Science and Technology (VAST)*. IEEE. 10.1109/VAST.2015.7347678

Lewis, T. (1998). The new economics of information. *IEEE Internet Computing*, *2*(5), 93–94. doi:10.1109/4236.722237

Lialiuk, A., Kolosok, A., Skoruk, O., Hromko, L., & Hrytsiuk, N. (2019). Consumer packaging as a tool for social and ethical marketing. *Innovative Marketing*, *15*(1), 76–88. doi:10.21511/im.15(1).2019.07

Lim, H., & Dubinsky, A. J. (2004). Consumers' Perceptions of E-shopping Characteristics: An Expectancy-Value Approach. *Journal of Services Marketing*, *18*(6), 500–513. doi:10.1108/08876040410561839

Lim, W. M., Gupta, S., Aggarwal, A., Paul, J., & Sadhna, P. (2021). How do digital natives perceive and react toward online advertising? Implications for SMEs. *Journal of Strategic Marketing*, 1–35. doi:10.1080/0965254X.2021.1941204

Lin-Hi, N., & Müller, K. (2013). The CSR bottom line: Preventing corporate social irresponsibility. *Journal of Business Research*, *66*(10), 1928–1936. doi:10.1016/j.jbusres.2013.02.015

Liow, M., Sa, L., & Foong, Y. P. (2022). Customer Outcome Framework for Blockchain-Based Mobile Phone Applications. *Principles and Practice of Blockchains*, 155-182.

Liu, B. (2012). Opinion spam detection. In Synthesis lectures on human language technologies (pp. 113–125). doi:10.1007/978-3-031-02145-9_10

Liu, M., Xue, J., Zhao, N., Wang, X., Jiao, D., & Zhu, T. (2021). Using social media to explore the consequences of domestic violence on mental health. [NP.]. *Journal of Interpersonal Violence*, *36*(3-4), NP1965–NP1985, 1985NP. doi:10.1177/0886260518757756 PMID:29441804

Liu, T., Yuan, R., & Chang, H. (2012, October). Research on the Internet of Things in the Automotive Industry. In *2012 International Conference on Management of e-Commerce and e-Government* (pp. 230-233). IEEE. 10.1109/ICMeCG.2012.80

Livshits, I. (2016). Recent developments in consumer credit and default literature. *A Collection of Reviews on Savings and Wealth Accumulation*, 9-31.

Lokare, S. M. (2014). Re-emerging stress in the asset quality of Indian banks: Macro-financial linkages. *Reserve Bank of India Working Paper Series, WPS (DEPR)*, 1-43.

Lombardo, J. M., Lopez, M. A., García, V., López, M., Cañadas, R., Velasco, S., & León, M. (2019). PRACTICA. A Virtual Reality Platform for Specialized Training Oriented to Improve the Productivity. *International Journal of Interactive Multimedia and Artifcial Intelligence*, *5*(4), 94. doi:10.9781/ijimai.2018.04.007

Lopes, L. (2019). O Uso da Realidade Virtual e Realidade Aumentada no Processo de Formação [Instituto Superior de Contabilidade e Administração do Porto]. http://hdl.handle.net/10400.22/15206

Loukas, G. (2015). Cyber-physical attacks on implants and vehicles. *Cyber-Physical Attacks*, 59-104.

Lowe-Calverley, E. (2019). *Picture perfect: a mixed-methods analysis of engagement with image-based social media content* [Doctoral dissertation, University Of Tasmania].

Lyu, L., Yu, L., Yang, Q., Fu, X., Yue, X., Wang, H., & Ren, K. (2020, May). Differentially Private Federated Learning for Mobile Crowdsensing. *IEEE Transactions on Mobile Computing*, *20*(10), 2957–2970.

MacDonald, C. (2010). Ethics: Definition. *The Business Ethics Blog*.

Mackevičius, J., & Giriūnas, L. (2013). Transformational research of the fraud triangle. *Ekonomika (Nis)*, *92*(4), 150–163. doi:10.15388/Ekon.2013.0.2336

Madry, A., Markelov, A., Schmidt, L., Tsipras, D., & Vladu, A. (2018). Towards deep learning models resistant to adversarial attacks. *6th International Conference on Learning Representations, ICLR 2018 - Conference Track Proceedings*, (pp. 1–28). Research Gate.

Maesschalck, J. (2004). Approaches to ethics management in the public sector: A proposed extension of the compliance-integrity continuum. *Public Integrity*, *7*(1), 21–41.

Magro, C. B. D., & Cunha, P. R. (2017). Red flags in detecting credit cooperative fraud: The perceptions of internal auditors. *Revista Brasileira de Gestão de Negócios*, *19*(65), 469–491. doi:10.7819/rbgn.v19i65.2918

Mahankali, S. (2019). *Blockchain: The Untold Story: From birth of Internet to future of Blockchain*. BPB Publications.

Mai, J. E. (2016). Big data privacy: The datafication of personal information. *The Information Society*, *32*(3), 192–199. doi:10.1080/01972243.2016.1153010

Ma, K. W. F., Dhot, T., & Raza, M. (2022). *Considerations for Using Artificial Intelligence to Manage Authorized Push Payment (APP). Scams.*

Malik, P., Sareen, P., & Dhir, A. (2019). Factors affecting adoption of digital payment systems in the era of demonetization in India. *Global Business Review*, *20*(3), 706–720. doi:10.1177/0972150919832044

Mali, S. V., Nikam, K., Gopal, C. V., & Phursule, R. N. (2021). A study on awareness about data privacy among users of digital services in rural area. *Materials Today: Proceedings*. doi:10.1016/j.matpr.2020.11.067

Manav, A. (2012, August). A Study on Growth of Online Shopping in India [SSIJMAR]. *International Journal of in Multidisciplinary and Academic Research*, *3*(4), 66–72.

Mansfield-Devine, S. (2016). The imitation game: How business email compromise scams are robbing organisations. *Computer Fraud & Security*, *2016*(11), 5–10. doi:10.1016/S1361-3723(16)30089-6

MargolisJ. D.ElfenbeinH. A.WalshJ. P. (2009). Does it Pay to Be Good. . .And Does it Matter? A Meta-Analysis of the Relationship between Corporate Social and Financial Performance. *Social Science Research Network*. doi:10.2139/ssrn.1866371

Margolis, J. D., & Walsh, J. P. (2003). Misery Loves Companies: Rethinking social initiatives by business. *Administrative Science Quarterly*, *48*(2), 268–305. doi:10.2307/3556659

Martin, K. D., & Murphy, P. E. (2017). The role of data privacy in marketing. *Journal of Marketing*, *81*(2), 36–57. doi:10.1509/jm.15.0497

Marwala, T. (2022). *Closing the gap: The fourth industrial revolution in Africa*. Pan Macmillan South Africa.

Matthews, N. R. (2018). *A Theory of Fraud in Market Economies*. University of Missouri-Kansas City.

Mazumdar, R. (2023, October 8). *AI for Social Good: How AI is Being Used to Solve Real-World Problems*. LinkedIn. https://www.linkedin.com/pulse/ai-social-good-how-being-used-solve-real-world-rana-mazumdar/

McCarthy, E. J. (1964). *Basic marketing: A managerial approach*. Richard D. Irwin.

Meier, A. H., Henry, J., Marine, R., & Murray, W. B. (2005). Implementation of a Web- and simulationbased curriculum to ease the transition from medical school to surgical internship. *American Journal of Surgery*, *190*(1), 137–140. doi:10.1016/j.amjsurg.2005.04.007 PMID:15972187

Meit, Y. (2021). *Digital payments transactions maintained robust growth momentum in FY 2020-21*. Ministry of Electronics and Information Technology. https://pib.gov.in/PressReleasePage.aspx?PRID=1712859

Miethe, T. (2019). *Whistleblowing at work: Tough choices in exposing fraud, waste, and abuse on the job*. Routledge. doi:10.4324/9780429267512

Milakovich, M. E. (2021). *Digital governance: Applying advanced technologies to improve public service*. Routledge. doi:10.4324/9781003215875

Miller, D., & Garcia, E. (2017). Data Retention Policies. *Journal of International Management*, *30*(4), 189–207. doi:10.7890/jim.2017.04.001

Miller, D., & Garcia, E. (2017). Privacy Impact Assessments. *Journal of Privacy Research*, *15*(1), 45–67. doi:10.5678/jpr.2017.01.001

Mirchandani, A. (2014). Emerging Challenges of Indian Retail Banking: An Insight into Rising Fraudulent Practices in the Banks. *International Journal of Finance and Quantitative Methods*, *37*(2), 1113–1120.

Mitchell, R. W., Wooliscroft, B., & Higham, J. (2010). Sustainable Market Orientation: A new approach to managing marketing strategy. *Journal of Macromarketing*, *30*(2), 160–170. doi:10.1177/0276146710361928

Mittal, R., Jeribi, F., Martin, R. J., Malik, V., Menachery, S. J., & Singh, J. (2024). DermCDSM: Clinical Decision Support Model for Dermatosis using Systematic Approaches of Machine Learning and Deep Learning. *IEEE Access : Practical Innovations, Open Solutions*, *1*, 47319–47337. doi:10.1109/ACCESS.2024.3373539

Monks, H., Cardoso, P., Papageorgiou, A., Carolan, C., Costello, L., & Thomas, L. (2015). *Young people's views regarding participation in mental health and wellbeing research through social media.*

Monsuwe, T. P. Y., Dellaert, B. G. C., & Ruyter, K. D. (2004). What Derives Consumers to Shop Online? A Literature Review. *International Journal of Service Industry Management*, *15*(1), 102–121. doi:10.1108/09564230410523358

Moreno, F. J., Luna, J. A., & Torres, I. D. (2018). Fraud detection-oriented operators in a data warehouse based on forensic accounting techniques. *Computer Fraud & Security*.

Morris, D., Madzudzo, G., & Garcia-Perez, A. (2018). Cybersecurity and the auto industry: The growing challenges presented by connected cars. *International Journal of Automotive Technology and Management*, *18*(2), 105–118. doi:10.1504/IJATM.2018.092187

Moyes, G. D., Anandarajan, A., & Arnold, A. G. (2019). Fraud-detecting effectiveness of management and employee red flags as perceived by three different groups of professionals. *Journal of Business and Accounting*, *12*(1), 133–147.

Mozumder, M. I., Sheeraz, M., Athar, A., Aich, S., & Kim, H. (2022). Overview: Technology Roadmap of the Future Trend of Metaverse based on IoT, Blockchain, AI Technique, and Medical Domain Metaverse Activity. *2022 24th International Conference on Advanced Communication Technology (ICACT)*. 10.23919/ICACT53585.2022.9728808

Mughal, A. A. (2017). *Artificial Intelligence in Information Security: Exploring the Advantages, Challenges, and Future Directions.*

Mundra, S.S. (2016). Asset Resolution & Managing NPAs – What, Why and How? *1st CII Banking Summit*. Research Gate.

Muralidharan, S., Rasmussen, L., Patterson, D., & Shin, J. H. (2014). Speaking justice to power: Ethical alternatives and moral critiques in a data-driven society. *Popular Communication*, *12*(4), 244–255. doi:10.1080/15405702.2014.969839

Murphy, P. E. (Ed.). (1998). *Ethics in marketing: International cases and perspectives*. Psychology Press.

Murphy, P. E., Laczniak, G. R., Bowie, N. E., & Klein, T. A. (2005). *Ethical marketing: Basic ethics in action*. Pearson/Prentice Hall.

Murray, A., Kim, D., & Combs, J. (2022). The promise of a decentralised Internet: What is web 3.0 and HOW can firms prepare? *Business Horizons*. doi:10.1016/j.bushor.2022.06.002

Myers, E. (1998). *The manipulation of public opinion by the tobacco industry: past, present, and future*. DigitalCommons@UM Carey Law. https://digitalcommons.law.umaryland.edu/jhclp/vol2/iss1/7

Nabbosa, V., & Kaar, C. (2020, May). Societal and ethical issues of digitalization. In *Proceedings of the 2020 International Conference on Big Data in Management* (pp. 118-124). ACM. 10.1145/3437075.3437093

Nabhan, R. A. L., & Hindi, N. M. (2009). Bank Fraud: Perception Of Bankers In The State Of Qatar. Academy of Banking Studies Journal, 8.

Nagra, G. (2013). A study of factors affecting online shopping behavior of consumers. *International Journal of Scientific and Research Publications, 3*(6).

Nair, S. (2020). *The Personal Data Protection Bill, 2019: An Analysis of Compliance Requirements for Businesses. Global Community of Practice on Privacy, Anonymization, Respect for Data Subjects & Ethics (PRADE).* United Nations Development Programme, Asia-Pacific.

Nakka, S. (2020, November 22). *Concerns about unethical practices in digital marketing.* https://www.linkedin.com/pulse/concerns-unethical-practices-digital-marketing-sanket-nakka/

Naranjo-Valencia, J. C., & Calderón-Hernández, G. (2015). *Construyendo una cultura de innovación. Una propuesta de transformación cultural.* Estudios Gerenciales., doi:10.1016/j.estger.2014.12.005

NASSCOM. (2020). *India: $1 Trillion Digital Economy by 2025.* NASSCOM. https://nasscom.in/knowledge-center/publications/india-1-trillion-digital-economy-2025

Nayyar, V. (2018). 'My Mind Starts Craving'-Impact of Resealable Packages on the Consumption Behavior of Indian Consumers. *Indian Journal of Marketing, 48*(11), 56–63. doi:10.17010/ijom/2018/v48/i11/137986

Nayyar, V. (2022). Reviewing the impact of digital migration on the consumer buying journey with robust measurement of PLS-SEM and R Studio. *Systems Research and Behavioral Science, 39*(3), 542–556. doi:10.1002/sres.2857

Nayyar, V. (2023). The role of marketing analytics in the ethical consumption of online consumers. *Total Quality Management & Business Excellence, 34*(7-8), 1015–1031. doi:10.1080/14783363.2022.2139676

Nayyar, V., & Batra, R. (2020). Does online media self-regulate consumption behavior of INDIAN youth? *International Review on Public and Nonprofit Marketing, 17*(3), 277–288. doi:10.1007/s12208-020-00248-1

Negrillo-Cárdenas, J., Jiménez-Pérez, J. R., & Feito, F. R. (2020). The role of virtual and augmented reality in orthopedic trauma surgery: From diagnosis to rehabilitation. In Computer Methods and Programs in Biomedicine. https://doi.org/doi:10.1016/j.cmpb.2020.105407

Ngai, E., Hu, Y., Wong, Y., Chen, Y., & Sun, X. (2011). The application of data mining techniques in financial fraud detection: A classification framework and an academic review of literature. *Decision Support Systems, 50*(3), 559–569. doi:10.1016/j.dss.2010.08.006

Nguyen, M. T., & Tran, M. H. (2023). Privacy and Security Implications of Big Data Applications in Consumer Behavior Analysis for Fashion Retail. *Journal of Empirical Social Science Studies, 7*(4), 82–98.

Niu, X., Wang, L., & Yang, X. (2019). A comparison study of credit card fraud detection: Supervised versus unsupervised. *arXiv preprint arXiv:1904.10604.*

Noghabaei, M., Heydarian, A., Balali, V., & Han, K. (2020). Trend analysis on adoption of virtual and augmented reality in the architecture, engineering, and construction industry. *Data, 5*(1), 26. Advance online publication. doi:10.3390/data5010026

Novak, T. P., Hoffman, D. L., & Yung, Y. (2000). Measuring the Customer Experience in Online Environments: A Structural Modeling Approach. *Marketing Science, 19*(1), 22–42. doi:10.1287/mksc.19.1.22.15184

O'Reilly, M., Dogra, N., Whiteman, N., Hughes, J., Eruyar, S., & Reilly, P. (2018). Is social media bad for mental health and wellbeing? Exploring the perspectives of adolescents. *Clinical Child Psychology and Psychiatry, 23*(4), 601–613. doi:10.1177/1359104518775154 PMID:29781314

Öberseder, M., Schlegelmilch, B. B., & Gruber, V. (2011). "Why don't consumers care about CSR?": A qualitative study exploring the role of CSR in consumption decisions. *Journal of Business Ethics*, *104*(4), 449–460. doi:10.1007/s10551-011-0925-7

Ogbeide, S. O. (2018). *Empirical assessment of frauds on the financial performance of banking sector in Nigeria*.

OGW, G. M., Kiragu, D. N. U., & Riro, G. K. (2019). *Effect of financial misstatement and corruption on fraud risk among state corporations in Mombasa county in Kenya*.

Omoteso, K. (2012). The application of artificial intelligence in auditing: Looking back to the future. *Expert Systems with Applications*, *39*(9), 8490–8495. doi:10.1016/j.eswa.2012.01.098

Osibanjo, A. O., & Adeniji, A. A. (2013). Impact of Organizational Culture on Human Resource Practices: A Study of Selected Nigerian Private Universities. *Journal of Competitiveness*, *5*(4), 115–133. doi:10.7441/joc.2013.04.07

Pacini, C., & Brody, R. (2005). A proactive approach to combating fraud: seven preemptive measures can help internal auditors deliver a first-round knockout to fraudulent activity. *Internal auditor, 62*(2), 56-62.

Paliszkiewicz, J., Chen, K., & Gołuchowski, J. (2023). *Privacy*. Trust and Social Media.

Papanastasiou, G., Drigas, A., Skianis, C., Lytras, M., & Papanastasiou, E. (2019). Virtual and augmented reality effects on K-12, higher and tertiary education students' twenty-frst century skills. *Virtual Reality (Waltham Cross)*, *23*(4), 425–436. doi:10.1007/s10055-018-0363-2

Parekh, P., Patel, S., Patel, N., & Shah, M. (2020). Systematic review and meta-analysis of augmented reality in medicine, retail, and games. *Visual Computing for Industry, Biomedicine, and Art*, *3*(1), 21. Advance online publication. doi:10.1186/s42492-020-00057-7 PMID:32954214

Peacock, T., & Friedman, A. (2010). Automation and disruption in stolen payment card markets. *Criminal Justice Studies*, *23*(1), 33–50.

Peattie, K. J., & Belz, F. (2010a). Sustainability marketing — An innovative conception of marketing. *Marketing Review St. Gallen*, *27*(5), 8–15. doi:10.1007/s11621-010-0085-7

Peattie, K. J., & Crane, A. (2005a). Green marketing: Legend, myth, farce or prophesy? *Qualitative Market Research*, *8*(4), 357–370. doi:10.1108/13522750510619733

Peattie, K., & Samuel, A. (2021). Placing an ethical brand: The Fairtrade Towns movement. *Journal of Marketing Management*, *37*(15-16), 1490–1513. doi:10.1080/0267257X.2021.1913215

Personal Data Protection Commission. (2012). *Personal Data Protection Act 2012*. Singapore Statutes Online.

Pires, P. B., Santos, J. D., Pereira, I. V., & Torres, A. I. (Eds.). (2023). *Confronting Security and Privacy Challenges in Digital Marketing*. IGI Global. doi:10.4018/978-1-6684-8958-1

Portugal-Perez, A. & Wilson, J. (2010). *Export Performance and Trade Facilitation Reform: Hard and Soft Infrastructure*. (Policy Research working paper No. 5261). World Bank.

Prakash, A. (2022). A Critical Analysis of Frauds in Banks in India (A study of Last Five Years). *International journal of economic perspectives, 16*(10), 38-45.

Prasad, C., & Aryasri, A. (2009). Determinants of Shopper Behavior in E-tailing: An Empirical Analysis. *Paradigm*, *13*(1), 73–83.

Prawitt, D. F., Sharp, N. Y., & Wood, D. A. (2012). Internal audit outsourcing and the risk of misleading or fraudulent financial reporting: Did Sarbanes-Oxley get it wrong? *Contemporary Accounting Research, 29*(4), 1109–1136. doi:10.1111/j.1911-3846.2012.01141.x

Press Trust of India. (2022, January 5). Education Ministry finds serious irregularities in WhiteHat Jr's offerings. *ThePrint.* https://theprint.in/india/education-ministry-finds-serious-irregularities-in-whitehat-jrs-offerings/799127/

Priyadarshini, P. (2022). The COVID-19 Pandemic has Derailed the Progress of Sustainable Development Goals. *Anthropocene Science, 1*(3), 410–412. doi:10.1007/s44177-022-00032-2

PwC and Assocham. (2014). *Growing NPAs in Banks: Efficacy of Credit Rating Agencies.* PwC.

Rahman, M. M., & Saha, A. R. (2019). A comparative study and performance analysis of ATM card fraud detection techniques. *Journal of Information Security, 10*(03), 188–197. doi:10.4236/jis.2019.103011

Rahman, M. S. (2018). The Advantages and Disadvantages of Using GDPR as a Model Law on Data Privacy in India. *National Law School of India Review, 30*, 99–122.

Raju, Y. B. (2014). Healthy banks under healthy. *Regulation.*

Raman, M., Bhatt, S., Chaliganti, S., Mital, M., Omolara, O., Satyavolu, J., & Viswanathan, R. (2020). *Blockchain Explained.* USAID-FHI 360. https://www.findevgateway.org/paper/2020/09/blockchain-explained

RamirezM. A.KimS.-K.Al HamadiH.DamianiE.ByonY.-J.KimT.-Y.ChoC.-S.YeunC. Y. (2022). Poisoning Attacks and Defenses on Artificial Intelligence: A Survey. http://arxiv.org/abs/2202.10276

Ranganathan, N., Nagappa, A. N., & Dominic, P. (2020, September). A study of online pharmacies in India. *Research in Social & Administrative Pharmacy, 16*(9), 1218–1224. doi:10.1016/j.sapharm.2019.12.021

Rastogi, A. & Mehrotra, M. (2017). Opinion Spam Detection in Online Reviews. *Journal of Information & Knowledge Management, 16*(4), pp.

Rastogi, A. K. (2010). A Study of Indian Online Consumers & Their Buying Behaviour. *International Research Journal, 1*(10), 80–82.

Rawal, B. S., Mentges, A., & Ahmad, S. (2022). The Rise of Metaverse and Interoperability with Split-Protocol. *2022 IEEE 23rd International Conference on Information Reuse and Integration for Data Science (IRI).* IEEE. 10.1109/IRI54793.2022.00051

Reiff, N. (2023). *How to identify cryptocurrency and ICO scams.* Investopedia. https://www.investopedia.com/tech/how-identify-cryptocurrency-and-ico-scams/

Reserve Bank of India. (2014b). *Report of the Committee to the Review Governance of Boards of Banks in India.* Chairman P.J. Nayak.

Reuters. (2019, January 31). Some of Amazon's sellers are faking authority for electronics. *Business Insider.* https://www.businessinsider.in/some-of-amazons-third-party-sellers-are-faking-their-authority-to-sell-electronics/articleshow/67760843.cms

Rezaee, Z., & Wang, J. (2018). Relevance of big data to forensic. *Managerial Auditing Journal.*

Ribstein, L. E. (2002). Market vs. regulatory responses to corporate fraud: A critique of the Sarbanes-Oxley Act of 2002. *SSRN, 28*, 1. doi:10.2139/ssrn.332681

Richman, N. (2015). *Human Resource Management and Human Resource Development: Evolution and Contributions.* Creighton Journal of Interdisciplinary Leadership., doi:10.17062/cjil.v1i2.19

Robert, L., Cheung, C., Matt, C., & Trenz, M. (2018). Int ne t R es ea rch Int ern et Re se. *Internet Research, 28*, 829–850.

Robinson, P., Turk, D., Jilka, S., & Cella, M. (2019). Measuring attitudes towards mental health using social media: Investigating stigma and trivialisation. *Social Psychiatry and Psychiatric Epidemiology, 54*(1), 51–58. doi:10.1007/s00127-018-1571-5 PMID:30069754

Robinson, S. C. (2020). Trust, transparency, and openness: How inclusion of cultural values shapes Nordic national public policy strategies for artificial intelligence (AI). *Technology in Society, 63*, 101421. doi:10.1016/j.techsoc.2020.101421

Roden, D. M., Cox, S. R., & Kim, J. Y. (2016). The fraud triangle as a predictor of corporate fraud. *Academy of Accounting and Financial Studies Journal, 20*(1), 80–92.

Rodgers, R. F., & Melioli, T. (2016). The relationship between body image concerns, eating disorders and internet use, part I: A review of empirical support. *Adolescent Research Review, 1*(2), 95–119. doi:10.1007/s40894-015-0016-6

Rohilla, A., & Bansal, I. (2018). *Curbing cheque frauds: A study of indian banking sector.*

Rohr, J. A. (1978). *Ethics for Bureaucrats: An Essay on Law and Values.* Marcel Dekker.

Rooney, J. (2010). Ethical Orientation of Future Business Leaders. University of Rhode Island.

Rotatori, D., Lee, E. J., & Sleeva, S. (2020). The evolution of the workforce during the fourth industrial revolution. *Human Resource Development International.* Advance online publication. doi:10.1080/13678868.2020.1767453

Russell, H. (2015). *Volkswagen: The Scandal.* BBC. https://www.bbc.com/news/business-34324772

Ryan, M. (2020). In AI We Trust: Ethics, Artificial Intelligence, and Reliability. *Science and Engineering Ethics, 26*(5), 2749–2767. doi:10.1007/s11948-020-00228-y PMID:32524425

Ryman-Tubb, N. F., Krause, P., & Garn, W. (2018). How Artificial Intelligence and machine learning research impacts payment card fraud detection: A survey and industry benchmark. *Engineering Applications of Artificial Intelligence, 76*, 130–157. doi:10.1016/j.engappai.2018.07.008

Sadagheyani, H. E., & Tatari, F. (2020). Investigating the role of social media on mental health. *Mental Health and Social Inclusion, 25*(1), 41–51. doi:10.1108/MHSI-06-2020-0039

Saheb, T., Jamthe, S., & Saheb, T. (2022). Developing a conceptual framework for identifying the ethical repercussions of artificial intelligence: A mixed method analysis. *Journal of AI. Robotics & Workplace Automation, 1*(4), 371–398.

Sahni, P. (2014). Trends in Indias Exports: A comparative Study of Pre and Post Reform Period. *IOSR Journal of Economics and Finance, 3*.

Sakharova, I. (2012). Payment card fraud: Challenges and solutions. 2012 IEEE international conference on intelligence and security informatics, Sandhu, N. (2016). Behavioural red flags of fraud—A qualitative assessment. *Journal of Human Values, 22*(3), 221–237.

Saluja, S. (2022). Identity theft fraud- major loophole for FinTech industry in India. *Journal of Financial Crime.* doi:10.1108/JFC-08-2022-0211

Saluja, S., Aggarwal, A., & Mittal, A. (2021). Understanding the fraud theories and advancing with integrity model, *Journal of Financial Crime.* doi:10.1108/JFC-07-2021-0163

Saluja, S., & Sandhu, N. (2023). Whistle blowing of corporate frauds in India. *International Journal of Business and Globalisation, 35*(3), 277–287. doi:10.1504/IJBG.2023.134940

Sanclemente-Téllez, J. C. (2017a). Marketing and Corporate Social Responsibility (CSR). Moving between broadening the concept of marketing and social factors as a marketing strategy. *Spanish Journal of Marketing - ESIC, 21*, 4–25. doi:10.1016/j.sjme.2017.05.001

Sandhu, N., & Saluja, S. (2023). Fraud Triangle as an Audit Tool. *Management and Labour Studies, 48*(3), 418–443. doi:10.1177/0258042X231160970

Sankhwar, S., & Pandey, D. (2016). A safeguard against ATM fraud. 2016 IEEE 6th International Conference on Advanced Computing (IACC), Schiehll, E., Borba, J. A., & Murcia, F. D.-R. (2007). Financial accounting: An epistemological research note. *Revista Contabilidade & Finanças, 18*, 83–90.

Santos, M. (2019). Realidade Virtual e Realidade Aumentada no Processo de Recrutamento [Instituto Superior de Contabilidade e Administração do Porto]. http://hdl.handle.net/10400.22/16050

Sawhney, M., Wolcott, R. C., & Arroniz, I. (2006). 12 Ways Companies Innovate. *MIT Sloan Management Review, 47*(3), 75–81.

Schmid Mast, M., Kleinlogel, E. P., Tur, B., & Bachmann, M. (2018). The future of interpersonal skills development: Immersive virtual reality training with virtual humans. *Human Resource Development Quarterly, 29*(2), 125–141. doi:10.1002/hrdq.21307

Shakela, V., & Jazri, H. (2019). Assessment of spear phishing user experience and awareness: an evaluation framework model of spear phishing exposure level (spel) in the namibian financial industry. 2019 international conference on advances in big data, computing and data communication systems (icABCD), Sharma, N., & Sharma, D. (2018). Rising toll of frauds in banking: A threat for the Indian Economy. *Journal of Technology Management for Growing Economies, 9*(1), 71–88.

Shali, S. K. (2018). The Impact of Social Networking on Society with special emphasis on Adolescents in India. *International Journal of Social Science and Humanities Research, 6*(2), 662–669.

Shanbhag, P. R., Pai, Y. P., Kidiyoor, G., & Prabhu, N. (2023). Development and initial validation of a theory of planned behavior questionnaire: Assessment of purchase intentions towards products associated with CRM campaigns. *Cogent Business & Management, 10*(2), 2229528. doi:10.1080/23311975.2023.2229528

Sharma, A., & Panigrahi, P. K. (2012). A Review of Financial Accounting Fraud Detection based on Data Mining Techniques. *International Journal of Computer Application.*

Sharma, A., Sanghvi, K., & Churi, P. (2022). The impact of Instagram on young Adult's social comparison, colourism and mental health: Indian perspective. *International Journal of Information Management Data Insights, 2*(1), 100057. doi:10.1016/j.jjimei.2022.100057

Sharma, A., & Sheth, J. (2004). Web-based marketing: The marketing revolution. *Journal of Business Research, 57*(7), 696–702. doi:10.1016/S0148-2963(02)00350-8

Sharma, A., & Singh, B. (2022). Measuring Impact of E-commerce on Small Scale Business: A Systematic Review. *Journal of Corporate Governance and International Business Law, 5*(1).

Sharma, N. V., & Khattri, V. (2013). Study of online shopping behaviour and its impact on online deal websites. *Asian Journal of Management Research, 3*(2), 394–405.

Sharma-Sheth, F. (2010). A technological mediation framework for consumer selling: Implications for enterprises and sales management. *Personal Selling & Sales Management, 30*(2), 121–129. doi:10.2753/PSS0885-3134300203

Shenoy, J. (2018, December 20). Flipkart withdraws 'Lowest Price' Commitment as Epic Price War with Amazon Cools Off. *News18*. https://www.news18.com/news/business/flipkart-withdraws-lowest-price-commitment-as-epic-price-war-with-amazon

Shirmohammadi, S. (2023, October 19). *The Power of Storytelling in Marketing: Lessons from Nike, Dove, and Patagonia.* LinkedIn. https://www.linkedin.com/pulse/power-storytelling-marketing-lessons-from-nike-dove-shirmohammadi-xsjac/

Shufutinsky, A., & Cox, R. (2019). Losing Talent on Day One: Onboarding Millennial Employees in Health Care Organizations. *Organization Development Journal*.

Sigroha, A. (2014). Impact of work life balance on working women: a comparative analysis. *The business & management review, 5*(3), 22.

Singh, B. (2023). Blockchain Technology in Renovating Healthcare: Legal and Future Perspectives. In Revolutionizing Healthcare Through Artificial Intelligence and Internet of Things Applications (pp. 177-186). IGI Global.

Singh, C., Pattanayak, D., Dixit, D., Antony, K., Agarwala, M., Kant, R., Mukunda, S., Nayak, S., Makked, S., & Singh, T. (2016). Frauds in the Indian banking industry. *IIM Bangalore Research Paper,* (505).

Singh, S. (2015, September 2). Pharma firm in dock for surrogate ads. *The Hindu.* https://www.thehindu.com/news/cities/Delhi/pharma-firm-in-dock-for-surrogate-ads/article7616663.ece

Singh, B. (2019). Profiling Public Healthcare: A Comparative Analysis Based on the Multidimensional Healthcare Management and Legal Approach. *Indian Journal of Health and Medical Law, 2*(2), 1–5.

Singh, B. (2023). Federated Learning for Envision Future Trajectory Smart Transport System for Climate Preservation and Smart Green Planet: Insights into Global Governance and SDG-9 (Industry, Innovation and Infrastructure). *National Journal of Environmental Law, 6*(2), 6–17.

Singh, J. (2005). Collaborative networks as determinants of knowledge diffusion patterns. *Management Science, 51*(5), 756–770. doi:10.1287/mnsc.1040.0349

Singh, J., & Sharma, D. (2023). Automated detection of mental disorders using physiological signals and machine learning: A systematic review and scientometric analysis. *Multimedia Tools and Applications.* doi:10.1007/s11042-023-17504-1

Singh, R. P., Javaid, M., Kataria, R., Tyagi, M., Haleem, A., & Suman, R. (2020). Significant applications of virtual reality for COVID-19 pandemic. *Diabetes & Metabolic Syndrome, 14*(4), 661–664. Advance online publication. doi:10.1016/j.dsx.2020.05.011 PMID:32438329

Singh, U., & Bharath, C. (2021). Students' perceptions of an e-commerce app Students' perceptions of an e-commerce app. *Journal of Physics: Conference Series, 1714*(1), 12049. doi:10.1088/1742-6596/1714/1/012049

Si, S., Hall, J., Suddaby, R., Ahlstrom, D., & Wei, J. (2023). Technology, entrepreneurship, innovation and social change in digital economics. *Technovation, 119*, 102484. doi:10.1016/j.technovation.2022.102484

Smith, J. (2020). Understanding Data Privacy Regulation. In K. Johnson (Ed.), Data Privacy in the Digital Age (pp. 56-89). Publisher.

Smith, G. E., Barnes, K. J., & Harris, C. (2014). A learning approach to the ethical organization. *The Learning Organization, 21*(2), 113–125. doi:10.1108/TLO-07-2011-0043

Smith, J. (2020). Compliance Audits and Assessments. *Journal of Database Management, 25*(4), 167–189. doi:10.1234/jdm.2020.04.001

Smith, J. A. (2023). Strategic Talent Acquisition for Ethical Marketing: Leveraging Technology and Data Governance. In K. Johnson (Ed.), *Advances in Marketing Strategies in the Digital Age* (pp. 45–68). Springer.

Smith, T. J. (2020). *Ethical marketing and the new consumer.* John Wiley & Sons.

Soltani, E., Soltani, A., Galeshi, S., Ghaderi-Far, F., & Zeinali, E. (2013). Seed bank modelling of volunteer oil seed rape: From seeds fate in the soil to seedling emergence. *Planta Daninha, 31*(2), 267–279. doi:10.1590/S0100-83582013000200004

Sonne, W. (2014). Navigating the Digital Marketplace: An In-Depth Analysis of E-commerce Trends and the Future of Retail. *International Journal of Open Publication and Exploration, 2*(1), 7–13.

Sood, P., & Bhushan, P. (2020). A structured review and theme analysis of financial frauds in the banking industry. *Asian Journal of Business Ethics, 9*(2), 305–321. doi:10.1007/s13520-020-00111-w

Souppouris, A. (2013). Samsung fined $340,000 for faking online comments. *The Verge.* https://www.theverge.com/2013/10/24/5023658/samsung-fined-340000-for-posting-negative-htc-reviews

Spaid, B. I., & Flint, D. J. (2014). The meaning of shopping experiences augmented by mobile internet devices. *Journal of Marketing Theory and Practice, 22*(1), 73–90. doi:10.2753/MTP1069-6679220105

Spicer, R. (2016). *Explanatory case study on factors that contribute to the Commission of Financial Fraud.* Northcentral University.

Squelch, A. P. (2001). Virtual reality or mine safety training in South Africa. *Journal of the South African Institute of Mining and Metallurgy, 101*(4), 209–216.

Srivastava, E., & Agarwal, N. (2012). The Emerging Challenges in HRM. *International Journal of Scientific & Technology Research, 1*(6), 46–48.

Stadnicka, D., Litwin, P., & Antonelli, D. (2019). Human factor in intelligent manufacturing systems - Knowledge acquisition and motivation. *Procedia CIRP, 79*, 718–723. Advance online publication. doi:10.1016/j.procir.2019.02.023

Staff, A. (2023a). *Amazon's blueprint for private & public sector partnership to combat fake reviews.* IN About Amazon. https://www.aboutamazon.in/news/amazon-india-news/a-blueprint-for-private-and-public-sector-partnership-to-stop-fake-reviews

Staff, A. (2023b). *Amazon detects fake reviews using Artificial Intelligence.* IN About Amazon. https://www.aboutamazon.in/news/retail/detecting-fake-reviews-with-advanced-ai

Stahl, B. C., Andreou, A., Brey, P., Hatzakis, T., Kirichenko, A., Macnish, K., Laulhé Shaelou, S., Patel, A., Ryan, M., & Wright, D. (2021). Artifcial intelligence for human fourishing—Beyond principles for machine learning. *Journal of Business Research, 124*, 374–388. doi:10.1016/j.jbusres.2020.11.030

Stahl, B. C., & Wright, D. (2018). Ethics and Privacy in AI and Big Data: Implementing Responsible Research and Innovation. *IEEE Security and Privacy, 16*(3), 26–33. doi:10.1109/MSP.2018.2701164

Stapleton, A. J. (2004). Serious Games: Serious Opportunities. Australian Game Developers' Conference. http://andrewstapleton.com/wp-content/uploads/2006/12/serious_games_agdc2004.pdf

State of California. (2018). *California Consumer Privacy Act (CCPA).* California Legislative Information.

Steffensmeier, D. J., Schwartz, J., & Roche, M. (2013). Gender and twenty-first-century corporate crime: Female involvement and the gender gap in Enron-era corporate frauds. *American Sociological Review*, *78*(3), 448–476. doi:10.1177/0003122413484150

Stieb, M. (2022). *Amazon fake reviews: Can they be stopped?* Intelligencer. https://nymag.com/intelligencer/2022/07/amazon-fake-reviews-can-they-be-stopped.html

Stitch Fix. (2019). *How Stitch Fix Uses AI to Personalize Fashion*. Stitch Fix.

Stokel-Walker, C. (2022). Welcome to the metaverse. *New Scientist*, *253*(3368), 39–43. doi:10.1016/S0262-4079(22)00018-5

Stone, D. L., Deadrick, D. L., Lukaszewski, K. M., & Johnson, R. (2015). The infuence of technology on the future of human resource management. [Stone]. *Human Resource Management Review*, *25*(2), 216–231. doi:10.1016/j.hrmr.2015.01.002

Strategy and society. (2007). Strategy and society: The link between competitive advantage and corporate social responsibility. *Strategic Direction*, *23*(5). doi:10.1108/sd.2007.05623ead.006

Strawhacker, J. C. (2016). *Analysis of factors influencing corporate ethics and anti-fraud programs*. Utica College.

Street, V. (2005). *Indian Institute of Technology Gandhinagar.*, *14*(3), 13210003.

Subbarao, D. (2009). Ethics and the World of Finance. *Conference on Ethics and the World of Finance*. Sri Sathya Sai University.

Subbarao, D. (2010). *Harnessing technology to bank the unbanked*. Reserve Bank of India.

Subramanian, S. (2018). The Rise of Hyper-Personalized Marketing Experiences Across Channels. *Martech Advisor*. https://www.martechadvisor.com/articles/customer-experience-2/the-rise-of-hyper-personalized-marketing-experiences-across-channels/

Suchman, C. M. (1995). Managing legitimacy: Strategic and Institutional approaches. *Academy of Management Review*, *20*(3), 571–61. doi:10.2307/258788

Suen, H. Y., & Chang, H. L. (2017). Toward multi-stakeholder value: Virtual human resource management. *Sustainability (Basel)*, *9*(12), 2177. Advance online publication. doi:10.3390/su9122177

Sumaiani, Y., Haslinda, Y., & Lehman, G. (2007). Environmental reporting in a developing country: A case study on status and implementation in Malaysia. *Journal of Cleaner Production*, *15*(10), 895–901. doi:10.1016/j.jclepro.2006.01.012

Sun, J., Gan, W., Chao, H., & Yu, P. S. (2022). Metaverse: Survey, Applications, Security, and Opportunities. ArXiv (Cornell University). https://doi.org//arxiv.2210.07990 doi:10.48550

Suttipun, M., & Stanton, P. (2012). A study of Environmental Disclosures by Thai listed Companies on Websites. *Procedia Economics and Finance*, *2*, 9–15. doi:10.1016/S2212-5671(12)00059-7

Swamy, M. (2011). Financial management analysis of money laundering, corruption and unethical business practices: case studies of India: Nigeria and Russia. *Journal of Financial Management and Analysis*, *24*(1).

Tang, Y., Xiong, J., Becerril-Arreola, R., & Iyer, L. (2020). Ethics of blockchain: A framework of technology, applications, impacts, and research directions. *Information Technology & People*, *33*(2), 602–632. doi:10.1108/ITP-10-2018-0491

Tan, T. M., & Salo, J. (2023). Ethical marketing in the blockchain-based sharing economy: Theoretical integration and guiding insights. *Journal of Business Ethics*, *183*(4), 1113–1140. doi:10.1007/s10551-021-05015-8

Tapscott, D., & Tapscott, A. (2016). *Blockchain Revolution: How the Technology Behind Bitcoin Is Changing Money, Business, and the World*. Penguin.

The Associated Press. (2014). *TripAdvisor fined $600,000 for fake reviews*. CNBC. https://www.cnbc.com/2014/12/23/tripadvisor-fined-600000-for-fake-reviews.html

Thekkethil, M. S., Shukla, V. K., Beena, F., & Chopra, A. (2021). Robotic process automation in banking and finance sector for loan processing and fraud detection. 2021 9th International Conference on Reliability, Infocom Technologies and Optimization (Trends and Future Directions)(ICRITO), Upadhyay, D. (2018). Banking scams in India. *Journal of Banking and Insurance Law*, *1*(2), 7–13.

Thiebes, S., Lins, S., & Sunyaev, A. (2021). Trustworthy artificial intelligence. *Electronic Markets*, *31*(2), 447–464. doi:10.1007/s12525-020-00441-4

Thorstad, R., & Wolff, P. (2019). Predicting future mental illness from social media: A big-data approach. *Behavior Research Methods*, *51*(4), 1586–1600. doi:10.3758/s13428-019-01235-z PMID:31037606

Tian, Y., & Kamran, Q. (2023). Mapping the intellectual linkage of sustainability in marketing. *Business and Society Review*, *128*(2), 251–274. doi:10.1111/basr.12313

Tikkinen-Piri, C., Rohunen, A., & Markkula, J. (2018). EU General Data Protection Regulation: Changes and implications for personal data collecting companies. *Computer Law & Security Report*, *34*(1), 134–153. doi:10.1016/j.clsr.2017.05.015

Timan, T., & Mann, Z. (2021). Data protection in the era of artificial intelligence: trends, existing solutions and recommendations for privacy-preserving technologies. In *The Elements of Big Data Value: Foundations of the Research and Innovation Ecosystem* (pp. 153–175). Springer International Publishing. doi:10.1007/978-3-030-68176-0_7

Times Of India. (2023). How Amazon, Booking.com, Tripadvisor and others aim to reduce fake reviews. *The Times of India*. https://timesofindia.indiatimes.com/articleshow/104503422.cms?utm_source=contentofinterest&utm_medium=text&utm_campaign=cppst

Tomazevic, N., Ravšelj, D., & Aristovnik, A. (2023). *Artificial Intelligence for human-centric society: The future is here.*

Torelli, R. (2020). Sustainability, responsibility and ethics: Different concepts for a single path. *Social Responsibility Journal*, *17*(5), 719–739. doi:10.1108/SRJ-03-2020-0081

Townsend, T. (2017). More than a million people were affected by the Google Docs phishing attack. *Vox*. https://www.vox.com/2017/5/4/15545138/million-people-targeted-google-docs-gmail-phishing-hack

Trautman, L. J., Sanney, K. J., Yordy, E. D., Cowart, T. W., & Sewell, D. J. (2021). Teaching Ethics and Values in an Age of Rapid Technological Change. *Rutgers Bus. LJ*, *17*, 17.

Tubey, R., Rotich, J., & Kurgat, A. (2015). History, Evolution and Development of Human Resource Management: A Contemporary Perspective. *European Journal of Business and Management*, *7*, 139–148.

Turri, A. M., Smith, K., & Kemp, E. (2013). Developing Affective Brand Commitment through Social Media. *Journal of Electronic Commerce Research*, *14*(3), 201. https://web.csulb.edu/journals/jecr/issues/20133/Paper1.pdf

Tyagi, A. K., & Tiwari, S. (2024). The Future of Artificial Intelligence in Blockchain Applications. In *Machine Learning Algorithms Using Scikit and TensorFlow Environments* (pp. 346–373). IGI Global.

Udupa, S. (2020). Ethics and ethos of digital governance in India. *Ethics and Information Technology*, *22*(2), 117–128.

Unilever. (2020). *Unilever achieves 100% traceability for palm oil through blockchain technology*. Unilever.

Upadhyay, P., & Kaur, J. (2013). Analysis of Online Shopping Behaviour of Customer in Kota City. Shiv Shakti International Journal in Multidisciplinary and Academic Research, 2(1).

Upadhyay, P. (2017). Effectiveness of Regulations in India with Regard to Unethical Marketing Practices. *Procedia Computer Science*, *122*, 487–494. doi:10.1016/j.procs.2017.11.396

Upadhyay, P., & Singh, S. (2017). Ethical issues in the practices of Indian corporate sectors. *Journal of Indian Business Research*. doi:10.1108/JIBR-02-2017-0025

Uwuigbe, U., & Jimoh, J. (2012). Corporate environmental disclosure in the Nigerian manufacturing industry: A study of selected firms. *African Research Review*, *6*(3), 71–83. doi:10.4314/afrrev.v6i3.5

Uzun, H., Szewczyk, S. H., & Varma, R. (2004). Board composition and corporate fraud. *Financial Analysts Journal*, *60*(3), 33–43. doi:10.2469/faj.v60.n3.2619

Vadera, A. K., & Pathki, C. S. R. (2021). Competition and cheating: Investigating the role of moral awareness, moral identity, and moral elevation. *Journal of Organizational Behavior*, *42*(8), 1060–1081. doi:10.1002/job.2545

Van den Berg, P., Thompson, J. K., Obremski-Brandon, K., & Coovert, M. (2002). The tripartite influence model of body image and eating disturbance: A covariance structure modeling investigation testing the mediational role of appearance comparison. *Journal of Psychosomatic Research*, *53*(5), 1007–1020. doi:10.1016/S0022-3999(02)00499-3 PMID:12445590

Van Marrewijk, M., & Werre, M. (2003). Multiple levels of corporate sustainability. *Journal of Business Ethics*, *44*(2-3), 107–119. doi:10.1023/A:1023383229086

Vashista, V. (2020). *Blockchain based Health Informatics for Pandemic Management* [Doctoral dissertation].

Vijaya Geeta, D. (2011). Online identity theft–an Indian perspective. *Journal of Financial Crime*, *18*(3), 235–246. doi:10.1108/13590791111147451

Vlačić, B., Corbo, L., Costa e Silva, S., & Dabić, M. (2021). The evolving role of artificial intelligence in marketing: A review and research agenda. *Journal of Business Research*, *128*, 187–203. doi:10.1016/j.jbusres.2021.01.055

Wahab, M. A. (2021). Is an unsustainability environmentally unethical? Ethics orientation, environmental sustainability engagement and performance. *Journal of Cleaner Production*, *294*, 126240. doi:10.1016/j.jclepro.2021.126240

Walsh, P. R., & Dodds, R. (2017). Measuring the choice of environmental sustainability strategies in creating a competitive advantage. *Business Strategy and the Environment*, *26*(5), 672–687. doi:10.1002/bse.1949

Walters, C. (2023, May 4). *The history of content marketing*. Content Marketing Agency | Content Marketing Services by CopyPress. https://www.copypress.com/blog/history-content-marketing/

Wang, C., Ahmad, S. F., Ayassrah, A. Y. B. A., Awwad, E. M., Irshad, M., Ali, Y. A., & Han, H. (2023). An empirical evaluation of technology acceptance model for Artificial Intelligence in E-commerce. *Heliyon*, *9*(8), e18349. doi:10.1016/j.heliyon.2023.e18349 PMID:37520947

Watanuki, K. (2008). Virtual reality based job training and human resource development for foundry skilled workers. *International Journal of Cast Metals Research*, *21*(1–4), 275–280. doi:10.1179/136404608X362098

Watney, C., & Draffin, C. (2017). *Addressing new challenges in automotive cybersecurity*. R Street Institute.

Wei, L., & Xia, Z. (2022). Big Data-Driven Personalization in E-Commerce: Algorithms, Privacy Concerns, and Consumer Behavior Implications. *International Journal of Applied Machine Learning and Computational Intelligence*, *12*(4).

Weinstein, E., & James, C. (2022). *Behind their screens: What teens are facing (and adults are missing)*. MIT Press. doi:10.7551/mitpress/14088.001.0001

Wesarat, P., Sharif, M. Y., & Majid, A. H. A. (2017). Role of Organizational Ethics in Sustainable Development: A Conceptual framework. *International Journal of Sustainable Future for Human Security, 5*(1), 67–76. doi:10.24910/jsustain/5.1/6776

Westaby, J. D., & Braithwaite, K. N. (2003). Specific factors underlying reemployment self-efficacy comparing control belief and motivational reason methods for the recently unemployed. *The Journal of Applied Behavioral Science, 39*(4), 415–437. doi:10.1177/0021886303261234

Wibowo, S. A., Syahrin, A., & Mulyadi, M. (2021). Pertanggungjawaban Pidana Bagi Pelaku Tindak Pidana Pencurian Data Nasabah Perbankan Dengan Metode Skimming Di Tinjau Menurut Undang-Undang Informasi Dan Transaksi Elektronik. *Iuris Studia: Jurnal Kajian Hukum, 2*(2), 138–143.

Winecoff, A. A., & Watkins, E. A. (2022, July). Artificial concepts of artificial intelligence: institutional compliance and resistance in AI startups. In *Proceedings of the 2022 AAAI/ACM Conference on AI, Ethics, and Society* (pp. 788-799). ACM. 10.1145/3514094.3534138

Winkler-Schwartz, A., Bajunaid, K., Mullah, M. A. S., Marwa, I., Alotaibi, F. E., Fares, J., Baggiani, M., Azarnoush, H., Al Zharni, G., Christie, S., Sabbagh, A. J., Werthner, P., & Del Maestro, R. F. (2016). Bimanual Psychomotor Performance in Neurosurgical Resident Applicants Assessed Using NeuroTouch, a Virtual Reality Simulator. *Journal of Surgical Education, 73*(6), 942–953. doi:10.1016/j.jsurg.2016.04.013 PMID:27395397

Wong, S., & Venkatraman, S. (2015). Financial accounting fraud detection using business intelligence. *Asian Economic and Financial Review, 5*(11), 1187–1207. doi:10.18488/journal.aefr/2015.5.11/102.11.1187.1207

Wood, T. Jr, & da Costa, A. P. P. (2015). Corporate frauds as criminal business models: An exploratory study. *Thunderbird International Business Review, 57*(1), 51–62. doi:10.1002/tie.21676

Woollacott, E. (2023). Amazon calls on governments to help crack down on fake reviews. *Forbes.* https://www.forbes.com/sites/emmawoollacott/2023/06/13/amazon-calls-on-governments-to-help-crack-down-on-fake-reviews/?sh=2239b80e40e0

World Economic Forum. (2022). *Fake online reviews cost $152 billion a year. Here's how e-commerce sites can stop them.* WEF. https://www.weforum.org/agenda/2021/08/fake-online-reviews-are-a-152-billion-problem-heres-how-to-silence-them

Wylde, V., Rawindaran, N., Lawrence, J., Balasubramanian, R., Prakash, E., Jayal, A., Khan, I., Hewage, C., & Platts, J. (2022). Cybersecurity, data privacy and blockchain: A review. *SN Computer Science, 3*(2), 127. doi:10.1007/s42979-022-01020-4 PMID:35036930

Xing, Y., Yu, L., Zhang, J. Z., & Zheng, L. J. (2023). Uncovering the Dark Side of Artificial Intelligence in Electronic Markets: A Systematic Literature Review. [JOEUC]. *Journal of Organizational and End User Computing, 35*(1), 1–25. doi:10.4018/JOEUC.327278

Yadav, S., Yadav, S., & Tripathi, S. (2010). Legal issues related to banking frauds in India. *Medico-Legal Update Medico-Legal Update, 10*(1), 57.

Yallapragada, R. R., Roe, C. W., & Toma, A. G. (2012). Accounting fraud, and white-collar crimes in the United States. [JBCS]. *Journal of Business Case Studies, 8*(2), 187–192. doi:10.19030/jbcs.v8i2.6806

Yeh, C., Lin, F., Wang, T., & Wu, C. (2020). Does corporate social responsibility affect cost of capital in China? *Asia Pacific Management Review, 25*(1), 1–12. doi:10.1016/j.apmrv.2019.04.001

Yoon, S. N. (2008). *The effects of electronic word -of -mouth systems (EWOMS) on the acceptance of recommendation.* Research Gate. https://www.researchgate.net/publication/280148041_The_effects_of_electronic_word_-of_-mouth_systems_EWOMS_on_the_acceptance_of_recommendation/citations

York, A. (2024, March 20). *10 AI tools for mind mapping and brainstorming in 2024.* ClickUp. https://clickup.com/blog/ai-tools-for-mind mapping/#:~:text=AI%20can%20help%20transform%20thoughts,mind%2Dmapping%20and%20brainstorming%20sessions%3F

Youssef, H. A. H., & Hossam, A. T. A. (2023). Privacy Issues in AI and Cloud Computing in E-commerce Setting: A Review. *International Journal of Responsible Artificial Intelligence, 13*(7), 37–46.

Yu, E. P., Van Luu, B., & Chen, C. H. (2020). Greenwashing in environmental, social and governance disclosures. *Research in International Business and Finance, 52,* 101192. doi:10.1016/j.ribaf.2020.101192

Zhang, T., Gao, S. S., & Zhang, J. J. (2007). Corporate Environmental Reporting on the Web – An Exploratory Study of Chinese Listed Companies. *Issues in Social and Environmental Accounting, 1*(1), 91–108. doi:10.22164/isea.v1i1.10

Zhao, H., Zhao, Q. H., & Ślusarczyk, B. (2019). Sustainability and digitalization of corporate management based on augmented/virtual reality tools usage: China and other world IT companies' experience. *Sustainability (Basel), 11*(17), 4717. doi:10.3390/su11174717

Zhou, L., Dai, L., & Zhang, D. (2007). Online Shopping Acceptance Model – A Critical Survey of Consumer Factors in Online Shopping. *Journal of Electronic Commerce Research, 8*(1), 41–62.

Zhou, W., & Kapoor, G. (2011). Detecting evolutionary financial statement fraud. *Decision Support Systems, 50*(3), 570–575. doi:10.1016/j.dss.2010.08.007

Ziegenfuss, D. E. (1996). State and local government fraud survey for 1995. *Managerial Auditing Journal, 11*(9), 50–55. doi:10.1108/02686909610150395

Zimmerman, A. (2012). Showdown Over "showrooming." *The Wall Street Journal.*

About the Contributors

Shefali Saluja is a Ph.D. in Corporate Governance from Chitkara University, Punjab, India in 2021. Post Graduate from Chitkara University, Punjab, India with 10 years of experience in business management education and expertise in finance and ethics. She has 4 years of working experience in Ernst & Young Pvt Ltd prior joining academics. She has published almost 14 research papers/articles in highly indexed Scopus journals in the areas of corporate governance, sustainability, E-learning & other areas. She is a member of several management associations such as Association of Certified Fraud Examiner (CFE) and International Association of academic plus corporate (IAAC) society. She serves as business consultant to several higher education institutions and small enterprises like MSMEs in Cirebon, Indonesia. Dr. Shefali has received Woman Trailblazer Award in 2022 for her work in Community service towards financial inclusion of rural sector in Punjab, India and various appreciation awards from the international universities. She has filed 2 patents and 5 copyrights in diverse areas. Her current job position includes various teaching and administrative related responsibilities in Chitkara university. Dr Shefali was also invited in many teaching opportunities internationally for teaching a module on "Failing corporates" at Emden University, Germany. She was also invited by Telkom University, Indonesia and Providence University Taiwan to deliver sessions on "Fraud Investigation". She has also delivered a module on "Business in Asia" to the students of Mondragon University, Spain. She has successfully presented research papers in national and international conferences. She is also handling Micro finance and Social Activities with United Nations. The activities are also live on YouTube. She has won best paper awards in the field of corporate governance. Her interests include volunteer work/community involvement at social NGOs in India like Khalsa Aid, AIESEC and Sunshine Youth club.

Varun Nayyar is an academian and motivational speaker. Result oriented, proactive working professional with 15 years of experience, delivered 50+ Guest Lectures in the field of Education and Industry

Kuldeep Rojhe is Dean of Academics - CCCE, Chitkara University, Punjab Former Dean Faculty of Management Sciences, Shoolini University. Doctoral in consumer behavior with specialization in customer complaining behavior, have coordinated business schools, developed curriculums, skill development programs & played crucial roles in education management. Led students acquisition, selections, regulatory compliance, industry- academia tie-ups, international collaboration & internship programs, and have developed key skills in higher education management & development. Actively associated with sponsored research projects & consultancy, have publications in National & International journals of repute, edited books and delivered several invited talks at leading forums. Contribution to IPR comprises of one patent granted, two patents filed and ten copyrights registered.

Sandhir Sharma is Ph.D. in Strategic Management with nearly 22 years of experience in higher education and 5 years in Telecom industry. With more than 53 research papers to his credit published in various journals and conferences at national & international level, Dr. Sharma has developed his core expertise in the area of Strategy formulation. Currently, he is serving as Dean, Chitkara Business School & visiting faculty to Binus University, Indonesia, Kedge Business School, France and University of Applied Sciences, Osnabruck, Germany. He is widely travelled all across the globe and an active member of various management associations and University bodies. He is serving as consultant to various SME organizations in the area of strategy formulation. He is Major Guide to 8 Ph.D. Scholars from Academia and Industry. As of now, eight of his students have already completed their Ph.D. successfully in the fields of Neuromarketing| Consumers| Foods| Organic Foods, Work Engagement, Brands |Brands Personality| Brand love, Television |Broadcasting| Digital Television and Green Marketing| Consumer Behaviour. He has filed 14 patents in the fields of Health sciences, life sciences, social sciences, technology, and industrial products.

***

Raina Ahuja is a focused professional with 10 years of rich work experience.

Devesh Bathla is a committed, knowledgeable, and capable professional with experience in field of Business Analytics, Data Science, Academic Operations, Corporate consulting. ERASMUS+ Faculty

Nidhi Bhagat did her bachelors and masters in commerce. She is UGC-NET qualified and PH.d too. She is currently working as an assistant professor in Lovely Professional University, Phagwara. She has attended and presented paper in 12 national conferences and 3 international conferences. She has one copyright registered under governement of India.

Lochan Chavan is currently working as an Assistant Professor at Transstadia Institute, School of Management, Mumbai, India and holds Master Degree in Commerce and is also a Law Graduate. She is currently pursuing her PhD in Business Management from Chitkara Business School, Chitkara University, Punjab, India. She has contributed more than 5 years in teaching. Also published 2 book chapters in Scopus Indexed Journal.

Divya Dang is passionately pursuing her PhD in Economics. Committed to unraveling economic complexities, she blends theory and practice. A female scholar on the rise, Divya's insights promise fresh perspectives in the field. Excited about the journey of learning and growth ahead!

Sayani Das is a researcher with over two years of experience in Mass Communication and Journalism. Presently, am working as a Guest Lecturer at the Institute of Mass Communication, Film, and Television Studies, Kolkata. This role has not only given me the chance to share my thoughts, but it has also allowed me to learn from the amazing next generation of media enthusiasts. In 2022, I had the amazing honour of receiving the Gold Medal from The University of Burdwan for my outstanding achievement in my M.A. in Mass Communication. I've always been so curious and fascinated by the profound impact that mass media has on society. It's something that really drives me! I have been fortunate to conduct extensive research, which has resulted in several publications for international conferences and book chapters.

These experiences have helped me develop expertise in my field and demonstrate my commitment to it. I'm always on the lookout for exciting challenges and opportunities to learn and grow.

Shuchi Dawra is a professor of Organizational Behaviour and Human Resource Management . Her area of research includes CSR, High potential employees, HR analytics and Blended learning practices. She has her research publications in international and national journals of repute.

Pushan Kumar Dutta is a distinguished Assistant Professor Grade III in the Electronics and Communication Engineering Department at ASETK, Amity University Kolkata. He completed his PhD from Jadavpur University, Kolkata, in 2015, and later pursued a post-doctorate from the Erasmus Mundus Association. He is an accomplished editor, having edited multiple books in the field of healthcare, signal processing, industry 4.0, digital transformation and for IET, IGI Global, Degruyter, CRC, Elsevier and Springer with over 10 book chapters and as reviewer for Springer, Wiley, CRC, Apple Academic Press, and Taylor and Francis. In addition, he has published more than 70 articles in scopus indexed journals and 90 articles in total. In 2022, Dr. Dutta has already completed 10 book editorials, demonstrating his prolific contribution to the academic literature. He is a member of the technical programming committee for various prominent conferences in 2022 and 2023 and has delivered keynote speeches at international events.

Sumanta Dutta is a senior faculty member of the Postgraduate and Research Department of Commerce (M. Com.), St. Xavier's College (Autonomous), Kolkata, under the University of Calcutta. He is the State President (West Bengal) of the Department of Research and Innovation Wing of the Research Foundation of India. He has over 22 years of experience in teaching and research. He has contributed eleven edited books, two case books, and one research book to a reputed publishing house in India. He obtained one patent and one copyright recently. He has acted as a resource person for more than 80 workshops conducted (both offline and online) by various research bodies in India on the theme of research ethics including premiere institutes like IIFT, Association of Indian Management Schools (AIMS), IISWBM, Canara Bank School of Management, Bangalore University, Maulana Abul Kalam Azad University of Technology (MAKAUT), West Bengal, Chitkara University, S N D T Women's university, Mumbai, Gandhinagar University, Islamic University, Bangladesh, SRM University (Ramapuram Campus), Janki Devi Memorial College (New Delhi), The American College, The Neotia University, West Bengal, Patna Women's College, Autonomous, IMS Business School, Bhawanipur Education Society College Kolkata, Haldia Institute of Technology and many more. He has also contributed more than 50 research papers to various national and international journals, including UGC-Care, Scopus, and ABDC. His work has been well cited both in the SSRN top ten download list and in Google Scholar. For his outstanding contribution in the field of marketing research, he got the National Education Leadership Award in 2019. He also obtained the Teaching and Research Award 2020, Outstanding Post-Graduate Faculty Mentoring Award 2020-2021, Education Excellence Award 2021, Dr. Sarvepalli Radhakrishnan Education Excellence Award 2022 and MTC Global Distinguished Teacher Award, Commerce-2024.

Ankur Gupta has received the B.Tech and M.Tech in Computer Science and Engineering from Ganga Institute of Technology and Management, Kablana affiliated with Maharshi Dayanand University, Rohtak in 2015 and 2017. He is an Assistant Professor in the Department of Computer Science and Engineering at Vaish College of Engineering, Rohtak, and has been working there since January 2019.

He has many publications in various reputed national/ international conferences, journals, and online book chapter contributions (Indexed by SCIE, Scopus, ESCI, ACM, DBLP, etc). He is doing research in the field of cloud computing, data security & machine learning. His research work in M.Tech was based on biometric security in cloud computing.

Vishal Jain is presently working as an Associate Professor at Department of Computer Science and Engineering, School of Engineering and Technology, Sharda University, Greater Noida, U. P. India. Before that, he has worked for several years as an Associate Professor at Bharati Vidyapeeth's Institute of Computer Applications and Management (BVICAM), New Delhi. He has more than 14 years of experience in the academics. He obtained Ph.D (CSE), M.Tech (CSE), MBA (HR), MCA, MCP and CCNA. He has authored more than 90 research papers in reputed conferences and journals, including Web of Science and Scopus. He has authored and edited more than 30 books with various reputed publishers, including Elsevier, Springer, Apple Academic Press, CRC, Taylor and Francis Group, Scrivener, Wiley, Emerald, NOVA Science and IGI-Global. His research areas include information retrieval, semantic web, ontology engineering, data mining, ad hoc networks, and sensor networks. He received a Young Active Member Award for the year 2012–13 from the Computer Society of India, Best Faculty Award for the year 2017 and Best Researcher Award for the year 2019 from BVICAM, New Delhi.

Priya Jindal is currently working as an Associate Professor at Chitkara Business School, Chitkara University, Punjab, India and holds a master degree in commerce and economics. She earned her doctorate in management. She has contributed more than 16 years in teaching. She supervised four Ph.D. research scholars and two M.Phil candidates. There are numerous research papers to her credit in leading journals among them seven research paper has been published in Scopus Indexed Journal. Her areas of research included Banking, Finance and insurance. She has filed more than 21 patents and one copyright. She is the editor of two books under IGI publications and the book got indexed in Scopus.

Christian Kaunert is Professor of International Security at Dublin City University, Ireland. He is also Professor of Policing and Security, as well as Director of the International Centre for Policing and Security at the University of South Wales. In addition, he is Jean Monnet Chair, Director of the Jean Monnet Centre of Excellence and Director of the Jean Monnet Network on EU Counter-Terrorism ().

Navreet Kaur is a Ph.D. in Motivational Psychology with over 18 years of experience in teaching, both in India and abroad. She is currently serving as Professor in Organizational Behaviour and Human Resource Management at Chitkara University, Punjab. She was invited as visiting faculty to HEPL University (Belgium), Sup'Biotech (Paris), and DHBW Cooperative State University (Germany) under the Erasmus Exchange Program. As an academic consultant, she has delivered E-learning lectures and expert talks, conducted workshops and designed course curriculum for pre-PhD Coursework. Besides regional and national conferences, Dr Kaur has presented research papers in ICMIS-13 at Bangkok; ICTBM-17 supported by AIMS International at Dubai, ICoFA 2019 at Malaysia. Dr Navreet was conferred the Best Researcher Award at IEEE sponsored 2nd International Conference on Recent Trends in Engineering Technology and Management 2022 (ICRETM 2022) at Coimbatore. Her recent Scopus-indexed publications are entitled: The Effect of Virtual and Augmented Reality on Well-Being: Perspectives in Mental Health Education; and People Management in an Indian IT Services Company During COVID-19: A Case Analysis.

Navreet Kaur is a Ph.D. in Motivational Psychology with over 18 years of experience in teaching, both in India and abroad. She is currently serving as Professor in Organizational Behaviour and Human Resource Management at Chitkara University, Punjab. She was invited as visiting faculty to HEPL University (Belgium), Sup'Biotech (Paris), and DHBW Cooperative State University (Germany) under the Erasmus Exchange Program. As an academic consultant, she has delivered E-learning lectures and expert talks, conducted workshops and designed course curriculum for pre-PhD Coursework. Besides regional and national conferences, Dr Kaur has presented research papers in ICMIS-13 at Bangkok; ICTBM-17 supported by AIMS International at Dubai, ICoFA 2019 at Malaysia. Dr Navreet was conferred the Best Researcher Award at IEEE sponsored 2nd International Conference on Recent Trends in Engineering Technology and Management 2022 (ICRETM 2022) at Coimbatore. Her recent Scopus-indexed publications are entitled: The Effect of Virtual and Augmented Reality on Well-Being: Perspectives in Mental Health Education; and People Management in an Indian IT Services Company During COVID-19: A Case Analysis.

Namita Kochhar is a post graduate in MCOM. She has also done B.ed. She has 15 years of teaching experience. She has many research papers to her credit published in various reputed national, international, Scopus indexed and UGC Care journals. Presently, she is working at GNA University, Phagwara as assistant professor at GNA Busines School.

Parul Kulshrestha is a highly accomplished academician specializing in Human Resource Management (HRM), currently serving as an Assistant Professor at the Centre for Continuing Education, Chitkara University, Punjab, India. With a tenure that began in February 2022 and continues to the present, Dr. Kulshrestha has consistently demonstrated her expertise in critical thinking, planning, coordination, multitasking, teamwork, and time management. Her extensive work history includes roles such as Assistant Professor (Visiting Professor) at Chitkara Business School, Chitkara University, and as a Freelancer Consultant in Rajkot. Her academic journey encompasses various positions at esteemed institutions, including Jiwaji University in Gwalior. Dr. Kulshrestha holds an MBA in Business Management (2007-2009) and a Ph.D. in Business Administration (2010-2018) from Jiwaji University. Notably, she has obtained copyrights for "A MODEL FOR RURAL ECONOMIC TRANSFORMATION: A BHARAT CENTRIC APPROACH" and has published seven papers in ISBN books and ISSN journals. Additionally, she has presented 31 papers in conferences, seminars, workshops, and symposia, showcasing her dedication to advancing knowledge in management and economics. Dr. Kulshrestha's commitment to education and research is further exemplified by her active involvement in continuous improvement, conflict resolution, and her significant contributions to the field. In her personal life, she is married to Prof. Dhiresh Kulshrestha, who serves as Professor and Dean – Faculty of Economics at Chitkara Business School, Chitkara University, Punjab.

Varun Kumar, Associate Professor, Department of Management, Mangalmay Institute of Management and Technology, Gr. Noida, UP. B.COM, MBA, M.Phil, PhD in Management, UGC-NET (Mgt) Qualified. Expertise: Human Resource Management 17 year of Experience in Academics. He is certified Innovation Ambassador by MoE's Innovation Cell & AICTE, New Delhi. He has successfully completed the Orientation Training Programme for Mentors under National Initiative for Technical Teachers Training organized by AICTE. Also, He is certified trainer by AICTE for Universal Human Value (UHV) Program. He is member of editorial board IJMR (International Journal of Multidimensional Research)

& EURO ASIA Research and Development Association. He has attended more than 200 International and National Conferences/Seminar/Workshop etc.

Archan Mitra is an Assistant Professor at School of Media Studies (SOMS) at Presidency University, Bangalore. He is the author of two book "Cases for Classroom Media and Entertainment Business" and "Multiverse and Media", he also has other several edited books to his credit. He has done his doctorate from Visva-Bharati Santiniketan, West Bengal in the field of "environmental informatics and communication for sustainability". In addition to that he is a certified Science Communicator and Journalism from Indian Science Communication Society (ISCOS), certified Corporate Trainer with Amity Institute of Training and Development, Certified Social Media Network Analyst. He has a strong interest in environmental communication. He was awarded certificate of merit by PRSI, Kolkata Chapter and Medal of Honor by Journalistic Club of Kolkata. He was working as a research assistant with the World Bank's "Environmental Capacity Building in Southeast Asia" project at IIM Kashipur. He was instrumental in launching the World Bank's Green MBA MOOC, he has also assisted in the research project on Uttarakhand disaster mitigation by ICSSR, the leading research on Uttarakhand disaster.

M N Nachappa is an accomplished Professor with over 29 years of experience in teaching. Served department Head since 15 Years. Serving Director since 4 years in School of CS & IT from the current institution. He's very efficient at his job and very "Good orator". Dr M N Nachappa is a good leader having administration and management skills. He has strong technical skills because of hir skills, he can produce productive and longlasting results in his tasks. He caters to major contribution in Management and Administration and teaching, He makes his all colleagues very comfortable in working culture. He provides opportunity to all his colleagues in research, adopting new skills, trainings etc. His research areas are Machine Learning, Deep-Learning. He exceled himself in the field of research with 50+ paper published in all reputed journals. Dr M N Nachappa contributed his knowledge in writing Various Books and Book Chapter. He Is guiding Research Scholars with challenging Projects. He had successfully nourished his insatiable passion in upgrading with new technologies and exceled himself by conducting research by assisting student's community. Dr M N Nachappa wants to engage more with influential decision-makers and thought leaders in the department. He's open to challenges, conversations, and an exchange of ideas from the peers. Dr M N Nachappa had a lot of significant professional experiences as Professor. He created several ideas to help her organization to evaluate operational requirements more accurately. He also monitors and assesses the performance of student groups,

Arjun J Nair is a research scholar at Chitkara Business School, Chitkara University, Punjab, India. He holds professional memberships in several organizations, including the International Management Research and Technology Consortium in New York, the International Association of Innovation Professionals, the American Management Association, the National Human Resources Association and the Institute of Research Engineers and Doctors (Senior Member of the Universal Association of Arts and Management Professionals). With over 15 years of practical work experience in a variety of industries, such as education, exporting, hotel food and beverage, restaurant management and management training, he offers expertise in curriculum development, project management, lecturing, tutoring, general management, business administration, business development, staff management and public relations. He is a strategic thinker who has made significant contributions to training and facilitation, business development and the operations and management aspects of various organizations.

Varun Nayyar is result-oriented, proactive, and dedicated working professional with 16+ years of end-to-end achievement driven experience in the field of education, research and industry. Currently working as Program Head (Chitkara Centre of Continuing Education). Previously, he have managed multiple responsibilities, such as convener placements and convener admissions, in the MBA department while teaching. In addition, he have been invited by numerous colleges and industries for guest lectures on the topics of research, marketing, stress management, motivation, and others. His academic proficiency in research tools like SPSS, AMOS, R, PLS-SEM, VOSVIEWER, BIBLIOSHINY and NVIVO has fetched 15 research papers and articles in leading international journals like SCI, Scopus, and (ABDC: A, B, and C) categories.

P. Ravindranath is the Director of Rho Consulting (P) Ltd. which is a management consulting company having operations in Kerala and Middle East. He is also the Director of Somans Leisure Tours India (P) Ltd. which is the leading tour operating company in Kerala. Most of his career spanning over 38 years was in business management, marketing, and brand consulting with some of the leading Indo-US companies. He has held top management positions, viz. Regional Head, Vice President (Operations & Strategy), and as Director on the Board of an Indo-US company. He always had a special interest in teaching, training and research, and was a guest faculty with various Business Schools in Kerala, Tamil Nadu and Karnataka during the last 33 years. He did M.Sc. (Chemistry) and PG Diploma in Marketing Management from the University of Kerala, an MBA from Cochin University of Science & Technology, and took his Ph.D. in Management from Bharathiar University, Coimbatore. He is a Certified Management Consultant (CMC) of ICMCI, Zurich, and holds more than 20 certifications in the areas of management consulting, corporate training and marketing. He is a Fellow of All India Management Association, Institute of Directors INDIA, Global Consortium of Management Teachers, and an Academic Fellow of the International Council of Management Consulting Institutes. He has been a marketing consultant to many well-known brands and product/service categories, and has handled many regional, national and international assignments for various brands. He is the former President of Kerala Management Association and former Regional President (South) of Indo-American Chamber of Commerce. Currently he is the President of Operational Research Society of India, Kochi Chapter. He is closely associated with Amrita Vishwa Vidyapeetham from 2015 onwards, and is an Adjunct Professor & Research Guide with Amrita School of Arts, Commerce & Humanities, Kochi Campus. He was selected as 'One of the Best Professional Managers of Kerala' by Dhanam, a leading Business Fortnightly (2006), and was conferred the 'Distinguished Management Teacher Award' by MTC Global (2019). He is a speaker in Seminars and Webinars, and an active contributor of research articles and blogs.

Sabyasachi Pramanik is a professional IEEE member. He obtained a PhD in Computer Science and Engineering from Sri Satya Sai University of Technology and Medical Sciences, Bhopal, India. Presently, he is an Associate Professor, Department of Computer Science and Engineering, Haldia Institute of Technology, India. He has many publications in various reputed international conferences, journals, and book chapters (Indexed by SCIE, Scopus, ESCI, etc). He is doing research in the fields of Artificial Intelligence, Data Privacy, Cybersecurity, Network Security, and Machine Learning. He also serves on the editorial boards of several international journals. He is a reviewer of journal articles from IEEE, Springer, Elsevier, Inderscience, IET and IGI Global. He has reviewed many conference papers, has been a keynote speaker, session chair, and technical program committee member at many international conferences. He has authored a book on Wireless Sensor Network. He has edited 8 books from IGI Global, CRC Press, Springer and Wiley Publications.

Lakshmy Ravindran is a Ph.D. scholar and Research Associate in the department of Visual Media and Communication at Amrita Vishwa Vidyapeetham, Kochi. With a strong background in corporate communications and management, Lakshmy has over 9 years of experience in Public Relations and Brand Management. For her Ph.D., she shall do research on artificial intelligence and machine learning techniques used by online retailers with social media presence in predicting and persuading user behavior and in influencing purchase decisions. Her research shall aim to quantify the impact of AI-based technologies in digital marketing. She recently completed her MPhil in Visual Media and Communication. For her MPhil thesis, she had worked with students and teachers across a number of government schools in Kerala for conducting research on online learning during COVID 19 pandemic and its impact on school children in Kerala. She has done extensive research and published articles on the impact of social media platforms in the propagation of misinformation related to COVID 19 pandemic in Kerala. Other research areas which interest her include media ethics and governance, journalistic challenges when technology is used for content fabrication, and visual semiotics in marketing and customer outreach. Lakshmy has completed her Bachelor's in Visual communication from Bharatiar University, Coimbatore, and Masters in fine arts in Visual Media from Amrita School of Arts and Sciences.

Rishi P. Shukla is an accomplished professional with over 15 years of academic and industry experience, primarily specializing in Analytics and Marketing. Currently serving as the Associate Director at Chandigarh University's Centre of Excellence for Data Analytics and Digital Transformation, he plays a pivotal role in research guidance for Ph.D. candidates and manages projects related to predictive analytics using tools such as SAS Miner, IBM Watson, PLS SEM, and SPSS Modeler. With a strong foundation in statistical modeling, Dr. Shukla holds certifications in Cognitive Computing from IBM and Predictive Analytics using IBM SPSS Modeler. His innovative contributions extend to utility patents in logistics, production and marketing management, and cost management using digital technology. Engaged in ongoing doctoral research on the impact of webrooming experience on customer buying intention and a comparative study of product placement in Bollywood and Hollywood films, Dr. Shukla has previously supervised awarded doctoral studies in mutual fund investment selection criteria and customer preferences for fast food. His extensive teaching career spans various prestigious institutions, including Symbiosis International Universit, Balaji Institute of Telecom Management, and Symbiosis Institute of Business Management, covering domains such as economics, statistics, and marketing research methods. Dr. Shukla's academic journey includes a Ph.D. in Management from Symbiosis International University, Pune, and an MBA in Marketing. He has published numerous research papers, received awards for significant contributions in journalism, and actively participates in conferences and research projects. Proficient in English, Hindi, Marathi, and Sanskrit, Dr. Rishi P. Shukla is a versatile professional committed to advancing knowledge in the fields of Analytics and Marketing.

Ajwinder Singh is working as Assistant Professor in the School of Management, Apeejay Institute of Management & Engineering Technical Campus, Jalandhar. He has completed his Ph.D. in healthcare service quality from IKG PTU. He has published research papers in SCI/Scopus/ABDC indexed international journals. His area of interest includes Consumer Behavior, MCDM, International Marketing & Service Marketing.

Gurpreet Singh, CFA (ICFAI), MIFA, M.COM, CTMS-HBSP, (IIM Ahmedabad), UGC-NET and JRF, PhD Pursuing Currently working as an Assistant Professor in the School of Management, Apeejay Institute of Management and Engineering Technical Campus, Jalandhar. He has done CFA from ICFAI University, one of the premier institutes in India. He has also completed M.com from Lyallpur Khalsa College, Jalandhar. He did various academic certifications like Case Method Teaching (CMT) from Harvard Business Publishing-IIM Ahmedabad, Goods and services tax (GST) certification from the Ministry of skill development and Entrepreneurship, Government of India. He has more than 11 years of experience in academics and his area of expertise is Accounting and Finance. He has presented papers at reputed National and International Conferences and published 9 research papers (Including SCOPUS, and DOI indexed Journals). He has attended various FDP and Refresher courses and organized various academic events like Case-based teaching, Short Term Programs and workshops.

Bhupinder Singh working as Professor at Sharda University, India. Also, Honorary Professor in University of South Wales UK and Santo Tomas University Tunja, Colombia. His areas of publications as Smart Healthcare, Medicines, fuzzy logics, artificial intelligence, robotics, machine learning, deep learning, federated learning, IoT, PV Glasses, metaverse and many more. He has 3 books, 139 paper publications, 163 paper presentations in international/national conferences and seminars, participated in more than 40 workshops/FDP's/QIP's, 25 courses from international universities of repute, organized more than 59 events with international and national academicians and industry people's, editor-in-chief and co-editor in journals, developed new courses. He has given talks at international universities, resource person in international conferences such as in Nanyang Technological University Singapore, Tashkent State University of Law Uzbekistan; KIMEP University Kazakhstan, All'ah meh Tabatabi University Iran, the Iranian Association of International Criminal law, Iran and Hague Center for International Law and Investment, The Netherlands, Northumbria University Newcastle UK, Taylor's University Malaysia, AFM Krakow University Poland, European Institute for Research and Development Georgia, Business and Technology University Georgia, Texas A & M University US name a few. His leadership, teaching, research and industry experience is of 16 years and 3 Months. His research interests are health law, criminal law, research methodology and emerging multidisciplinary areas as Blockchain Technology, IoT, Machine Learning, Artificial Intelligence, Genome-editing, Photovoltaic PV Glass, SDG's and many more.

Sanjay Taneja is currently an Associate Professor in Research at Graphic Era University, Dehradun, India. His significant thrust areas are Banking Regulations, Banking and Finance (Fin Tech, Green Finance), Risks, Insurance Management, Green Economics and Management of Innovation in Insurance. He holds a double master's degree (MBA &M.Com.) in management with a specialization in Finance and Marketing. He received his PG degrees in Management (Gold Medalist) from Chaudhary Devi University, Sirsa, India in 2012. He earned his Doctor of Philosophy (Sponsored By ICSSR) in Banking and Finance entitled "An Appraisal of financial performance of Indian Banking Sector: A Comparative study of Public, Private and Foreign banks in 2016 from Chaudhary Devi University, Sirsa, India. He received his Post Doctoral Degree from faculty of Social Sciences, Department of Banking and Insurance, Usak University, Turkey entitled on "Impact of the European Green Deal on Carbon (CO_2) Emission in Turkey" in 2023. He has published research papers in reputed SCOPUS/Web of Science/SCI/ABDC/UGC Care Journals. Prof. Taneja has more than fifty publications in total (Scopus/ABDC/Web of Science- 27)

Index

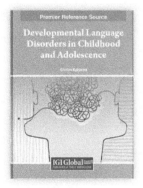

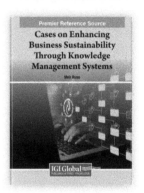

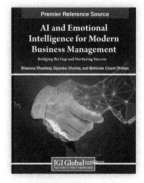
 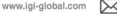

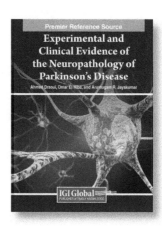
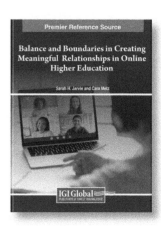

 www.igi-global.com

9 798369 346129